The Art and Practice of Mediation

Second Edition

Peter Bishop
Cheryl Picard
Rena Ramkay
Neil Sargent

emp 2015 • EMOND MONTGOMERY PUBLICATIONS • TORONTO, CANADA

Emond Montgomery Publications Limited
60 Shaftesbury Avenue
Toronto ON M4T 1A3
http://www.emp.ca/highered

Printed in Canada.

Reprinted April 2019.

We acknowledge the financial support of the Government of Canada through the Canada Book Fund for our publishing activities.

Publisher: Mike Thompson
Managing editor, development: Kelly Dickson
Director, editorial and production: Jim Lyons
Developmental editor: Katy Littlejohn
Copy editor: Jamie Bush
Production editor: Laura Bast
Proofreader: Nancy Ennis
Indexer: Paula Pike
Text designer: Tara Wells
Cover designers: Stephen Cribbin & Simon Evers
Cover image: © Skyscan Photolibrary / Alamy

Library and Archives Canada Cataloguing in Publication

Picard, Cheryl Ann
[Art and science of mediation]
The art and practice of mediation / Peter Bishop, Cheryl Picard, Rena Ramkay, Neil Sargent. — Second edition.

Includes index.
Revision of: The art and science of mediation. Toronto : Emond Montgomery Publications, 2004.
ISBN 978-1-55239-562-2 (pbk.)

1. Mediation—Textbooks. 2. Conflict management—Textbooks.
I. Sargent, N. (Neil), author II. Bishop, Peter J. (Peter Jason), 1950-, author
III. Ramkay, Rena, author IV. Title. V. Title: Art and science of mediation.

HM1126.P52 2015 303.6'9 C2014-904540-9

Brief Contents

Detailed Contents v
Scenarios ix
Preface xi
About the Authors xv

1 Introduction to the Art and Practice of Mediation 1
2 Dispute Resolution Processes 31
3 Mediation as a Dispute Resolution Process 63
4 Understanding Conflict Behaviour 93
5 Conflict and Communication 125
6 Convening and Preparing for a Mediation 155
7 Cultivating Constructive Dialogue in Mediation 189
8 Getting to the Heart of Conflict 225
9 Reaching Decisions and Completing the Mediation Process 253
10 Restorative and Reconciliation Processes 287
11 Using Mediation in Organizations and Communities 325
Appendix A Agreement to Mediate 367
Appendix B Memorandum of Understanding (MOU) 369
Appendix C Standards of Practice 371
Index 387

Detailed Contents

Brief Contents iii

Scenarios ix

Preface xi

About the Authors xv

1 **Introduction to the Art and Practice of Mediation** 1

Introduction 1

Mediation Applications 2

Different Approaches to the Practice of Mediation 4

The Goals of Mediation 5

A Mediator's Framework 6

The Art of Mediation 9

Developing Skills in Mediation 17

An Overview of Key Terms and Concepts Used in This Text 20

Summary 27

Discussion Questions and Exercises 28

Further Reading 29

References 29

2 **Dispute Resolution Processes** 31

Introduction 31

The Relationship Between Power, Rights, and Interests 32

The Dispute Resolution Spectrum 33

Power-Based Dispute Resolution Methods 34

Rights-Based Dispute Resolution Methods 38

Interest-Based Dispute Resolution Methods 40

Negotiation 42

Mediation 52

Summary 57

Discussion Questions and Exercises 58

Further Reading 59

References 60

3 **Mediation as a Dispute Resolution Process** 63

Introduction 63

Core Elements of Mediation 64

The Idea of Mediator Neutrality 67
Forms of Mediation Practice 68
Why Choose Mediation? 78
Defining Success in Mediation 81
Benefits of Mediation 82
Summary 87
Discussion Questions and Exercises 88
Further Reading 89
References 90

4 **Understanding Conflict Behaviour** 93
Introduction 93
What Is Conflict? 93
Three Constructs for Understanding Conflict 95
How People Respond to Conflict 98
Conflict Behaviour 102
Conflicts and Choices 104
Why People Behave as They Do 108
Summary 120
Discussion Questions and Exercises 120
Further Reading 121
References 122

5 **Conflict and Communication** 125
Introduction 125
Understanding Communication 125
Communication and Interaction 128
Communication Blockers 131
Non-Verbal Communication 134
The Communication Skills of a Mediator 136
Summary 151
Discussion Questions and Exercises 151
Further Reading 152
References 153

6 **Convening and Preparing for a Mediation** 155
Introduction 155
What Is Convening? 155
What Does Convening Entail? 158
The Convening Process 162
How Convening Varies in Different Situations 164
A Framework for Convening 165
Mediator Selection 178

Pre-Mediation: Preparing for Mediation 182
Summary 185
Discussion Questions and Exercises 186
Further Reading 187
References 187

7 **Cultivating Constructive Dialogue in Mediation** 189
Introduction 189
Understanding the Sources of Conflict 190
Cooperative Behaviour 194
How Mediators Cultivate Dialogue 197
The Parties' Conflicting Perspectives 200
Beginning the Mediation 201
Exploring the Parties' Narratives 205
Strategies for Transforming Adversarial Dialogue 207
Participation of Parties' Advisers in Mediation 217
Summary 220
Discussion Questions and Exercises 221
Further Reading 222
References 223

8 **Getting to the Heart of Conflict** 225
Introduction 225
The Logic of the Mediation Process 225
Strategies for Getting to the Heart of the Problem 229
What Makes a Mediation Work? 230
Expanding Parties' Ways of Understanding 232
The Creative Communicator 239
Summary 248
Discussion Questions and Exercises 249
Further Reading 251
References 252

9 **Reaching Decisions and Completing the Mediation Process** 253
Introduction 253
Generating Options to Resolve the Problem 254
Strategies for the Resolution Phase 263
Reaching a Final Decision or Resolution 270
Stage 5: Post-Mediation Action 280
Summary 283
Discussion Questions and Exercises 284
Further Reading 285
References 286

10 Restorative and Reconciliation Processes 287
Introduction 287
Conflict and the Perception of Justice 288
What Is Justice? 289
Restorative Justice Processes 302
Summary 319
Discussion Questions and Exercises 319
Further Reading 320
References 321

11 Using Mediation in Organizations and Communities 325
Introduction 325
Measuring the Costs of Conflict 326
Types of Workplace: Competitive Versus Collaborative 328
What Is a Mediation Program? 330
Conflict Management Systems 336
Community Mediation Programs in Canada 338
Evaluation of Processes, Programs, and Systems 342
Challenges and Risks of Mediation 344
The Profession of Mediation 350
Summary 358
Discussion Questions and Exercises 359
Further Reading 361
References 363

A Agreement to Mediate 367

B Memorandum of Understanding (MOU) 369

C Standards of Practice 371

Index 387

Scenarios

Chapter 1
Car Repair Blues (see also Chapter 7) 20

Chapter 2
Garage Sale 44
Fruit Exchange 51
Haven Homes (Exercise 1) 58

Chapter 3
An Unhappy Customer 74
Divorcing Spouses (Exercise 1; see also Chapter 7) 88

Chapter 4
Open House 105
The Band Next Door (Exercise 2) 120

Chapter 5
High-Context Communications 127
Performance Review 135
Workplace Change (see also Chapter 8) 138

Chapter 6
Not in My Backyard 159

Chapter 7
Car Repair Blues (see also Chapter 1) 202
Divorcing Spouses (Exercise 5; see also Chapter 3) 221

Chapter 8
Workplace Change 233
Workplace Change (Exercise 6) 249

Chapter 9
An Aging Parent (Exercise 6) 285

Chapter 10
Separating Spouses 294
Victim–Offender Mediation in a Drunk Driving Death Case 304
The Cadman–Deas Case 310

Chapter 11
Student Mediation Services Program 331
Mediation with Recent Immigrants (Exercise 6) 360

Preface

This text aims to introduce you to the art and practice of mediation in a way that illustrates the complexity and diversity of mediation contexts and practices. Mediation research and development have significantly progressed from where they were a decade ago, when the earlier edition of this book (*The Art and Science of Mediation*) was published. This new edition incorporates some of these recent findings and perspectives. While retaining a significant amount of text from the previous edition, *The Art and Practice of Mediation* provides updated materials, and it works from a more inclusive framework for thinking about mediation and its various applications.

The Learning Plan of This Book

We open this book with an overview of the mediation field, examining both its breadth and depth. In Chapters 2 through 4, we focus on different aspects of conflict, communication, and dispute resolution. These chapters explore the implications of using different dispute resolution methods, discuss key principles of conflict, consider the influence of psychological and emotional factors on behaviour, and introduce you to the various approaches to mediation and their underlying theories. Chapter 5 deals with the subject of communication in conflict, examining both verbal and non-verbal communication as processes that are socially constructed, culturally rooted, relational, and interactive.

Chapters 6, 7, 8, and 9 provide an in-depth examination of the stages of the mediation process. We begin with the convening and pre-mediation stage (Chapter 6), then move through the stages of cultivating dialogue (Chapter 7) and getting to the heart of conflict (Chapter 8), before arriving at the final stage of exploring options and reaching decisions (Chapter 9). In these chapters, we explore a range of strategies and skills that mediators may use throughout all stages of the process, illustrating our discussion with concrete examples and case studies.

Chapter 10 is devoted to the subject of restorative justice—how it compares with other notions of justice and how it is expressed in a variety of practices, from victim–offender mediation (VOM), to sentencing circles, to the large-scale reconciliation processes that are needed in the aftermath of civil war. Finally, in Chapter 11, we introduce you to the design, operations, and evaluation of mediation programs and integrated conflict management systems within organizations and communities. This chapter addresses some of the challenges and risks involved in mediation, as well as the different ways that the profession of mediation has responded to these challenges and risks.

We have organized the book in such a way that you can easily apply what you learn and further your study of particular areas. We use conflict scenarios and examples, taken from different contexts, to illustrate the varied goals, strategies, and skills of mediation. You will encounter public disputes over development plans, international conflict situations, workplace conflict, restorative justice processes, legal disputes, consumer conflicts, disputes related to family law, and many other areas where mediation is practised. Discussion questions and exercises at the end of each chapter enable you to test your new-found knowledge and skills. The end of each chapter includes a listing of additional readings and websites relevant to the subject matter of the chapter. These are intended for those who have a particular interest in the area and are interested in researching it further.

In working through the material in this book, you should consider setting specific learning goals for yourself. These goals could include the following:

- learning new ways of thinking about conflict—of understanding conflict and conflict interaction;
- developing skills and tools for analyzing and understanding conflict;
- learning new skills and approaches for mediating or dealing with conflict;
- developing your conflict competence; and
- pursuing any other goals that led you to purchase this book.

It is our hope that the knowledge you develop by pursuing these goals will be of practical value to you. In particular, we hope you will develop your own methods and abilities for analyzing conflict and applying strategies and techniques that you find particularly relevant. We also hope you will develop your ability to understand and explain why the approach you use can lead to success, whatever success may mean in a particular case.

Peter Bishop
Cheryl Picard
Rena Ramkay
Neil Sargent

A Note from the Publisher

The publisher wishes to thank the following people for providing their feedback and suggestions during the development of this book: Gary Furlong, Roger Gunn (NAIT), Joanne Hagger-Perritt (Northern College), Virginia Harwood (Durham College), Robyn Jacobson (UOIT), Nancy Riopel (Northern College), Sharon Wilson, and Craig Zelizer (Georgetown University).

For Instructors

For more information on this book, please visit the accompanying website at **www.emp.ca/mediation2e**. Supplemental teaching resources, including role-plays, test bank, and more, are also available for instructors who have chosen this book for their courses. Instructors should contact their Emond Montgomery representative for more information, or contact us via the website.

About the Authors

Peter Bishop is an Ottawa-based mediator, lawyer, and conflict management practitioner, trainer, and consultant. He has extensive experience with conflict intervening and learning, particularly in the context of organizations in the public, private, and non-profit sectors. He currently teaches mediation in the Department of Law and Legal Studies at Carleton University and is active in Carleton's Graduate Diploma Program in Conflict Resolution.

Dr. Cheryl Picard, professor emeritus, Department of Law, Carleton University, is a practitioner, educator, and researcher in conflict management and mediation. She has been mediating one-on-one conflicts and group conflicts since 1978, and while at Carleton founded the Mediation Centre, the Centre for Conflict Education and Research, and the Graduate Diploma in Conflict Resolution program. Her teaching and research were instrumental in the development of insight mediation and the insight approach to conflict. She now works in private practice from her home in Prince Edward Island.

Rena Ramkay works in the fields of mediation, conflict prevention, and resolution for a number of organizations. Her current focus is international and involves the design and delivery of training in ADR aligned with human rights' instruments, the development of community mediation programming, and monitoring and overseeing programming for conflict-affected youth and children. She has been teaching in Carleton University's Department of Law and the Graduate Certificate Program in Conflict Resolution since 1996. Rena sits on the board of Peacebuild as secretary and represents Canada in the North American region of the Global Partnership for the Prevention of Armed Conflict (GPPAC).

Neil Sargent has been a member of the Department of Law at Carleton University since 1974. He received his LLB from Nottingham University, his LLM from Osgoode Hall Law School, and a graduate diploma in European Integration from the University of Amsterdam. He is director of both the Graduate Diploma in Conflict Resolution and the Centre for Conflict Education and Research in Carleton's Department of Law and Legal Studies.

CHAPTER 1
Introduction to the Art and Practice of Mediation

LEARNING OBJECTIVES

After reading this chapter, you will be able to:

- Understand the wide range of contexts in which mediation is used
- Identify three main goals of mediation
- Explain the five-phase framework of the mediation process
- Understand the significance of adopting a holistic approach for developing mediator competency
- Identify at least three ways that you can develop your mediation competence
- Understand a number of key mediation terms and concepts

CHAPTER OUTLINE

Introduction 1
Mediation Applications 2
Different Approaches to the Practice of Mediation 4
The Goals of Mediation 5
A Mediator's Framework 6
The Art of Mediation 9
Developing Skills in Mediation 17
An Overview of Key Terms and Concepts Used in This Text 20
Summary 27

In the middle of every difficulty lies opportunity.

Albert Einstein

Introduction

Violent **conflict*** stubbornly persists all over the world. **Disputes** arise over natural resources, governance arrangements, and the keys to power. Such disputes result in significant casualties—human ones, most importantly, but also environmental and economic ones. As individuals, we confront conflict in our day-to-day lives on a regular basis. While conflict can be positive, driving us to adapt and change for the better, many of us experience conflict as something negative, to be avoided at all

* This term and other key terms and concepts are defined later in this chapter under the heading "An Overview of Key Terms and Concepts Used in This Text."

costs. Some of our most serious disputes—determining custody and access to children after divorce; resolving human rights complaints; reconciling victim and offenders after a horrific crime—are best resolved with the help of third parties who have expertise in conflict resolution. These experts are commonly known as mediators. Without their assistance, peace can be elusive.

In this chapter, we examine various aspects of mediation, with the aim of providing the reader with a general picture before we go into more detail in the following chapters. We discuss the many contexts in which mediation is used, provide an overview of the mediation process and different approaches to its practice, reflect on the "art" of mediation and its significance to new mediators, and define key mediation terms and concepts so as to provide the reader with a general orientation to the book.

Mediation Applications

Mediation is now used in a variety of contexts and has many different applications, including the following:

- insurance claims;
- land-use planning and development;
- trade and commerce;
- separation and divorce;
- family conflict, including parent–child, intergenerational, and elder conflicts;
- organizational and workplace conflicts;
- civilian interaction with police;
- schoolyard squabbles;
- contractual disputes;
- human rights complaints;
- immigration and refugee issues;
- environmental assessments;
- banking and real estate disputes;
- community and neighbourhood issues;
- criminal and civil cases;
- peace negotiations in the aftermath of war; and
- reconciliation processes following mass human rights violations.

Wherever conflict exists, mediation is becoming a preferred option for dealing with it. New applications for mediation are emerging all the time.

Mediation is becoming an integral part of organizational and institutional conflict management systems. Organizations are increasingly adopting it and other informal processes to resolve disputes internally. In workplaces, mediation is used to address a variety of internal grievances—for example, conflicts arising from staff relations or organizational restructuring. Among the reasons for resolving workplace conflict through interest-based, dialogic processes such as mediation are that they improve morale and help build effective teams and team consensus.

In November 2003, the Canadian Parliament passed Bill C-25, the *Public Service Modernization Act*. This Act requires that mediation services be provided for labour relations and that informal conflict management systems be established in every federal department. (See the Treasury Board's website, listed at the end of this chapter.) Many public sector organizations, such as the Royal Canadian Mounted Police, the Department of Justice, the Canada Revenue Agency, the Department of National Defence/Canadian Forces, and Public Works and Government Services have established integrated conflict management systems (Lynch, 1997). No doubt this trend will continue, and mediation will become more broadly institutionalized.

As well as being used to address conflict *within* organizations, mediation has become the preferred process for resolving disputes between organizations and members of the public. For example, disputes between civilians and police officers increasingly go to mediation before more formal disciplinary procedures are undertaken. Mediation is more and more often relied on, as well, in physician–patient disputes. Research has shown that many costly medical malpractice lawsuits can be avoided if patients, before commencing a lawsuit, try mediation with representatives of their health organization (Liebman, 2011). Mediation provides patients with the opportunity to express their concerns, to officials from the relevant health organization, about the way they have been treated in the medical system. In the United States, where research on these cases has been completed, physicians do not participate in the mediations but are represented by their hospitals, clinics, or medical associations. Nevertheless, even without physicians' direct participation, all **parties** come to a better understanding of the difficult decisions and the complex human costs associated with various forms of medical intervention. This sometimes leads health-care representatives to review policies in hospitals or clinics in order to improve patient experiences and safety. In the province of Ontario, the Dentists Association has also adopted mediation to resolve its patient–dentist complaints (see the ODA website, listed at the end of the chapter).

People have become aware of the considerable savings involved in using mediation. This has led to the incorporation of mediation into the formal legal system. In Ontario, for example, many civil lawsuits now require parties to attempt mediation prior to a judicial hearing in a formal trial process. Mediation at an early stage in civil litigation often helps the parties reach a mediated **settlement** of their legal dispute without the costly step of going to trial. While most civil law disputes are settled through pretrial negotiations between the parties' lawyers, the use of mediation at an early stage in the litigation process has resulted in more cases being settled earlier, which means lower costs both for the parties and for the legal system (Macfarlane, 1995).

Information technology has recently opened up new fields of mediation. Sessions now take place via email, instant messaging, chat rooms, and video conferencing. Some of the advantages of using online dispute resolution (ODR) include the following: its low cost (people do not have to travel to participate); reduction of time-zone differences; and its speed and availability. For some, ODR is less confrontational than face-to-face mediation. On the other hand, communicating about contentious and emotional subjects without being face to face with the other person can be difficult. In the absence of facial expressions and body language, online or telephone communication can even cause the conflict to escalate. However, as technology develops, innovators will no doubt find new ways to deal with these challenges. ODR will be an ongoing area of development, and a potential market niche for some mediators. (See references to ODR in the websites listed at the end of this chapter.)

The field of mediation has broadened on many levels. In Canada, our rich multicultural context has influenced mediation practice. Many newcomers to this country have brought their former societies' traditions of using social network mediators (Moore, 1996, pp. 43–47) to resolve community and neighbourhood disputes. Canada's First Nations have traditionally employed forms of community **justice** and sentencing circles, and these have influenced the practice of mediation. International diplomacy, which influences parties with the carrot-and-the-stick technique, has affected the form that mediation takes in trade and human rights tribunals. The legal profession, too, has placed its stamp on the process, as varied applications have brought mediation into the justice system.

The growing institutionalization of mediation has brought concerns that it is being adopted simply because it is more cost-effective than litigation. Efficiency arguments do favour mediation, but they are not the most compelling arguments for it. The deepest benefit of mediation is its potential to transform relationships and transform the parties' future orientations toward conflict (Bush & Folger, 2005). The economic rationale for establishing mediation systems should not obscure the full potential of the process.

Different Approaches to the Practice of Mediation

Mediation's use in the varied contexts described above has enriched the field. Professional conferences now offer workshops on narrative mediation practice, human rights mediations, workplace conflict resolution, and numerous other models of practice particular to a mediation context or ideology. Some educational institutions now specifically identify the type of mediation training they supply. For example, the Institute for the Study of Conflict Transformation promotes Bush and Folger's transformative mediation (see the website provided at the end of this chapter).

As we will examine in Chapter 3, there are many different approaches to the practice of mediation, including problem-solving, evaluative, or settlement types; and transformative, holistic, or inclusive types, which bring together shared ideals while recognizing multiple goals and a multiplicity of practices (Picard, 2004). The growth of mediation over the past 20 years has largely been in areas, including civil and family disputes, in which problem-solving, evaluative, or settlement mediation is used. This trend is a concern to some proponents of mediation. They have concerns whether consumers of mediation are making knowledgeable and informed choices about which type of mediation they prefer to use. They also fear that it could lead to mediation's becoming a subsidiary of the legal profession rather than an alternative to it. Picard and Saunders (2002, pp. 235–236) worry that,

> given the increasing involvement of the state in mediation through mandated schemes attached to the courts, and the strong presence of lawyers within these schemes, both as practitioners and as consumers (via their clients), … control of the field [is in danger of] falling into the hands of the legal profession.

We believe that having different types of mediation is a good thing, with the settlement approach used for legal disputes and the transformative or holistic approaches (including insight, transformative, and narrative mediation) used for "relational" conflicts. It is problematic, however, that people who opt for mediation, regardless of the nature of their conflict, often expect the settlement approach rather than a more transformative or holistic one. Mayer (2000, pp. 195–198) has observed that clients often want and expect a settlement approach, and these expectations may be at odds with the mediator's actual process goals and intentions.

According to a market-driven view of mediation, a settlement approach should be used if that is what people want and expect in legal or other contexts. The rationale here is that if mediators fail to deliver what clients want, mediation will not be used at all.

Mediators who endorse a transformative perspective counter that mediation's potential for individual, relational, and social growth will never be realized if market-driven criteria are given priority. Such mediators say that the settlement approach should not be used at all, because it simply maintains the status quo and extinguishes any transformative potential inherent in the conflict situation. Bush (1989), a proponent of transformative mediation, has said that if settlement-type mediation is to be the only kind used in court-connected programs, it would be better that mediation not be used at all in the civil justice system.

The Goals of Mediation

In this text, we do not attempt to resolve the debate over whether mediation is primarily a relational or a problem-solving endeavour, or whether one of these perspectives has more value than the other. Our basic position is that mediation should address conflict as a relational, dynamic, and value-based phenomenon, with solving conflict problems as its primary outcome.

The three main goals of mediation, as we see it, are to

1. resolve or settle disputes;
2. facilitate understanding, learning, and growth; and
3. restore relationships after they have been harmed.

The conceptual framework we provide here is based on the mediator's understanding the parties' goals and having sound theoretical and experiential knowledge to determine which approach to mediation would be most effective. Depending on which of the three goals identified above is driving the process, the mediation is likely to have different characteristics.

Which of the three goals is driving the mediation process depends, in turn, on the nature of the dispute context. For example, when mediation is being used to establish peace agreements after violent conflict, the dispute-settling goal is likely to be paramount. The same is true for mediation that takes place "in the shadow of the courts," such as mediation for environmental, human rights, or civil disputes. Community or workplace mediations, on the other hand, are more naturally suited to the goal of facilitating understanding, learning, and growth, so that the disputing parties can peacefully interact in the future. Victim–offender mediation, restorative justice dialogues, and reconciliation processes usually have the goal of restoring relationships and harmony after people have been harmed.

The three goals of mediation are not mutually exclusive, and there are situations where it is appropriate to combine them. For instance, it may be necessary to promote understanding and learning before a dispute can be settled. Consider a conflict involving two spouses who are negotiating child custody arrangements. Before they settle these arrangements, they will need to understand their children's needs and learn more about one another's parenting values. The mediation process, in this instance, would aim both to promote understanding and growth in the parties and to settle the dispute. It may even come to involve the third goal of mediation—restoring the spouses' broken relationship so that they can implement their custody arrangements amicably.

A Mediator's Framework

All mediators have a framework for their mediation process. In our experience, most mediators follow a process framework like the one we present in this book (in Chapters 7, 8, and 9), which includes the following stages:

- pre-mediation,
- cultivating dialogue,
- getting to the heart of the conflict,
- reaching decisions and completing the mediation process, and
- post-mediation.

Figure 1.1 Framework of the Mediation Process

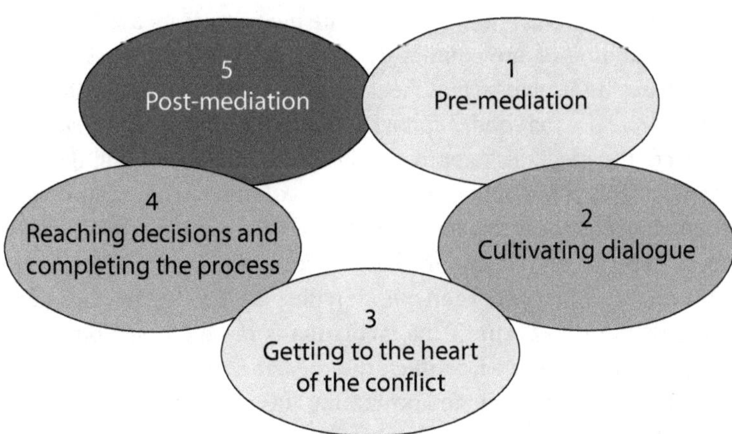

Pre-Mediation

There will be tasks to complete prior to conducting any mediation. These tasks may include the following: reviewing parties' statements of facts, in the case of a civil litigation; meeting individually with each party, in the case of a restorative justice process; facilitating consensus-building processes with groups of **stakeholders**, in the case of a public policy mediation; or speaking with individuals over the phone, in the case of a workplace conflict.

During pre-mediation, the mediator determines whether the particular dispute situation is suitable for mediation and whether the participants are ready for mediation. In some cases, a mediator may even spend time preparing parties to go to mediation. The practical tasks involved in setting up mediation will also be completed during pre-mediation: determining a place, time, and date; preparing a room and breakout rooms; discussing fees and other issues, if appropriate; removing barriers to participation in mediation and furnishing parties with the technology and supplies they require to discuss and resolve their situation.

Cultivating Dialogue

This phase opens the mediation process and usually begins with a mediator providing introductory remarks. These remarks will cover process information, guidance for discussions, logistical information, and other important tone-setting items. The parties themselves will usually begin by presenting their respective versions of the conflict and its causes. Next comes some attention to the parties' perspective—how they view events and why. This will unfold differently depending on the mediator's approach and on his or her goals. The party's values, consciousness, and culture will shape their perception of the conflict. The mediator's response to the adversarial narratives will aim at promoting collaborative dialogue.

Getting to the Heart of the Conflict

In trying to get to the heart of the conflict, the mediator is focused on achieving a deeper understanding of the conflict dynamics and of the interests, needs, and values underlying the dispute, so that she can unlock the keys to **resolution**. Mediators typically use strategies that both support and question the parties' understandings of the conflict. The mediator's approach and the parties' goals will determine the particular shape this phase of the process takes—what types of questions are asked, what information she seeks to elicit from the parties, and how she listens to them. For example, if the parties' goals in mediation are to solve a problem in a contractual dispute, the mediator may listen and question the parties to learn which needs must be met for resolution to occur. If the mediation is more focused on preserving a relationship, as in a co-worker conflict, the mediator's focus will be on revealing misperceptions about behaviour and promoting alternative understandings. Getting to the heart of the conflict involves the real work of mediation.

Reaching Decisions and Completing the Mediation Process

Typically, in the "resolution" phase, the mediator leads or facilitates a process in which the parties generate, consider, and assess various resolution options and then, moving through a process of negotiation, make one or more decisions that will fully resolve their dispute. How the resolution phase of mediation proceeds will vary depending on the nature and the context of the dispute. For example, the resolution phase of a divorce mediation likely will be very different from that of a mediation of a civil personal injury dispute. In the latter case, most of the resolution phase probably will consist of the mediator shuttling back and forth between the parties and their lawyers, seeking to complete their negotiation process. On the other hand, in divorce mediation, the resolution phase is often done with the parties together in joint session, enabling them to fully discuss the implications of all resolution options.

Post-Mediation

Post-mediation can take many forms, depending upon the context of the conflict, the mediator's reporting requirements, the legal nature of the **issues** in dispute, and other matters needing to be settled after mediation has ended. In legal cases, there may be formal requirements to file a written agreement with the courts or to have parties' lawyers look over and sign off on agreements. In community mediation cases, the mediator may only need to follow up with a phone call to the parties to check in on how the resolution or agreement is holding up. For some "insider" mediators—those who work within an institution and need to consider institutional needs—post-mediation may involve filing agreements with a certain office in the institution. The particulars of the post-mediation stage also vary with the dispute context. Yet all mediators will have some task or tasks to complete following a mediation, even if simply a process of self-reflection about what went well in the mediation and what did not go well.

The Art of Mediation

How does one become a competent mediator? People who are just learning about mediation may be told to "trust the process" or to "let the magic of mediation work." However, these words do not provide much guidance to a new mediator.

So far in this chapter, we have considered a wide range of contexts in which mediation is used, as well as different approaches and goals adopted by mediators in different situations. Regardless of what approach a mediator uses, he or she needs to do more than merely follow the science of mediation—the process stages, the strategies, and the communication skills and techniques. A successful mediator needs to have and to develop artistry. Mediation artistry comes from the skillful employment of intuition, artfulness, empathy, connectedness, and creativity. Both the science and the art of mediation are prerequisites for successful practice. Both elements must feature in *a holistic approach to mediation.* In the following section, we discuss the new science paradigm required for this approach.

The Traditional Scientific Method

The traditional scientific method relies on the detailed analysis of what can be known through our physical senses. We know what we can see, hear, smell, taste, and touch; we understand larger systems by understanding their basic components. In the case of a machine, for example, the scientific method posits that by studying the parts of this machine, we can understand how it works. In other words, we can take the machine apart and examine the workings of each component to learn how the whole machine functions.

Or take the Western scientific approach to medicine. A doctor observes symptoms (the parts), takes tests (verifies), analyzes the data, diagnoses the cause of the disease, and prescribes or performs the appropriate treatment. This approach is based on the premise that the root cause of the disease can be determined and then resolved through prescribed medicine or medical procedures. This is a linear, causal chain of inquiry.

A fundamental principle of Western scientific theory is that, with complete knowledge of a patient's condition and of current medical science, a doctor can determine the optimal treatment for the patient. In practice, different medical experts may disagree on what that optimal treatment is. Consider, for example, a patient with an apparent wrist injury. The wrist problem experienced by the patient may be only one manifestation of a completely separate condition, such as a damaged disc in the patient's spine.

"New" Science: The Holistic Approach

Wheatley (1999, pp. 10–11) proposes that the new science focuses on holistic understanding, rather than on an understanding of the parts. Systems are seen as a network of relationships, and knowledge is derived from understanding the relationships and their interconnectedness within the system. Returning to our machine example, the new science does not take the machine apart, but rather studies it in operation, trying to discover links and understand relationships between the component parts. This is a holistic approach to knowing, and it is non-linear, with unpredictable causal links.

If we return to our medical example of the patient with a wrist problem, a holistic medical practitioner might begin her intervention by seeking links between the wrist concerns and other bodily symptoms. She would analyze the body's whole system of interaction—how the wrist is linked to other parts of the body, such as the shoulder, the spine, and the musculature. She might study the patient's hair follicles, eyes, or other systems for information about the wrist. The conclusion she arrives at may be that there is a stomach hernia (or a muscle tear) that is affecting the patient's posture. The poor posture is particularly evident when the patient works on the computer, and the resulting spine misalignment has led to damage of the wrist tendon. Without a systemic (holistic) analysis, this doctor could have arrived at very different conclusions; she might have treated only a symptom instead of looking for ways to eliminate its cause. Treatment in this instance involves strengthening the musculature around the spine and having the patient practise proper posture alignment when on the computer, as well as more conventional therapies designed to ease wrist pain.

This approach, known as a *holistic* approach, requires that we continue to use analysis, but that we use it differently than we did before. To understand the causes of conflict, we need to understand its sources; however, more importantly, we need to understand how those sources interact or coexist with other elements of the conflict.

What Is a Holistic Approach to Mediation?

A holistic approach to mediation is based on a number of premises. First of all, holistic practitioners view conflict as a relational phenomenon. Conflict arises from and is manifested as a feature of the interactions and relations among two or more people or groups of people. Any attempt to explain, understand, or resolve conflict as an individual phenomenon will be incomplete. Conflict is a complex, multidimensional phenomenon. In a particular case, it is impossible to isolate or identify all causes, manifestations, and effects of the conflict. How individuals respond to conflict and how people and groups interact in conflict situations are uniquely determined by historical, cultural, psychological, environmental, economic, social, political, and other factors.

Conflict, from the holistic perspective, is a phenomenon arising from the mind, heart, body, and spirit (LeBaron, 2002). People in the midst of conflict experience it with and through their minds, their emotions, their physical sensations, and their souls. Likewise, people influence the conflict situation—and other people and groups involved in it—through ways of the mind, heart, body, and spirit. This inevitably means that logic and rational discussion alone are inadequate to understanding, describing, and dealing with conflict (Benjamin, 1995a, pp. 143–144; Benjamin, 1995b, pp. 3–4; Fisher, 2000, p. 88).

The more that parties and intervenors know about the people and their conflict situation and relationships, the greater their capacity for resolving or managing the conflict productively. An understanding of the connections and the relationship—historical and contextual—between the parties will be most informative in the approach to mediation. The mediator must see the conflict and the parties through a systems lens. This involves observing and sensing the interconnections between the parties and the elements of the conflict.

The mediator should expect a process of inquiry and discovery that will be non-linear and unpredictable. Conflict conditions tend to cause people to think and behave in ways that may be contrary to their rational best interests, both individually and relationally. As Benjamin (1995b, p. 6) says, "virtually every conflict, whether a business or a family dispute, has subjective, non-rational aspects that must be addressed."

It is thus important to remember that, while an understanding of the parts is important, a holistic approach advises us to observe, feel, and understand the relationships. In addition to individual characteristics of conflict, the mediator must always consider how connections and relationships are affecting each party's willingness and ability to negotiate effectively. It is this understanding that can move a conflict from its destructive to its constructive nature. The mediator is simultaneously observing the individual (the part) in mediation at the same time that he is observing the entire relationship (the system). To practise holistically, the mediator must interact with the parties in conflict in both rational and non-rational ways. He often starts with logical, analytical frameworks and integrates what he knows intuitively into his reactions and responses. Figure 1.2 shows the assumptions about knowledge and how we know what we know under the old science and new science paradigms.

The Dynamics of Conflict Intervention

As we can see from Figure 1.2, one of the key assumptions of a holistic approach to mediation is that the observer or "knower" can never stand completely outside whatever is being observed. Interestingly, this claim comes to us from theoretical physics, the heartland of the old scientific method—not from the social sciences.

Figure 1.2 The "Old" and "New" Science: A Comparison

The "old" (traditional) scientific method	The "new" scientific method
Knowledge is based on observation and analysis. We can "know" through our physical senses.	Knowledge can be based on observation and analysis and the physical senses. But we can also "know" through experience and insight.
The observer stands outside the activity or phenomenon that is being observed—a "standpoint of objectivity."	The observer can never stand completely outside that which is being observed. There is always some interaction between the observer and what is being observed.
The observer (investigator) must take care not to influence or interact with the data or information being analyzed—the observer is passive and non-interactive with the thing that is being observed.	The observer ("knower") is actively engaged in the creation of knowledge. The observer is not just a passive observer of objective data, but consciously or unconsciously influences the selection and interpretation of information or data.
Conflict is a social phenomenon that can be objectively observed and analyzed.	Conflict is a form of social interaction that may be experienced subjectively by the participants in ways that are not always evident to an objective observer.
Conflict behaviour can also be observed and analyzed objectively.	It is not enough to rely on observation and analysis alone to understand conflict behaviour. We also have to rely on experience and insight to understand how the conflict is experienced subjectively by the participants.
The emphasis is on the search for objective knowledge—the "truth" about the conflict.	The emphasis is on gaining insight into the different ways in which the participants experience the conflict—the different "truths" about the conflict.
Observer neutrality is a crucial process value to prevent observer bias.	An interactive observer can never be strictly neutral, in the sense of having no influence on the data or information being observed. Instead, the observer strives to be conscious of his or her influence on the selection and interpretation of data, and to act in an ethically responsible manner.
That which can be objectively known through observation and analysis can also be modified in predictable ways through external intervention. The "purpose" of conflict intervention, therefore, is to treat or cure the conflict situation.	Because observation and analysis alone will not enable us to obtain the full truth about the conflict, any external intervention based on this assumption is likely to have unanticipated consequences. Intervention should therefore be directed at transforming or changing the parties' subjective experience of the conflict.

It was Einstein who taught us that there is no Archimedean point from which we can obtain a completely unbiased and objective view of reality. Our perceptions of reality are always influenced, knowingly or unknowingly, by a pre-existing framework of ideas, expectations, and beliefs about the way the world is ordered. We see and hear through filters. We may disregard or fail to perceive information that is incompatible with our pre-existing assumptions, or we may interpret it in a subjective, self-serving way.

Imagine, for example, an anthropologist doing fieldwork among a tribal people who had never before had contact with modern society. The anthropologist is excited because he is able to observe the organization and rituals of a society that has developed over centuries, free of external social or technological influences. The anthropologist believes that the data obtained from this research will provide crucial information about how societies adapt to their natural environment and about whether humans are naturally peaceful social actors or are naturally aggressive. However, by arriving on the island armed with notebooks, computers, recording equipment, cameras, food supplies, a tent, and a hundred other basic supplies, the anthropologist has already influenced the very society he set out to study. It is no longer a society that has developed "with no contact with the outside world." The tribal people are likely to behave and interact in the anthropologist's presence differently, if only slightly differently, than they would in his absence. The problem is that the anthropologist can never know this for sure. His very presence has altered the dynamics of the society he has come to observe. What he observes has therefore been affected by his presence.

What is a problematic principle for our anthropologist may be a benefit to mediators and a key element in the art of mediation. As mediators, we recognize that the presence of a third party in a conflict situation is likely to alter the dynamics of the conflict and the relationships between the participants. Indeed, this is the main purpose of the mediator's intervention. The mediator cannot impose a decision on the parties if they are unable to reach agreement. Yet the intervention of an impartial third party may help the parties alter their perceptions of the conflict and of each other, and may help them move from an adversarial stance to a more collaborative one. The focus of the mediator's intervention is thus to change the dynamics of the conflict relationship, to unblock obstacles to communication, to enable the parties to generate new insights into their own conflict, and to alter or transform the parties' subjective experience of the conflict they are engaged in. A mediator is *always* actively engaged in the communication process between the disputants and in the creation of knowledge about the conflict. Mediation is a form of interactive engagement in a conflict relationship. The mediator can never be strictly neutral between the participants in the sense of being a passive observer. Instead, the mediator strives to act impartially with respect to the disputants, to build trust with all the participants, and to allow all the participants to tell their own stories or truths about the conflict.

Now, compare the interactive involvement of a mediator with that of a neutral judge in a courtroom hearing. In the adversarial system, the judge is supposed to be a passive observer while the litigants introduce evidence and cross-examine each other's witnesses. Judicial neutrality requires that the judge not identify with or assist the litigants in their case presentations. A mediator's role, by contrast, is to assist both participants in presenting their case (so to speak), or in telling their stories. Moreover, the parties in mediation are not telling their stories to the mediator—even if it often appears this way—so much as to each other. In explaining their interests, cares, or fears, the parties may be talking to the mediator, but they are being heard by the other party. Indeed, as we will explore in later chapters, one of the key roles of a mediator is to act as a communication bridge between the parties.

This brings us to a second core element of a holistic approach to mediation, and one that we wish to emphasize: the importance of incorporating the *subjective experiences* of the parties into any resolution to the conflict. A holistic approach to mediation is premised on the belief that there is always more than one truth about any conflict situation or relationship. Each party will have his or her own perspective. A mediator needs to understand the various truths about the conflict; he or she needs to obtain information about the parties' subjective experiences of the conflict—their perceptions, hopes, fears, emotions, values, beliefs, or expectations. Once again, we can contrast this holistic approach to mediation with the assumptions about the "truth" that underpin the litigation process, where the emphasis is placed on the objective facts of the conflict—that is, what actually happened—rather than on the subjective experiences of the parties themselves.

A key objective in litigation is to determine the "truth" of the conflict. Anything that does not assist in determining the core truth is considered irrelevant to the proceedings. Most especially, the parties' subjective beliefs, emotions, interpretations, or experiences are dismissed. This is one of the main reasons that the parties are represented by lawyers in the litigation process. Lawyers can present the parties' arguments in a more objective, unemotional manner than the parties themselves are generally able to do. In addition to professional expertise and knowledge of the law, the capacity to be objective and unemotional about the facts of the case is highly prized in the legal profession.

For most mediators, however, the capacity to be responsive to the subjective, emotional needs of the disputants is as important as the capacity to manage the objective dimensions of the conflict. This is one reason that participants in mediation tend to express satisfaction with the process, even if it does not necessarily result in resolution. All conflicts have both objective and subjective dimensions. Any proposed agreement that is not attentive to the latter—to the subjective beliefs, values, and experiences of the participants—is unlikely to be lasting. Indeed, much of a mediator's intervention is focused on adjusting the parties' subjective experience of their own conflict so as to help them move from an adversarial to a more collaborative approach to resolving the conflict.

As you work through the material in this textbook, we encourage you to use the holistic approach as you examine the issues that you encounter in the case studies and examples we provide. You will need to be slow to make judgments, and you will need to stay open to different opinions and points of view, including those you are inclined to reject. This does not mean agreeing with all that others say with respect to a conflict situation. It does mean respecting others (especially those you disagree with) as intelligent and well-meaning people whose opinions and perspectives are worthy of consideration. It means seeking to understand the deeper meaning and truth of others' apparently opposing perspectives. By doing so, you will arrive at a new, more valuable understanding of the issues underlying a conflict. With this approach, you will be able to learn from those whose ideas and points of view you would otherwise have rejected.

Mediators' Ways of Knowing

According to Michelle LeBaron, a mediator derives knowledge through his or her analytical skills, as well as through more creative "ways of knowing" (LeBaron, 2002). Intellectual ways of knowing are well developed in mediation education, research, and practice—through theories about human behaviour, communication, negotiation, and conflict. More emotional, physical, or intuitive ways of knowing have not received much discussion in this field. They are not readily trusted because they do not follow the linear methods of discovery traditionally used in science. They are a part of the "new" science or the holistic understanding of conflict and human interaction.

LeBaron (2002) outlines four types of intelligence that are important to those working in conflict resolution:

1. emotional,
2. somatic,
3. intuitive-imaginative, and
4. "connected" intelligence.

Emotional fluency (or intelligence)—in other words, the awareness and capacity to develop insights into one's own and other's emotions—enables the mediator to recognize, understand, and respond to emotion that is connected to the conflict. What this ability means and how we may develop it have been widely discussed since the publication in 1995 of Daniel Goleman's book *Emotional Intelligence.* To understand this ability in the context of mediation, consider the following example. Let's say that one party begins to physically withdraw from the mediator and from the other party by moving back in her chair and breaking eye contact with them. An emotionally fluent mediator will recognize that a deeper emotion, a feeling of isolation, is behind the withdrawal. The party does not articulate this feeling verbally, but the mediator's fluency or emotional intelligence enables him to "hear" the sentiment as strongly as if it were spoken.

Somatic intelligence is the capacity to "read" and flow with the body's instincts—to perceive when one party is physically withdrawing, reacting, or connecting. Again, consider a party who is physically withdrawing from the mediator and from the other party. A mediator will be responding somatically to this development if he moves his body closer to the receding party, offering a form of physical support and encouragement with his proximity and his open, attentive posture.

Using imagination and visualization—and guided by our intuitive senses—we are able to disconnect from old ways of seeing so that we can consider new paths forward. Consider, for example, two co-workers who are in conflict. The mediator asks each of them to picture their working relationship in the future. If both are able to visualize an effective partnership and to describe what they will contribute and what they need to receive, they are using imagination and visualization to help overcome their deadlock.

A faculty for making and responding to metaphor is part of intuitive-imaginative intelligence. This is a key tool for getting to know—and for fully addressing—important conflict experiences. For example, imagine that we describe a mediation process as an expedition that started in a desert, crossed rocky ground, moved into a thick jungle, and eventually emerged on wide, fertile fields. This metaphor speaks volumes about what people have experienced and achieved in this mediation. The use of metaphor and stories is covered more fully in Chapter 8.

Connected intelligence, or connected ways of knowing, is essential for understanding conflict as part of a relational system. These ways of knowing emerge from the ties we have with others and from our acknowledging and understanding the influence of those ties. Again, consider two co-workers who are in conflict. The two parties would demonstrate connected knowing if they could be brought to recognize each other's importance in carrying out their work and to discuss each other's relative strengths in doing so.

Like Benjamin (1995a, 1995b), LeBaron (2002) recognizes the need for resourcefulness and flexibility in mediation; she explains how mediators draw on various creative sources of knowledge, in addition to traditional analytic ways of understanding, to guide their actions. Developing these other ways of knowing is critical to the mediator's effectiveness. We believe that creative tools are essential for fully knowing and expressing the human conflict experience. Indeed, many forms of artistic expression—music, painting, dance, and so on—are ways of expressing aspects of human experience that cannot be described with words.

Developing Skills in Mediation

This text aims to impart knowledge that has both theoretical and practical value for readers. Our hope is to provide knowledge sufficient to enable the reader to

- diagnose conflict in future,
- consider and apply techniques that may be useful in its resolution, and
- understand why these techniques succeed.

People who read this book may never become *professional* mediators. All of us, however, take on the role of a mediator from time to time in the sense that we find ourselves periodically trying to resolve conflict. The contexts vary: issues among friends, roommates, or co-workers; a group project in school or at work; a political issue in the community. In these situations, a mediator will seek to respond to conflict assertively and respectfully; to achieve a resolution that is fair and beneficial for all; to build up, not break down; in other words, to make peace, not war.

We hope this book will help you learn the skills you need to take on the role of a mediator—to discover and develop your mediation talents and generally to enhance your existing skills for responding to conflict. This process may be challenging; individual talent may be wrapped in inhibitions, doubts, fears, and confusion. Time and experience are needed to unpack this talent. As with most human endeavours, people often need help to discover and develop their talent for mediation. Good instruction, coaching and honest self-assessment all will contribute to this process.

Attributes of a Skilled Mediator

What are some essential attributes of a good mediator? Our list includes being empathetic, non-judgmental, tolerant, fair-minded, flexible, creative, patient yet persistent, optimistic, and having a healthy sense of humour. Maggiolo (1971) presents an interesting list of characteristics that mediators need:

- the patience of Job;
- the sincerity and bulldog characteristics of the English and the wit of the Irish;
- the physical endurance of a marathon runner;
- the broken-field dodging abilities of a halfback;
- the guile of Machiavelli;
- the personality-probing skills of a good psychiatrist;
- the confidence-retaining characteristics of a mute;
- the hide of a rhinoceros;
- the wisdom of Solomon;
- demonstrated integrity and impartiality;

- fundamental beliefs in human values and potential, tempered by the ability to assess personal weaknesses as well as strengths;
- the hard-nosed ability to analyze what is available in contrast to what might be desirable; and
- sufficient personal drive and ego, qualified by a willingness to be self-effacing.

Reflective Practice

Reflective practice is what moves mediators from mediocrity to artistry (Lang & Taylor, 2000). It is how mediators acquire confidence and competence; it enables them to be creative, flexible, and to think outside the box, so they are not simply following a prescribed set of actions within a particular framework. Becoming a competent mediator requires commitment and openness to learning from mistakes. It requires mediators to review their performances, with the aim of improving their ability to better serve those who call on them for help. They assess their actions and strategies, then enter into discussions with others about how they can enhance their performance.

Lang and Taylor (2000, p. 47) say that being reflective is essential to achieving competence and artistry as a mediator. They say that

> [t]he ability to learn from each experience; to refine, adjust and enhance one's skills; and to respond thoughtfully to the unique and surprising events in professional practice can be achieved through the consistent, thoughtful and intentional application of the methods and principles of reflective practice.

They list six characteristics of reflective practitioners (2000, p. 123):

1. engaging in a continual process of self-reflection;
2. relying on theory to guide and inform their practice;
3. using experimentation to test observations, perceptions, and formulations of the experience, beliefs, and needs of their clients;
4. being willing to see through perspectives other than their own, to experience surprise;
5. being open to new information about their practices—as lifelong learners, they are open to new strategies and techniques; and
6. not seeing themselves as experts—acknowledging that both they and their clients have expertise to bring to bear on the conflict situation.

The concept of "reflecting in action" comes from the work of Schon (1987). It means that the mediator is able to carry on an internal conversation about the unexpected. Reflecting in action is based on the premise that professionals usually know more than they say about their actions, more than the theory they are using. In other words, intelligent practice is more than an application of knowledge. As Schon

(1987, p. 50) writes, "know-how is *in* the action." While we may think before acting, much of the spontaneous behaviour of a skillful practitioner comes from somewhere other than prior knowledge. Taking the time to reflect upon our actions can lead us to examine the tacit norms underlying a judgment, the theories implicit in patterns of behaviour, the feelings linked to courses of action, the roles being played out, and the contextual framing of a problem, to name some reflection-in-action objects.

Becoming an Advanced Practitioner

To separate the novice, apprentice, and practitioner, Lang and Taylor (2000, p. 12) use the concept of developing artistry. Picard (2002, pp. 140–141) also says that being a skilled mediator involves the integration of skills, knowledge, and self-reflection. She sets out five hallmarks of advanced practitioners.

1. *Knowledge and skills.* These are required, along with assessment, timing, intuition, empathy, judgment risk, patience, confidence, and the ability to assume the many roles of a mediator.
2. *Critical mind.* This means that advanced practitioners are able to do the following: distinguish their orientation from other mediation approaches; reflect on how a mediation could have been improved; assess the possible good and harm that can come out of a mediation; know when it is time to consult or bring in the experts; and know when it is time to terminate a mediation.
3. *Flexible, creative, and inquisitive.* Advanced practitioners are flexible in that they are willing to change their style of mediating to accommodate parties' needs and abilities; they are creative in that they use humour, metaphor, drama, drawing, language, sculpting, and other creative tools to help parties present their points of view, understand each other, and continue negotiating; and they are inquisitive in that they stay curious and non-judgmental.
4. *Reflective.* This means that advanced practitioners recognize personal limits, biases, values, and world views; that they are in touch with and can manage their own emotions; and that they can "think outside the box."
5. *Lifelong learner.* This means that advanced practitioners are familiar with developments in theory and research; they read books, academic journals, and professional newsletters; they frequently attend professional conferences, workshops, and courses; they are members of professional associations, and they network with other professionals in the field.

Developing Mediation Competence

Achieving artistry as a mediator requires lifelong learning. It requires experience, reflection, and a continuous stream of new knowledge and insights.

One of the most powerful ways for mediators to advance their skills is to observe themselves mediating. A simulated mediation can be videotaped. As part of the debriefing, the mediator discusses the mediation with the role players, stopping at various points to get their reactions to the interventions. The mediator identifies his or her own strengths and weaknesses and, if possible, compares this assessment with other assessments. Less experienced mediators can learn much by asking a more senior mediator to debrief a video with them.

A mediator may give back to the field and advance his or her own skills by coaching new mediators and by participating as a role-player in private sessions. Some communities have organized coaching groups for ongoing skill development.

Another way to develop your **conflict competence** is to keep a regular journal of your relevant experiences with conflict and of your reflections, insights, and learning in connection with these experiences. A reflective journal is a tool for experiential learning. You can use the journaling process to learn more about conflict, about how you deal with conflict, and about your own conflict competencies and practices—both those you have and those you don't have but may choose to develop.

Experienced and prospective mediators alike should approach their practices with open, yet critical, minds. Being *mindful* in the work of mediation means drawing upon both theory and practice. A mediator needs sufficient knowledge and confidence to be transparent, strategic, and intentional. Artistry in mediation comes through competence, creativity, intuition, and resourcefulness.

An Overview of Key Terms and Concepts Used in This Text

What follows is a brief introduction to some of the key terms used in this text. It is not an inclusive glossary of all the new and important terms you will encounter throughout this book. Its main aim is clarification; it is a list of terms that other writers in the area may define slightly differently. We will return to these terms in more detail as we move through the text, deepening your understanding and appreciation of them. To illustrate these terms, we refer to the various conflict scenarios included in this book, the first of which is the Car Repair Blues scenario (see Box 1.1).

BOX 1.1 » Scenario: Car Repair Blues

Chris is the owner-operator of the ARCO service station. Dale lives in the neighbourhood, and occasionally she gets her gas at the ARCO station. But she has never had her car fixed there—until yesterday. Early in the morning, she came to the station with her seven-year-old Ford. She told Chris that it needed its six-month check and that it was running a bit "rough" and probably needed a tune-up. She asked Chris if he could do her a real favour and fix it by the end of the day; she needs her car for work and really can't be without it. Chris said that he would have to "move things around" but that he would try to accommodate her. He said a tune-up would likely run her about $150.

When Dale returned later that day, Chris told her that their thorough inspection revealed that her radiator was almost shot, and then he handed her a bill for $1,200. He had just begun telling her about the rebuilt radiator they'd managed to locate when Dale hit the roof, interrupting him angrily. The following exchange ensued:

> *Dale*: What is this, a licence to print money?
> *Chris*: What do you mean? You wanted me to fix your car right away and I did.
> *Dale*: I don't think so. I never agreed to this—there is no way I can, or will, pay that kind of money.
> *Chris*: Well, you're not going to get your car until you do.

Chris refused to release the car until Dale paid the bill. She stormed out.

Conflict

Conflict exists when a person perceives another person, group, organization, nation, or people as a threat and therefore as an adversary. It involves a subjective perception and belief. Brian may have adversarial perceptions of Alice and be in conflict with her even though Alice does not know how Brian thinks, and she does not have such adversarial perceptions of him. To say that Brian perceives Alice as an adversary means that Brian believes that Alice has or may hurt him somehow, that she has had or may have some adverse effect on him.

Conflict can occur between people who have generally good, cooperative relations. In such a case, it probably will be mild, temporary, and related only to one aspect of the relationship. In other cases, conflict may be much more serious, long-standing, and intractable. In those cases, the adversaries probably view each other as enemies and their adversarial perceptions and emotions (which we call "hostility") will probably permeate all aspects of their relationship.

Conflict may exist without there being any recognized dispute or disagreement between the parties involved. On the other hand, people may have a dispute without there being conflict—in other words, without any adversarial perceptions or emotions developing between the parties. For example, good friends may disagree about what movie or what restaurant to go to without being in conflict.

Conflict Competence

Conflict competence is the measure of a person's ability to successfully respond to and resolve interpersonal conflict. As in other areas of human endeavour, conflict competence requires innate talent and aptitude as well as the skill and artistry that come from ongoing learning and reflective practice. An important goal for any mediator is to help the parties develop conflict competence.

Conflict Narratives

In every conflict situation, there are different **conflict narratives**, or stories, from the people, groups, or organizations involved. These differing interpretations of the conflict are based on each party's values, assumptions, and beliefs, which influence how they make meaning and how they think. Among other things, a conflict narrative will present a protagonist (the good guy, or hero) and an antagonist (the bad guy, or villain). For example, in the Car Repair Blues scenario (see Box 1.1), Dale's conflict narrative will be very different from Chris's; each side will villainize the other according to a particular "justice perspective."

What is a *justice perspective*? It is a narrative perspective on the events that precipitated the dispute, and it determines the form of the conflict narrative. A justice perspective may yield, for example, one of the following:

- an *oppression* story (he/she/they are oppressing me, putting or keeping me down, making my life miserable);
- an *exploitation* story (he/she/they are exploiting me; using me in an oppressive way for his/her/their own gain or profit but to my disadvantage, loss, or hurt);
- a story of *persecution* (he/she/they are persecuting me; *wrongfully* attacking me, accusing me, blaming me, scapegoating me); or
- a story of *subversion* or *sabotage* (he/she/they are working behind the scenes to do me in, to defeat me), or a *conspiracy* (they have a deliberate plan or scheme to do me in, to defeat me).

Convening

Convening is the process for determining the best method for the parties to use to resolve their dispute. In this process, an impartial third party known as the "convenor" will help the parties consider various process options, including the following: negotiation, mediation, conciliation, arbitration, adjudication, or some combination of these processes. Mediation is not always the best choice. It is the convenor's job to discuss the process options with each party and help them determine what process is best for their situation.

There are two ways for a convenor to become involved in a dispute. It may be consensual; that is to say, he or she may intervene at the request of and with the consent of the parties. In other circumstances, convening may be mandatory—a process required by certain procedural rules or regulations that apply to disputes in a particular context.

Let's consider an example of convening that occurs on a consensual basis. In the Divorcing Spouses scenario (see Exercise 1 at the end of Chapter 3), either Jo-Anne or Paul may contact a private practice family mediator to explore the possibility of using mediation to resolve their dispute. Before starting a mediation process with Paul and Jo-Anne, the mediator will need to conduct a convening process that consists of one or more private meetings (in person or by telephone) with each of the parties to determine whether mediation is an appropriate dispute resolution process, agreeable to both of them. If either party refuses to speak to and meet with the convenor/mediator, then the process will not go ahead.

In the Workplace Change scenario (see Box 8.1, in Chapter 8), the convening process provided for in the company's mediation program policy is not really a consensual one. Under this policy, each party is required to meet privately and confidentially with the mediation coordinator. However, neither party is compelled to proceed with mediation. Mediation will be used only if both parties agree to it. In this instance, then, the convening process is not a consensual process, but the mediation is. In the case of the Sonata Development scenario (see Exercise 1 at the end of Chapter 2), a convening process could be initiated by either of the parties (Haven Homes or Sonata Preservation Society (SPS)), or by the City. Whichever party initiates the process, the person conducting the convening process will need to be an independent consultant with expertise and experience in the multi-party mediation of public land-use disputes.

Decision-Making Authority

Decision-making authorities are individuals or entities (groups, organizations, or nations) with legitimate and generally recognized power and authority to determine the outcome of a dispute in the event that the parties fail to do so on their own. An authority may impose a decision or outcome on the parties. Or an authority may help the parties make their own decisions on the issue between them. In the Band Next Door scenario (see Exercise 2 at the end of Chapter 4), the apartment building landlord or superintendent would be an *authority* with the authority or legal power to enforce the rules of the apartment building about loud noise between the hours of 10:00 p.m. and 7:00 a.m.

In the Sonata Development scenario (see Exercise 1 at the end of Chapter 2), the City Council has legal authority to decide what new zoning designation and conditions will apply to the land owned by Haven Homes. The City Council will exercise its decision-making authority on a rezoning application that is submitted by Haven Homes and that is opposed by the SPS. If any party is dissatisfied with the Council's decision on the rezoning application, that party may be entitled to appeal the decision to the Ontario Municipal Board, the body with the statutory power to review and decide disputed land-use issues in Ontario.

Dispute

A **dispute** is a disagreement between two or more persons, groups, organizations, or nations about what action they will take in a specific situation, individually or collectively. For instance, in the Car Repair Blues scenario (Box 1.1), the dispute between Dale and Chris is a disagreement over the costs charged for the repair of a car, and what action should now be taken. Each party has adopted a position that is unacceptable to the other side. Dale refuses to pay Chris the $1,200 he has charged her for fixing her car. Chris refuses to return Dale's car to her until she pays his bill. Until Chris and Dale reach a mutual decision, they will remain in conflict.

Dispute Resolution Processes

Dispute resolution processes are processes for resolving disputes. They fall into two categories:

1. With a *consensual* process, the parties decide the outcome. The two main consensual processes are negotiation and mediation.
2. With a *formal, legal*, or *third-party* process, a third-party authority decides the outcome of the dispute. Third-party dispute resolution processes include adjudication, arbitration, and authoritative command.

The Integrative Paradigm

The **integrative paradigm** of dispute resolution is fundamentally different from the *positional paradigm* to which most people refer when involved in a dispute. With the positional paradigm, people present arguments in support of their own position and try to rebut or undermine an opposing position. Through this process of debate, all arguments are presented and tested. In theory, right shall prevail. Indeed, this is the "adversarial" process that is the basis of our legal system. This is what Deborah Tannen (1999) calls the "argument culture."

The integrative paradigm is based on the premise that there is some validity to both sides' points of view. In pursuing this paradigm, you will explore and try to understand all conflicting points of view. Having done that, you will seek a conclusion that draws on and, so far as possible, integrates the different perspectives.

Issue

In a dispute or conflict among two or more people, we refer to the basic subject of their disagreement as the **issue** between them. In the Car Repair Blues scenario (Box 1.1), the disputed issue is that Dale has refused to pay Chris's bill for $1,200. In some disputes, there are two or more issues. For example, in the Divorcing Spouses dispute between Jo-Anne and Paul, there are at least three issues between the parties: (1) custody of their children, (2) division of their property, and (3) support payments by Paul. The issues that need to be settled for the dispute to be resolved are referred to as the *substantive* or *material* issues between the parties. In any legal analysis of a dispute, a lawyer should be able to identify and describe the substantive issue or issues between the parties in such a way that any other lawyer would concur and say, "Yes, those are indeed the issues between these parties."

Justice and Justice Perspectives

Justice is a complex concept that has different meanings in different situations. It is both a subjective perception (as is injustice) as well as an objective ideal. In most situations of conflict, a sense of injustice will be an element in one party's perception of the other. Party A invariably believes, for example, that Party B has committed, or is in the process of committing, some wrong against Party A. Depending on the context, we may refer to a party's alleged wrong as either an *offence*, a *violation of another's rights*, or a *breach of a duty* or *obligation* or a *liability*.

A primary purpose of our legal or justice system is to apply the rule of law—our established system of laws, procedures, and processes for determining legal liability. In this way, we aim to hold people accountable for actions they commit that are contrary to law. This is the principle of retributive justice: wrongful actions are subject to legal sanction.

The notion of justice may be examined at different levels, with the view changing as the level shifts. We can use the Google Earth program as a metaphor. From the Street View, we examine what happens in detail in a specific case and assess to what extent justice is achieved there, in terms both of outcome and process—in other words, procedural justice. If we go to a higher level, we may view and assess the justice of a given organization or community (for example, an ethnic or faith community). At a still higher level, we may view, examine, and assess the overall justice of a national justice system. At this national level, we can consider to what extent a nation is a "just society." Pierre Trudeau was a lifelong advocate for a just society in Canada.

Another concept of justice is known as *restorative justice*. Some of its fundamental assumptions and premises are different from those of the traditional *retributive* justice system. Restorative justice is achieved through the active responsibility and accountability of the offender, which bring healing and reconciliation for victims, offenders, and the community.

Mediation Programs

A **mediation program** is a system of resources, personnel, procedures, and practices for providing mediation services to people within an organization, school, institution, or community. Typically, an organizational mediation program will have a permanent manager or administrator. There are organized mediation programs in many different organizations, including workplaces, schools, non-profit organizations, and government departments and agencies. Many communities have mediation programs, such as victim–offender mediation programs or neighbourhood mediation services.

Parties and Stakeholders

Both conflicts and disputes involve two or more parties. A **party** is a person, group, organization, or nation that is engaged in and has some responsibility to act in relation to the subject matter of the dispute. Parties have both rights and responsibilities with respect to all other parties in relation to the subject matter of the dispute. These may be legal rights and responsibilities, defined according to the applicable legal system, or they may be moral rights and responsibilities, defined according to a relevant code of conduct or established social practice. An example of the latter would be the universal expectations that people generally have when they line up to purchase tickets at a theatre or to be served at a bank, coffee shop, or grocery store. Party A has rights vis-à-vis Party B (legal or moral) when Party A has a legitimate and generally recognized expectation about what Party B should or should not do in relation to the subject matter of that dispute. Conversely, to say that Party A has responsibilities vis-à-vis Party B (legal or moral) means that Party B has a legitimate and generally recognized expectation about what Party A should or should not do in relation to the subject matter of that dispute.

A **stakeholder** is a person, group, organization, or nation that is affected by a dispute but generally does not have responsibilities to, or claims on, others in relation to the subject matter of the dispute. In the Car Repair Blues scenario (see Box 1.1), Dale and Chris are the parties to the dispute, whereas Dale's family, friends, and employer might be considered stakeholders. In the Sonata Development scenario (see Exercise 1 at the end of Chapter 2), community groups or, for example, the local school board could be involved as stakeholders rather than as parties.

In a multi-party public dispute, stakeholders may participate in a dispute resolution process. Mediation is a consensual process, so the parties would need to consent to their participation. With a formal or legal process (for example, adjudication), a stakeholder would generally be allowed to participate as an intervenor if the procedural rules or the process authority allows for such participation.

Principle of Self-Determination

The principle of **self-determination** is a fundamental principle of mediation. It applies to most (but not all) forms of mediation in North America. According to this principle, it is better for the parties themselves to determine the outcome of their dispute than for others to make decisions for them. Ideally, the parties will do this by a process of negotiation, with only the assistance they need, but not more. This assistance often takes the form of mediation. A mediator who applies the principle of self-determination does only what is required to help the parties decide for themselves the outcome or resolution of their dispute.

Resolution and Settlement

Resolution refers to the outcome, result, or conclusion of a dispute or conflict. The resolution of a dispute is often referred to as a **settlement**. In the Car Repair Blues scenario (Box 1.1), if Chris and Dale agree that Dale will pay Chris $800 in full satisfaction of his bill, we would say that their dispute has been *settled* and that their agreement on the disputed amount was their *settlement*. Reaching a settlement usually means that there is no further legal claim for either party to pursue; any such legal claims have also been settled. In a case with multiple issues, such as Paul and Jo-Anne's divorce dispute (see Exercise 1 at the end of Chapter 3), it is possible to settle one issue—for instance, child custody—without settling the other issues.

The resolution of conflict can also be subjective and interpretive. For instance, Party A's conflict with Party B is resolved when Party A no longer perceives Party B as an adversary, or when Party A's adversarial perception of Party B is reduced, even if that perception is not eliminated altogether.

Response to Conflict

Conflicting parties' perceptions, emotions, and thought processes produce behaviours that are a **response** to these experiences. While we always have a choice in how we respond to conflict, sometimes we respond without thinking—in an instinctive or knee-jerk way. A person will typically have one or some of the following responses to conflict: ignore it and do nothing; flee or withdraw; fight; accommodate; or collaborate with the other party by engaging in dialogue.

For example, in the Car Repair Blues scenario (Box 1.1), Dale could have ignored her conflict with Chris and not acted on her perception that he ripped her off. She could have accommodated him and paid the bill and carried on without even mentioning her negative feelings. If she had done that, she would likely have decided never to take her car back to the ARCO service station, a withdrawal or "flight" response. Alternatively, she could have ignored the conflict as a small blip and continued to patronize Chris and his business. Instead, Dale chose to respond to the conflict by communicating her adversarial perceptions and angry feelings to Chris. Had she not been so aggressive, her communications with Chris might have resulted in a more collaborative, cooperative outcome.

Summary

In this chapter we introduced the reader to the wide variety of mediation applications, including the following: organizations or institutions; public complaints; the formal justice system. We also discussed the new fields of mediation opened up by innovations in information technology. Mediation can achieve various goals. They range from dispute settlement or resolution to understanding, learning, and growing, to restoring or repairing relations after grievous harm has been inflicted. All mediators follow the five-phase approach we have outlined in this chapter, with adaptations within each phase depending upon the goals of the mediation.

Regardless of what particular approach or approaches a mediator may use, the effectiveness of mediation largely stems from its holistic orientation toward understanding conflict and toward helping parties to transform their relationship. A holistic orientation is based on the "new science" paradigm, which seeks knowledge not through examining a system's parts in isolation but through an understanding of the relationships between the parts—their interconnectedness. Logic and rational discussion alone are not sufficient to understand the subjective experience of parties in conflict. Mediators do need to use traditional scientific methods of analysis and strategic planning. At the same time, they need to rely equally on emotional, somatic, intuitive-imaginative, and "connected" ways of knowing to interpret and understand events and experiences. Mediators work to influence parties' ways of understanding, thus promoting relational change. This is done through the heart, mind, body, and spirit.

A key component in the development of mediator competence and artistry is ongoing reflective practice, and we provided some tips as to how you might go about integrating reflective practice into your handling of conflict in order to improve your mediation competence. Finally, we included a list of key terms that we will be using throughout the book. This is not a comprehensive list, but rather a collection of some of the terms and concepts we use frequently in this text.

DISCUSSION QUESTIONS AND EXERCISES

1. How and where will you apply what you learn in this course (be as specific as you can)?
2. Why is it important for the mediator to clarify the goals of the mediation?
3. Think of a conflict you have been involved in. Now, think of a metaphor or analogy that describes how you viewed that situation. Think creatively. Was it like a "pot boiling over," "walking on eggshells," "a cold Canadian winter"? How evocative—and successful—is your metaphor in describing what it felt like to be in the situation? What emotions does it evoke? How rich and full is the picture you have painted?
4. Read the Car Repair Blues scenario (Box 1.1) and then answer the following questions:
    a. What is the conflict between Dale and Chris?
    b. What is Dale's conflict narrative? What is her justice perspective? What is Chris's conflict narrative? What is his justice perspective?
    c. Who are some third-party decision-making authorities in this case?

5. Think of a conflict situation that you are or have been involved in. Write a two-page reflective journal about this conflict, including what you said and did, some of the challenges you experienced and what you could do differently in this case to be more conflict competent.

FURTHER READING

Lang, M., & Taylor, A. (2000). *The making of a mediator*. San Francisco: Jossey-Bass.

LeBaron, M. (2002). *Bridging troubled waters: Conflict resolution from the heart*. San Francisco: Jossey-Bass.

Picard, C.A. (2002). *Mediating interpersonal and small group conflict* (2nd ed.). Ottawa: Golden Dog Press.

Wheatley, M.J. (1999). *Leadership and the new science*. San Francisco: Berrett-Koehler Publications.

Websites

The Association for Conflict Resolution (ACR): http://www.acrnet.org
This is a professional organization dedicated to enhancing the practice and public understanding of conflict resolution. ACR gives voice to the choices for quality conflict resolution.

The Institute for the Study of Conflict Transformation, Inc.: http://www.transformativemediation.org
This is a professional organization dedicated to the study of transformative mediation.

National Center for Technology and Dispute Resolution: http://www.odr.info

Ontario Dentists Association. ODA Mediation Service: http://www.oda.on.ca/you-your-dentist/oda-mediation-service60

Treasury Board of Canada Secretariat. Report of the Review of the *Public Service Modernization Act, 2003*: http://www.tbs-sct.gc.ca/reports-rapports/psma-lmfp/psma-lmfptb-eng.asp

REFERENCES

Benjamin, R. (1995a). The constructive uses of deception: Skills, strategies, and techniques of the folkloric trickster figure and their application by mediators. *Mediation Quarterly*, *13*, 3–18.

Benjamin, R. (1995b). The mediator as trickster: The folkloric figure as professional role model. *Mediation Quarterly*, *13*, 131–149.

Bronson, S. (2000). Improving mediator competence through self-assessment. *Mediation Quarterly*, *18*, 171–179.

Burton, J. (1990). *Conflict: Resolution and prevention*. San Francisco: St. Martin's Press.

Bush, R.A.B. (1989). Mediation and adjudication, dispute resolution and ideology: An imaginary conversation. *Journal of Contemporary Legal Issues*, *3*, 1–35.

Bush, R.A.B., & Folger, J.P. (2005). *The Promise of mediation: The transformative approach to conflict* (rev. ed.). San Francisco: Jossey-Bass.

Fisher, J. (2000). Symbol in mediation. *Mediation Quarterly, 18*, 87–107.

Lang, M., & Taylor, A. (2000). *The making of a mediator*. San Francisco: Jossey-Bass.

LeBaron, M. (2002). *Bridging troubled waters: Conflict resolution from the heart*. San Francisco: Jossey-Bass.

Liebman, Carol B. (2011). Medical malpractice mediation: Benefits gained, opportunities lost. *Law and Contemporary Problems, 74*, 135-149.

Lynch, J. (1997). *RCMP: Revitalizing culture, motivating people: Innovations in conflict management system design at the Royal Canadian Mounted Police*. Ottawa: RCMP.

Macfarlane, J. (1995). *Court-based mediation of civil cases: An evaluation of the Ontario Court (General Division) ADR centre*. Toronto: Ministry of the Attorney General.

Maggiolo, W. (1971). *Techniques of mediation*. Dobbs Ferry, NY: Oceana.

Mayer, (2000). *The dynamics of conflict resolution: A practitioner's guide*. San Francisco: Jossey-Bass.

Moore, C.W. (1996). *The mediation process: Practical strategies for resolving conflict* (2nd ed.). San Francisco: Jossey-Bass.

Picard, C.A. (2002). *Mediating interpersonal and small group conflict* (2nd ed.). Ottawa: Golden Dog Press.

Picard, C.A. (2004). Exploring an integrated framework for understanding mediation. *Conflict Resolution Quarterly, 21*(3), 295–311.

Picard, C.A., & Saunders, R.P. (2002). The regulation of mediation. In M. MacNeil, N. Sargent, & P. Swan (Eds.), *Law, regulation and governance* (pp. 223–238). Toronto: Oxford University Press.

Schon, D.A. (1987). *The reflective practitioner*. San Francisco: Jossey-Bass.

Tannen, D. (1999). *The argument culture: Stopping America's war of words*. New York: Random House.

Wheatley, M.J. (1999). *Leadership and the new science*. San Francisco: Berrett-Koehler Publications.

CHAPTER 2

Dispute Resolution Processes

LEARNING OBJECTIVES

After reading this chapter, you will be able to:

- Understand the nature of each of the following types of dispute resolution processes—adjudication, authoritative command, arbitration, conciliation, mediation, and negotiation
- Identify the differences between positional and principled approaches to negotiation, and the differences between interest-based processes, such as negotiation and mediation, and rights-based processes, such as adjudication and arbitration
- Explain what is meant by mediation and by certain hybrid mediation processes, and how the approach known as principled negotiation can satisfy the interests of all parties

CHAPTER OUTLINE

Introduction 31
The Relationship Between Power, Rights, and Interests 32
The Dispute Resolution Spectrum 33
Power-Based Dispute Resolution Methods 34
Rights-Based Dispute Resolution Methods 38
Interest-Based Dispute Resolution Methods 40
Negotiation 42
Mediation 52
Summary 57

You've got to know when to hold 'em, know when to fold 'em, know when to walk away, know when to run.

Kenny Rogers, "The Gambler"

Introduction

All societies develop social arrangements for dealing with conflicts. No society could function for very long without doing so. Indeed, the success of a society is often contingent on its capacity for developing fair, just, and efficient methods for resolving disputes among its members. Without effective institutional arrangements for managing conflicts peacefully, social conflicts can escalate and become destructive and unmanageable.

Most of us are familiar with the feud between the Hatfields and the McCoys. The original cause of the conflict was long forgotten as the conflict generated its own momentum, drawing in new members of both families in a never-ending cycle of grievance, hostility, and counter-aggression. We can observe similar patterns of destructive behaviour in many conflict situations, from small, interpersonal, family disputes, to long-standing inter-ethnic or inter-regional conflicts involving entire communities. A primary goal in designing dispute resolution methods is to manage conflict peacefully and thereby avoid these destructive patterns.

There are a number of different **dispute resolution processes**. In this chapter, we examine power-based, rights-based, and interest-based methods. We locate these different processes on a dispute resolution spectrum and identify the differences between them. Primarily, we focus on the interest-based process of negotiation, discussing two different negotiation approaches and the practical implications of applying them in particular cases. Then, after considering some negotiation challenges and strategies, we conclude with a brief introduction to the mediation process.

The Relationship Between Power, Rights, and Interests

One way of looking at how conflict is resolved is by examining the power, rights, and interests of the parties involved (Ury, Brett, & Goldberg, 1988). In a power-dominant system, power is generally confined to coercive power and does not include other more positive or cooperative forms of power such as restorative or creative power.

During the so-called Dark Ages, or Middle Ages (about 400 to 1500 CE), in Western civilization, the use of force or power-based methods was common. Rights-based and interest-based methods did exist. However, without a well-established system of laws and a functioning government to implement them, people resorted mostly to power-based methods to deal with conflict.

In the last half of the second millennium, emerging Western nations developed the laws and the government institutions required to implement what is referred to as the "rule of law." By the 20th century, Canadian society, along with most other Western nations, recognized the state's legitimate power or authority to establish and apply an elaborate system of laws for regulating virtually all aspects of our lives. The rights-based system and rights-based methods for dealing with conflicts became all-pervasive. Rights-based methods for dealing with conflict require a well-established and functional government that includes courts, tribunals, and police forces, as well as the government departments and agencies to administer and support them.

Rights-based methods are established on a foundation of authoritative power. This concept applies in private contexts as well. Within any community, organization, or family, there are recognized rules or norms that govern people's interactions, and there are persons with legitimate authority or power to apply these rules or norms. In other words, they have **decision-making authority**. For example, a university student residence will have rules that govern the activities in the residence between 11:00 p.m. and 7:00 a.m., as well as a person with the recognized authority to enforce those rules. However, as many university dons, school teachers, and parents have experienced, having the authority to enforce standards of good behaviour and having the power to actually do it are often very different.

The interest-based approach to conflict is one that seeks to resolve the conflict by satisfying the interests of each party. "Interests" are the parties' needs, concerns, and values—what is most important to them in the context of the conflict. Consider, for example, a typical conflict that occurs when a small group of students in residence party loudly at 1:00 am. Their interests may be to express themselves freely and to have a well-rounded social life—the complete university experience. On the other hand, the interests of the students in conflict with them probably are to be well-rested so they can do their academic work as well as possible. Later in this chapter, we discuss negotiation and mediation as interest-based processes.

Very few conflicts are one-dimensional; power, rights, and interests are elements that are interconnected in many conflict situations. As Ury, Brett, and Goldberg (1988, p. 6) remind us, even in negotiation and mediation, where the emphasis is placed on reconciling the interests of the disputants, the relative bargaining *power* of the parties may often play a significant role in the negotiation process. Indeed, these authors suggest that some negotiations, which they refer to as "power-based negotiations," may be explicitly concerned with establishing who is the more powerful party. Examples of this can be found in the negotiations over the terms of a peace treaty between two countries that have recently been at war, or the negotiations between management and a union over the terms of a new agreement.

Other negotiations, such as an out-of-court settlement negotiation between two parties involved in a lawsuit, may be explicitly concerned with the *rights* of the parties and how a judge would likely decide the case should negotiations fail. In this negotiating context, the rights of the parties and their relative strength or bargaining power, as well as their relative interest in reaching a settlement, are all likely to be factors in the negotiation process and will influence the final outcome of the conflict.

Ury, Brett, and Goldberg believe that contemporary society is dominated primarily by power-based dispute resolution processes, then by rights-based ones, and, to a lesser extent, by interest-based ones. They call this a "distressed system"; and they suggest that a better model would be one where interest-based processes are more commonplace than either power- or rights-based processes. Their vision for an "interests dominant system" is depicted in Figure 2.1.

The Dispute Resolution Spectrum

Figure 2.2 is a "resolution wheel" showing the spectrum of dispute resolution methods and the three basic categories—power-based, rights-based, and interest-based—into which they fall. It consists of three concentric circles. The outer circle shows the three

Figure 2.1 Moving from a Distressed to an E ective Dispute Resolution System

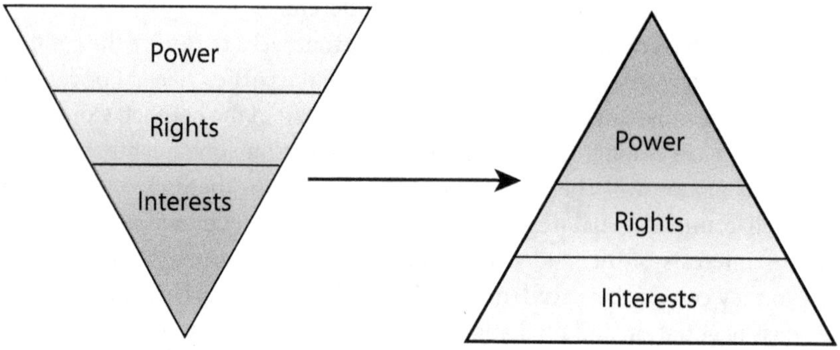

Source: Ury, Brett, and Goldberg (1988, p. 19).

basic approaches: power, rights, and interests. The middle circle has the six methods. The inner circle indicates the "nature" of the decision maker for each method—that is, who decides the outcome. In negotiation and mediation, the parties decide the outcome. For arbitration, adjudication, and authoritative command, the authority decides. And for unilateral action, one party decides. Note that the methods on the lower half of the wheel are those in which "Authority Decides"; those on the upper half are ones in which "Parties Decide," either together or unilaterally. As we will discuss, with arbitration the parties decide on the authority (they select the arbitrator) and the arbitrator decides the outcome.

The three categories and six methods shown in Figure 2.2 are not mutually exclusive. Parties may choose one dispute resolution method as their primary one while using some or all of the others in different combinations, variations, or hybrids. Practitioners often use various methods in order to meet the needs of the parties in a particular dispute.

Power-Based Dispute Resolution Methods

Jessie and her younger brother Tim are fighting over a toy. Tim says he had it first, but Jessie says it belongs to her. Who will get the toy? How will their argument be resolved? One method is by *unilateral action*—one of them will physically take the toy and keep it from the other. Since Jessie is bigger and stronger than Tim, she has the power to do that.

Unilateral Action

Unilateral action is one party acting to achieve a desired outcome without the cooperation or participation of the other party. This may involve force or coercion.

Figure 2.2 The Dispute Resolution Spectrum

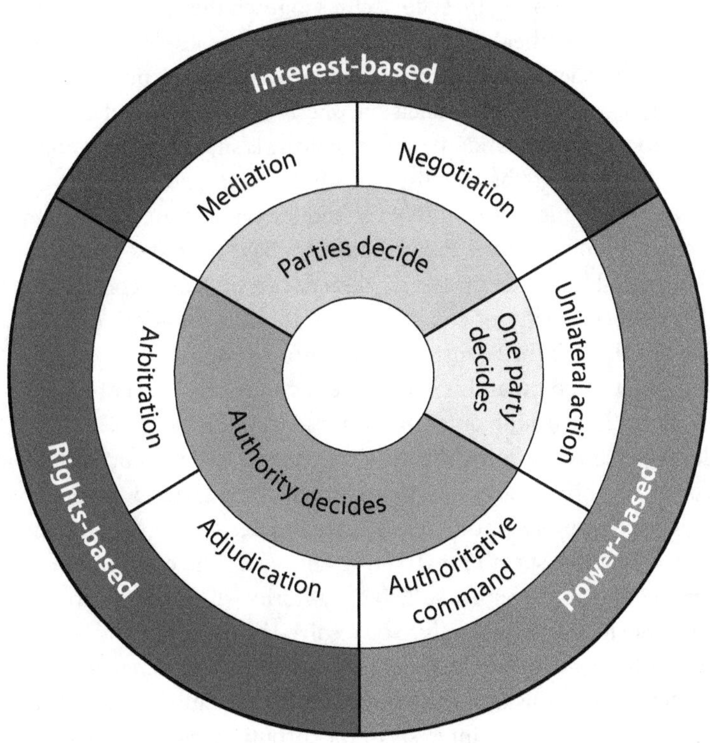

Strikes, lockouts, peaceful protests, and boycotts are all forms of unilateral action and are intended to pressure the other party into making concessions in a conflict situation. Often, unilateral action by one party results in escalated conflict, as the other party retaliates with coercive action or pressure tactics of its own. Other examples of unilateral action are military or armed intervention, including intervention by peacekeeping forces, or action taken by a coast guard unit to protect local fisheries.

Authoritative Command

Another power-based method for dealing with disputes is *authoritative command.* Let's return to Jessie and Tim. Their mother hears their argument and intervenes. Each child claims the toy. Tim pleads, "I had it first"; Jessie counters, "I don't care, it belongs to me." They are both right—it does belong to Jessie, and Tim did have it first. The mother listens to the two children and then considers what to do. She may decide that Jessie can have it, since it belongs to her. On the other hand, the mother may say, "Young lady, in this house we share our things, so you are going to have to let Tim keep it, at least for the rest of the morning." Or, she may be so exasperated by their constant fighting that she decides to teach them both a lesson and takes the toy away so that neither child can have it.

The mother's decision-making power derives from her position of authority over the children. In making her decision, she is not constrained by their arguments. There is no particular standard or rule that she is supposed to rely on in making her decision. She does not have to listen to all the facts before making up her mind, or to give each child the opportunity to introduce evidence or cross-examine the other. Even more significantly, the mother does not have to justify her decision to the two squabbling children; she can even make a decision, such as confiscating the toy, that satisfies neither. Finally, of course, the children have no right of appeal against the mother's decision if they consider it unfair or wrong.

Authoritative command is used to resolve various types of conflicts and issues within all kinds of groups, organizations, and institutions. Consider the following example. Two managers from different departments within a corporation are involved in a conflict over how the corporation's budget should be allocated. Manager A wants to see more money spent on the research and design of new products; Manager B wants more money spent on marketing and sales. The corporation's budget is limited, and neither manager has sufficient authority within the corporation to overrule the other. Such a conflict is likely to be resolved by the command of a senior manager who has authority over both of these managers. The senior manager decides the issue based on what she considers to be best for the corporation. The decision is not based on either the rights or the interests of the disputing managers. We might call this a "management decision."

In a public or government context, "policy" or "administrative" decisions are another form of authoritative command. In Canada's government, the authority of the Queen, as head of state, is exercised through the principles and practices of our parliamentary democracy.

Majority Vote

One of the most common democratic processes for resolving public policy conflicts—and another form of authoritative command—is the process of majority vote. Consider the following scenario. A developer has applied to city council to rezone a parcel of land in a residential area, so the developer can build a new shopping mall. City council is considering this application. The developer argues that the mall will bring new jobs and new residents to the area, and will contribute to the process of urban regeneration. A neighbourhood coalition, concerned about the increased traffic that the mall is likely to bring into the area, seeks the support of a city councillor to prevent the development from going ahead. Council listens to arguments both for and against the proposed development, and then votes on the rezoning application. In the end, the policy dispute will be decided by council vote. If a majority of the city councillors vote in favour of the motion, the rezoning application will be approved. If, however, a majority of councillors are opposed to the rezoning application, the motion will fail, and the developer will have to reconsider its plans for the shopping mall, perhaps cancel the project altogether. The councillors do not have to justify their individual decisions to vote in favour of or against the proposal.

The principle of majority vote is considered to be an effective process for resolving many kinds of public and private policy disputes because it is fair, just, and efficient. It is *fair*, because each party in the process has an equal opportunity to present voters with arguments in support of its position. (This applies whether the vote is a council decision on a rezoning application or a municipal election to decide who will be the next mayor.) It is *just*, because all the participants accept that this is a legitimate way to decide the outcome of the dispute, and thus they are unlikely to contest the outcome even if they are disappointed in the result. Finally, it is *efficient*, because the outcome of the voting procedure is final and will be determined as soon as the votes are counted and the result is announced.

Problems with Authoritative Command

Authoritative command is often an efficient mechanism for resolving organizational conflicts, but it may not always be fair or just. Consider the situation of a young female employee who is subjected to harassing behaviour by her supervisor. She may be justifiably concerned about submitting her complaint to a senior manager in the organization. What if the senior manager favours the supervisor, with whom he or she may have had a working relationship over a number of years? Are there any assurances that the employee's complaint will be listened to seriously or investigated? Even if the senior manager does take the complaint seriously, what criteria should govern his or her decision? Does the manager have the authority to suspend the supervisor for his improper behaviour, or even to dismiss him on disciplinary grounds? Or could this action by the manager expose the organization to a potential lawsuit by the supervisor for wrongful dismissal? What if the manager responds to the employee's complaint by transferring the supervisor to another position in the organization, or by suggesting to the employee that perhaps she should transfer to another position in the organization?

We can quickly see that relying on a power-based process to resolve workplace harassment disputes may sometimes produce very unjust outcomes. In the scenario described above, the outcome may be unjust for the complainant or, potentially, for the supervisor. In these circumstances, it may be preferable for all those directly involved in the conflict situation (and this includes not only the complainant and the supervisor but also the manager and the organization as a whole) to utilize a different type of dispute resolution mechanism. The two leading possibilities are *rights-based processes*, such as adjudication or arbitration, and *interest-based processes*, which are based on negotiation.

Rights-Based Dispute Resolution Methods

Rights-based methods of resolving conflict normally entail formal adjudicative processes involving courts and tribunals. These processes rely on evidence-based methods of fact-finding to determine whether the allegations made by the complainant can be verified, and the court or tribunal determines what legal or arbitral consequences should follow. Processes of this kind typically have certain features in common:

1. an objective fact-finding process that is often adversarial in form;
2. relatively formal procedural rules governing the disputants' participation in the fact-finding process;
3. a relatively time-consuming process for gathering and organizing relevant evidence;
4. a third party with authority to make a decision that is binding on the disputants;
5. zero-sum outcomes, with a clear winner and a loser; and
6. an expectation (or requirement) that the third party should provide reasons for his or her decision.

We will see all six of these elements at work in the litigation process, in which a judge *adjudicates* a legal dispute between two litigants. We will also see them in the *arbitration* process, which involves a less formal adjudicative mechanism for deciding a dispute between two parties.

Adjudication

Adjudication is a formal, rights-based process in which an impartial third party (adjudicator), with no personal interest in the outcome of the dispute, makes an authoritative ruling on contested questions of law or fact. Adjudication differs from authoritative command. In the cases of authoritative command cited above—those of the mother with the children and of the senior manager with the supervisor—the decision-making power is based on the two figures' pre-existing position of authority over the disputants. An adjudicator, by contrast, has no authority over the disputants except insofar as he or she is required to make a decision about the issues in dispute. This means that the adjudicator's decision-making power is restricted to the specific questions of law or fact that are presented by the parties for decision, and cannot normally extend beyond this. (For a classic discussion of the elements of adjudication, see Fuller, 1978, pp. 353–409.)

The most familiar context for adjudication is the court system. Here, the judge, who is a state-appointed official, has the primary responsibility to decide the issues in dispute between the litigants in accordance with formal rules of law. Adjudication is also frequently used in rights-based administrative tribunal proceedings, such as an immigration review board hearing, a municipal board hearing, or a complaint before a human rights tribunal.

Because the adjudicator can only make a decision on the issues presented by the parties, the issues in dispute must be *narrowly defined* so that the adjudicator can make a decision. Within the litigation process, this means that the dispute becomes translated into a set of legal and factual issues. Aspects of the conflict that cannot be narrowly defined tend to be treated as irrelevant to the adjudication process, no matter how important they may be to the disputants (Emond, 1989, pp. 8–9; Boulle & Kelly, 1998, p. 41). One consequence of this restrictive orientation is that the disputants may feel they have lost control over their own conflict. In many contexts, the disputants do not participate directly in the adjudication process. Instead, their lawyers represent them in the legal proceedings and make arguments and present evidence on their behalf. In these cases, the only opportunity a disputant has to participate directly is when he or she is called to testify as a witness.

Adjudication is known as an "adversarial process." Both parties have an opportunity to present evidence and arguments in support of their respective positions. They also have an opportunity to attack the evidence and credibility of the other party. The adjudicator then must make a decision on the issues in dispute, based on the evidence and arguments that have been presented. The adjudicator must decide in favour of one party or the other—a win–lose outcome in which one party wins and the other loses. In most cases, the adjudicator cannot try to find a compromise or base his or her decision on any external factors or information that was not presented by the parties themselves. With this adversarial process, each party emphasizes or exaggerates the strong points of its own case and attacks the other party's case, including the credibility and character of that party. In addition to being a long and expensive process, adjudication tends to damage or even destroy the relationship between the parties.

Arbitration

Arbitration is a private, confidential dispute resolution process. Like adjudication, arbitration is a process whereby parties submit their dispute to an impartial third party who is authorized to make a decision that resolves the issues between the parties. Unlike a judge or other state-appointed adjudicator, the arbitrator is selected by the parties, who are responsible for paying his or her fees (McLaren & Sanderson, 1995, p. 104).

Unless it is mandated by statute (for example, under the *Labour Relations Act*), arbitration is "consensual" in that both parties must agree to the process. In many cases, that agreement is in place before the dispute arises; it is made pursuant to a clause in a pre-existing contract that governs the parties' relationship. Examples of contracts that include such clauses are collective bargaining agreements, construction contracts, commercial leases, employment agreements, and other corporate or commercial agreements. In the absence of such a pre-existing clause, arbitration can be used only if the parties agree to it after their dispute has arisen. In Ontario, such arbitration agreements are governed by the *Arbitration Act, 1991*.

Arbitration provides a more *flexible* dispute resolution process than the court system does, since it is not bound by the court's formal rules of fact-finding and procedure. In addition, the parties are able to select an arbitrator with expertise in a particular area, such as labour–management relations or international commercial arbitration, rather than having to deal with an appointed judge who may not be an expert in the relevant area. Arbitration is generally quicker and cheaper than the court system, since the parties are able to arrange the timing of the arbitration hearing by agreement, rather than being forced to wait until their case comes up on the court docket (McLaren & Sanderson, 1995, p. 105; Stitt, Handy, & Simm, 1996, p. 455).

Interest-Based Dispute Resolution Methods

Arbitration and adjudication are referred to as "rights-based" processes because the criteria for deciding the issues between the disputants are legal ones. The decisions of the third party—arbitrator or adjudicator—are based on an analysis of the rights and obligations of the parties. With a rights-based approach, in other words, the parties will present their claims and positions in legal terms—in terms of their rights and obligations. With interest-based processes such as mediation and conciliation, on the other hand, the parties themselves decide the issues based on what they determine to be their best interests. Parties that take an interest-based approach will think outside the "legal box" and consider a wider range of factors—that is, their interests.

An example will clarify this distinction between rights-based processes and interest-based ones. Consider the Car Repair Blues dispute from Chapter 1 (Box 1.1). In a rights-based process, Dale could claim that Chris has no right to be paid for repairs that she (Dale) never agreed to. Dale (or her lawyer) could apply a contract law analysis to the facts of the case. She could say that because there was no agreement that Chris would replace her radiator, he has no right to claim any payment for this repair to her car. This analysis is a narrow one that only considers legal factors. If, on the other hand, Dale and Chris were to take an interest-based approach, they could consider factors such as Chris's business reputation, Dale's need to be treated fairly, and their future business relationship. We will discuss in greater detail below (under the heading "Principled Negotiation") how an interest-based approach would work in the case of Dale and Chris.

The distinguishing feature of interest-based processes is the high degree of input and control over outcomes that the parties themselves have. In a negotiation, the parties may negotiate directly with each other, or they may negotiate through representatives, such as lawyers or agents. Mediation and conciliation are both assisted negotiation processes in which an impartial third party intervenes to help the parties reach a negotiated agreement (Boulle & Kelly, 1998, p. 74).

The role of a conciliator falls somewhere between that of a mediator and that of an arbitrator. A conciliator may actively create and propose terms of settlement, which the parties are then free to accept or reject. In most forms of mediation, the mediator will leave it to the parties themselves to generate their own terms of settlement, though he or she may explore various settlement options with them. As Boulle and Kelly (1998, p. 74) observe, there is a lot of overlap between the role of a mediator and that of a conciliator. In this book, we focus on mediation as the most common form of assisted negotiation process.

The key presumption of all interest-based processes for resolving conflict is that a decision that satisfies the interests of all the disputants is likely to provide a better resolution to the conflict than a decision imposed by a third party. This presumption is relevant to everything we will have to say about mediation, so it is useful to stop and reflect on it now. The following arguments underlie it:

1. Interest-based processes for resolving conflict tend to promote integrative or win–win outcomes, as compared with the tendency of rights-based or power-based processes to result in zero–sum or win–lose outcomes.
2. A decision that is made by the disputants themselves is more participatory and democratic than a decision imposed by a third party. Interest-based processes, therefore, encourage greater autonomy and **self-determination** by disputants than rights-based processes do.
3. By focusing on the disputants' *interests* rather than on their *rights*, a wider range of potential settlement options may be opened up. Interest-based processes, therefore, tend to promote more creative decision making than rights-based processes do.
4. In reaching a decision or choosing between a range of settlement options, the disputants are likely to be better judges of their own interests than a third party (Mnookin & Kornhauser, 1979).
5. Collaborative or joint decision making, by its very nature, requires the voluntary participation of the disputants. A decision that is arrived at voluntarily is likely to result in a more *satisfying* outcome for all disputants, and, consequently, one that is likely to be more stable and long-lasting than a decision that is externally imposed and does not necessarily satisfy all parties' interests.
6. A collaborative process that addresses the interests of all parties is much more likely to preserve or even promote a good relationship between the parties than an adversarial, rights-based process.

Negotiation

Negotiation occurs when people communicate for the purpose of reaching agreement on some action that one or more of them will take. By this definition, negotiation includes a discussion you may have with a friend about what to watch on TV, or what to have for dinner, or what movie to go to, or about who will do the laundry, wash the dishes, or clean the bathroom. In the workplace, we negotiate deadlines with our bosses, the division of tasks with our colleagues, and the details of a project's scope with our clients. Living and working with other people require that we be able to negotiate.

Often, negotiation occurs without any *apparent* conflict—without any disagreement, argument, or the sorts of emotions, communications, and behaviour typically associated with disagreements or fights. Yet, there is always the potential for a negotiation to become a full-blown conflict if we do not meet one another's needs in a satisfactory way. Think of how easily a negotiation over who will do the dinner dishes can escalate into a shouting match during which each party, in order to make his or her point, ends up airing a list of past grievances. Negotiation, like mediation, requires a good deal of skill and artistry, particularly in situations where the potential for negative conflict is high.

Any negotiation includes several essential elements:

1. Negotiation is a process of communication between two or more parties. The communication may be direct or indirect—where a party communicates through an agent or representative.
2. The parties are communicating for the purpose of trying to reach an agreement.
3. The subject matter of the parties' negotiation must be some proposed *joint or reciprocal action*. Joint action is an activity in which both parties are active participants—for example, going to a movie together. Reciprocal action implies that one person does something for the other, and the other does something in return. For example, in a workplace negotiation, one person might agree to draft the content of a project proposal if the other takes on the task of developing a budget for the project.

Discussions in which one person attempts to convince another about who the greatest hockey player of all time was or what caused the decline and fall of the Roman Empire are not negotiations.

Negotiation is defined by Pruitt and Carnevale (1993, pp. xv, 2) as "a discussion between two or more parties aimed at resolving incompatible goals." Likewise, Fisher and Ury (1991, p. xvii) define negotiation as "back and forth communication designed to reach an agreement when you and the other side have some interests that are shared and others that are opposed." We have developed the following definition, based on these earlier ones:

> Negotiation is a process of communication between two or more parties seeking to reach agreement on some joint or reciprocal action to be taken by them.

Negotiation is used both to enter into contractual relations (for example, to sell an asset or to begin employment) and to deal with issues or disagreements that may arise within existing relationships. Disagreements arise within contractual relationships (for example, buyer–seller, employer–employee, partner–partner) and within other types of relationships, such as the following: family relationships, where (for example) divorcing spouses are trying to divide assets; community relationships, where neighbours have disagreements over noise or property use; and tort relationships, where accident victims and other involved parties (or their insurance companies) contest damages sustained in a car accident.

Types of Negotiation

Fisher and Ury (1981) distinguish between two broad types of negotiation: positional and principled. In the following, we will describe each of these two types of negotiation and will illustrate, with case studies, how each would proceed.

Positional Negotiation

You have experienced positional negotiation countless times since childhood. You want someone to do something, and you try to persuade him or her to agree to your proposal. You want the family car for the weekend or you want your roommate to clean the kitchen. Any time you try to persuade someone to agree to your proposal, you are engaged in positional negotiation. Your position is your desired outcome—your demands, or what you want the other person to do. This is a distributive approach to negotiation. The English legal system uses this adversarial principle, pitting opposing positions against each other and determining the "truth" according to which of the two positions appears the best or the strongest. Forceful advocacy and debating prowess are major assets in this system.

Positional negotiation typically involves strategies and tactics that most of us are familiar with. Competing behaviour will likely be present. In our Garage Sale scenario (Box 2.1), Mario makes a "lowball" offer as his opening position, concealing the extent of his interest in the piece and his desire to have it. Nadia responds, insisting on her original price, and conceals any willingness to take less. Both responses are positional.

Principled Negotiation

In their seminal book *Getting to Yes*, first published in 1981, Fisher and Ury developed an approach to negotiation that is fundamentally different from positional negotiation. They call it "principled negotiation." It is based on the assumption that it is possible to integrate the needs of all parties in determining best outcomes.

BOX 2.1 » Scenario: Garage Sale

At a garage sale, Mario sees a white pine cabinet that he'd like to buy. The sticker price is $400, but he wants to get it for no more than $150. He initiates the negotiation by saying to the vendor, Nadia, that he will pay $80 for the item. That is Mario's position, which, in his mind, is his "opening position." Nadia frowns, shakes her head, and says that she might accept "a bit less than $400, but not $80—no way." She shows and describes several features of the piece and says how and when it was made. Mario shrugs his shoulders and decides to leave and come back later in the day. When he returns, the item is still there, but now the price tag is $300 (Nadia has changed her position from $400 to $300). Mario says: "I'll take that thing off your hands for $120." Nadia says: "It's worth three times that—I'd accept $260, but that'd be highway robbery." They continue to haggle, eventually agreeing that Mario will buy the cabinet for $215.

Principled negotiation is sometimes called "interest-based negotiation," "integrative negotiation," or "collaborative negotiation." In this book, we use these terms interchangeably.

According to Fisher and Ury, principled negotiation is based on four essential principles:

1. Separate the people from the problem.
2. Focus on interests, not positions.
3. Generate options for mutual gain.
4. Use objective criteria.

In examining each of these principles, we will revisit the Car Repair Blues scenario that we considered in Chapter 1 (Box 1.1).

Dale and Chris have a dispute over what Chris is going to do with Dale's car and how much she must pay (or what she must do) to get it back. Walking home from the ARCO garage, Dale may cool down enough to decide to negotiate further with Chris, in an attempt to get her car back. At this point, Dale can pursue either a *positional approach* or a *principled approach.*

Car Repair Blues: The Positional Approach

Dale takes the position that Chris should return the car to her upon her paying $150. She argues that Chris was wrong in charging her $900 for work he did (or claims to have done) and that she is therefore entitled to get her car back upon payment of a fair and reasonable amount for the repair. Dale believes that Chris was unreasonable and inconsiderate (she may even have doubts about his honesty and business ethics).

Clearly, she is very upset with what he did, and her behaviour toward him is angry and sarcastic. In pressing her position with Chris, Dale not only presents her arguments as to why she is right, but attacks Chris's position, his actions toward her, and even his character. Whether she really intends it, her words and manner come across to Chris as being insulting and hostile. Dale hopes that Chris will feel bad about what he has done and perhaps fearful of what she might do in response, so he will give in to her demands.

Car Repair Blues: The Principled Approach

Instead of taking a positional negotiation approach, Chris could pursue principled negotiation. To do that, he would prepare for and approach his negotiation with Dale in accordance with the four principles explained in *Getting to Yes* (Fisher & Ury, 1991), listed above.

1. Separate the People from the Problem

Although Chris is upset by Dale's behaviour and her statement that she is being "ripped off," he accepts that she probably sees the situation very differently than he does. He is willing to respect and listen to her view, though he disagrees with it. He wants to have a meaningful dialogue so that he can gain a better understanding of Dale's experience and her perspective. He also hopes that Dale will be able to understand and respect his perspective. He gives considerable thought to how he can express his perspective to Dale in such a way that she will hear and appreciate it. Chris realizes that the negative perceptions and feelings he has toward Dale (and that she probably has toward him) will affect their negotiation. He resolves to do what he can to overcome their negative impact.

To this end, Chris might say something like the following, early in his discussion with Dale:

> I recognize that your view of this situation is very different from mine. We just see things differently. I want to give you a chance to talk about how you see the situation. Then I'd like to do the same. I would like each of us to talk about our hopes and concerns and, in particular, what is really important to each of us. If we do this, I think we'll be able to figure out the best way to resolve our differences.

Chris's aim in using this approach is to overcome his and Dale's inclination to attack each other—to blame, insult, or intimidate. He knows that such attacks result in an escalation of the conflict. By separating the people from the problem, the parties can "attack the problem, not each other"; they can be soft on the people and hard on the problem. Successful application of this principle will enable parties in conflict to move on to the second tenet of the principled approach: Focus on interests, not positions. This is the heart of the interest-based negotiation process.

2. Focus on Interests, Not Positions

Positions are what people say they want—their preferred outcomes. In Car Repair Blues, Chris wants Dale to pay him $1,200 for the repairs he made to her car. His position is that Dale must pay him $1,200. He can present various reasons or arguments why she should do that. On the other hand, Dale's position is that Chris should let her have her car for payment of $150, which was his original estimate for a tune-up. Like Chris, she also has arguments in support of her position—reasons for her thinking her outcome is the right one.

What are Chris's and Dale's *interests*? What do they really need in this situation? What is really motivating them? What is most important to each of them in relation to the settlement of this issue? Why do they want what they say they want? According to the theory of interest-based negotiation, discovering each party's interests—that is, the underlying needs or motivations beneath their positions—is the key to unlocking their dispute. Some of these interests will be apparent, some hidden. In many cases, it may not be at all clear to a particular party what his or her most important interests are in relation to the disputed issue. How then do we discover the parties' key interests?

In pursuing the interest-based approach, Chris's goal would be for both Dale and himself to receive all relevant information, including a full understanding of their respective perceptions, needs, expectations, beliefs, and concerns. To this end, he would give Dale a full opportunity to express her perspective, and he would ask appropriate questions to clarify and probe her concerns, assumptions, and expectations. Then he would invite her to give him the opportunity to fully express his own perspective and to answer any questions she might have about his concerns.

Chris's ultimate objective would be the following: the understanding and insights that he and Dale gain from this interest-based discussion would enable them to go on and reach an agreement that fully satisfies both of their interests. The terms of this *win–win* agreement would come from applying the next principle.

3. Generate Options for Mutual Gain

After the parties have gained a full understanding of each other's perspectives and key interests, they need to move on to discuss the options for satisfying their interests. As Fisher and Ury explain (1991, pp. 57–59), most people at this point are inclined to move directly to a discussion of their proposed solution. In other words, one or both parties will want to discuss what they believe is the *best* way to resolve their disagreement and thereby solve their problem. Fisher and Ury point out that such an approach will invariably lead to a narrow, positional negotiation. They recommend that, at this point in the process, negotiators brainstorm options instead of looking for the nearest solution; that they seek all possible actions or agreements that could be part of the agreed outcome; and that they do so without judgment or evaluation. Only through such a process can the parties find a broad, integrative, and creative solution.

For example, when the negotiation process described in Car Repair Blues has reached the point where Dale and Chris have a good understanding of each other and their key interests, they could move directly to a narrow negotiation of how much money Dale should pay Chris. Imagine, for example, that Chris has acknowledged that he should not have done the work without Dale's authorization and has apologized for doing so. Likewise, Dale has acknowledged that Chris was well intentioned and did work that was of some value to her, although she would not have chosen to have the work done at that point. Based on these preliminary concessions, the two parties might quite quickly come to an agreement that Dale pay some compromise amount, say $500, to settle their dispute.

If, however, instead of coming to a quick agreement, they use a brainstorming process to think of all possible options before they try to make their deal, they might come up with the following list of options:

- Dale will agree to say to others (for example, friends and associates) that Chris is a competent, honest, and reliable mechanic, and she will agree never to make disparaging comments about his work or customer service;
- Dale will make an initial payment of $100 and will pay the balance of the agreed invoice amount in monthly installments of, say, $50 per month;
- Chris will give Dale a credit note (or even two or three) for a routine six-month servicing of her car (including the labour for routine checks, oil changes, and the like);
- Dale will agree to give Chris at least two days' notice before bringing her car in for service, and Chris will agree to take Dale's car any time on two days' notice.

We can see that, by taking the time and effort to generate options, Dale and Chris would clearly end up with a better agreement, one that is fully responsive to their needs. They would have achieved a truly win–win outcome.

4. Use Objective Criteria

In every dispute, there are disputed issues that must be answered to resolve the dispute. In Car Repair Blues, we might frame these issues as follows:

- What repair work needed to be done on Dale's car?
- What would have been a fair and reasonable price for such work by Chris?

The answers to each of these questions would be based on relevant objective criteria—standard practices, prevailing opinions, and the pricing conventions of the local car repair industry. In most cases, the difficulty would be to identify and obtain information of this kind that both parties would find acceptable. In this particular scenario, Chris would be able to answer both of these questions based on his experience of the car repair industry, and Dale could probably determine for herself how fair and reliable Chris's information was. If necessary, Dale could get a second opinion from another auto mechanic.

Principled negotiation can be an excellent process; however, people in conflict may not be ready or able to pursue it effectively. This is why people often need the assistance of a mediator—to enable them to engage in this process in situations where they would otherwise be inclined to revert to positional negotiation. Now let's examine the tension between principled and positional negotiating.

The Negotiator's Dilemma: To Cooperate or to Compete?

As students of mediation and conflict resolution, we must be aware of the fundamental reality of every negotiation. Lax and Sebenius, of the Harvard Program on Negotiation, call this fundamental reality "the negotiator's dilemma." In *The Manager as Negotiator* (1986), Lax and Sebenius explain how all negotiation involves different degrees of cooperation and competition. It entails trying to reach agreement in a situation where both parties have partly compatible and partly incompatible goals. For instance, I may want to see an action movie, but my partner prefers to go to the theatre to watch a dance performance. Both of us want to relax on a Friday night after a stressful week at work, but our respective preferences about how to do so are different. How should we reconcile our different preferences? How much should each of us give up in order to accommodate the other person's preferences? Or how much should we insist on our own preferred outcome, at the expense of the other party?

In a domestic context such as this, both parties may be aware that there are costs to competing too much. But even in a more "arm's-length" negotiation context, the same tension exists. On one hand, how much is each party prepared to compete to satisfy its own demands so far as it possibly can? On the other hand, how willing is each side to cooperate so that the other party also satisfies some of its negotiation goals? If one party to a negotiation is so uncompromisingly competitive that it claims nearly all the available benefits, there is little incentive for the losing party to continue with the negotiation, and the negotiation will probably fail. In this case, the "winners" of the negotiation may eventually end up paying a higher price for winning than they anticipated; their competitive standpoint and win-at-all-costs attitude may make their negotiating partner resentful, diminishing that party's willingness to negotiate or cooperate in the future.

The efficiency of negotiation as a mode of resolving disputes therefore depends on whether the parties can reach an understanding about two matters: (1) how much they want to compete, and (2) how much they want to cooperate to enable the other party to reach some or all of its negotiating goals. Lax and Sebenius (1986) call this the tension between "claiming value" and "creating value" in negotiation. Value-claiming behaviour is associated with positional bargaining in which each side seeks at once to claim as much from the negotiation as possible and to concede as little as possible to the other side.

Value-claiming tactics may include

- overstating the value of your holdings (goods, services);
- understating or distorting your preferences or needs;
- minimizing or discounting the value of the other party's holdings;
- minimizing, downplaying, or depreciating the other party's alternative;
- bargaining hard—starting high, conceding slowly;
- exaggerating the value of your own concessions;
- bluffing;
- attacking the other party with threats, intimidation, criticism, and ridicule; and
- deceiving.

On the other hand, actions to create value may include

- sharing information;
- revealing preferences and needs;
- revealing your honest opinions, doubts, and uncertainties;
- discussing your past contributions to the problem (that is, admitting your mistakes);
- looking for a better way, rather than "your" way; and
- being cooperative by looking for ways that you can help each other.

Figure 2.3 depicts the negotiator's dilemma. If both negotiators cooperate to create value, which they share fairly, they both achieve a "good" result from their negotiation. However, each party faces a risk: if party B is primarily competing and claiming (especially if doing so in a secretive, deceptive way), party A faces the prospect of a "bad" result. In that case, party B gets a "great" result at party A's expense. To avoid that risk, there is a tendency for both parties to compete and to pursue mainly value-claiming tactics, which puts them in the lower right quadrant of Figure 2.3, with a result that is mediocre for both.

Even though, in theory, parties may use principled negotiation to create value and to achieve a better result overall, a party may believe, for various reasons, that he or she will be better off pursuing a positional, adversarial approach. That party may believe that his or her maximum benefit will be achieved by making demands, applying pressure, opposing or resisting the other, and, generally, trying to achieve a good outcome at the expense of the other party.

Figure 2.3 The Negotiator's Dilemma

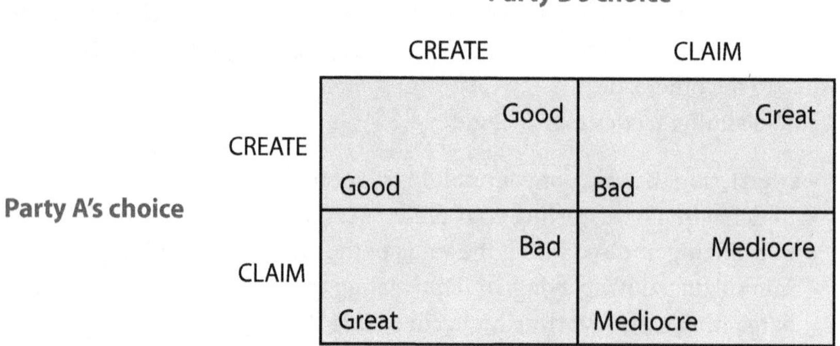

Creating Value

The positional negotiation approach generally leads to an outcome where a "fixed pie" is divided between the parties. It is a distributive process, whereby something of value is divided between the parties. As we noted above, positional negotiation is primarily a process of value claiming. In our Garage Sale scenario (see Box 2.1), Nadia has the pine cabinet and Mario has some money, before their negotiation. Mario wants the cabinet, and the main question is how much he will pay for it. They negotiate, haggling over the price, and the outcome is that Mario gets the cabinet for $215. Nadia may believe it is really worth between $275 and $300, in which case she would believe that Mario has claimed value from her of between $60 and $85. That is, she has lost that amount, which, in turn, Mario has won. For this reason, we refer to positional negotiation as a *win–lose* process.

Principled negotiation, by contrast, is said to be a *win–win* process—a process whereby value is created; the pie is expanded. As Lax and Sebenius say (1986, p. 32): "We create value by finding joint gains for all negotiating parties." To do that, negotiators need to be "inventive and cooperative" (p. 30). We will use the following example of children with fruit, as did Lax and Sebenius, to illustrate the basic principles behind creating value.

The negotiations in the Fruit Exchange scenario (Box 2.2) have created value, producing mutual gains for everyone—Sally, Marc, and Judy. Yet this could happen only if Sally knows that Marc likes bananas and that Judy likes apples. As the example illustrates, value creation occurs only if parties have good information about one another's preferences or interests. In fact, if you consider the Fruit Exchange scenario further, you will find that if Sally, Mark, and Judy have complete information about one another's interests or preferences, they can make further trades to achieve even more joint gains, and all three will be even better off.

BOX 2.2 » Scenario: Fruit Exchange

Sally has six apples. Her friend Marc has three pears, and her other friend Judy has four bananas. Sally prefers pears to apples and doesn't like bananas at all. Marc likes bananas the most and pears second, and eats an apple only once in a while. Judy likes all fruit about the same.

If Sally wants one of Marc's pears, it seems unlikely that Marc will agree to trade a pear for one or more of Sally's apples. It seems unlikely that Sally could persuade Marc to trade one of his pears for one or more of her apples. In other words, there is a problem in the negotiation that Sally would like to have with Marc. It appears unlikely that either Sally or Marc will be able to achieve their negotiation goals of trading some of their fruit for other fruit they prefer.

However, if Sally discovers that Marc prefers bananas to pears, and that she could trade with Judy for a banana, then all of a sudden more possibilities open up for each of them to achieve their negotiation goals. This illustrates the theory of mutual gains. Sally trades with Judy, an apple for a banana. Since Judy already has four bananas, she probably prefers getting an apple for one of her bananas. Then Sally trades her banana (which she doesn't like at all) to Marc for a pear. Marc is happy that he now has a banana instead of his pear, and Sally is happy that she now has a pear for one of her apples. Everybody is better off. The two negotiated exchanges have created value for all three of them.

This scenario illustrates a basic principle of value creation: that cooperation among negotiating parties—and open and honest communication of their interests by all parties—will lead to mutual gains.

Another classic example of value creation is two sisters fighting over an orange. Gail has the orange, but Glenda is yelling at her: "Give it back, it's mine. I put it in the fridge, and you knew it." They argue on and on until finally their mother comes in, cuts it in half, and gives each of them half of the orange. While the mother thinks the solution was fair, both children go away angry and dissatisfied, without saying anything more. However, if their mother had intervened as mediator, rather than as arbiter, and asked each of them why they wanted the orange, the result could have been very different. In fact, Gail wanted the rind from the orange peel to make an orange cake, whereas Glenda wanted the pulp to make juice. If they had taken time to determine the girls' respective interests in the orange—in other words, what each of them really wanted from it—they could have come up with a solution that fully satisfied both girls' interests. They could have realized greater value from the orange.

As the orange example illustrates, creating value really means finding ways to realize the potential value inherent in a conflict situation. When the parties' compatible or common interests are discovered, the way to expand the pie and create value becomes apparent. To the extent that principled negotiation creates value, it results in *better outcomes* than positional negotiation does. That is what "creating value" means: the overall value or well-being realized by *both* parties is greater than it would otherwise be.

In comparing principled and positional negotiation, we also need to consider the costs or negative effects of positional negotiation. Positional negotiation is a value-claiming process, and when parties use it, they divide their existing value or assets. Through negotiation, in other words, they simply redistribute what they both already have. It is what game theorists refer to as a *zero-sum game*—one person gains what the other gives up, and the total of all gains and losses is zero. Further, the competitive positional bargaining process has costs and negative effects that may result in its being a *value-negating* process. Whereas value claiming divides a fixed pie and value creating expands the pie, value negating *shrinks* the pie. The costs and negative effects of positional negotiation may reduce the overall value available to the parties (Bishop, 1995).

Negotiating Power: BATNA

Whenever we are negotiating, we should always know and assess what Fisher and Ury (1991, p. 97) refer to as our "best alternative to a negotiated agreement," known by its acronym BATNA. A party's BATNA is its best, most advantageous course of action should it not reach agreement with the other party. In many dispute situations, a claimant's BATNA may be the outcome they would achieve by proceeding with litigation—by going to court.

For example, a plaintiff claiming compensation from an insurance company for personal injuries in a car accident may believe that, if the case goes to court, she will likely achieve a net monetary recovery (after all legal costs) of between \$20,000 and \$50,000. If the plaintiff has accurately assessed the merits, costs, and risks of her court action, she may well be advised to accept a negotiated settlement that would provide her with a net recovery of between \$20,000 and \$50,000. If the most she can achieve by negotiating is less than \$20,000, she should proceed with her best alternative action—that is, her BATNA—and take the case to court. On the other side of the table, the insurance company, if it believes that the plaintiff could recover \$50,000 or more by going to court, would be willing to negotiate a settlement of between \$20,000 and \$50,000 (plus legal costs). That is why we say that a party's BATNA is a substantial component of its negotiating power.

Mediation

Often the parties to a negotiation will not be able to reach an understanding about how much to cooperate and how much to compete in order to satisfy their respective goals. Incompatible positions, different communication styles, unresolved or unexpressed emotions, lack of trust—these may all be obstacles to successful negotiations between the parties. In such circumstances, the parties may need the intervention of a neutral third party to facilitate the negotiation. With mediation, which is a form of third-party intervention, a mediator helps the parties negotiate a resolution to the conflict. The mediator's role is to facilitate the negotiation process by helping the parties exchange information and learn more about each other's preferences, interests, goals, and values. The mediator does not try to resolve the conflict for the parties or to impose an outcome on the negotiations; it is up to the parties to make their own decisions and reach their own agreement.

Mediation is a very flexible form of dispute resolution process that is used in a wide variety of disputing contexts—from remote village communities to the United Nations, from community youth justice programs to labour–management disputes, from international peacekeeping efforts in war-torn countries to interpersonal family conflicts. The value of mediation as a non-coercive process that empowers the disputants to resolve their own conflicts has made it the fastest growing dispute resolution method in the whole dispute resolution field (McLaren & Sanderson, 1995, p. 56).

In Canada, mediation is still in its "defining phase" (Boule & Kelly, 1998, p. 4). Although it is one of the oldest and most traditional forms of dispute resolution, with roots in many cultures extending back thousands of years (Picard, 2002, p. 19; Folberg & Taylor, 1990, pp. 1–5; Moore, 2003, pp. 20–22), the modern mediation movement in Canada and the United states has only emerged in the past 30 to 40 years, and in many respects is still in its infancy.

As Picard (2002, pp. 40–41) has observed, the rapid development and diversification of mediation practice has caused it to outstrip the existing mediation theory. As a result, there is no standard, generally accepted definition of the process and its goals that applies to all forms of mediation. The role of peacekeeping troops as mediators in the aftermath of an inter-ethnic conflict will be very different from that of a mediator who is handling a dispute between an insurance company and a claimant injured in an automobile accident. A professional family mediator who is paid for her services will describe her work very differently than will a volunteer peer mediator in a school **mediation program** or a community elder in an Aboriginal community.

Despite these differences in practice style, all forms of mediation have one thing in common: mediators work with the disputing parties to enable them to resolve their own conflicts. The American scholar Lon Fuller (1971, p. 325; cited in Picard, 2002, p. 22) has observed that what makes mediation different from other forms of dispute resolution is

> its capacity to reorient the parties toward each other, not by imposing rules on them, but by helping them to achieve a new and shared perception of their relationship, a perception that will redirect their attitudes and disposition towards one another.

Picard (2002, p. 21) says that mediation is

> a form of assisted negotiation where an impartial person facilitates the negotiation process while the parties determine the outcome. The goal is to help the parties gain insight into the cares and concerns that underlie the conflict

> situation and that are affecting their lives and the lives of others. This insight enables parties to reach consensual decisions that accommodate their needs. It is a self-empowering process that emphasizes self-determination and interconnectedness.

Along similar lines, Kruk (1997, p. 4; cited in Picard, 2002, p. 22) defines mediation in normative terms as

> a collaborative conflict resolution process in which two or more parties in dispute are assisted in their negotiation by a neutral and impartial third party and empowered to voluntarily reach their own mutually acceptable settlement of the issues in dispute. The mediators structure and facilitate the process by which the parties make their own decisions and determine the outcome, in a way that satisfies the interests of all parties in the dispute.

Hybrid Methods of Mediation

Dispute resolution methods are not mutually exclusive, and practitioners use them in various combinations or hybrids. The possible variations or combinations are limited only by the imaginations of the participants. For example, a hybrid method known as *neutral evaluation* is a cross between evaluative mediation and arbitration. With this hybrid method, the neutral third party considers all the facts and the evidence and then expresses an opinion as to the likely outcome of an adjudication. The parties then seek to negotiate or settle their differences based on the opinion expressed by the neutral evaluator.

In some cases, parties and their advisers may combine different methods in different ways. For example, in a divorce dispute, the parties may start with mediation and use that process to deal only with the issues between them over child care and parenting and sharing childcare expenses. However, in a separate process for dividing their property, they may choose to involve their lawyers and agree to jointly select a neutral business evaluator to arbitrate in the valuation of the wife's business.

Mediation, arbitration, and adjudication have given rise to two hybrid forms of mediation practice: mediation-arbitration and court-connected mediation.

Mediation-Arbitration ("Med-Arb")

Mediation-arbitration, or med-arb, is a hybrid form of mediation practice that, as its name suggests, combines elements of both mediation and arbitration. In choosing this process, the parties effectively agree in advance to a two-step process. First, they attempt to negotiate a resolution to their conflict with the assistance of a mediator. Second, those issues that cannot be resolved through mediation are submitted to arbitration (McLaren & Sanderson, 1995, p. 192). The parties may agree that the same person who acted as mediator will act as arbitrator in the second stage of the process. However, this is not necessary; the parties could select a different person to arbitrate the outstanding issues. The advantage of using the same person to act as both mediator and arbitrator is that, should the process get to the second stage, this person will already be familiar with the issues remaining to be resolved and will be able to complete the arbitration component quickly and at a lower cost to the parties than a new arbitrator would (McLaren & Sanderson, 1995, p. 193).

Med-arb, like mediation and arbitration, is a private, informal process based on the consent of the parties. By using this hybrid process, the parties are simply deciding in advance what will happen if the mediation is unsuccessful or only partly successful. It enables the disputants and the mediator to know from the outset what process will be used to resolve the outstanding issues. In short, the parties are assured of having the advantages of arbitration for the second stage and thereby avoiding the costs and risks of litigation.

Limitations of Med-Arb

Keep in mind that, in important respects, mediation and arbitration are distinct dispute resolution techniques. Arbitrators and mediators both act as impartial third parties, but their roles are very different. Where an arbitrator is authorized to make a decision and impose a settlement that resolves the issues between the parties, a mediator tries to assist the parties to reach their own negotiated settlement. The mediator may become involved in exploring the parties' options for settlement. But it is the parties who remain in control of the outcome; the mediator cannot impose any terms of settlement.

In the second stage of med-arb, the third party is required to impose terms of settlement. If the same person who acts as a mediator in stage one is to take on the role of the arbitrator in stage two, will it be possible for that person to be non-judgmental and impartial as a mediator? The significance of this question will become clearer in Chapter 3, when we look at different mediator orientations or approaches to mediation. For now, we will note the tendency within med-arb for the first-stage mediator to adopt a problem-solving or settlement orientation toward mediation, in the hope of narrowing the issues that remain to be decided by arbitration. The question this raises for mediation theorists and practitioners is whether the hybrid nature of med-arb will indirectly pressure mediators to be settlement-oriented rather than to adopt a transformative or facilitative orientation to mediation practice.

Another potential concern with med-arb is that parties may be constrained in what they say and reveal in the mediation stage, if they know that the mediator will be their arbitrator in the second phase of the process. Open, honest, unguarded communication is an important goal of mediation.

Court-Connected Mediation

Court-connected mediation is another hybrid form of mediation. It is a hybrid insofar as the mediation process takes place within the institutional confines of the court system. Most court-connected mediation programs have been introduced as part of an institutional court reform process designed to reduce the delays, complexities, and costs of litigation. Under the rules of practice governing Ontario's mandatory mediation program (OMMP), for example, some litigants engaged in a private, non-family, civil lawsuit are required to try mediation at an early stage in the trial proceedings, in the hope that they might arrive at a mediated settlement before they reach the litigation stage.

The costs of these mediation sessions are divided between the two parties, with the mediator being selected from a court-approved roster. These mediators are not required to have legal training, but the majority of them are lawyers. This enables them to provide the disputing parties with a reality check concerning the likely costs and outcomes of further litigation. This reality check may provide, in turn, a significant motivation to reach a negotiated settlement. If the dispute is settled with the assistance of a mediator, the case is withdrawn from the court's trial docket. If the parties are unable to resolve their dispute through mediation, the case will continue through the normal litigation process until it is heard by a judge (or settled out of court).

While the Ontario civil mediation program is mandatory, other court-connected mediation programs offer more flexibility, allowing the parties to choose between mediation and adjudication. They often make this choice after consulting with a court official who has the authority to refer them to mediation (Boulle & Kelly, 1998, pp. 203, 206). Increasingly, judges in provincial family courts and small claims courts are taking on active case management roles, in which they may even discuss settlement options with the parties, in an effort to promote early settlement. If no settlement is reached, the same judge will formally adjudicate the dispute. Additionally, in cases heard before many administrative boards and tribunals, settlement conferences and other mediation-type procedures are being introduced as a more flexible alternative to a formal adjudicative process. Likewise, many professional associations, such as the Canadian Bankers Association, the Canadian Medical Association, and even provincial law societies, are urging that informal, non-adversarial processes, based on mediation, be used to resolve professional–client disputes over issues such as complaints of professional misconduct (Boulle & Kelly, 1998, pp. 213, 217; McLaren & Sanderson, 1995, pp. 414–417).

The rapid growth of such court-connected and voluntary professional mediation programs is, in part, a response to a public perception that the courts have become too costly and inaccessible to the average litigant. The *Report of the Ontario Courts Inquiry* (1987) into court reform in Ontario found that the legal costs incurred by a successful litigant in a civil trial total, on average, more than half of any damages awarded. In family law, the situation is even worse, since the costs of continuing to litigate are potentially unlimited, while the assets accumulated by the separating couple are always finite (1987, p. 52). This means that, for many litigants, the costs of going to court may exceed the amount claimed, especially if the court case involves any contested legal issues that may be appealed by the unsuccessful litigant. Even if the parties are able to reach an out-of-court settlement agreement before going to court, the legal fees incurred by both sides in preparing for trial are often significant, especially since most cases settle only at a relatively late stage in the proceedings, often on the very steps of the courthouse (Stitt, Handy, & Simm, 1996, pp. 459, 464). Court-connected mediation programs are therefore designed to provide the parties with a relatively low-cost alternative to the court system, but one that preserves their rights to sue if the mediation process proves unsuccessful.

Limitations of Court-Connected Mediation

Like med-arb, court-connected mediation has given rise to some concerns (Picard & Saunders, 2002, p. 231; Welsh, 2001). Some mediation practitioners and theorists are concerned that the close link between mediation and litigation (within most court-connected mediation programs) may serve to diminish the process differences between these two dispute resolution techniques. Within many of these court-connected programs, mediation is not so much viewed as an alternative to the formal legal system as an integral part of it. Court-connected mediation programs, like med-arb, can be seen as involving a two-stage dispute resolution process, with mediation as the first stage and adjudication as the second stage. Because adjudication is a rights-based process, court-connected mediation programs also tend to adopt a rights-based, or evaluative, orientation. As a result, the third-party mediator, in order to encourage the parties to settle, tends to discuss with them the likely outcomes if the case goes on to trial. This tendency may be more pronounced where court-connected mediators have training or experience as practising lawyers. Ironically, the very success of court-connected mediation programs raises questions about the effectiveness of this form of mediation in transforming the ways in which we approach and understand conflict (Picard & Saunders, 2002; Bush & Folger, 1994; Welsh, 2001).

Summary

There is a wide spectrum of power-based, rights-based, and interest-based dispute resolution processes. There are primary processes, such as adjudication, negotiation, and mediation, and there are hybrid processes, such as mediation-arbitration (med-arb) and court-connected mediation, which have characteristics of both rights-based and interest-based processes. Of course, the focus of this book is interest-based resolution processes, especially mediation. In this chapter, we have considered the elements of principled negotiation, which, when it was introduced over 30 years ago, formed the basis of the interest-based approach. As we move forward in the book, we will examine subsequent theories and approaches. By doing so, we will develop our understanding of how mediation can best meet the diverse needs of people in our society.

DISCUSSION QUESTIONS AND EXERCISES

1. Haven Homes owns 200 acres of raw land on the western boundary of Sonata, a suburb on the outskirts of the City. Haven Homes has applied to the City for rezoning of the land from R1 to R3 and for approval of its development plan. The company is proposing a high-density subdivision with a high proportion of semi-detached and multiple unit buildings. The present R1 zoning permits only single-family homes with 18-metre lots. With R3 zoning, a developer can build semi-detached (2 or 3 units together) and multiple unit buildings (i.e. townhouses) and single homes on smaller (10-metre) lots. Haven Homes' proposed subdivision would add up to 5,000 people to the population of Sonata. The Sonata Preservation Society (SPS) is a community group that wants to preserve the small-town character and ambience of Sonata. SPS opposes Haven Homes' development plan and rezoning application. The two opposing views are presented at a public meeting. Alex is the president of SPS. Grant is the general manager of Haven Homes.

   > *Alex*: This is ridiculous. Haven Homes has done this other places and there is no bloody way we're going to let them do it here. It will destroy our community—traffic, congestion, noise, garbage, pollution. We might as well be in the middle of the city. There is a perfectly good place for their low-end, high density housing in the other end of the city.

   > *Grant*: Our proposed development will be very beneficial for this community. There is a real shortage of lower-cost, affordable housing—especially for younger families. In trying to block this project, the SPS is considering only their own selfish interests and couldn't care less about the well-being of the wider community.

   a. What different possible dispute resolution methods might the parties use in this case?
   b. Imagine that you are Alex or Alex's adviser. What strategy would you employ for dealing with this dispute with Haven Homes? What will you need to consider in deciding what your best strategy or approach will be in this case? What strategy do you think Haven Homes intends to use?
   c. Imagine you are Grant or Grant's adviser. What strategy would you employ for dealing with this dispute with SPS? What will you need to consider in deciding what your best strategy or approach will be in this case? What strategy do you think SPS intends to use?
2. In the Garage Sale scenario, what are some of the strategies and tactics employed by Mario and by Nadia? What are some other strategies and tactics they could have used? List as many as you can think of. Which of these are positional and which, if any, are interest-based?

3. Make a list of all of the negotiations that you have been involved in over the past two weeks (include informal negotiations with family and friends). In which of those negotiations did you use any interest-based methods? What interest-based methods could you use in these cases?
4. Think of a negotiation that you are or have been involved in. Write a two-page reflective journal about this negotiation, including what you said and did, some of the strategies and tactics you used (positional or interest-based), some of the challenges you experienced, and some specific ways you might develop your competence as a principled negotiator.
5. What does it mean to consider the interests of a party in a dispute situation? What can be achieved by doing this?
6. Do this exercise in groups of 4–5 students each, using the Car Repair Blues scenario (Box 1.1, in Chapter 1). In your group, have one person volunteer to be Dale and one person volunteer to be Chris. You will role play a negotiation between Dale and Chris. Imagine that Dale has returned to Chris's garage to negotiate with him to get her car back. Before negotiating, take 2 minutes on your own to prepare to negotiate. In the role play, Dale will be a positional negotiator. Chris, on the other hand, will be a principled negotiator. When ready, Dale and Chris will negotiate for 5–10 minutes and the rest of the group will observe. Then, in your group, discuss the following:
   a. What different negotiating behaviours, strategies, and tactics did Dale and Chris use?
   b. What would you have done as mediator to help Dale and Chris with their negotiation?

FURTHER READING

Boulle, L., & Kelly, K.J. (1998). *Mediation: Principles, process, practice.* Toronto: Butterworths.

Chornenki, G., & Hart, C. (1996). *Bypass court.* Toronto: Butterworths.

Emond, D.P. (1989). Alternative dispute resolution: A conceptual overview. In D.P. Emond (Ed.), *Commercial dispute resolution* (pp. 1–25). Aurora, ON: Canada Law Book.

Fisher, R., & Ury, W. *Getting to yes: Negotiating agreement without giving in.* (2nd ed.). New York: Penguin Books, 1991.

McLaren, R.H., & Sanderson, J.P. (1995). *Innovative dispute resolution: The alternative.* Toronto: Carswell.

Websites

ADR Institute of Canada, Inc.: http://www.adrcanada.ca

This is a national non-profit organization that provides leadership in the development and promotion of alternative dispute resolution in Canada and internationally. In concert with seven regional affiliates across the country, ADR Canada represents and supports professionals who provide dispute resolution services as well as the individuals and organizations that use those services.

Program on Negotiation at Harvard University Law School: http://www.pon.harvard.edu
The Program on Negotiation (PON) is a consortium program of Harvard University, Massachusetts Institute of Technology, and Tufts University. It serves as an interdisciplinary research center dedicated to developing the theory and practice of negotiation and dispute resolution in a range of public and private settings. PON's mission includes nurturing the next generation of negotiation teachers and scholars, helping students become more effective negotiators, and providing a forum for the discussion of ideas.

REFERENCES

Bishop, P. (1995). *Winning in the workplace: ADR strategies for employment disputes.* Scarborough, ON: Carswell.

Boulle, L., & Kelly, K.J. (1998). *Mediation: Principles, process, practice.* Toronto: Butterworths.

Bush, R.A.B., & Folger, J.P. (1994). *The promise of mediation.* San Francisco: Jossey-Bass.

Emond, D.P. (1989). Alternative dispute resolution: A conceptual overview. In D.P. Emond (Ed.), *Commercial dispute resolution* (pp. 1–25). Aurora, ON: Canada Law Book.

Fisher, R., & Ury, W. (1981). *Getting to yes: Negotiating agreement without giving in.* Boston: Houghton Mifflin.

Fisher, R., & Ury, W. (1991). *Getting to yes: Negotiating agreement without giving in* (2nd ed.). New York: Penguin Books. Copyright © 1981, 1991 by Roger Fisher and William Ury. Reprinted by permission of Houghton Mifflin Company. All rights reserved.

Folberg, J., & Taylor, A. (1990). *Mediation: A comprehensive guide to resolving conflicts without litigation.* San Francisco: Jossey-Bass.

Fuller, L.L. (1971). Mediation: Its forms and functions. *Southern California Law Review, 44,* 305–339.

Fuller, L.L. (1978). The forms and limits of adjudication. *Harvard Law Review, 92,* 353–409.

Kruk, E. (1997). *Mediation and conflict resolution in social work and the human services.* Chicago: Nelson Hall.

Lax, D., & Sebenius, J.K. (1986). *The manager as negotiator.* New York: Free Press.

McLaren, R.H., & Sanderson, J.P. (1995). *Innovative dispute resolution: The alternative.* Scarborough, ON: Carswell.

Mnookin, R., & Kornhauser, L. (1979). Bargaining in the shadow of the law: The case of divorce. *Yale Law Journal, 88,* 950–997.

Moore, C.W. (2003). *The mediation process: Practical strategies for resolving conflict* (3rd ed.). San Francisco: Jossey-Bass.

Picard, C.A. (2002). *Mediating interpersonal and small group conflict* (2nd ed.). Ottawa: Golden Dog Press.

Picard, C.A., & Saunders, R.P. (2002). The regulation of mediation. In M. MacNeil, N. Sargent, & P. Swan (Eds.), *Law, regulation and governance* (pp. 223–238). Toronto: Oxford University Press.

Pruitt, D., & Carnevale, P. (1993). *Negotiation in social conflict*. Pacific Grove, CA: Brooks/Cole.

Report of the Ontario Courts Inquiry. (1987). Toronto: Ministry of the Attorney General.

Stitt, A., Handy, F., & Simm, P.A. (1996). Alternative dispute resolution and the Ontario civil justice system. In *Rethinking civil justice: Research studies for the Civil Justice Review: Vol. 21* (pp. 449–490). Toronto: Ontario Law Reform Commission.

Ury, W., Brett, J., & Goldberg, S. (1988). *Getting disputes resolved: Designing systems to cut the costs of conflict*. San Francisco: Jossey-Bass.

Welsh, N. (2001). The thinning vision of self-determination in court-connected mediation: The inevitable price of institutionalization? *Harvard Negotiation Law Review*, *6*, 1–96.

CHAPTER 3

Mediation as a Dispute Resolution Process

LEARNING OBJECTIVES

After reading this chapter, you will be able to:

- Understand the core elements of the mediation process
- Identify three types of mediators and a variety of different approaches to mediation, from pragmatic problem-solving processes to processes that influence individual and social transformation
- Explain why a person might choose to use mediation
- Explain some of the benefits and limitations of mediation

CHAPTER OUTLINE

Introduction 63
Core Elements of Mediation 64
The Idea of Mediator Neutrality 67
Forms of Mediation Practice 68
Why Choose Mediation? 78
Defining Success in Mediation 81
Benefits of Mediation 82
Summary 87

Resolving conflict is rarely about who is right. It is about acknowledgment and appreciation of differences.

Thomas Crum

Introduction

Mediation is a very flexible form of dispute resolution process that is used in a wide variety of disputing contexts. There are many different forms of it. What a community elder does in mediating a community dispute in Nigeria may be very different, for example, from what a professional family mediator does in Canada.

Mediation is an ancient form of dispute resolution, used for millennia in a wide range of cultures (Picard, 2002, p. 19; Folberg & Taylor, 1984, pp. 1–5; Moore, 2003, pp. 20–22). However, the modern mediation movement in Canada and the United States has only emerged in the past 30 to 40 years, and we may regard it as being still in its infancy. Consequently, there is no generally accepted definition of the process and its goals—no definition that covers all forms of mediation practice.

Some definitions emphasize mediation's practical techniques for managing conflict while de-emphasizing the goals of collaborative decision making and conflict resolution. Others take a normative approach to defining mediation, viewing it as a field of practice that is based on principles of collaborative decision making, interconnectedness, and the disputants' self-empowerment (Boulle & Kelly, 1998, pp. 4–6). Still other definitions identify mediation as a learning process rather than as a problem-solving one (Melchin & Picard, 2008), or they focus on how language plays a central role in constructing who we are and how we engage with others (Winslade & Monk, 2000). The American scholar Lon Fuller has suggested that what makes mediation different from other forms of dispute resolution is that it changes the parties' orientation toward each other by helping them establish a shared perspective on their relationship, a perspective that serves to alter their attitudes and approaches to one another (Fuller, 1971, p. 325; cited in Picard, 2002, p. 22).

In this text, we define mediation as a process that uses a third party from outside the dispute to assist two or more parties to settle, resolve, or transform conflict.

Core Elements of Mediation

Certain basic features are common to many forms of mediation practice. The following may be considered core elements:

- The process is consensual in that the parties must be willing to accept the intervention of a mediator to assist them in the negotiating process (Moore, 2003, p. 16). Without such willingness on both sides, the mediator can do little to facilitate a joint resolution of their dispute. In this sense, the mediator's authority is always contingent on the consent of the parties, even if there has been a mandatory referral to mediation.
- The process is normally private and confidential.
- The mediator plays an active role in facilitating the parties' communication and negotiation but remains impartial as to the outcome.
- Any agreement reached in mediation is based on the decision of the parties. The mediator has no decision-making power—no authority to impose a decision on the parties that they have not agreed to.
- As a collaborative approach to conflict, mediation's goal is to achieve an agreed outcome that, as much as possible, satisfies the needs and interests of all of the parties.

Consensus

The process of mediation is consensual, but that does not mean that the parties always voluntarily choose to enter into mediation. There may be situations in which the disputants are required by law to accept the mediation process. For example, a government may pass legislation forcing striking workers back to their jobs and may appoint a labour mediator to assist in the negotiation between the disputants. Ontario's court-connected mediation program for civil litigation is another example of mandatory mediation. However, though the parties may be required to enter the mediation process, the mediator cannot compel them to negotiate if they are not prepared to talk to each other. A mediator can try to promote dialogue between the parties in order to increase the chances for a successful resolution of the conflict, but he or she cannot create a dialogue where no willingness to engage in dialogue exists (Moore, 2003, p. 16).

Confidentiality

While confidentiality is usually a feature of the mediation process, the parties may decide themselves, in consultation with the mediator, what degree of confidentiality they desire. In other words, they may decide whether they want relatively strict confidentiality to apply or whether disclosures emerging from the mediation process may be used in other forums. For example, one party in a mediation session may admit to something that could result in legal or disciplinary consequences for him or her outside the mediation room. It is important for the parties to discuss the possibility of this situation in advance, since mediation promotes disclosure between disputants, and the participants need to feel comfortable about this openness. It is an improper use of mediation for one party to enter the process in the hope of the second party's disclosing information that the first party can use in another process. (For an extended discussion of the legal protection of confidentiality in mediation, see Boulle & Kelly, 1998, pp. 300–314.)

Impartiality

To be impartial, the mediator must not favour one party over another or allow personal preference or bias to influence the mediation process. This is what we mean by *impartial.* Moore (2003, p. 53) defines impartiality similarly: "[I]mpartiality refers to the absence of bias or preference in favor of one or more negotiators, their interests, or the specific solutions that they are advocating." Acting impartially and being perceived as impartial are vital if the mediator is to build trust with both parties. If one party believes, correctly or incorrectly, that the mediator is showing bias toward or undue sympathy for the other side, then that party is likely to withdraw his or her trust from the mediator. This will inevitably interfere with the mediator's ability to facilitate an agreement between the parties. So the mediator must be mindful of this responsibility at all times.

The requirement of impartiality involves a number of competing considerations. The first is how far a mediator should go in trying to treat the parties with strict equality. If one disputant is less skilled in negotiation than the other disputant, or if there appears to be an imbalance in bargaining power between the disputants, how far is it permissible for the mediator to depart from the principle of strict equality—for example, by trying to balance the power between the parties or by trying to influence the negotiating style of the less experienced disputant?

The impartiality of mediators varies depending on their proximity to the conflict. For some types of dispute resolution processes, the mediator is an "insider-partial." This term was coined by John Paul Lederach and Paul Wehr in reference to their work in Central America (1991), and it refers to a process whereby one party to the conflict plays a role in facilitating negotiations. Though this person may not be a central actor in the conflict, he or she tends to be involved in it and often has an interest in the dispute outcome.

For other types of dispute resolution processes, the mediator is an "outsider-partial." The "outsider-partial" is someone not directly involved in the conflict, but not entirely impartial and more likely to favour a status quo outcome. In traditional forms of community mediation, for example, it is common for a respected community member to take on a mediating role, despite the fact that he or she has an overriding interest or concern in community stability and harmony.

In the field of mediation, there is often confusion between impartiality and neutrality. Some use the terms interchangeably; however, according to our use of the terms, they have distinct meanings, which we discuss below under the heading "The Idea of Mediator Neutrality."

Decision-Making Power and Agreed Outcomes

Mediation is a process whereby the parties retain final authority over the outcome of the conflict. As a third-party intervenor, the mediator may be called upon to play many different roles at different stages of the process. Building trust between the disputants; clarifying the issues that need resolution; helping the parties learn more about each other's interests, needs, and values; designing a negotiation process; creating options for resolution; even assisting the parties in drawing up a final agreement—all of these are functions of a mediator. Yet these functions are secondary to the mediator's primary role—that of helping the parties to reach their own decision. The benefit of the disputants' self-empowerment is one of the normative values underlying the whole process of mediation. By modelling good communication skills and by helping the parties identify their true interests and values, a mediator may help the parties navigate the process of achieving resolution. Ultimately, however, the decision to achieve resolution must come from the parties themselves.

The mediator, then, is responsible for the *process* of the negotiation, while the parties retain control over its outcome. This control is crucial. If one party feels pressure from a mediator to settle on terms that he or she would not otherwise accept, that person is likely to feel aggrieved by the outcome and will be less likely to comply with the settlement over time.

In their lack of authoritative decision-making power, mediators differ from judges or arbitrators operating in a rights-based process. The judge or arbitrator is required to make a binding decision on the particular facts or issues that are in dispute. The role of the judge is not to reconcile the interests of the disputants, but to determine who is right (Eckhoff, 1969).

The judge's decision looks back at the past conduct of the parties to determine what happened and who is right and who is wrong. The judge does not examine the deeper causes of the conflict, except insofar as they are relevant to reaching a judgment about whether the alleged conduct of either of the disputants violated any legal rule. Nor does the judge inquire into the motivations or beliefs underlying the disputants' actions, or into the nature of their relationship. The judge must decide only whether any legal wrongdoing has been proven, and, if so, what legal consequences should follow from this. As a result, the root causes of the conflict are all too often left unresolved (Irving & Benjamin, 1987, p. 39).

By contrast, a mediator seeks to help parties uncover the sources of the conflict and to explore the reasons, beliefs, values, and motivations that underlie their behaviour. When a mediator looks to the past, it is not in order to judge the parties' conduct; it is to gain insight into the conflict and to understand better the disputants' interactions. Often, the key to helping the parties resolve their dispute in a mutually satisfying way is the mediator's ability to build a relationship of trust with both of them. Both need to feel that they are being listened to by the mediator, and that their interests are regarded as legitimate and worthy of attention. Therefore, the mediator needs to be non-judgmental; he or she needs to create an environment in which all parties are able to express their fears, concerns, and emotions to a sympathetic, curious, and impartial third party.

The mediator's role is more facilitative and future-oriented than that of a judge or arbitrator. The mediator seeks to open lines of communication between the disputants, and to promote a constructive dialogue through which the parties may come to a joint understanding of the issues that divide them as well as of their common interests. A mediator also acts as a problem solver, helping to find creative ways around some of the obstacles that impede the parties' progress toward a consensual resolution. The mediator may also act as a sounding board against which each party can test two things: (1) the accuracy of his or her perceptions of the actions and motives of the other, and (2) the reasonableness or feasibility of his or her own claims and demands. The mediator must also be able to help parties set priorities, evaluate options, and reach decisions that are agreeable to all parties. In all of these ways, the mediator acts as a facilitator to help parties find ways to reconcile or live with their competing interests, needs, and values.

The Idea of Mediator Neutrality

The idea of the mediator being "neutral" is a source of much debate among mediators. Therefore, we thought it would be useful to explain how we understand the term and how it is used in this text. When it comes to the idea of mediator neutrality, we concur with Moore (2003, p. 53), who has said that neutral mediators "have often not had any previous relationship with disputing parties, or at least have not had a relationship from which they could directly and significantly benefit." In addition, as Moore says, "the mediator does not expect to obtain benefits or special payments from the parties as compensation for favors in conducting the mediation." In this narrow sense, a *neutral* mediator is one whose relationship with each party does not interfere or conflict with her role and responsibilities as mediator. That is what we mean by *neutral* when we use the term in this text.

Sometimes the term *neutrality* is used in a broader sense, to refer to the nature and degree of the mediator's influence on the mediation process. In this sense, a mediator is said to be "neutral" to the extent that her opinions or values do not influence the mediation process or its outcome. In our view, the idea of a mediator being "neutral" in this broader sense is misleading. With many others in the field, we believe that a mediator does have an impact, intentionally or not, on the direction and outcome of mediation through her very presence at it. Such influence is inevitable. The addition of the mediator to the conflict dynamic changes the parties' interactions. The questions mediators choose to ask and the way they listen to parties are influenced by, among other factors, their background, culture, and education. As humans with life experiences, we can never act with a totally "clean slate."

Forms of Mediation Practice

The consensus among mediation professionals is that there is no one unitary theory of mediation process and outcome, and that mediators rely on a variety of social, psychological, economic, and political understandings of conflict in order to guide their practice (Folger & Jones, 1994; Kressel, Pruitt, & Associates,1989). Ways of mediating vary. Some mediators have clearly defined, pragmatic, problem-solving process goals; others have broadly defined process goals focused on social and individual transformation. It is our belief that mediation has the potential to achieve both kinds of goals.

Different Types of Mediators

It is certainly the case that mediators can have very different roles, depending on the context and culture in which they work. One way to classify them is by the type of relationship they have with the parties. Moore (2003, p. 43) identifies three types—social network, independent, and authoritative.

Social Network Mediator

A social network mediator is generally part of an ongoing and shared social network—a friend, a family member, a colleague, a neighbour, a religious leader, or an elder. All parties involved in the conflict know this person. Often, the mediator has an ongoing relationship with one or all of the parties and some familiarity with the issues in dispute. Even though a social network mediator may have an ongoing relationship with one or both of the parties, the mediator needs to be impartial. In other words, the mediator must ensure that his relationship with either party does not interfere or conflict with his role and responsibilities as mediator—to be fair, impartial, and trustworthy. Social network mediators are common in societies where the resolution of conflict is understood to occur within the larger social context of family or community and is not solely the responsibility of those directly involved in the conflict.

In Somalia, for example, mediation is a common form of dispute resolution. However, it looks very different there. The mediator is not a distant or neutral party; he or she is a member of the community and is well known and respected by all parties. This person is considered to be very knowledgeable, influential, and powerful. The parties would not trust someone they did not know. The Somali concept of confidentiality is also very different. The mediation session is not considered a private matter at all. In fact, everyone who is connected to the parties attends, from siblings to distant relatives. On many occasions, the mediation room is not large enough to hold all the participants.

This example shows that social mediators have a role in other cultures. It also shows, more generally, how cultural expectations determine the mediator's role. The professional North American model of mediation, which rests on the principles of mediator anonymity, independence, and confidentiality, would not meet the Somali expectations of the process. Mediation in the Somali tradition is based on the assumption that the conflict between the parties only takes place within the context of the wider group. Therefore, social network mediators are the type expected in this culture. They bring their experience and values as a member of the wider group to the task of mediating the dispute between the parties.

Independent Mediator

In North American legal practice, the model of the independent mediator is the most familiar one. Most accredited professional bodies in the legal sphere have adopted this mediation model.

Independent mediators differ from social network mediators in that they are perceived to have no vested interest in the dispute and are not connected to the parties in any way. They are expected to be impartial, objective, and outside the dispute. They have no decision-making power and no authority to oversee or enforce any agreements that might be reached through the mediation process. In this type of mediation process, the mediator is often described as being in control of the process, but not of the outcome of the dispute. Independent mediators are often selected by the parties because of their expertise as professionals in dispute resolution, not because of their familiarity with the parties or their knowledge of community values.

People choose this kind of mediator because they want procedural help that will enable them to negotiate a resolution to the dispute. Often, the parties will have tried themselves to negotiate a resolution to their dispute, but without agreement. The role of this kind of mediator is to facilitate the communication between the parties, to help them clarify the issues that need to be agreed on, and to remove obstacles to reaching agreement that may have arisen because of their conflict-filled relationship. The independent mediator is by far the type most familiar to Canadians as they turn to mediation in ever growing numbers for help in a wide range of marital, workplace, and other disputes.

Authoritative Mediator

In some ways, authoritative mediators are a combination of social network mediators and independent mediators. They are often known to the parties, have some form of relationship with them, and are generally in a powerful position relative to them. For example, an authoritative mediator may be the parties' supervisor or employer. Authoritative mediators, like other types of mediators, do not make decisions for the parties, but they often exercise some influence over the outcome, in which they may have a vested interest.

The authoritative mediator is becoming more commonplace in large organizations, both in government and in private industry. Many managers and senior executive officers undertake training in mediation so they can intervene early in workplace disputes, before they turn into formal grievances. In such a case, the manager as mediator has a vested interest in maintaining or increasing productivity, and recognizes that productivity depends on good working relationships among employees.

Different Approaches to Mediation

In some early conceptions of mediation, approaches were often classified as being either *content* or *process* interventions. Content interventions focused on resolving the substantive issues in dispute; process interventions focused on communication and the relationship between the parties. Presenting mediation approaches in these dual or dichotomous terms has become a common way of distinguishing one approach from another. Kolb (1983), for example, has paired the metaphors "dealmaker" and "orchestrator" to differentiate mediators' functions, while Silbey and Merry (1986) have referred to "bargaining" and "therapeutic" mediation styles. Kenneth Kressel and his colleagues (1994) have identified the "settlement-oriented" style as opposed to the "problem-solving" style.

Commentators have used various other dualisms in mapping the different approaches to mediation. Kressel and Pruitt (1989) developed the *task-oriented* and *socioeconomic* mediation approaches. While working with Kolb (1994), Kressel determined that mediation espouses either a *transformative* vision or a *pragmatic problem-solving* vision. Similarly, Bush and Folger (1994) contrasted styles of mediation as *transformative* or *problem solving*; Schwerin (1995) identified mediators as being either *facilitator* or *activist*; and Riskin (1996) described mediators as *facilitative* or *evaluative*.

Other dualisms used to classify mediation approaches include *broad* versus *narrow*, *open* versus *closed*, *positional* versus *interest-based*, *settlement* versus *process-oriented*, and *individualist* versus *relational*. In most cases, these typologies depict a mediator as being either a passive facilitator or an active shaper of solutions. In some instances, however, the dualisms are based on very different frameworks for understanding conflict.

This style of contrasting the mediator's functions in dual or bipolar terms still dominates much of the existing literature on mediation. By way of illustration, Figure 3.1 shows the different labels and characteristics of a pragmatic problem-solving approach as opposed to one whose goal is social and individual transformation. As you consider this figure, however, keep in mind that the more recent literature on mediation has suggested that mediation approaches are likely more integrated than the various dichotomies shown in this figure would suggest.

Facilitative and Evaluative Approaches

Riskin (1996) created a grid to show what mediation is and what mediators do. (See Figure 3.2.) His typology of mediation styles was designed to help disputants determine what type of mediation they wished to undertake and what type of mediator to use. An important finding from Riskin's work is that, though mediators usually have a predominant orientation that is based on a combination of factors (personality, experiences, education, and training), mediation approaches are not tightly contained; there is fluidity within the concepts (1996, p. 113). Mediators may depart

Figure 3.1 Continuum of Mediation Goals

Pragmatic problem-solving process goals	⟷	Social & individual transformation process goals
• content		• process
• positional		• interest-based
• dealmaker		• orchestrator
• bargaining		• therapeutic
• problem solving		• transformative
• facilitator		• activist
• evaluative		• facilitative
• passive		• active
• individualist		• relational

from their orientation to respond to the dynamics of the conflict situation. This flexibility was likewise identified in Picard's (2000) research, which found mediators stating that they change their style according to the nature of the dispute and the parties.

Riskin's grids emphasize two contrasting features: how mediators view their role (evaluative or facilitative) and how mediators define the problem (narrow or broad).

Figure 3.2 Mediator Techniques

The following grid shows the principal techniques associated with each mediator orientation, arranged vertically with the most evaluative at the top and the most facilitative at the bottom. The horizontal axis shows the scope of problems to be addressed, from the narrowest issues to the broadest interests.

EVALUATIVE

NARROW Problem Definition

BROAD Problem Definition

NARROW Problem Definition	BROAD Problem Definition
Urges/pushes parties to accept narrow (position-based) settlement	**Urges/pushes parties** to accept broad (interest-based) settlement
Develops and proposes narrow (position-based) agreement	**Develops and proposes** broad (interest-based) settlement
Predicts court outcomes	**Predicts** impact (on interests) of not settling
Assesses strengths and weaknesses of legal claims	**Probes** parties' interests
Litigation Issues / Other Distributive Issues	Business (Substantive) Issues / Business Interests / Personal Interests / Societal Interests
Helps parties evaluate proposals	**Helps parties** evaluate proposals
Helps parties develop narrow (position-based) proposals	**Helps parties** develop broad (interest-based) proposals
Asks parties about consequences of not settling	**Helps parties** develop options
Asks about likely court outcomes	**Helps parties** understand issues and interests
Asks about strengths and weaknesses of legal claims	**Focuses discussion** on underlying interests (business, personal, societal)

FACILITATIVE

Source: Riskin (1996). Reprinted with permission.

Each of the various quadrants reflects a mediator's belief about the nature and scope of mediation and his or her assumption about the parties' expectations.

In most cases, with a narrow definition of the problem, the mediator and the parties frame the issues in terms of the parties' legal rights and obligations. This narrowing often occurs when the parties in dispute involve their lawyers. With a broad definition of the problem, a mediator will ensure there is an exploration of both parties' needs, interests, and values. This approach does not preclude consideration of the parties' rights and obligations; it just means that the discussion will not be confined to them.

An evaluative mediator assumes that the participants want and need the mediator to provide direction. An *evaluative-narrow* approach would involve a mediator assessing the strengths and weaknesses of parties' claims, predicting court outcomes, developing and proposing a settlement, and pushing parties to settle, based on his or her assessment of their claims. With an *evaluative-broad* perspective, the mediator actively works to develop proposed solutions that take into account the parties' interests, as well as their rights and obligations, and to move the parties toward a settlement based on all of that.

A facilitative mediator assumes that the parties themselves are capable of developing better solutions than those a mediator might create. A *facilitative-narrow* mediator will generally conduct a mediation in which the discussion is focused on the legal issues between the parties, with the negotiation confined to legally framed positions and outcomes. This type of mediator helps parties to become "realistic" about their situation and to do some reality testing based on their knowledge and experience, but does not use his or her own assessments, predictions, or proposals to construct agreements for them.

On the other hand, using a *facilitative-broad* approach, the mediator helps the parties to discuss and understand the issues in terms of their underlying interests, rather than just their legally framed positions. The parties are encouraged to generate and assess proposals that will accommodate those interests. At the broad end of the facilitative continuum, mediators see their role as helping parties communicate and understand one another. At the broad end of the evaluative continuum, the mediator, by virtue of his or her expertise, assumes that the parties want guidance in reaching an appropriate settlement.

To understand the problem-definition continuum—from narrow to broad—you need to know that there is always more than one interest underlying the issues in a dispute. With a narrow approach, one strives to settle the dispute in legal terms, as a court would. With a broad approach, by contrast, one strives not just for a legal settlement but also to reveal and respond to the personal, business, or community interests that might underlie the dispute. The scenario presented in Box 3.1 will illustrate this continuum.

BOX 3.1 » Scenario: An Unhappy Customer

A customer has launched a civil suit against a garage owner in a small rural town in Nova Scotia. The customer has been going to this garage because of its convenient proximity to his place of work and because, for the past 15 years, the work done by the mechanics has been quite acceptable. Now, however, he thinks that the work done on his car by a new employee was lacking and caused him to be in a car accident soon after he picked the car up from the garage.

The work done on the car involved installing four new winter tires. After leaving the shop, the car owner set out for Halifax, a distance of about 200 kilometres. About one hour into the trip, the car started to swerve out of control. With great effort, the driver was able to bring the car to a stop, but not before running through a guard rail and into a deep culvert. The front and side of the car were badly damaged, and the owner received minor injuries. The police determined that the accident had likely been caused by the wheel coming loose—a result of the wheel nuts not having been put on tightly.

The angry car owner has sued the garage owner for the cost of repairs to the car in the amount of $4,500. He would like to avoid an insurance claim because it would increase his premiums. The car owner also wants an apology from the garage owner for causing him trauma and inconvenience, and some reassurance that the owner will be more attentive in the future to the competence of the mechanics he hires to work in the shop.

The garage owner prides himself on good workmanship and stands by his solid reputation in the community. He does not accept that his shop should bear the full cost of the repairs, because the body of the car was not in good condition in the first place. He is concerned as much about losing his good reputation as about the lawsuit itself.

Assume that the customer and the garage owner described in Box 3.1 have agreed to mediation. If a narrow form of mediation were undertaken to resolve this dispute, the goal would be to settle the financial issues as expediently as possible, based on the legal merits of each side's case. In other words, the goal would be to determine how much, if anything, the garage owner would pay the customer. This decision would be based on the legal rights of the parties, and negotiations would take place in the "shadow of the law."

Now consider what would happen if the scope of the negotiations were to broaden, so that they took into account the business and personal interests of the two parties. In this case, we might imagine the discussions drawing out the garage owner's interest in continuing to do business with this customer and to maintain his good reputation, so as to not lose other customers. As for the customer, we would likely discover that he does not want to use another garage, given that this one is close to his work and therefore convenient. The customer is also mindful that the garage's work on his car has been satisfactory for the past 15 years; he still has confidence in the owner's competency despite his bad experience with one employee.

As a facilitative-broad mediator may find, both parties have an interest in restoring the customer's confidence in the future work of this garage. This mediation would include discussions about individual business and personal interests and would proceed to link them to the issues of financial settlement.

As the scope of the negotiations broadens further, community interests could also become a part of the discussions. In a small town, a long-standing, family-owned business may disappear if required to pay a substantial settlement. Jobs are at stake if the garage closes, and neighbours could become polarized as they are forced to take sides on the issue. As the discussion broadens, the issue of payment becomes linked to personal, business, and community interests, thus becoming less central to the overall negotiations.

Transformative Approach

In *The Promise of Mediation* (1994), Bush and Folger introduced their *transformative* approach to mediation, setting out its basic tenets. This approach is based on a more "relational" view of conflict than the facilitative and evaluative approaches are. In other words, rather than being solely focused on reaching settlement, the transformative approach emphasizes that people have an inherent form of consciousness that connects them to one another and allows a person to realize that others have needs and desires similar to one's own. It is this human capacity for relating to others that, according to this theory, should underpin a mediator's intervention, which should not merely be focused on settling the dispute. While a focus on settling the dispute can help to address the immediate issues facing the parties, it may not address their long-term need to be able to interact together successfully in the future.

Mediators following the transformative approach aim to foster in the disputing parties a greater sense of their own efficacy as well as a greater openness to others, based on a relational ideology. Disputes are viewed as opportunities for moral growth and transformation, rather than as problems to be solved.

With the transformative approach, a mediator pursues two goals: empowerment and recognition. These are thought to be the most important outcomes mediation can achieve. *Empowerment* involves strengthening individuals' abilities to reflect, to make choices, and to act in a conflict situation. It occurs when people come to understand more clearly their goals and their own importance. It also means that parties increase their skills in conflict resolution, gain a new awareness of their resources, and are able to make deliberate, conscious decisions about what they want to do. Bush and Folger tell us that when this process of empowerment happens, the parties experience a greater sense of self-worth, security, self-determination, and autonomy (1994, p. 87). Empowerment is independent of any particular outcome of the mediation. Solving problems for parties is *not* transformative mediation.

Recognition means becoming more sympathetic and responsive to the other party's situation. Parties achieve recognition in mediation when they are able to feel less threatened and more open to the other party. As well, they become sympathetic and have the desire to be responsive to the other party in their thoughts, words and actions.

Bush and Folger (1994, p. 94) provide the following concrete definition of successful mediation:

> A mediation is successful (1) if the parties have been made aware of the opportunities presented during the mediation for both empowerment and recognition; (2) if the parties have been helped to clarify goals, options, and resources, and then to make informed, deliberate and free choices regarding how to proceed at every decision point; and (3) if the parties have been helped to give recognition wherever it was their decision to do so.

Among mediation practitioners, the transformative model has become a popular and valued approach.

Narrative Approach

The narrative approach to mediation recognizes that the parties' conflict behaviours are often embedded in narratives, known as conflict narratives, concerning the history of their relationship. When that relationship has been full of conflict, it is often difficult to deal with the particular issues raised by the present dispute; the narratives of the past continue to influence the actions and perceptions of the parties in the present. This can occur between individuals in a family or in a small group—for example, between siblings or co-workers in a workplace setting. Such "conflict-soaked narratives" can also exist where there has been a long history of conflict and tension between members of different ethnic, religious, or even national groups, as with Israelis and Palestinians, or Catholics and Protestants in Northern Ireland.

Using the narrative approach, the mediator encourages parties to tell their personal "conflict stories," hoping they will be able to produce an "alternate" story that will lead them to a resolution of their dispute. This approach is based on social constructionist theory, which posits that people organize their experiences in story form as a way to make sense of their lives and relationships, and that "they act both out of and into these stories" (Winslade & Monk, 2000, p. 3). With this approach, mediators do not seek one "factual" story; instead, they find it more useful to accept each person's story as a lived reality and then "seek out the points where the story might incorporate some different approaches" (p. 3). A key task of the mediator is to make the parties question the rigid and negative motivations they attribute to each other's actions. The mediator accomplishes this by several means: by building the parties' trust in the mediator and in the mediation process; by developing conversations that externalize, as opposed to internalize, the conflict; by mapping the effects of the conflict on the respective parties; by deconstructing the dominant story lines; and by developing shared meanings about the conflict and its solutions. (For more information on social constructionist theory, see Burr, 1995, and Gergen, 1999.)

Important to narrative mediators is the belief that the parties' conflict stories are drawn from the cultural stories of the world around them. As a result, there are always multiple stories at play during a mediation session. Narrative mediation has three phases: engagement, deconstruction of the conflict-saturated story, and construction of an alternate story (Winslade & Monk, 2000, p. 58):

1. In the *engagement* phase, the mediator concentrates on establishing a relationship with the conflict parties by attending to the physical setting and the non-verbal behaviour displayed by all parties. Attention is also given to the roles that the mediator and the parties will take on as a result of the mediation.
2. In the stage of *deconstructing the conflict-saturated story*, the mediator works actively to separate the parties from their perceptions and understandings of the conflict by "undermining the certainties on which the conflict feeds, and inviting the parties to view the plot of the dispute from a different vantage point" (p. 72). The assumption is that elements of cooperation, points of agreement, and mutual respect have been left out of the conflict-saturated story. Deconstructing that story can lead to creating an alternate story that includes these areas.
3. The final stage of narrative mediation is to *construct an alternate story*. In this stage, the mediator is "occupied with crafting alternative, more preferred story lines with people who were previously captured by a conflict-saturated relationship" (p. 82). The development of a cooperative attitude may be more important than reaching an agreement.

Insight Approach

The insight approach to mediation has features in common with other approaches. Like other models of mediation, it has a beginning stage, in which the issues, parties, and positions are identified; a middle stage, in which the needs, values, and interests underlying parties' positions with respect to the issues are explored; and an end stage, in which resolution options that fulfill the parties' interests are generated, evaluated, and agreed upon. It has most in common with the transformative and narrative approaches because, like the insight mediator, mediators trained in transformative and narrative approaches focus on relational aspects, and their lines of questioning take the parties into diverse areas of personal and social experience.

The *insight* approach assumes a relational view of conflict in that it sees interactions and interdependence as cornerstones of conflict. Mediators applying the insight approach use communication skills similar to those used with the transformative and narrative approaches and with other interest-based approaches.

A key goal of the insight approach is to facilitate learning. To achieve this goal, the insight mediator uses certain types of questions and lines of questioning. For example, the mediator will endeavour to discover if one party's values must necessarily threaten the other party's values. The rationale here is that differing values can co-exist if they are not perceived as threats. The mediator's questions aim to discover how the parties' past experiences and fears of a dismal future are shaping their present interpretations and actions. They engage the parties in conversation to help them understand each other's meanings, particularly ill-expressed or misinterpreted meanings that create, exacerbate, and sustain conflict.

With the insight approach, mediators help facilitate parties' learning: about the conflict, about each other's cares and concerns, and about new possibilities for action. The goal of their questioning is to help parties achieve breakthroughs in perspectives and attitudes—breakthroughs that shift relations and interactions onto new ground. The questioning aims at a deeper understanding of the values that are threatened through the conflict dynamic.

The need for mediators to stay curious, non-judgmental, and transparent is emphasized in insight mediation. The aim is to help parties discover the causes, elements, emotions, and values—as well as the patterns of interaction and their relational nature—of the conflict situation in which they are involved. The essence of the insight practice is expressed in the following core statement:

> Conflict occurs when an individual or group experiences threats to their needs, desires, expected patterns of cooperation, or deeply held judgments about the good of society. These threats lead to defend responses. Defend responses feel like threats to others and they, in turn, also respond defensively. Through deepening conversations and emergent creativity a mediator helps parties gain insights that produce new understandings and alter defend patterns of interaction so that learning and change can occur. (Picard & Jull, 2011)

Why Choose Mediation?

Since the beginnings of the alternative dispute resolution (ADR) movement in North America, mediation has been lauded as a more efficient and cost-effective alternative to the courts. It came into prominence in the late 1960s and early 1970s in the United States, largely as a response to public dissatisfaction with the justice system (Scimecca, 1991), as well as from a desire for community self-reliance, social justice, and transformation (Picard, 2002, p. 9). Victim–offender reconciliation programs, family mediation, and community-based mediation centres emerged at around the same time in Canada. Canadian legal reform in the 1970s focused on alternatives to sentencing for young offenders, alternatives that recognized that adjudication was not addressing the root causes of crime. As well, those in the family law field sought more responsive and non-adversarial processes for divorcing couples with children. (For more history on the emergence of ADR in Canada, see Picard, 2002.) In the 1970s and early 1980s, mediation processes were not well known, and few people outside of those working in the field would have been able to define it. Today, mediation can be found in our everyday vernacular, and it is rare to encounter people who have not heard of it or have not been touched by mediated processes in some form. What has led to this immense growth?

Mediation as a form of dispute resolution appeals on many levels, both ideological and methodological. For us, mediation rests on a relational world view, as opposed to an individualist perspective. This world view posits that

> the highest values of the social enterprise are these two: first, the fulfillment of the individual's capacity for moral development, for going beyond self-interest and being concerned with others; and second, the discovery of a common good beyond any private vision of the good, through the encounter between self and others in shared political discourse and action. (Bush, 1989, p. 14)

There are also many good methodological reasons to adopt mediation for dispute resolution. Figure 3.3 reveals some of the many methodological differences between adjudication and mediation.

From the comparison in Figure 3.3, it is easy to see why individuals, companies, and organizations might prefer to use mediation over other methods of dispute resolution, particularly adjudication, for many conflicts. Mediation usually ensures that the conflict will not exacerbate with time; its private nature enables parties to speak freely and without fear that honesty will cost them their public reputations; and its non-judgmental, non-adversarial, and non-blaming nature guarantees "face saving." Outcomes of this process benefit all parties involved—they are considered win–win, because all parties' needs are considered and responded to in resolving the dispute. When agreements are arrived at through mediation, parties do tend to believe they are fair and cost-effective. (See Macfarlane, 1995; Bingham & Pitts, 2002; Tjersland, 1999; Burrell, Zirbel, & Allen, 2003.)

In many cases, mediation or negotiation is in fact the preferred choice, with a full 95 percent of all civil cases settling before they reach Superior Court. In very few cases does the suit actually proceed to court. Yet, the fundamental principles behind mediation are distinct from those of adjudication, and a great number of people expect a legal dispute resolution to follow the principles of adjudication (Macfarlane, 1995). The difference in approach and ideology are important to identify, particularly when a party is able to choose the process that best responds to his or her needs.

In addition to the process advantages of mediation noted above, parties who use mediation also report satisfaction with the quality of mediation. Aside from the clear benefits in efficiency and outcomes, mediation offers a number of other benefits to its users—namely, the beliefs and values inherent in mediation and the impact on those who go through the process. Reaching agreement is not necessarily the most

Figure 3.3 Adjudication Versus Mediation

Adjudication	Mediation
Third party has authoritative decision-making power—the judge or panel makes the decisions	Third party has no authoritative decision-making power—the parties to the conflict make the decisions
Lawyers represent and speak for their clients, who are directly affected by the conflict	Parties to the conflict speak on their own behalf, even when counsel attends the mediation session
Only legal principles can be argued—the conflict must be expressed as a legal issue and effects of the conflict must be legally recognized	No constraint on subjects discussed—parties may bring all points they believe relevant to the dispute, including emotion
Once litigation is begun, it is mandatory that all parties attend	Voluntary process for all parties
Aggressively adversarial in nature—objective is to "beat" your opponent (win-lose)	Non-adversarial—objective is to promote understanding and outcomes that benefit all (win-win)
Fact-finding process employing the principle of falsifiability	Dialogic process where facts are not judged to be true or false
Public process that is recorded	As confidential as the parties desire, without need for any record
Decisions are rendered based on positions argued—conflict can be "settled," but the cause may be left unaddressed	Decisions are arrived at based on party interests unearthed during the process—conflict causes are addressed, as well as parties' needs
Relationship ending for the parties involved—focused on blame	Relationship preserving for parties involved—focused on mutual understanding and acceptance
Long delays getting to hearing	Quickly scheduled and completed
Expensive process	Relatively cost-effective
Very little educational value, given that parties do not participate directly	Great potential for discovery, because parties learn about one another, as well as creating a better means for future interactions
Focus on the objective, rational, and measurable effects of the conflict = *linear*	Equal focus on the subjective, emotional, and non-measurable effects of the conflict = *holistic*

important index of mediation success. Evaluation research indicates that between 92 and 97 percent of parties are satisfied with the opportunity to participate in a mediation (Bingham & Pitts, 2002, p. 141). Gaining new knowledge, clarifying issues, having concerns heard, and being responsible for outcomes were equally important factors in parties' satisfaction (Jones & Bodtker, 1998; Burrell, Zirbel, & Allen, 2003).

Mediation puts the responsibility and control for resolving disputes back into the hands of those most intimately affected by it—the parties to the conflict. This is considered the empowering nature of mediation, because it upholds the individual in conflict as the one who is best placed to know what she or he needs for conflict closure. Mediation holds that durable outcomes come from processes that address the root causes of conflict, not merely the symptoms. Through mediation, conflict is resolved, not just managed. It is also biased in favour of collaborative, rather than competitive, interaction between individuals, because it is premised on the world view that people are inherently striving to relate and connect to other people.

Resolving conflict is thus about re-establishing connections broken by the conflict. Given the opportunity, people will and do recognize and understand the other party, because

> the individual is an agent of reflection, challenged by some implicit common standard to enlarge himself by connecting to and serving others, and society is an encouraging educator in that developmental process. (Bush, 1989, p. 14)

This world view is what makes mediation such an attractive option for dispute resolution. Indeed, many new mediators are drawn to the field for the values it reflects and inspires.

Unlike adjudication or other forms of conflict resolution that rely on the expertise of a third party to make decisions, mediation rests on the desire of parties to restore harmony to their relationships with others—and the subsequent capacity for humans to understand and empathize with others. Mediation can bring out the best in all of us. It works, in part, because it assumes that individuals are able to overcome selfishness in their relationships with the "other," and, as a result, a surprising number of people live up to these expectations.

Defining Success in Mediation

How should success be defined in mediation? Since the parties to the mediation are those who make the decisions, should success ultimately be defined by the parties themselves? Yet, the mediator also needs some template to determine whether he or she is meeting key objectives in practice. These are important questions for mediators and mediation evaluators to ask. In fact, success in mediation is often defined differently depending on which participant you ask (the parties, the mediator, or the parties' counsel).

Some parties might define success in terms of how much they "win" relative to the other party. A party's counsel, for example, might define success in terms of how much the process gives his or her client relative to what they could have got out of adjudication. In these instances, success is defined in terms of relative material gain. Other parties come to mediation with other goals in mind—such as to preserve their relationships. These parties may measure their success in terms of more collaborative outcomes.

Mediators have different measures for success depending on their particular approach. A mediator using the transformative approach will likely consider the mediation a success if the parties leave the session feeling empowered and having experienced recognition. Mediators who use a narrative approach may consider their sessions successful if an alternate narrative is created for the parties' understanding of their conflict. A mediator using the insight approach will consider the mediation a success if, through learning more about themselves and each other, the parties are freed from threat and so can change their patterns of interaction from defensive to something more constructive. Settlement-oriented mediators deem mediation successful if it ends in an agreement. This list could go on—there are as many definitions of success as there are types of mediators.

We think that mediation is, at its core, about transforming relationships. To determine how successful a mediation session has been in that regard, a mediator would need to obtain information from the parties about how their experience and understanding of their relationship may have changed and how that new insight might lead to a different and less problematic pattern of interaction now and in the future.

Benefits of Mediation

There are many reasons for the growing popularity of mediation. People have come to associate the process with certain benefits: informality and flexibility; openness and creativity; lower costs; and education and discovery.

Informality and Flexibility

Mediation is informal, not bound by the procedural requirements of a trial or an arbitration hearing, and is often quicker and less expensive. A mediation session can be held wherever the disputants and mediator are prepared to meet to facilitate a resolution to the conflict.

The mediation process is also comparatively flexible. For example, there is no procedural limit—as there often is with a formal adjudication process—on the number of parties who can participate (Emond, 1989, p. 8). Mediation can be used in two-party conflicts, such as a commercial dispute between two individuals or a divorce mediation, or it can be used in multi-party disputes involving many different stakeholders. The mediation process can have either a single mediator or co-mediators. The parties can bring representatives (such as lawyers or close family friends) into the mediation process, or they may participate directly, on their own.

The mediation process also allows for structural flexibility. The parties to a mediation may meet with the mediator either together or separately. In some international mediations, the process is structured in the form of separate meetings between the mediator and representatives from each country, often in different locations, with the parties only coming together at a later stage in the mediation process, if sufficient progress is being made. This example also shows that the mediation process is flexible enough to respond to changing circumstances, even within the context of a single mediation.

Mediation is flexible in other respects, too. For example, it can be used in disputes with either a high legal content or a low one. An example of a dispute with low legal content would be a volunteer peer mediation program for dealing with schoolyard bullying.

The mediation process is also more informal than other adjudication processes, encouraging direct participation by the parties in conflict. The disputants retain ownership of their conflict, both in terms of defining its nature and in terms of controlling the outcome. The litigation process, by contrast, requires the conflict to be translated into a legal dispute, involving technical questions of fact and law that can only be fully understood and determined by legal professionals. Consequently, the parties involved tend to lose control over their own disputes. With litigation, even the language in which the dispute is described undergoes a translation into technical legal jargon that most non-legal professionals cannot understand. Litigants therefore rely on their lawyers to navigate these unknown waters for them. Christie (1977, pp. 1–12) goes so far as to call lawyers "professional thieves" who rob disputants and communities of the opportunity and the skills to resolve their own conflicts peacefully.

In mediation, then, the parties define the nature of the dispute and the issues that need to be discussed. In a sense, the mediator acts as a moderator between the disputants, rather than as an umpire or referee. The mediator has no power to make a decision about what information or issues are relevant. What is relevant depends on the needs of the parties—and these needs may differ at different times during the mediation process. Mediators recognize that conflicts are often multidimensional, and therefore they allow space for the parties to address the psychological, relational, and emotional dimensions of the conflict, dimensions that would not normally be addressed in litigation or in an arbitration hearing. In many respects, mediation is unique in its capacity to incorporate the human and relational dimensions of a conflict into the dispute resolution process itself (Boulle & Kelly, 1998, p. 41; Bush & Folger, 1994, p. 2).

Openness and Creativity

Another benefit of the mediation process is that it promotes non-adversarial, open communication between the disputants. This gives it a critical advantage over adversarial processes such as litigation and arbitration. In an adversarial process, disputants tend to view information as a resource that becomes less valuable the more it is shared. (If I have more information than you, I should be able to extract a higher price from you for the value of my information.) Information is viewed as a commodity to be carefully hoarded, never shared for free. The litigation process tends to reinforce this view of information. Lawyers discourage their clients from communicating directly with the other party, lest they inadvertently make an admission they should not make, or give away "strategic" information about the strengths of their case.

Unlike litigation, a mediator tries to create a non-adversarial environment, so that the parties communicate openly with each other about the issues in dispute. Ultimately, mediation, like negotiation, can be seen as a communication process in which the parties try to reach a mutually acceptable agreement that is capable of satisfying their separate interests. Any negotiation involves a tension between the parties' desire to reach an agreement and the parties' competing interests. A mediator often "adds value" to the negotiating process by creating a non-adversarial environment that encourages joint decision making and collaborative problem solving. A basic premise of mediation is that the better the quality of the information jointly available to the participants in mediation, the better the outcome of any joint decision-making process. The mediator therefore focuses on trying to improve the quality of the information jointly available to the disputants by probing their interests and looking for creative options that could provide the basis for a mutual agreement. Information is therefore viewed as a common resource that increases in quality—and therefore also in value—the more it is *shared* between the parties.

The emphasis on open communication and collaborative decision making also opens the door to more creative outcomes than are normally possible in arbitration or litigation. The role of a mediator is not to hand down an authoritative decision on the issues in dispute but to assist the parties in crafting their own resolution to the conflict. The parties, not the mediator, are responsible for the outcome of the conflict. This means that the mediator has much more flexibility than either a judge or an arbitrator in examining settlement options, and in encouraging the parties to become joint decision makers in resolving their conflict. The range of potential outcomes is not constrained by legal precedents or by the particular facts of the conflict. Nor are the outcomes restricted to a limited number of specific legal remedies, as would be the case in litigation. Instead, the parties are free to craft outcomes that are uniquely tailored to their own particular needs and circumstances. In a workplace harassment mediation, for example, the parties could reach an agreement that responds to the complainant's interest in having the harassing behaviour of her supervisor acknowledged and stopped. But the outcomes could also extend to a broader organizational commitment to create a harassment-free workplace for the future. Mediation is thus a norm-creating process in which the parties themselves agree on the norms or standards to be used in settling their dispute and governing their future relationship (Boulle & Kelly, 1998, p. 42; Sander & Goldberg, 1994, p. 52).

Lower Costs

Another benefit of mediation is its relatively low cost. Because it is a consensual process, mediation often avoids many of the costs and risks of losing associated with more adversarial processes. In litigation and arbitration, the decision of the third party is imposed on the disputants, who are then expected to comply with the ruling of the third-party decision maker. Because litigation and arbitration tend to result in winners and losers, the costs for the loser may often be substantial. The unsuccessful disputant may have invested significant resources in these processes, in the expectation of obtaining a favourable outcome. If the outcome is unfavourable, not only does the disputant have to accept the result, but also the costs (such as legal fees) of pursuing the litigation or arbitration process, which may be very high.

By contrast, since mediation is based on reconciling the parties' interests and needs rather than determining who is right (or who is in the wrong), the risks and costs of "losing" tend to be significantly reduced. Even if mediation does not result in a negotiated settlement of all the issues that are outstanding between the parties, neither party will have "lost"—they cannot be forced to comply with a ruling that they disagree with. The consensual nature of the mediation process, therefore, also has a tendency to lower the risks of non-compliance that are sometimes associated with more coercive decision-making processes such as litigation.

Exemplifying the limitations of the courts' coercive jurisdiction is the problem of non-compliance with support and custody awards in family law. Non-compliance in this context sometimes results in child kidnapping or child abduction, with one parent rejecting the court's ruling over custody and access. Of course, we do not suggest that the consensual nature of the mediation process is likely to prevent any future disagreement between the parties over such contested issues. But the point is that the coercive nature of the litigation process does not prevent the costs of future conflict between the disputing parties in such circumstances. Indeed, it is arguable that the adversarial and coercive nature of the litigation process may sometimes accentuate the risks of future conflict (Irving & Benjamin, 1987, pp. 36–43).

Less obviously, mediation also reduces the costs of winning that are associated with more adversarial decision-making processes. In a legal process, the costs of being vindicated are sometimes quite high. Following an adversarial workplace harassment proceeding, for example, it may be difficult for a complainant to re-establish relationships with other co-workers or supervisors who were not directly involved in the complaint. Likewise, a business that becomes involved in highly publicized litigation with a customer or client may be concerned about the effect on its reputation, even if it wins its lawsuit. In such circumstances, the privacy and confidentiality of mediation offer significant procedural advantages over litigation. Where future relationships are important to the disputants, mediation can often minimize the collateral damage that may result from a hostile adversarial process (Sander & Goldberg, 1994, p. 52).

Education and Insight

Mediation offers the benefit of educating the parties about collaborative decision making and about constructive conflict management, and for Bush and Folger (1994, pp. 2, 4–5), the educative function of mediation is its most important characteristic; it is what makes it qualitatively distinct from all other dispute resolution processes. For Melchin and Picard (2008), the primary benefit of mediation is that of learning about oneself and others so that less threatening patterns of social interaction can be discovered. Mediation achieves both learning and education by providing disputing parties with opportunities to respond to conflict in more constructive ways. Instead of seeing the other disputant as an adversary who must be defeated, mediation teaches the twin values of empowerment and recognition. Individuals are empowered when they learn to solve problems through their own efforts rather than through outside agencies or the threat of force. Recognition involves seeing our own image reflected in the eyes of the other disputant, and thereby discovering our common humanity. For Bush and Folger (1994, pp. 2, 4–5), the disputants' discovery, through mediation, of their shared humanity is more important than the actual results of any mediation process. Even if the mediation does not result in a negotiated settlement, the experience of mediation is likely to equip the parties with improved communication skills, and thus with an increased capacity to resolve their own conflicts in the future. So too, the discovery of new patterns of social interaction that allow conflicting values to coexist without threat have long-ranging impacts far beyond the problem at hand.

Limitations of Mediation

Having identified some benefits of mediation, we should also point out that mediation has its limitations and will not be appropriate for every dispute resolution situation. These limitations may be summarized as follows:

- Collaborative decision making is only possible where all disputants are willing to participate actively in the decision-making process. Where that participation is not forthcoming, mediation is unlikely to result in an integrative resolution.
- Not all conflicts can be resolved through collaborative decision-making processes. In some cases, there may be public values at stake that a private, non-adjudicatory process may not adequately address.
- In a conflict in which the rights of the parties are uncertain, one or more of the parties may prefer to rely on a rights-based process in order to clarify their legal rights or entitlements.
- Where there is a large power imbalance between the disputants, mediation processes may lack sufficient procedural safeguards to ensure that the weaker party is protected from exploitation by the stronger party (Grillo, 1991).

- Mediation processes are typically private and informal, and therefore incapable of generating and publicizing legal norms or precedents. A disputant whose conflict goal is to create new legal rights or precedents—for example, in a case where the interests of others (of a class of people or even of the public at large) are at stake—may be better served by a process other than mediation (Fiss, 1984).

The limitations of mediation have generated a lively debate in the conflict resolution literature. This debate concerns how and by whom, in a given case, the method of dispute resolution should be determined. Should this decision be left to the disputants themselves? Are they—as much of our conflict resolution theory would suggest—in the best position to decide which dispute resolution process is in their own best interests? Are the parties *able* to make that decision? In many cases, the parties will probably need assistance in deciding how best to deal with their conflict or dispute. As mediation theorists and practitioners, however, we generally favour a self-determination approach, leaving it to the disputants to make the ultimate decision about which dispute resolution process is most suitable for their own conflict. For illustrative articles on this debate, see Chornecki & Hart (1996, pp. 1–17); Sander & Goldberg (1994, pp. 49–64); Fiss (1984); McThenia & Shaffer (1985); Bailey (1989); and Bush (1989). We will come back to this question in our Chapter 6 discussion of the process of convening a mediation.

Summary

In this chapter, we discussed some key features of mediation. We presented different approaches to mediation, from pragmatic problem-solving processes to processes that influence individual and social transformation. With the former, conflict is a problem to be solved; with the latter, it is an opportunity for growth and empowerment. We discussed the following approaches in particular: the evaluative approach, whereby the mediator provides parties with the direction they need to reach settlement; the facilitative approach, whereby the mediator's role is to help parties understand the problems they want to address; the transformative approach, whereby the mediator focuses on the empowerment and recognition of parties; the narrative approach, whereby the mediator focuses on creating a shared narrative alternative to the parties' conflict-saturated stories; and the insight approach, whereby the mediator focuses on helping parties gain insight into threats to each other's values in order to change problematic ways of interacting.

Regardless of what particular approach or approaches a mediator may use, the effectiveness of mediation largely stems from its orientation toward understanding conflict and toward helping parties to transform their relationship through an understanding of their interconnectedness. Unlike many other forms of dispute resolution, mediation is focused on the decisions of the parties rather than someone in authority who is distant from the impact and aftermath of the situation and the decision making. Research shows that it strengthens relationships, is relatively cost effective, and results in high levels of satisfaction.

DISCUSSION QUESTIONS AND EXERCISES

1. Paul and Jo-Anne are going through a divorce after a nine-year marriage. They have two children: Riley, seven, and Brianna, five. Paul works as a bureaucrat with the provincial Department of Health, while Jo-Anne has just gone back to work as an elementary school teacher after putting her career on hold until the children reached kindergarten age. Paul has moved into his own apartment, which is outside the school district where Jo-Anne works and where both children attend school. But there are good elementary schools in Paul's new neighbourhood, and he thinks the kids would do well in a new school environment where their mother is not a teacher. Paul is especially concerned about Riley, who has been getting into trouble at school since his mother and father decided to divorce. Jo-Anne, on the other hand, wants to keep the children at their present school, and she wants them to live with her in the house where they have lived thus far. She is concerned that Paul will contest custody of the children, which she feels would make it even harder for the children to adjust to their parents' divorce. For his part, Paul feels that Jo-Anne is putting her anger with him (at getting involved with another woman) over what is best for the children. He is concerned that Jo-Anne blames him for the divorce, and may try to alienate the children from him. So he wants to make sure, if it is legally possible, that Jo-Anne will not be in a position to jeopardize his future relationship with the children.

   Imagine that you are mediating this divorce dispute.

   a. What would you be seeking to achieve as a facilitative mediator? What specific aspects of this conflict situation would you explore with them? In the course of this exploration, what are some questions you would ask them?
   b. If you used an evaluative approach, what would your answers to the previous question be?
   c. How would your answer be different if you used a transformative approach, a narrative approach, or an insight approach?
2. Think of a situation in which you could be a social network mediator (within your family, with friends or fellow students, or with co-workers). What approach would you use in mediating that conflict? What challenges would you face as mediator in this case and what would you do to overcome these challenges?
3. With the insight approach to mediation, mediators help facilitate parties' learning: about the conflict, about each other's cares and concerns, and about new possibilities for action. Think again of the situation you considered in responding

to the previous question. What could the parties in that conflict learn about themselves and their situation that might help them resolve their conflict? As mediator, how could you help them gain such insights and learning?

4. Think of a conflict in which you have been involved. Keeping in mind the differences between mediation and adjudication, think about which process you would prefer to use. Why? What is it about the nature of your conflict situation that lends itself to your choice? What is it about your own nature that lends itself to your choice?
5. Refer to the Sonata Development scenario, described in the first exercise at the end of Chapter 2, then answer the following questions:
   a. As a mediator in this case, what would be your goals for the mediation process? What specifically would you hope to achieve for these parties as the mediation proceeds?
   b. How would you describe and explain the approach that you would use as mediator in this case?
   c. What specific aspects of this conflict situation would you explore with the parties? In doing this, what are some questions you would ask them?
6. Refer to the Unhappy Customer scenario described in Box 3.1. Then answer the following questions:
   a. As a mediator in this case, what would be your goals for the mediation process? What specifically would you hope to achieve for these parties as the mediation proceeds?
   b. How would you describe and explain the approach that you would use as mediator in this case?
   c. What specific aspects of this conflict situation would you explore with the parties? In doing this, what are some questions you would ask them?

FURTHER READING

Bush, R.B., & Folger, J. (1994). *The promise of mediation*. San Francisco: Jossey-Bass.

LeBaron, Michelle. (2002). *Bridging cultural conflicts: Conflict resolution from the heart*. San Francisco: Jossey-Bass.

Melchin, K.R., & Picard, C.A. (2008). *Transforming conflict through insight*. Toronto; University of Toronto Press.

Moore, C.W. (2003). *The mediation process: Practical strategies for resolving conflict* (3rd ed.). San Francisco: Jossey-Bass.

Picard, C.A. (2002). *Mediating interpersonal and small group conflict* (Rev. ed.). Ottawa: Golden Dog Press.

Picard, C.A. & Jull, M. (2011). Learning through deepening conversations: A key strategy of insight mediation. *Conflict Resolution Quarterly*, *29*(2), 151–176.

Winslade, J., & Monk, G. (2000). *Narrative mediation*. San Francisco: Jossey-Bass.

Websites

The Institute for the Study of Conflict Transformation, Inc.: http://www.transformativemediation.org
This institute was founded to promote the transformative approach, first articulated by Robert A. Baruch Bush and Joseph P. Folger in *The Promise of Mediation.*

The Lonergan Centre at University of Saint Paul: http://ustpaul.ca/en/lonergan-centre-home_371_131.htm
The Lonergan Centre at Saint Paul University connects scholars with expert practitioners in national and international collaborative research projects that develop, apply, and communicate the work of Bernard Lonergan. Established in the spring of 2007, the Centre focuses on research in areas that can make a difference to people's lives: peace and conflict; business and economics; ethics and community; insight and learning; science and religion; faith and life.

Mediate.com: Mediators & Everything Mediation: http://www.mediate.com
Mediate.com is a leading provider of online services to mediation professionals and programs. They offer such things as an ADR Directory, online courses, and a host of books, DVDs, articles, and other resources of interest to mediation clients and practitioners.

REFERENCES

Bailey, M. (1989). Unpacking the "rational alternative": A critical review of family mediation movement claims. *Canadian Journal of Family Law, 8,* 61–96.

Benjamin, R. (1995a). The constructive uses of deception: Skills, strategies, and techniques of the folkloric trickster figure and their application by mediators. *Mediation Quarterly, 13,* 3–18.

Benjamin, R. (1995b). The mediator as trickster: The folkloric figure as professional role model. *Mediation Quarterly, 13,* 131–149.

Bingham, L.B., & Pitts, D.W. (2002). Highlights of mediation at work: Studies of the national REDRESS evaluation project. *Negotiation Journal, 18,* 135–146.

Boulle, L., & Kelly, K.J. (1998). *Mediation: Principles, process, practice.* Toronto: Butterworths.

Burr, V. (1995). *An introduction to social constructionism.* New York: Routledge.

Burrell, N.A., Zirbel, C.S., & Allen, M. (2003). Evaluating peer mediation outcomes in educational settings: A meta-analytic review. *Conflict Resolution Quarterly, 21,* 7–26.

Bush, R.A.B. (1989). Mediation and adjudication, dispute resolution and ideology: An imaginary conversation. *Journal of Contemporary Legal Issues, 3,* 1–35.

Bush, R.A.B., & Folger, J.P. (1994). *The promise of mediation.* San Francisco: Jossey-Bass.

Chornecki, G., & Hart, C. (1996). *Bypass court.* Toronto: Butterworths.

Christie, N. (1977). Conflicts as property. *British Journal of Criminology, 17,* 1–15.

Eckhoff, T. (1969). The mediator and the judge. In V. Aubert (Ed.), *Sociology of law* (pp. 171–181). London: Penguin Books.

Emond, D.P. (1989). Alternative dispute resolution: A conceptual overview. In D.P. Emond (Ed.), *Commercial dispute resolution* (pp. 1-25). Aurora, ON: Canada Law Book.

Fisher, J. (2000). Symbol in mediation. *Mediation Quarterly, 18,* 87–107.

Fiss, O.M. (1984). Against settlement. *Yale Law Journal, 93,* 1073–1091.

Folberg, J., & Taylor, A. (1984). Mediation: A comprehensive guide to resolving conflicts without litigation. San Francisco: Jossey-Bass.

Folger, J.P., & Jones, T.S. (Eds.). (1994). *New directions in mediation: Communication, research, and perspectives.* Thousand Oaks, CA: Sage.

Fuller, L.L. (1971). Mediation: Its forms and functions. *Southern California Law Review, 44,* 305–339.

Gergen, K.J. (1999). *An invitation to social constructionism.* Thousand Oaks, CA: Sage Publications.

Goleman, D. (1995). *Emotional intelligence.* New York: Bantam.

Grillo, T. (1991). The mediation alternative: Process dangers for women. *Yale Law Journal, 100,* 1545–1610.

Irving, H.H., & Benjamin, M. (1987). *Family mediation: Theory and practice of dispute resolution.* Toronto: Carswell.

Jones, T.S., & Bodtker, A. (1998). Satisfaction with custody mediation: Results from the York county mediation program. *Mediation Quarterly, 16,* 185–200.

Kolb, D.M. (1983). Strategy and the tactics of mediation. *Human Relations, 36,* 247–268.

Kolb, D.M. (1994). *When talk works: Profiles of mediators.* San Francisco: Jossey-Bass.

Kressel, K., Frontera, E., Forlenza, S., Butler, F., & Fish, L. (1994). The settlement-orientation vs. the problem-solving style in custody mediation. *Journal of Social Issues, 50,* 67–84.

Kressel, K., Pruitt, D., & Associates. (1989). *Mediation research.* New Brunswick, NJ: Centre for Negotiation and Conflict Resolution at Rutgers, State University of New Jersey.

Kruk, E. (1997). *Mediation and conflict resolution in social work and the human services.* Chicago: Nelson Hall.

LeBaron, M. (2002). *Bridging troubled waters: Conflict resolution from the heart.* San Francisco: Jossey-Bass.

Lederach, J.P., & Wehr, P. (1991). Mediating conflict in Central America. *Journal of Peace Research, 28*(1), 85–98.

Macfarlane, J. (1995). *Court-based mediation of civil cases: An evaluation of the Ontario Court (General Division) ADR centre.* Toronto: Ministry of the Attorney General.

McLaren, R.H., & Sanderson, J.P. (1995). *Innovative dispute resolution: The alternative.* Scarborough, ON: Carswell.

McThenia, A.W., & Shaffer, T.L. (1985). For reconciliation. *Yale Law Journal, 94,* 1660–1668.

Melchin, K.R., & Picard, C.A. (2008). *Transforming conflict through insight.* Toronto: University of Toronto Press.

Moore, C.W. (1996). *The mediation process: Practical strategies for resolving conflict* (2nd ed.). San Francisco: Jossey-Bass.

Moore, C.W. (2003). *The mediation process: Practical strategies for resolving conflict* (3rd ed.). San Francisco: Jossey-Bass.

Picard, C.A. (2000). The many meanings of mediation: A sociological study of mediation in Canada. PhD dissertation. Ottawa: Carleton University.

Picard, C.A. (2002). *Mediating interpersonal and small group conflict* (2nd ed.). Ottawa: Golden Dog Press.

Picard, C.A., & Jull, M. (2011, Winter). Learning through deepening conversations: A key strategy of insight mediation. *Conflict Resolution Quarterly, 29*(2), 151–176.

Riskin, L. (1996). Understanding mediator orientations, strategies and techniques: A grid for the perplexed. *Harvard Negotiation Law Review, 7,* 25–35. Please note that the copyright in the Negotiation Law Review is held by the President and Fellows of Harvard College, and that the copyright in the article is held by the author.

Sander, F.E.A., & Goldberg, S.B. (1994, January). Fitting the forum to the fuss: User-friendly guide to selecting an ADR procedure. *Negotiation Journal,* 49–67.

Schwerin, E.W. (1995). *Mediation, citizen empowerment and transformational politics.* Westport, CT: Praeger.

Scimecca, J.A. (1991). Conflict resolution and a critique of alternative dispute resolution. In H. Pepinsky & R. Quinney (Eds.) *Criminology as peacemaking* (pp. 263–279). Indianapolis, IN: Indiana University Press.

Silbey, S., & Merry, S.E. (1986). Mediator settlement strategies. *Law and Policy, 8,* 7–32.

Taylor, A. (1997). Concepts of neutrality in family mediation: Contexts, ethics, influence, and transformative process. *Mediation Quarterly, 14,* 215–235.

Tjersland, O.A. (1999). Evaluation of mediation and parental cooperation based on observations and interviews with the clients of a mediation project. *Mediation Quarterly, 16,* 407–423.

Wheatley, M.J. (1999). *Leadership and the new science.* San Francisco: Berrett-Koehler Publications.

Winslade, J., & Monk, G. (2000). *Narrative mediation.* San Francisco: Jossey-Bass.

CHAPTER 4

Understanding Conflict Behaviour

LEARNING OBJECTIVES

After reading this chapter, you will be able to:

- Understand conflict from the perspective of a mediator
- Identify the five different ways that people may respond to conflict
- Identify five different conflict behaviours and recognize these behaviours in yourself and others
- Explain conflict behaviour in terms of some of the cognitive and emotional processes that influence it

CHAPTER OUTLINE

Introduction 93
What Is Conflict? 93
Three Constructs for Understanding Conflict 95
How People Respond to Conflict 98
Conflict Behaviour 102
Conflicts and Choices 104
Why People Behave as They Do 108
Summary 120

An eye for an eye will only make the whole world blind.

Mahatma Ghandi

Introduction

In this chapter, we examine how conflict affects people, their relationships, and their interactions. We discuss how conflict arises from various sources and how people experience conflict and respond to it. Our aim is to help you understand how different people in different circumstances have different ways of dealing with conflict. We also want you to become familiar with some basic concepts and tools for analyzing conflict.

The term *conflict behaviour* refers to the perceptions, emotions, thoughts, attitudes, communications, and actions of people in conflict. The more we can understand conflict behaviour in a given situation—our own and others'—the better we can respond to and deal with the conflict constructively.

What Is Conflict?

Conflict—an inevitable and integral part of social and political life—happens in and between families, communities, organizations, and governments. Any day's news reports on a wide array of conflict situations. Well-known examples include custody battles, proposed building developments, union–management issues, and wars. A comprehensive list would be endless.

Conflict, though we generally think of it in negative terms, also serves to enhance relations, increase productivity, and create new understandings, as well as to reinforce societal standards and provide opportunity for growth and moral development. The idea that conflict is not always dysfunctional is relatively new. Classical philosophers such as Plato and Aristotle viewed conflict as a threat to the success of the state. This view led to the belief that conflict needed to be kept to a minimum, if not totally eliminated. The 17th-century philosophers Hobbes and Locke posited the social contract theory, according to which order was seen as essential for a proper society.

Later theorists have taken a different view. Both Marx and Coser argue that conflict is an important aspect of group formation and that group conflict helps establish or re-establish cohesion. Coser (1956) identifies conflict as a constructive form of socialization, telling us that a certain degree of conflict is an ally in the formation and satisfactory continuation of group life. Theorists such as Simmel (1903) and Dahrendorf (1958), argue that it is the absence of conflict in a society, not its presence, that is surprising and abnormal; there is good reason to be suspicious of a society or social organization that shows no evidence of conflict. As we discuss in this chapter, whether conflict is productive or dysfunctional depends on how people respond to it.

Defining Conflict

Definitions of conflict vary. For instance, Boulding (1962, p. 5) defines conflict as "a situation of competition in which the parties are *aware* of the incompatibility of potential future positions and in which each party *wishes* to occupy a position which is incompatible with the wishes of the other." According to Coser (1968, p. 232), "Conflict is a struggle over values or claims to status, power, and scarce resources, in which the aims of the conflicting parties are not only to gain the desired values but also to neutralize, injure or eliminate their rivals." Himes (1980, p. 14) defines conflict as "the purposeful struggles between collective actors who use social power to defeat or remove opponents and to gain status, power, resources and scarce values." And Hocker and Wilmot (1995, p. 21) say that conflict is "an expressed struggle between at least two interdependent parties who perceive incompatible goals, scarce resources, and interference from others in achieving their goals." More recently, conflict has been defined as emerging from defensive patterns of interaction caused by the disputants' experiencing threat to deep levels of value (Melchin & Picard, 2008).

A number of scholars distinguish between *latent* conflict and *manifest* conflict (Boulding, 1962; Rummell, 1976; Moore, 2003). If one or more of the parties is unaware that its goals or interests are incompatible with those of the other party, the conflict is latent. On the other hand, when *both* parties are aware of the incompatibility of their goals and interests and consciously adopt incompatible positions toward each other, their conflict becomes manifest. Manifest conflict usually involves some communication or interaction between the parties; it results in a *struggle*.

Deutsch (1973), too, distinguishes between manifest and latent conflict. According to him, manifest conflict occurs when issues are expressed or at least known by both parties. With latent conflict, on the other hand, the issues are hidden and unknown by one or even both of the parties. Many conflict situations are both manifest and latent: some of the issues involved are expressed and known while others are hidden and unknown. We often refer to manifest conflict as the *presenting problem* and latent conflict as the *underlying problem*.

Some definitions of conflict use terms that include manifest conflict but exclude latent conflict. We prefer a broader definition such as the following, which includes both kinds of conflict:

> Conflict exists when a person perceives that another person's actions or intended actions threaten to harm his or her needs, interests, relationships, or values.

Conflict involves subjective perceptions. As we discuss below, it involves an emotional response to threatening stimuli or perceptions. Brian may have adversarial perceptions of Alice, even though Alice does not know how Brian thinks about her. We would refer to this as a situation of latent conflict between Brian and Alice. If Alice becomes aware of Brian's adversarial perception of her and consequently begins to develop adversarial perceptions of Brian or to consider him a threat to her in some way, the conflict between them becomes manifest.

Three Constructs for Understanding Conflict

This book aims to develop general conceptual models of conflict resolution; awareness of the conditions that make particular conflict resolution techniques effective; and knowledge about the causal processes that produce successful or unsuccessful interventions. Our orientation to conflict is based on three key constructs:

1. Conflict is relational.
2. Conflict is dynamic and emergent.
3. Conflicts are value-based.

Construct One: Conflict Is Relational

To say that *conflict is relational* means that parties in conflict are social actors who function in different social environments and are always engaged in networks of social relationships that are meaningful to them. The conflicts we will be considering throughout this book arise out of these interactions with others. Any attempt to explain, understand, or intervene in a conflict as a mediator requires the mediator to have some awareness of the dynamics of the interactions that have given rise to the conflict. Focusing only on the interests or needs of the parties as individuals, without having some understanding of the complexity of the relationships between them, is likely to result in inadequate or incomplete outcomes, which often do not address the underlying issues behind the conflict.

The simplest type of relational conflict arises when one party misinterprets another party's action. For example, let's say a woman closes the open back door on her husband and children, who are playing in the yard. Her husband and children interpret her action as disapproval of their play. She might have a myriad reasons for closing the door. She may have been listening to the radio and could not hear the weather update over the noise of her family. Or she might have been worried that mosquitoes were coming into the house. But her family believes she is angry with them. Complicating the situation is the fact that she herself has no idea that they have perceived her action in this way. When the family re-enters the house, they tiptoe around her and avoid speaking to her so as not to anger her further. She does not know why her family is not engaging with her and feels that she is being ignored.

A cascade of reaction and misinterpretation, as this example shows, can easily arise from a single action. This is because all our actions take place in social contexts where these actions have meaning for others, as theirs do for us. The mother in the above example is only thinking of her own immediate concerns—to listen to the radio, or to keep mosquitoes out of the house. But her husband and her children interpret her action as if it had meaning in relation to them.

We frequently interpret others' actions as if they were directed at us, and attribute meanings to them that the actors themselves did not intend. Imagine how easily this kind of mistaken attribution occurs when the parties are in a situation of overt conflict. When the listener already fears and distrusts the speaker, an innocent remark can easily be interpreted as concealing a hostile intention. Mistaken attribution of intentions can be a damaging factor in any kind of conflict situation, from interpersonal disputes between family members to large-scale international conflicts.

Construct Two: Conflict Is Dynamic and Emergent

Our second construct—that *conflict is dynamic and emergent*—follows from our first principle. To return to the example given above—of the mother closing the door—her action has produced a reaction from her family that, in turn, produces a further misunderstanding in her; when they are quiet on re-entering the house, she believes they are ignoring her. This conflict is likely to continue transforming the longer it remains in existence. What is true for relatively minor interpersonal conflict situations is also true for large-scale ones. Conflicts tend to transform and change over time. So there is an emergent property to many conflict situations. We cannot always predict in advance the ways in which a conflict situation may develop or change.

This unpredictability stems from the fact that we as social actors do not merely act on a world that is already fixed or knowable in relation to ourselves. As self-reflexive, goal-directed actors, we first have to try to make sense of the conditions in the particular environment—social, political, workplace, or family—that we inhabit, so that we can make decisions or choices about how to achieve our aims. The problem is that we can never fully predict the effects of our actions on others. As we have seen, others may interpret our actions differently than we intended, and their misinterpretation may determine their response.

The consequences of our actions are often very different from what we expect. This dynamic is exaggerated in conflict situations. One party's action to de-escalate the conflict may be interpreted by the other party as an attempt to gain a future advantage. For example, one party's calling for a truce in a military conflict may be interpreted by the other side as a sign of weakness or as a way of buying time to build up reinforcements. Even a well-intentioned effort by one party to reduce or avoid further conflict can sometimes result in increased aggression from the other side. And when one side sees its conciliatory efforts being misinterpreted and responded to in this way, it is likely to respond with greater aggression itself, or to become less willing to engage in future dialogue with the other party.

Mediators need to be aware of the complex dynamics of conflict interactions. Conflicts, if they are left unaddressed, can often escalate and transform in the ways described above. Changing the parties' perceptions or interpretations of each other's conflict behaviour can open the door to more positive or constructive conflict behaviour. This is a big part of what mediators do. They help the parties come to a deeper understanding of each other's needs, goals, values, and interests, so they can work cooperatively to arrive at their own resolution to the conflict.

Construct Three: Conflicts Are Value-Based

The third construct, that *conflicts are value-based*, illustrates three things: the complex nature of justice and other norms; the role that subjective perceptions play in parties' behaviour; and the importance of *deep culture* (Galtung, 1996) in understanding what is at stake in conflict situations. Values encompass the cognitive, emotional, somatic, and spiritual engagement of the self in conflict, and they play a significant role in both creating and unravelling conflicts. Values often manifest themselves in the feelings that are connected to our experiences and ideals, as well as to futures we imagine that hold dire consequences. When we refer to values, we are examining the different motivations for human action.

Abraham Maslow (1943) postulated that human beings have five levels of need. They are as follows, descending in order from the most basic:

1. physiological,
2. safety,
3. love and belonging,
4. self-esteem, and
5. self-actualization.

The first two levels refer to basic needs such as food, shelter, security, and health. The next three are related to our interpersonal and social needs: the need to belong to groups and families; the need to have a sense of value and contribution in relation to others; and the need to live up to our fullest potential in relation to society. Maslow believed that these needs are a hierarchy and that human beings need to meet the more basic needs before moving up the scale to achieve self-esteem and self-actualization.

John Burton (1990) and other human-needs theorists who work in conflict resolution (Rothman, 1997; Northrup, 1989; Coate & Rosati, 1988) have adapted Maslow's hierarchy to conflict theory. They see these needs not in terms of a hierarchy but as a collective of requirements that humans need in order to fully develop. To Maslow's list, they add values such as identity, cultural security, freedom, distributive justice, and participation. Their view, in other words, is that every citizen in every country, in order to develop fully, must meet both the basic needs identified by Maslow and other needs related to identity, cultural security, freedom, distributive justice, and participation.

Because of their inseparable connection with human values, emotions play an essential role in a person's understanding of a conflict situation and how she responds to the situation. As we discuss in more detail below, we cannot separate emotion from cognition and reason. Many of our traditional dichotomies—between emotion and reason, left brain and right brain, head and heart—no longer hold. Damasio and others (Damasio, 1999; LeDoux, 1996; Cozolino, 2006) have shown that emotion is essential to *all* decision making, including decisions related to conflict. For this reason, a holistic approach to conflict and mediation is needed, one that draws on all of our capacities and talents.

All of the constructs we have described in this section—conflicts are relational; conflicts are dynamic and emergent; conflicts are value-based—apply to conflict situations, and the mediator will have to address all of them. The conceptual framework that this text provides is broad enough to enable mediators to do this—to design interventions that recognize the relational nature of conflict, respect its dynamic and ever-changing nature, and respond to the values that are at stake.

How People Respond to Conflict

People respond to conflict in five basic ways:

1. They *ignore* it and thus tolerate the continuing conflict.
2. They *withdraw*, removing themselves from the conflict situation (the "flight" response).
3. They *fight*, using physical force, coercion, intimidation, threats, or subversive action to get what they want.
4. They *appeal* to a higher authority to decide what will be done to respond to and change the conflict situation.

5. They *negotiate* by communicating with others about the conflict in order to effect some change that will improve or resolve the conflict situation.

A person may respond to conflict with one of these actions or with more than one. Any one of them may be useful, depending on the circumstances, and any one of them will be affected by two factors, present in every conflict. The first factor is the degree to which a party tries to achieve his or her goal, which is characterized as "assertiveness." The second factor is the degree to which a party tries to satisfy the other person's goal, which is characterized as "cooperativeness." Let us examine more closely these five basic ways of responding to conflict.

Ignore

Perhaps the most frequent **response** to a conflict situation is to *ignore* it and thus avoid dealing with it. People avoid conflict for different reasons and in different ways. For example, a young female employee, Melissa, may be experiencing heightened levels of tension with a male supervisor at work named Arnold. She feels that he is too hard on her and too demanding. She may avoid confronting Arnold about this tension because she is concerned about the consequences of doing so. For instance, Arnold may be in a position to write a negative employment review, which could limit her chances for promotion. To Melissa, this and other risks seem to outweigh the possible benefits of confronting Arnold personally or complaining to someone else in authority. As a result, Melissa tries to ignore his behaviour and to continue doing her job as if the conflict situation does not exist. By responding to conflict in this way, Melissa aims to smooth over the differences or tensions between Arnold and herself. In so doing, she is choosing to suppress the conflict and accommodate the other party's needs and expectations.

Withdraw

Another avoiding response to a conflict situation is to *withdraw* from it. Melissa may find, for example, that she is unable to ignore Arnold's conduct toward her; she may decide that it is just easier to leave the organization, even though she would prefer not to. By deciding to leave, Melissa has removed herself from the conflict situation. However, the conflict itself has not been resolved. Withdrawal is an avoidance strategy; it is not a response to conflict aimed at addressing the issues that caused it. *Ignoring* and *withdrawing* are passive responses. The parties do not engage with the conflict.

Fight

When a person seeks to confront conflict, he or she may act in an active, aggressive manner. This is known as the *fight* response. A "fight" is not necessarily a physical contest of strength. Fighting may consist of coercive tactics aimed at threatening or intimidating the other party in non-physical ways; it may consist of subversive (hidden) efforts to weaken, neutralize, or defeat the opposition. With a fight response to conflict, a party uses his or her strength or resources, directly or indirectly, overtly or covertly, to triumph over his or her opponent.

A fight response to conflict typically involves a unilateral action or threat of action by one party, with the objective of pressuring the other party to accede to the first party's position—to unilaterally impose its will. A fight response is both unilateral (initiated by one side with the aim of producing a response by the other) and coercive (involving the exercise of power or the threat of doing so).

Power is exercised in many ways in conflict situations. In the context of a fight response to conflict, power is defined by Ury, Brett, and Goldberg as "the ability to coerce someone to do something he would not otherwise do" (1988, p. 7). This implies the capacity to impose costs on another party. These costs can be imposed in financial or economic terms, in terms of physical threats, and in terms of material costs, such as the threatened loss or destruction of something of value to the other party. These costs may also include damage to a person's reputation, relationships, or psychological health.

We often think that the disputant with the greater resources or capacity to impose costs will be more likely to win in any extended power struggle. Sometimes, however, the disputant with the greater capacity to absorb costs will ultimately prove to be the more powerful. Whatever the relative power balance between the disputants, it is important to realize that a fight response tends to result in escalating costs for all parties the longer the conflict goes on.

By its very nature, a fight response tends to result in winners and losers, since each disputant involved is seeking to unilaterally impose its will on the other. If one side wins, the other side is not likely to be happy about the outcome. If neither party is sufficiently powerful to obtain a clear victory, a stalemate results, which means that neither party is satisfied with the outcome. In these circumstances, disputants may seek another approach to resolving the conflict, or they may agree to a truce, only to resume their fight at some time in the future. If fight is the only response, the conflict will never be resolved satisfactorily for all parties.

Appeal to Authority

The fourth response to conflict is to appeal to authority—that is, to a person or body that has authority over the parties and over the subject matter of the dispute. For example, if your neighbour is making too much noise late at night, you may phone your landlord (if you live in an apartment building) or the police, either of whom can restore the peace. Or consider our example from Chapter 2, where Jessie and her younger brother Tim are fighting over a toy. Tim may respond to this conflict by asking their mother to intervene. In both of these examples, the person appealing to authority is seeking what is, in effect, power-based action by the authority. In Chapter 2, we referred to this power-based action as authoritative command.

Now consider Melissa again, the female employee we discussed above. Melissa finds that her supervisor, Arnold, is too hard on her, too demanding. She may speak to their manager, Alison, in the hope that Alison will talk to Arnold and get him to act in a more reasonable manner towards her. In doing this, Melissa is invoking the power-based authoritative command of their manager Alison. Of course, Melissa will do this only if she believes that Alison will be sympathetic and will support her in her conflict with Arnold.

On the other hand, if Melissa believes that Arnold's behaviour is bad enough to qualify as harassment, she could pursue a formal rights-based appeal to authority. She could make a formal harassment complaint under the organization's workplace harassment policy. In that case, an independent investigator or reviewer would decide, based on evidence submitted by both sides, whether Arnold's behaviour towards Melissa was harassment. If the investigator finds Melissa's complaint to be well-founded, then the organization's management could impose disciplinary sanctions on Arnold.

With an informal power-based appeal to authority, one that invokes authoritative command, a person is relying on the authority's power to resolve a conflict that the person alone would be powerless (or so he or she believes) to resolve. A formal rights-based appeal to authority is different. The introduction of an authoritative, third-party decision maker will alter the dynamics of a conflict in several important respects. Instead of a determination based on power or resources, the focus in a third-party decision-making process such as arbitration or litigation shifts to the question of who has the better argument or claim. Ury, Brett, and Goldberg refer to this as a shift away from a focus on power to a focus on rights (1988, p. 7). Two parents locked in a custody battle will each try to persuade the judge that their own proposed arrangements are in the children's best interests and that the other parent's are not. The judge then has to decide which side to believe, and which set of proposed custody arrangements are most likely to benefit the children (or, as is more often the concern, least likely to disrupt the children's well-being).

A key element of any rights-based approach to resolving conflict is that, in deciding between the disputants' competing claims, the third-party decision maker should use an independent standard that all parties can accept as legitimate (Ury, Brett, & Goldberg, 1988, p. 7). In the case of the parental custody dispute, for example, the judge's decision will be based on what would be in the best interests of the children.

This is one of the strengths of a rights-based approach to conflict, as compared with a power-based or fight response. The fair application of an appropriate, mutually acceptable rule or standard will lead to a just result. At the same time, however, a rights-based approach to conflict also tends to result in win–lose or zero-sum outcomes, whereby one side's gains are perceived as coming at the other side's expense. In other words, rights-based approaches to conflict resolution provide relatively little opportunity for collaborative or win–win outcomes.

Negotiate

A fifth response to conflict is to *negotiate.*

For a person in conflict, negotiating involves engaging the other party in a discussion of the conflict between them. The purpose of this discussion is to find a way to reconcile or live with each other's competing interests, needs, or values. By negotiating, the parties enter into a relationship of *interdependence.* Neither party can act completely independently of the other (Gulliver, 1979, pp. 5–6). The parties enter the negotiating process with competing objectives; each wants different things. At the same time, each negotiating party needs the other's agreement in order to achieve his or her conflict objectives. If either party is in a position to obtain what he or she wants without the other's agreement, there would be no need to negotiate.

In most cases of negotiation, neither party is in a position to compel the other's agreement. (A peace negotiation after a defeat in war might be an exception.) Consequently, the process of negotiation involves a complex dynamic in which each party seeks to influence the beliefs, expectations, or preferences of the other, with the aim of reaching an agreement that satisfies his or her own interests on the best possible terms.

In this chapter, we are primarily interested in *how* people negotiate and how people behave when they find themselves in conflict. We have now considered the five basic ways that people respond to conflict. Next, we will consider five types of conflict behaviour—in other words, how people actually behave while engaged in conflict.

Conflict Behaviour

How do people behave in conflict situations? What causes them to act as they do? What is going on inside them when they run, or fight, or look the other way? Why is it that some people will behave in these ways while others will try to work things out? How do people in conflict situations communicate? Are their words easily understood? Are they accusatory? Or do they primarily express themselves in nonverbal language? Is what they say and do constructive or destructive? Are they passive, aggressive, or assertive? These are some of the many questions we may ask about conflict behaviour.

Types of Conflict Behaviours

There are many ways that people behave in conflict. Some people are assertive or aggressive, and some are passive. Some people may be passive or even timid in some situations, but can become "tigers" in others. Thomas and Kilmann (1974) identified five key types of conflict behaviour: competing, avoiding, accommodating, compromising, and collaborating.

Avoiding

A person who is *avoiding* tends to suppress or conceal feelings and concerns that may create conflict. Avoiders do not raise or discuss issues, fearful of what others may say or do. Avoiding behaviour prolongs problems to everyone's detriment, and is considered a *lose–lose* proposition because nothing changes through this approach.

Competing

A person who is *competing* is pursuing his or her own demands, wants, or claims at the expense of the other. People who are competing engage in adversarial, aggressive actions such as attacking and criticizing the other's position, exaggerating their own position, and blaming, threatening, intimidating, or manipulating the other party. They give the impression that their primary motive is to defeat their opponent. Fisher and Ury (1991, pp. 7–9) call this type of behaviour "hard bargaining." Lax and Sebenius (1986, p. 34) refer to it as "claiming tactics," as we discussed in Chapter 2. This behaviour may also feature the following: insulting or demeaning the other party; displaying impatience, irritation, or disgust; interrupting or tuning out the other party, or responding to them in a negative way; being stubborn and rigid; and bluffing or bottom-lining. Competing produces a *win–lose* outcome—one person gains at the other's expense.

Accommodating

A person who is accommodating tends, at his or her own expense, to surrender to the other's demands or wants. An accommodator accepts the other's views and tends to go along with proposals that satisfy the other party's interests, without pursuing or asserting his or her own. Fisher and Ury (1991, pp. 7–9) consider this behaviour to be "soft bargaining." It includes making excessive concessions, being overly agreeable and trusting, and being too flexible and "nice," as well as giving in. Accommodating is considered *lose–win*, since the accommodator gives up his or her goals and the other party gains everything.

Compromising

A person who is compromising seeks an outcome that partly satisfies each party's demands or wants. They "split the difference," looking for fairly quick and easy solutions somewhere between the two positions of the conflicting parties. Both parties sacrifice to some extent. Compromising is *win–lose-for-all*, because both the compromiser and the other party end up giving a little to get a little.

Collaborating

A person who is collaborating is being assertive and expressing his or her own interests while, at the same time, seeking to understand and respond constructively to the other person's interests. Through creative problem solving, this collaborative person seeks an outcome that maximizes his or her own interests but that also satisfies, as much as possible, the other's interests. Fisher and Ury (1991) coined the term "principled bargaining" to describe this behaviour. They consider this approach to be assertive. It does not mean being nice and polite and letting someone else dominate the discussion. Collaborating requires that all parties be assertive in expressing their concerns and beliefs, especially those concerns and beliefs that differ from the other parties'. In other words, collaborative interaction demands the assertive expression of disagreement, concerns, or conflicting beliefs. However, it is important that parties go about this assertiveness in a mutually respectful manner—not in the insulting, intimidating, or aggressive manner typical of a competing or hard-bargaining style. Collaborating is viewed as *win–win*, in that all parties achieve their goals.

Conflicts and Choices

In the real world, people's responses to conflict do not always fall neatly into the categories we have set out. People rarely choose one particular response to a conflict situation and then pursue this course to the exclusion of all others. As individuals—and as members of larger groups and organizations—we often behave according to the responses of those around us. Another factor is that, in many conflict situations, our responses vary at different times. Whether we decide to fight, to withdraw, to negotiate, or to litigate depends on a host of factors. Not the least of these is our perception of the other party's response to our own behaviour.

By way of example, let's return to Melissa—the young female employee who initially sought to avoid a confrontation with her supervisor Arnold. After talking to her friends and family, Melissa may decide to lay a complaint of harassment against Arnold. In other words, her response to conflict may change from avoidance to a more rights-based response, and this happens after she obtains advice from people who are not direct participants in the conflict situation. Her formal complaint may, in turn, elicit a new response from Arnold, now faced with a formal, legal investigation and the possibility of disciplinary sanctions. Arnold may choose to negotiate, proposing that Melissa and he enter into mediation. How the conflict is eventually resolved—whether through negotiation, litigation, or otherwise—depends very much on how each of the parties responds to the moves of the other.

As the Open House scenario (Box 4.1) demonstrates, different responses by people in conflict lead to different outcomes—some good, some not so good. Some responses are *functional*—that is, they will likely lead to beneficial or productive outcomes and a resolution of the conflict. Other responses may result in no improvement or resolution—or they may make the situation worse and cause the conflict to escalate. These responses are *dysfunctional*.

Sam and Terry's competing behaviour could continue beyond this point. Sam may recount to Maria his version of the earlier meeting with Terry, trying to convince

BOX 4.1 » Scenario: Open House

Sam and Terry have joint responsibility to organize an open house for current and potential corporate sponsors of their non-profit organization. They have been working on the project for six weeks, and the event is now four weeks away. They meet with Maria, the organization's executive director, for a project status review and the following exchange occurs:

> *Terry*: "By the way, Sam, when are you going to give me the final list of corporate contacts?"
>
> *Sam*: "What do you mean? That's not my job."
>
> *Terry*: "We talked about it three weeks ago. You were supposed to get the old list, make corrections and additions, and get the final list back to me a week ago."
>
> *Sam*: "No way! We never said that."
>
> *Terry*: "That was the understanding. How could you screw this up? You knew that I was waiting for the list—that I couldn't do the invitations until I got it!"
>
> *Sam*: "I didn't screw up. You weren't waiting for me. That's a bloody lie and you know it! This is so typical of you! Drop the ball and then come up with some hogwash to blame somebody else."

Maria that Terry is wrong. He may list all the things he is doing in comparison with Terry, attempting to prove how unreasonable it is for him (Sam) to be burdened with this additional responsibility.

Terry, for her part, may try to point out inconsistencies in Sam's version of events. Also, she might recall other times when Sam was unreliable or made mistakes. Clearly, such actions by Terry and Sam, with the thoughts and emotions that go with them, will take a real toll on their relationship. Regardless of what they do to complete this project, they will likely clash again if they continue working together.

Let's consider how this scenario would have played out differently if one or both of them had behaved differently. For example, if Sam had been accommodating, it might have gone as follows:

> *Terry*: "By the way, Sam, when are you going to give me the final list of corporate contacts?"
>
> *Sam*: "What do you mean? I didn't think that was my job."
>
> *Terry*: "We talked about it three weeks ago. You were supposed to get the old list, make corrections and additions, and get the final list back to me a week ago."

> *Sam*: "Sorry, I don't recall that at all. I don't know where my head was at. Obviously I've messed up. I'll get right on it and get it to you by Wednesday."

Consider the following questions. What specific aspects of Sam's accommodating behaviour can you identify in this version? What are some possible consequences of Sam's accommodating response for Sam and his ongoing relationship with Terry? What are some possible consequences for Terry? What if Terry's recollection or account was inaccurate?

Sam's response would be an avoiding one if, despite thinking Terry is wrong, he says nothing to that effect. In this case, he would doubt that it was ever agreed he would prepare the corporate contact list, but he does not want to cause trouble (as he sees it) between Terry and himself, so does not express this doubt. His response might go something like the following:

> *Terry*: "By the way, Sam, when are you going to give me the final list of corporate contacts?"
>
> *Sam*: "I'm working on it. I'll get it to you tomorrow or Wednesday at the latest."

The avoiding response is different from the accommodating response in that there is no expression of any conflict, disagreement, or misunderstanding between Sam and Terry.

What are some possible consequences of Sam's avoiding response for each individual at the meeting, and for their working relationship? How might those differ from the consequences of the accommodating response?

In terms of negotiation, Sam's avoiding response precludes any negotiation concerning who ought to prepare the corporate contact list. With the accommodating response, this question does get discussed—although the negotiation is little more than a brief exchange between Sam and Terry before they quickly agree that Sam will do the work.

If, on the other hand, Sam and Terry adopted compromising or collaborating behaviours, they might have a significant negotiation. The two exchanges that follow illustrate what compromising and collaborating might look like. Pay particular attention to the differences between the two behaviours and to their consequences.

A compromising approach by Sam might proceed as follows:

> *Terry*: "By the way, Sam, when are you going to give me the final list of corporate contacts?"
>
> *Sam*: "What do you mean? I didn't think that was my job."
>
> *Terry*: "We talked about it three weeks ago. You were supposed to get the old list, make corrections and additions, and get the final list back to me a week ago."

> *Sam*: "That's not how I recall it. There seems to have been a misunderstanding between us. But I don't think there's much point in going back and rehashing it. The important thing now is for us to get the job done."
>
> *Terry*: "I suppose. What do you suggest?"
>
> *Sam*: "What do you say we split the list in two—you take A to L, I'll take M to Z, and we get it done by tomorrow?"
>
> *Terry*: "Yeah, okay. I'll have to adjust my schedule, but I guess I can do it."

What specific aspects of each person's compromising behaviour can you identify in this exchange?

In this approach, there is some negotiation between Sam and Terry, but without much discussion of the issues between them, of their concerns, or of the various options they may have for resolving their issues. For example, the issues of misunderstanding, of miscommunication, or of breakdown in their working relationship (that is, the element that caused them both to miss this task) are not really addressed or discussed. What they have done or failed to do in this regard is not addressed. Nor are the negative perceptions, doubts, irritations, and attitudes that each may have concerning the other. They have resolved very little. Therefore, we can expect that similar problems may arise between Sam and Terry in the future, and that their unresolved feelings or concerns may not only affect their ongoing relationship, but erupt into more serious trouble at some point.

The disputed issue between Sam and Terry was how the contact list would be done. Without further discussion of that issue, of each person's relevant interests, and of the various options for resolving it, we have no way of knowing whether their agreed outcome (to split the list) is the best one. In fact, it may be the case that some other solution would be better all around, given the quantity of work each of them has, as well as the skills, abilities, and resources each may have to draw on to compile the list—and how this contact list is actually going to be used.

A collaborative approach, which would probably require more time than a compromising approach, might start off with an exchange like the following:

> *Terry*: "By the way, Sam, when are you going to give me the final list of corporate contacts?"
>
> *Sam*: "Terry, I don't know what you're referring to. I don't recall us deciding that I would do that. I think there may have been a misunderstanding between us."
>
> *Terry*: "Yes, so it seems. I'd suggest we talk about that to see how that might have happened. What do you think?"
>
> *Sam*: "Yeah, I think we should."

What specific aspects of each person's collaborating behaviour can you identify in this version?

If both Sam and Terry take a collaborating approach to this conflict, they will identify and discuss the issues between them thoroughly. They will recognize and discuss the issue of miscommunication, and both will accept some responsibility for contributing to it and for the need to interact differently in the future. They will discuss and explore their own and each other's perceptions, assumptions, expectations, and concerns, seeking to understand each other's differing perspective and experience. They will recognize that discussing and resolving their common concerns or issues between them will improve their working relationship in the future. To resolve the issue of the contact list, they will discuss and explore each of their relevant interests and then consider various options for meeting the interests of both. Through collaborative negotiations, Sam and Terry would very likely devise a solution that is better for both of them.

We have presented the five conflict behaviours as distinct. However, rarely does a person adopt one behaviour alone when negotiating. Instead, that person is likely to adopt some or all of the five in a single negotiation, depending on what is happening at the moment. In the Open House scenario involving Sam and Terry, there might be some "tit for tat" in the negotiation. If Terry becomes blaming, for example, Sam may respond in kind, adopting a more competitive approach to assert his needs. When Terry seems accommodating, Sam may open up and become more collaborating. It is important to recognize that each of the five conflict behaviours has particular advantages and may be appropriate depending on the circumstances.

Why People Behave as They Do

People behave as they do for many reasons. We will now examine the psychological and social factors that influence how people in conflict behave. First, we will consider cognitive factors—in other words, factors that influence how we think about, interpret, and understand a conflict situation. Second, we examine emotion, focusing on how our emotional operating systems influence how we think and act in conflict.

Cognitive Dimensions of the Conflict Response

What causes a person involved in conflict to interpret it as he or she does? Each person involved in a conflict has a "story" concerning it. We refer to that story as the person's conflict narrative. In the Open House scenario, for example, Terry and Sam each have their own conflict narrative based on the history or background of their relationship and on the events of their dispute described above. Each person is the protagonist (the "good guy") in his or her own conflict narrative, and the other person is the antagonist ("adversary"). The setting for this story is Sam and Terry's workplace; therefore, the conflict could affect the employment, careers, and economic well-being of both parties. Another element of the setting is the community of co-workers and corporate clients who may know the parties and who may learn about this drama between them. This may affect Sam and Terry's professional reputations and standing. Finally, each person's conflict narrative has a value or justice perspective that is shaped by that person's personal, social, and cultural identity.

The following processes, paradigms, and concepts from the field of cognitive psychology can help us understand how people interpret conflict and how they compose the conflict narratives that influence their behaviour:

- the social nature of cognition;
- mental programming and cognitive schemas;
- the conflict cycle; and
- insight and learning.

The Social Nature of Cognition

Fiske and Taylor (1991) emphasize that the study of cognition is concerned not only with our own internal consciousness, but also with how we process information from our environment. As social actors, we are constantly interacting with others in a variety of contexts—with family members in the domestic sphere, with colleagues in the workplace, or with strangers when commuting to and from work.

Social interaction is an element in our cognition even when we are not face to face with others. While driving, for example, we have to be conscious not only of our own goals (where we want to go and what we will do when we get there) and of road conditions (for example, what the traffic is like), but also of other drivers' intentions—for example, whether the car coming by us on the inside lane is likely to move into our lane when it catches up with a slower car ahead of it. Whether at work, at home, or on the road, we are constantly "reading" our environment and trying to anticipate others' behaviour. If we fail to do so, we are likely to get into conflicts with others. Fiske and Taylor (1991) refer to this necessary attentiveness as the social dimension of cognition. They maintain that much of our everyday, practical decision making is not just focused on our own goals; it also takes into account the actual, implied, or imagined presence of others (Fiske & Taylor, 1991; Fiske, 2004).

Mental Programming and Cognitive Schemas

As social actors, we are continuously trying to understand and anticipate the actions or intentions of others. However, there is often too much information coming in for us to process all of it. So our minds select; we pay attention to informational stimuli that are significant to our goals or activities. In his groundbreaking work on psychology, William James (1890) referred to this as the concept of selective attention. Fiske and Taylor built on James's concept of selective attention by referring to humans as "cognitive misers" (Fiske & Taylor, 1991, p. 176; Pruitt & Carnevale, 1993, p. 83).

The concept of cognitive misers refers to the human tendency to use as little information as possible to define a situation, to plan a course of action, to make a judgment, or to imagine other people's responses to our own actions. Rather than seeking more information to test our operating assumptions, we often rely on cognitive shortcuts; our brains use what are called *cognitive schemas* to speed up the information-processing stage.

A cognitive schema is a mental structure that a person's brain uses to organize and categorize knowledge. It is a "building block of cognition" (Rumelhart, 1980). As we develop through childhood, our brains store our acquired knowledge in cognitive schemas (Bartlett, 1932; Piaget, 1952) and subsequently use these schemas to process new information and form new knowledge. These schemas generally operate below the level of conscious awareness. We recognize a person's face, for example, by mentally referencing it against the database of faces and identities we already have stored in memory.

Schemas do not just operate at the visual or auditory level. They also comprise sets of ideas or associations about personal or social identity. Janice Gross Stein (2005, p. 293) states that people make use of schemas to define situations or to make sense of themselves or others. My schema of myself is my self-concept. My schema of you is my concept of you in relation to myself, or to others. My schema of a boss or a co-worker may combine some of the following attributes: hard-working, efficient, demanding, self-sacrificing, honest, insensitive to others, unforgiving, calculating, friendly, unassuming, good-looking, or always on the make. A schema is built up over time through memories of past encounters, and it can be transferred from one person to another.

Schemas can operate at the individual level or at the level of a group, or collective. Such group, or collective, schemas may underlie cultural patterns of thought and behaviour. For example, a stereotype is a collective schema that members of one social group may hold about members of another social group. The stereotype operates as a schema by selectively filtering the one group's information about the other (Fiske, 2004, pp. 423–424). Such schemas block our learning by excluding information about others that does not conform to our existing knowledge.

Once created, schemas of the self and of others often become entrenched and hard to change. Information that is consistent with a pre-existing schema tends to be received, while incompatible information is discarded. Though unaware of doing so, we automatically discount incompatible information as "unreliable" or "probably untrue"; we explain it away as "unusual" or "atypical," perhaps a consequence of circumstantial factors. Let us say, for instance, that we have a negative schema of a certain person, and then we see him behaving graciously in a social situation. Because this information is incompatible with our schema, we might look for ways to discount it. "Well, he would have to be nice, wouldn't he? He was meeting his mother-in-law for the first time." Or: "He was trying to impress the boss" (Pruitt & Carnevale, 1993, p. 144; Gross Stein, 2005, pp. 293–294).

As we can see, our cognitive schemas are instrumental in how we interpret a conflict situation, our adversaries, and their actions and intentions. They inform our conflict narratives.

The Conflict Cycle

The schemas we use to make sense of our social encounters often have a self-reinforcing quality; they filter out information that challenges or contradicts them. This may result in the psychological effect known as the "self-fulfilling prophecy" (Pruitt & Carnevale, 1993, p. 143; Fiske, 2004, pp. 421–422). The self-fulfilling prophecy works through a process of circular causality whereby one person's pre-existing beliefs about another person or group produce behavioural responses in the other person or group that, in turn, confirm the first person in their initial beliefs. This is behind what we refer to as the conflict cycle.

Figure 4.1 illustrates the conflict cycle. Consider a family situation in which A (a teenage daughter) is feeling alienated from B (her parents). She believes they don't understand or care about her. So she withdraws from them and from other family members, behaving toward them in ways that seem rude or abrupt or uncaring. Her parents respond to this rude behaviour by attempting to discipline their daughter. She experiences this as her parents being harsh and critical; it confirms her belief that her parents don't understand or care about her at all. This cycle feeds and escalates the conflict situation.

Figure 4.1 The Conflict Cyle

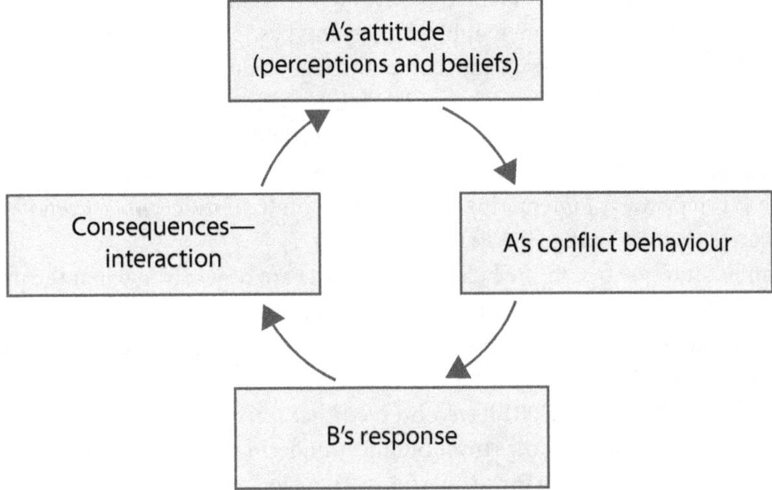

This example might seem to describe a commonplace phenomenon, a teenager going through a phase. But the mechanism of the self-fulfilling prophecy is at work in many conflict situations where the parties have settled schemas of self and other. In such situations, everything the other party does or says tends to be filtered through the pre-existing schema or narrative that each person has developed for making sense of the conflict. This reinforces the parties' pre-existing beliefs about each other. As a result, parties in conflict often have difficulty communicating with each other. One of the mediator's most important functions is to alter or to disrupt the self-reinforcing dynamics of such negative communication patterns.

Keep in mind that every message we send operates on at least two levels (Watzlawick et al., 1967, pp. 51–53): the level of *content*, or the surface information of the message; and the level of *context*, which contains information about how the parties view their relations with each other. How we respond to messages often depends not only on their content but also on how we interpret their context—that is, what we believe they tell us about how the other person views us in relation to them. This is why the teenage daughter, in our example above, responds with such hostility to her parents' criticism of her rude behaviour. Apart from the actual content of the parents' criticism, there is—as the daughter sees it—the contextual message that they are self-righteous and judgmental toward her. This is the perception that made the daughter feel so alienated from her parents in the first place.

Insight and Learning

Conflict theorists advance our understanding of what people in conflict are actually doing. They have made us aware that people engaged in resolving conflict are also engaged in a process of learning. This notion is particularly prominent in the insight approach to conflict resolution. This approach (which we discussed in Chapter 3) emphasizes that a mediator can help parties attain insights and new understanding to overcome their *learned* mental blocks, stereotypes, prejudices, and self-serving biases. The new learning, or insight, comes through dialogue between the parties in dispute, and it contributes to a change in their behaviours and thus to a change in the conflict situation. Parties who acquire new insight in this way gain a new perspective on themselves and on others. This insight, in turn, empowers them to search for new ways of interacting and dealing with their differences, even if doing so requires them to change the way they live.

Conflict intervenors, in the belief that conflicts are best solved when the parties involved are free to learn, see it as one of their key roles to facilitate new understandings and insight. To fulfill this role, they need to understand something about the learning process.

Melchin and Picard (2008) have observed that learning takes place through a sequence of operations that arise from genuine wondering. It emerges from questions, and insight is the answer to those questions. To really know something, we must

- have the information,
- understand what the information means,
- ensure that our understanding is correct, and
- be able to use the information in taking responsibility for our actions.

Learning theorists tell us that the desire to understand the meaning of our experience is a defining condition of being human. To be human is to want to know. It is this strong desire that generates the curiosity needed to engage in dialogue, and this dialogue, in turn, generates new insights. In conflict situations, these insights lead to new ideas for change. Learning involves much more than the passive reception of information. It arises from an active desire. This is an important idea for individuals trying to help parties resolve their conflicts through mediation or through other intervention processes.

Emotion and Its Influence on Conflict Behaviour

Until a few years ago, many of us tended to give emotion short shrift. We said things such as "His emotions got the better of him," or "She's got to put aside her emotions." Psychologists and neuroscientists used to talk about the emotional brain and the thinking or cognitive brain as if they were two separate sections or systems. And we believed that, except for artists and mothers, emotion got in the way of productive functioning. We thought that, for the most part, emotion should be set aside because it interfered with productive human thinking—the so-called "left brain" functions of analysis, critical thinking, and reasoning. We thought we had to do whatever we could to suppress emotion and minimize its negative influence on rational, intelligent thinking and decision making. Emotion had no place in the law offices and boardrooms of our nation. Even in most workplaces, the prevailing dictum was "Leave your personal feelings at home."

In much of the mediation and negotiation literature of the past 20 years, the explicit or implicit message has been to minimize emotion—either to keep it out of the room altogether or, at least, to manage it in such a way that it will no longer disrupt the parties' communication, collaboration, and decision making. The prevailing assumption among mediators was that, where conflict is concerned, emotion merely makes a bad situation worse and must be avoided or suppressed. For mediators, that has meant learning to manage emotion—deploying techniques to release or divert the force of "negative" emotions.

However, the neuroscience explosion of the past 10–15 years, led by researchers such as Damasio and LeDoux, has produced a dramatic change in our knowledge and understanding of emotion. We now know that our emotional systems and the emotions they produce are an integral and essential component of *all* human thought. As Damasio (1994) says, emotions are essential to *all* decision-making. When our emotional systems are functioning well, we make wise decisions. When they are not functioning well—when they are impaired or dysfunctional—we make bad decisions or we don't make decisions at all.

Emotion is a complex set of biological processes involving neurons in the brain and in the rest of the nervous system, and involving chemicals that flow into and through the cardiovascular system. Our emotional operating systems constitute our built-in physiological capacity to respond to the environmental stimuli we continuously confront—and to do so in ways that promote our safety, health, well-being, survival, and propagation as a species.

We are not conscious of much of our emotional processing. As Goleman says in *Social Intelligence*, much human emotion occurs on the "low road" of the human brain (2006, p. 16):

> The low road is circuitry that operates beneath our awareness, automatically and effortlessly, with immense speed. Most of what we do seems to be piloted by massive neural networks operating via the low road—particularly in our emotional life.

For example, as I drive a busy freeway on my way to a morning appointment, the anger I feel towards a slow driver in front of me may completely mask the underlying emotion that is motivating and influencing me in that moment. The emotion that is occurring within me, yet completely beneath my consciousness, could be fear at what other people at that morning meeting may think and do if I am late.

The Functions of Emotion

A fundamental evolutionary purpose of human emotions is to enable us to evaluate people and events that we encounter in our environment as "good" or "bad"—that is, as beneficial or harmful. Positive emotions (for example, joy, compassion, enthusiasm, and curiosity) cause us to move toward or be attracted to people and activities that will promote our safety, health, and well-being, individually and collectively. Negative emotions (for example, dislike, fear, suspicion, and resentment) cause us to avoid or reject people and activities that may harm our individual or collective safety, health, and well-being.

Our emotions and our emotional operating systems are essential for our day-to-day functioning. Emotions give us answers to the question each of us must constantly face: What will I do in this situation? When our emotions are functioning well, when we are operating with emotional intelligence, they help us to make good choices and to act in ways that benefit us. Consider the following examples:

- Curiosity and excitement can move us to actively engage our world.
- Love and affection can move us to get close to and to connect with another person.

- Anger can move us to fight to remedy an injustice.
- Fear can move us to flee or to withdraw from a situation of danger.
- Confidence and pride can cause us to come forward and assert ourselves.
- Shame and embarrassment can cause us to hold back and re-evaluate.
- Grief and sadness can cause us to withdraw and recharge.

When our emotional operating systems are functioning well, we will have sound opinions and will make good choices. Even if others do not agree with us or fully understand our choices, they can perceive that we are exercising "good judgment" or even "wisdom." We are being emotionally intelligent.

Emotions influence our decisions and actions in many different ways. As you read this section of text, you are experiencing some emotions that are influencing whether you read through the whole section and (if you do read it through) whether you are reading attentively or inattentively. If your emotion is curiosity or fascination, you will be reading and mentally processing this text in a certain way. Your reading will be different if your main emotion is resentment at being made to read this text. If your main response is resentment, confusion, or annoyance ("This makes no sense!"), you may nonetheless continue reading because of some combination of fear, pride, guilt, or shame ("I've got to get through this"). To the extent that you are forcing yourself through the text, you are probably experiencing frustration along with the other emotions. What this example illustrates is that there is a jungle of complex emotion underlying even the simplest activities in our day-to-day lives.

We humans have an amazing ability to know and to react to our environment. It is our emotional mechanisms—our built-in emotional operating systems—that, for the most part, give us this ability. Thanks to them, we are able, without consciously thinking about it, to react to our environment in ways that benefit our safety and well-being.

Emotions and Negotiation

Emotions have a significant effect on the interactions and relations of people in conflict. Studies of the intrapersonal effects of a person's emotions on his or her behaviour in negotiation have consistently demonstrated that positive moods and emotions lead to an increase in particular strategies and outcomes, such as concessions, cooperativeness (Forgas, 1998), and joint-gain seeking (Carnevale & Isen, 1986). In contrast, negative moods and emotions reduce the use of these strategies, and they diminished the desire for future interaction with the other party (Allred et al., 1997).

Early research into the link between negotiation and emotions at the *interpersonal* level relied upon field study, social psychology experiments, and game theory analysis. These studies identified three key functions of emotions with respect to negotiation:

1. Emotions convey three types of information to negotiating partners: how you feel about the issues at hand; your social intentions; and your orientation to the negotiating partner.
2. Emotions can evoke either complementary or reciprocal emotions in others, which may lead to an increase in either cooperative or competitive behaviour between the parties.
3. Emotions and the other side's reactions to them can lead to either joint gains or win–lose outcomes, and can either decrease or increase the parties' desire for future relationships with each other.

Studies of emotion undertaken in the area of conflict and negotiation have tended to focus on the effects of happiness and anger. Results indicate that expressions of anger from a negotiator consistently lead to larger concessions from the other party *if* the latter perceives himself to be in a lower power position (for example, with little support from superiors; with few options available outside of the negotiation; with low legitimate power in his hierarchical position) than the negotiator. At the same time demonstrations of anger can clearly have negative effects on negotiations. A party that has to deal with an angry negotiator is less likely to be happy with outcomes, less likely to engage in future relationships with the other side, and more apt to become angry themselves.

Expressions of happiness from a negotiator, by contrast, tend to elicit fewer and smaller concessions from the other side, according to some researchers—although (on the other hand) such expressions of happiness do not reduce the desire for a future relationship with the negotiator (Van Cleef et al., 2004; Morris & Keltner, 2000; Carnevale & Isen, 1986). Our own firsthand experiences in mediation have not always borne out these research findings; we have found that the expression of positive emotion by one party may actually elicit increased responsiveness and concessions from the other party.

Theorists have also tended to view emotions as a means of communication in negotiations—indirect communication that requires interpretation by the other side. An expression of disappointment from a negotiator, for example, might indicate to the other party that she is not achieving what she had hoped. This *might* influence the other party to concede more. Alternatively, an expression of guilt from a negotiator might signal to the other party that he should ask for more in the negotiation. In short, it is not merely the expression of emotion that changes a negotiation dynamic; it is how that emotion is interpreted and responded to.

The expression of emotion can strongly affect the level of trust between negotiating parties. Trust is a key factor in producing cooperative, as opposed to competitive, behaviours among negotiators (Deutsch & Krauss, 1960). The honest and effective communication of emotion, whether positive or negative, can lead to increased trust between negotiating parties (Boone & Buck, 2003). A mediator, by helping parties to honestly and accurately express their emotions, can increase the level of trust between them. One type of conflict that does not seem to be influenced significantly by the parties' emotions or emotional expression is conflict over values and norms. One explanation for this is that values and norms, because they go to the core of a person's identity and affiliations, are held very dear. Where such core values are concerned, trade-offs and concessions seem inappropriate and unacceptable to people (Wade-Benzoni et al., 2002).

Negotiations take place within a wide variety of social and cultural contexts, so it is difficult to accurately predict what impact emotional expression will have on a negotiation. This is particularly true of cross-cultural negotiations when, for some people, emotion and social context are deeply embedded in the meaning of relationships and environments. Standards and norms governing which emotional expressions are appropriate and which are proscribed vary according to cultural context. For example, in a cultural context where displays of anger are frowned upon, a show of anger during a negotiation will be differently received than it would be in a context where anger is routinely expressed.

The expression of anger in conflict is often a result of fear. Let's look at the fear response more closely.

The Fear Response

Consider the brain's mechanism for fear. When our eyes, ears, or other senses detect certain stimuli, signals are sent to a part of the brain called the amygdala. The amygdala in turn sends signals that activate the sympathetic nervous system to release hormones, such as adrenaline, that produce the "fight-or-flight" or acute stress response. All of this happens with little, if any, conscious awareness or control by our cognitive or thinking brain—that is, the cortex (see Figure 4.2).

The Physiology of Fight-or-Flight

When our fight-or-flight response is activated, the chemicals (adrenaline, cortisol, and other hormones) that are released into our bloodstream cause a series of dramatic physiological changes. Our heart and respiratory rates increase. Blood and nutrients are diverted from the centre of our body (for example, from the digestive system) to our arms and legs so they are energized for running and fighting. Our pupils dilate. Our awareness narrows and intensifies, as does our eyesight—that is, our peripheral vision is reduced. Our perception of pain diminishes. Our immune system mobilizes with new intensity. We become prepared—physically and psychologically—for fight-or-flight.

When it is activated, the fight-or-flight response triggers innate competitive instincts and behaviours. We tend to perceive persons or things in our environment as a threat. We tend to perceive others as adversaries. Our fears are exaggerated.

What makes this particularly problematic is that people in conflict are often not fully aware—sometimes they are not at all aware—that they are having this response.

In many cases, the fight-or-flight response will limit a person's ability to be fully rational; it will cause him or her to see and think narrowly and defensively. As a result, this person may appear to behave in irrational and dysfunctional ways.

As LeDoux and other neuroscientists have discovered, the data that our senses receive signalling potential danger goes to the thalamus, which sends it along two pathways:

1. to the amygdala, which triggers the fight-or-flight physiological reaction (as shown by the blue and red arrows in Figure 4.2); and
2. to the cortex, which takes more time to process and evaluate the information (see the orange arrows in Figure 4.2).

The results of the cognitive assessment that occurs via the second pathway are then sent to the amygdala. They either confirm the threat, in which case the fear-based reaction and behaviour will continue, or they negate it, in which case the fear response will be quelled and stopped (LeDoux, 2002, pp. 62–64).

The Fear Response and Mediation

When the fear response works as it is supposed to, it will "serve and protect" us. In many conflict situations, however, the fear response adversely affects how people think and act, producing counterproductive or dysfunctional behaviours.

Figure 4.2 The Fear Response

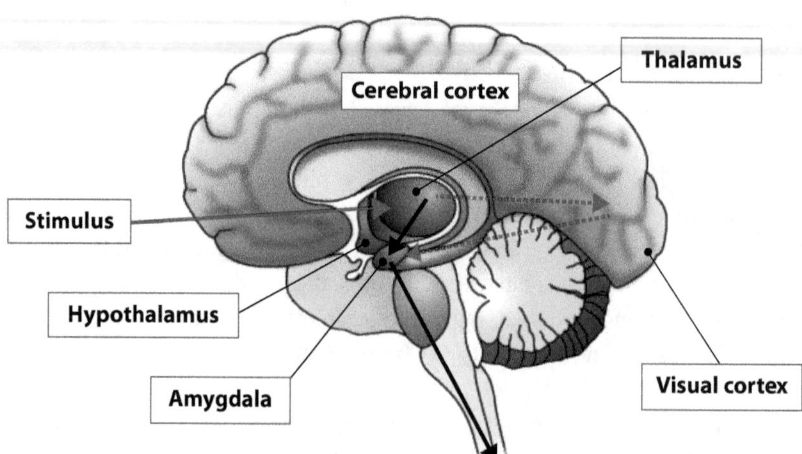

Source: Adapted from LeDoux (2002).

Mediators need to understand the effects of emotion and of the expression of emotion on how people think and behave in conflict. Mediators need to be especially clear about the fear response. Affecting a person unawares, the fear response will significantly influence his or her interpretation of a conflict situation—in other words, his or her conflict narrative. Conflict emotions, conflict narratives, and conflict behaviours are three mutually interdependent elements of any conflict (see Figure 4.3).

Although a person's behaviour may be viewed in isolation, usually we consider it in the context of the conflict relationship. That relationship will have a history, a status (that is, it will be a relationship in a marriage, in a family, or in a workplace), with typical attributes and dynamics of power and patterns of behaviour.

Consider your relationship with a person close to you—a spouse, partner, friend, sibling, parent, or child. How do you usually behave in conflict situations when you disagree with that person? Do you argue? Do you give in? How do you tend to respond to different things that person might say or do? What emotions do you feel? What emotional behaviour do you display? How would a third-party observer describe your emotions and your emotional behaviour at such times? How would you characterize your behaviour? Is it aggressive or passive or some combination of the two? What aspects of your behaviour would you say are constructive and which could be seen as destructive? What are the elements of power between you and the other person? How do you influence each other? What are some typical patterns of behaviour in this relationship?

Being able to analyze and understand conflict behaviour is a very valuable tool for successful mediation. We gain useful insights by seeking to understand why people behave and interact as they do. Various factors may influence behaviour:

Figure 4.3 Three Key Elements of Conflict

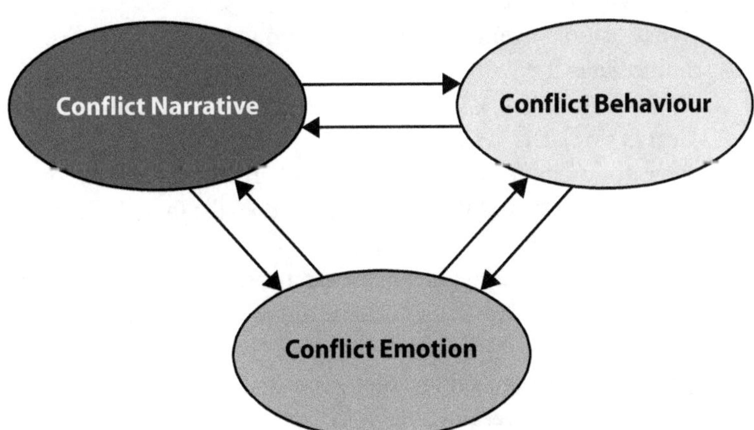

psychological makeup, culture, social influence, economics, law, and the media. However, despite our efforts to rationalize conflict behaviour and to understand it in scientific terms, it often seems to defy such analysis. Nonetheless, we continue trying to understand, knowing as we do that people often find ways to resolve conflicts they do not fully understand.

Summary

Conflict practitioners are primarily interested in the subjective experience of conflict. As we have seen in this chapter, people respond to conflict in five different ways—avoiding, withdrawing, fighting, appealing to authority, or negotiating. For a full understanding of people's behaviour in conflict, we need to examine the parties' underlying cognitive and emotional processes. In this chapter, we have cited some of the scholarship concerning why people in conflict interact as they do. With this theoretical understanding, a mediator will be better equipped to make sense of the complexities of parties' conflict interactions and, in turn, to help the parties themselves make sense of that interaction. In doing so, the mediator will help parties to collaborate rather than to engage in less productive interactions such as competing, avoiding, accommodating, or compromising.

DISCUSSION QUESTIONS AND EXERCISES

1. What are the effects of latent conflict in an ongoing relationship?
2. It is late Tuesday evening, and Farah is trying to relax. She is keyed up about an important presentation that she has to give the next morning. Suddenly she hears loud, pounding rock music coming from the apartment next door. Her neighbour Rocky—and some of his friends—are playing electric guitars and drums. As it goes on and on, Farah begins to wrestle with the problem of what course of action she should take.
   a. Imagine that you are Farah.
      i. What actions would you as an individual be inclined to take immediately?
      ii. What actions, if any, would you be inclined to take subsequently—the next day or later?
      iii. How do you think your neighbour might respond to the various actions you are considering? What effect, if any, does the thought of his response have on your plans to respond?
      iv. What other actions might you consider taking, either immediately (that is, while the music is actually going on) or subsequently?
   b. Imagine that you are Rocky. There are only a few times during the week that you and your mates can get together to practise.
      i. How would you feel and how would you respond to various actions that Farah might take with respect to your band practice?

After considering the above scenario from both Farah's perspective and Rocky's perspective, you will realize that there are numerous possible responses from both parties. All responses will likely fall within one or more of the five response categories presented in this chapter.

   c. Referring to the four stages of the conflict cycle (see Figure 4.1), describe what could occur if Farah were to go next door to confront Rocky about his loud music. How might this altercation affect the attitudes and behaviours of both parties?

3. Think of a conflict situation you have experienced in relation to a group project at school or work. How did you respond? How would you characterize your behaviour in that case? What were some of the factors that caused you to behave as you did?
4. Consider the Open House scenario described in Box 4.1. Then answer the following questions.
   a. What specific aspects of competitive behaviour can you identify or infer for each party (including their thoughts, emotions, perceptions, communications, and actions)?
5. What are some of the cognitive schemas (yours and/or others') that contribute to conflicts within your school community? How can you respond to these productively?
6. In this chapter, we suggested that any of the five conflict behaviours might be appropriate and advantageous depending on the conflict situation. Here are five conflict situations. Try to decide which behaviour you would use, and list reasons for your decision.
   a. Your seven-year-old child wants to stay up past her bedtime.
   b. You are confronted by a man who demands your money. He has no weapons. There's no-one else nearby.
   c. You're fairly sure you gave a cashier a $20 bill. She insists it was only $10.
   d. You and another customer reach for the last copy of a newspaper. It includes an article written by a friend of yours.
   e. You and a close friend each have favourite performers. These two performers are each giving a concert on the same evening—to which you both have bought two tickets (to treat the other)—and each event is for one night only.

FURTHER READING

Bunker, B., Rubin, J., & Associates. (1995). *Conflict, cooperation and justice*. San Francisco: Jossey-Bass.

Damasio, Antonio. (1999). *The feeling of what happens: Body and emotion on the making of consciousness*. Orlando, FL: Harcourt Books.

Folger, J.P., Poole, M.S., & Stutman, R.K. (1993). *Working through conflict* (2nd ed.). New York: Harper Collins.

Hocker, J., & Wilmot, W. (1995). *Interpersonal conflict*. Madison, WI: WCB Brown and Benchmark.

LeDoux, J. (1996). *The emotional brain: The mysterious underpinnings of emotional life*. New York: Simon & Schuster.

LeDoux, J. (2002) Emotion, memory, and the brain. *Scientific American, 12*, 62–71.

Mayer, B. (2000). *The dynamics of conflict resolution*. San Francisco: Jossey-Bass.

Websites

The Amygdaloids: http://www.amygdaloids.com
This is a New York City rock band of scientists, headed by neuroscientist Joseph LeDoux, who is the lead singer and songwriter. On this site you will find songs and other material about the workings of the human mind.

Brain and Creativity Institute: http://dornsife.usc.edu/bci/

Conflict Resolution Education Connection: http://www.creducation.org
This website is devoted to the promotion of conflict resolution education throughout the world.

Damasio, Antonio. (2011). The quest to understand consciousness [Video file]. TED: http://www.ted.com/speakers/antonio_damasio

Daniel Goleman: http://www.danielgoleman.info

The LeDoux Lab—Center for Neuroscience at NYU: http://www.cns.nyu.edu/home/ledoux/index.html

Peace Pledge Union. Understanding conflict: http://www.ppu.org.uk/learn/conflict/st_conflict.html

Rummell, R.J. (1975).*Understanding conflict and war* (Vol. 1). Beverley Hills: Sage. https://www.hawaii.edu/powerkills/NOTE10.HTM

REFERENCES

Allred , K.G., Mallozzi, J.S., Matsui, F., & Raia, C.P. (1997). The influence of anger and compassion on negotiation performance. *Organizational Behaviour and Human Decision Processes, 70*, 175–187.

Bartlett, F.A. (1932). *Remembering: A study in experimental and social psychology*. New York: Cambridge University Press

Boone, R.T., & Buck, R. (2003). Emotional expressivity and trustworthiness: The role of nonverbal behaviour in the evolution of cooperation. *Journal of Nonverbal Behaviour, 27*, 163–182.

Boulding, K.E. (1962). *Conflict and defense: A general theory*. New York: Harper & Row.

Burton, J. (1990). *Conflict: Resolution and provention*. New York: St. Martin's Press.

Carnevale, P.J.D., & Isen, A.M. (1986). The influence of positive affect and visual access on the discovery of integrative solutions in bilateral negotiation. *Organizational Behaviour and Human Decision Processes, 37*, 1–13.

Coate, R.A., & Rosati, J.A. (1988). Human needs in world society. In R.A. Coate & J.A. Rosati (Eds.), *The power of human needs in world society* (pp. 1–20). Boulder, CO: Lynne Rienner Publishers.

Coser, L. (1956). *The functions of social conflict*. New York: Free Press.

Coser, L. (1968). *Continuities in the study of social conflict*. New York: Free Press.

Cozolino, L. (2006). *The neuroscience of human relationships: Attachment and the developing brain*. New York: Norton.

Dahrendorf, R. (1958). Toward a theory of social conflict. *Journal of Conflict Resolution, 2*(2), 170–183.

Damasio, Antonio. (1994). *Descartes' error: Emotion, reason, and the human brain*. New York: Penguin Books.

Damasio, Antonio. (1999). *The feeling of what happens: Body and emotion on the making of consciousness*. Orlando, FL: Harcourt Books.

Deutsch, M. (1973). *The resolution of conflict*. New Haven, CT: Yale University Press.

Deutsch, M., & Krauss, R.M. (1960, September). The effect of threat upon interpersonal bargaining. *Journal of Abnormal and Social Psychology, 61*(2), 181–189.

Fisher, R., & Ury, W. (1991). *Getting to yes: Negotiating agreement without giving in* (2nd ed.). New York: Penguin Books. Copyright © 1981, 1991 by Roger Fisher and William Ury. Reprinted by permission of Houghton Mifflin Company. All rights reserved.

Fiske, Susan, T. (2004). *Social beings: A core motives approach to social psychology*. New York: John Wiley and Sons, Inc.

Fiske, S.T., & Taylor, S.E. (1991). *Social cognition*. (2nd ed.). New York: McGraw-Hill.

Forgas, J.P. (1998). On being happy and being mistaken: Mood effects on the fundamental attribution error. *Journal of Personality and Social Psychology, 75*(2), 318–331.

Galtung, J. (1996). *Peace by peaceful means: Peace and conflict, development and civilization*. Thousand Oaks, CA: Sage.

Goleman, D. (1995). *Emotional intelligence. Why it can matter more than IQ*. New York: Bantam.

Goleman, D. (2006). *Social intelligence. The revolutionary new science of human relationships*. New York: Bantam.

Gross Stein, J. (2005). Psychological explanations of international conflict. In W. Carlsnaes, T. Risse, & B.A. Simmonds (Eds.), *Handbook of international relations* (pp. 292–308). Thousand Oaks, CA: Sage.

Gulliver, P.H. (1979). *Dispute and negotiation: A cross-cultural perspective*. New York: Academic Press.

Himes, J. (1980). *The nature of social conflict in conflict and conflict management*. Athens, GA: The University of Georgia Press.

Hocker, J., & Wilmot, W. (1995). *Interpersonal conflict* (4th ed.). Madison, WI: WCB Brown and Benchmark.

James, W. (1890). *The principles of psychology* (Vol. 1). New York: Henry Holt.

Lax, D., & Sebenius, J.K. (1986). *The manager as negotiator*. New York: Free Press.

LeDoux, J. (1996). *The emotional brain: The mysterious underpinnings of emotional life*. New York: Simon and Shuster.

LeDoux, J. (2002). Emotion, memory, and the brain. *Scientific American, 12*, 62-71. Retrieved from http://people.brandeis.edu/~teuber/emotion.pdf.

Lonergan, B. (1957). *Insight: A study of human understanding*. New York: Philosophical Library.

Lonergan, B. (1992). *Collected works of Bernard Lonergan* (Vol. 3: *Insight: A study of human understanding*). Toronto: University of Toronto Press.

Maslow, A. (1943). A theory of human motivation. *Psychological Review, 50*(4), 370–396; available at: http://psychclassics.yorku.caMaslow/motivation.htm.

Melchin, K.R., & Picard, C.A. (2008). *Transforming conflict through insight*. Toronto: University of Toronto Press.

Moore, C.W. (2003). *The mediation process: Practical strategies for resolving conflict* (3rd ed.). San Francisco: Jossey-Bass.

Morris, M., & Keltner, D. (2000). How emotions work: The social functions of emotional expression in negotiation. *Research in Organizational Behaviour, 22*, 1–50.

Northrup, T.A. (1989). The dynamic of identity in personal and social conflict. In L. Kriesberg, T.A. Northrup, & S.J. Thorson (Eds.), *Intractable conflicts and their transformation* (pp. 55–82). Syracuse, NY: Syracuse University Press.

Piaget, J. (1952).*The origins of intelligence in children*. New York: Norton.

Pruitt, D., & Carnevale, P. (1993). *Negotiation in social conflict*. Pacific Grove, CA: Brooks/Cole.

Rothman, J. (1997). *Resolving identity-based conflict in nations, organizations, and communities*. San Francisco: Jossey-Bass.

Rumelhart, D.E. (1980). Schemata: The building blocks of cognition. In R.J. Spiro, B.C. Bruce, & W.F. Brewer. (Eds.), *Theoretical issues in reading comprehension*. Hillsdale, NJ: Lawrence Erlbaum.

Rummel, R.J. (1976). *Understanding conflict and war* (Vols. 1–2). New York: Wiley.

Simmel, G. (1903). The sociology of conflict. *American Journal of Sociology, 9*, 490–525.

Thomas, K.W., & Kilmann, R.K. (1974). *Conflict mode instrument*. New York: XICOM.

Ury, W., Brett, J., & Goldberg, S. (1988). *Getting disputes resolved: Designing systems to cut the costs of conflict*. San Francisco: Jossey-Bass.

Van Cleef, G.A., De Dreu, C.K.W., & Manstead, A.S.R. (2004). The interpersonal effects of anger and happiness in negotiations. *Journal of Personality and Social Psychology, 86*, 57–76.

Wade-Benzoni, K.A., Okamura, T., Bret, J.M., Morre, D., Tenbrunsel, A.E., & Bazerman, M.H. (2002). Cognitions and behaviour in asymmetric social dilemmas: A comparison of two cultures. *Journal of Applied Psychology, 87*, 87–95.

Watzlawick, P., Bavelas, J.B., & Jackson, D.D. (1967). *Pragmatics of human communication*. New York: W.W. Norton.

CHAPTER 5

Conflict and Communication

LEARNING OBJECTIVES	CHAPTER OUTLINE
After reading this chapter, you will be able to • Understand communication as a process of interaction, interpretation, and meaning making that is influenced by culture and emotion • Identify different types of conversations • Identify different types of communication blockers • Identify different forms of non-verbal communication • Explain the communication skills and tools that are essential to being a competent mediator	Introduction 125 Understanding Communication 125 Communication and Interaction 128 Communication Blockers 131 Non-Verbal Communication 134 The Communication Skills of a Mediator 136 Summary 151

Words are like spears: Once they leave your lips they can never come back.

Yoruban Proverb

Introduction

This chapter introduces communication principles and mediation techniques. We discuss both verbal and non-verbal communication from the basis that communication is socially constructed, culturally rooted, relational, and interactive. We consider different ways of understanding communication and some attitudes and responses that inhibit communication. In the last half of the chapter, we discuss communication skills commonly used by mediators, including the following: listening and questioning skills, connecting skills, and skills for assertive conflict communication that are essential for managing conflict.

Understanding Communication

Conflict resolution practitioners have long acknowledged the central role that communication plays in understanding and resolving conflict. Parties in conflict tend to develop communicative patterns that are counter productive, impeding the conflict's successful resolution. For example, one party may feel unheard because the other talks past, rather than with, him. Or he may feel that the language used by the other party in describing the conflict and its past events bears no relation to his own. In such cases, constructive communication between the parties is often very difficult.

A mediator (or other third party intervenor) can change the communication dynamic between the parties. Third parties become part of the communicative relationship; their presence influences the nature of the interaction; and they, like the parties, become changed by their involvement. Folger and Jones (1994, p. 37) say that "mediators are not third parties who act on others without being acted upon, yet most of our theory implicitly or explicitly confirms this view." The very nature of human interaction means that we cannot be part of an interaction without shaping, moving, directing, and being affected by it. The concept of the mediator as a "third party neutral" does not take fully into account the mediator's active role in managing or facilitating the parties' communication.

Good communication is both an art and a science. The science is understanding why certain communication patterns tend to evoke certain responses. The art is producing shared meanings and understandings. Communication occurs in a variety of ways: direct and indirect, intended and unintended, verbal and non-verbal, rational and intuitive. We all communicate differently depending on our different personalities, cultures, education, and life experiences, so there is infinite potential for miscommunication and misunderstanding. At the same time, there is no limit to our potential for becoming skilled and artful communicators in many contexts.

Through communication, we make meaning out of our experiences and share those meanings with others. It has been said that people spend about three-quarters of their waking moments communicating (Katz & Lawyer, 1994, p. 16). This suggests that human beings cannot *not* communicate. Our smiles, frowns, gestures, and other non-verbal cues reveal our thoughts and feelings. Actions and non-actions, including silence, can be perceived as meaningful, and can be interpreted. For example, a person's silence may convey a message: "She ignored me" or "He's upset." At times, we are unaware of the messages we send. At other times, our messages are imagined or misinterpreted by others.

Interpreting correctly the messages we are constantly receiving from others is not easy. The listener "can't possibly know what is in the sender's private world of meaning" (Gordon, 1977, p. 51). As listeners, we must "decode" messages to ascertain meaning. Sometimes this process requires that we disregard the words of the message itself and perceive its meaning elsewhere—in the sender's body language, tone of voice, or behaviour. We rely on these non-verbal signals to tell us whether he or she was communicating intentionally, jokingly, or evasively. Meaning is also influenced by context—that of the messenger and that of the listener. As individuals we are "conscious of how others respond to us, and we relate to others in ways that both generate and reinforce our own sense of identity" (Sargent et al., 2011, p. 347).

Cultural anthropologists such as Geert Hofstede, Edward T. Hall, and Philip Gulliver (Hofstede, Hofstede, & Minkov, 2010; Gulliver, 1979) have written about communication patterns in different cultures. Their studies have determined that these patterns can vary widely; they locate them along a spectrum. At one end of the spectrum are "low-context" communication patterns. At the other end are "high-context" communication patterns. Low-context communication generally encompasses direct verbal messages, plain and explicit language, a linear or sequential expression of thought, depersonalized and scientific statements, and a relative absence of—and resistance to—silence. In high-context communication, messages are delivered through indirect, coded, and implicit communication that is understood according to context, non-sequential expression of thoughts, personalized and intuitive statements, and non-verbal gestures and silence. The particular conventions of communication vary widely between cultures, but all cultures have both high-context and low-context communication patterns.

Individualist cultures, such as the United States and (to a lesser degree) Canada, value direct forms of communication—that is, low-context communication patterns (Gudykunst, 1991). In these societies, people are considered good communicators to the extent that they are able to convey a message accurately through explicit, verbal communication. The belief is that, with this kind of direct, low-context communication, the message is less likely to be misinterpreted.

In Asian cultures, by contrast, where high-context communication is favoured, direct verbal communication can be considered disrespectful. In such cultures, the message tends to be encoded within the context of the discussions, not explicitly conveyed by the verbal communication. The context depends on such factors as where the communication occurs (for example, where the parties meet or where they are sitting) or what the parties are wearing. In a high-context communication culture, the message varies according to a person's non-verbal expression, body gestures, or other behaviours. Communication is indirect; a relatively small part of the real message is communicated verbally. The scenario set out in Box 5.1 (adapted from Gudykunst, 1991) exemplifies high-context communication.

BOX 5.1 » Scenario: High-Context Communications

An Indonesian man from a remote village wants to marry an upper-caste woman. To do this, he must send his mother to visit the woman's mother to get permission for the marriage. He does so. During this visit, the prospective bride's mother serves the man's mother tea and bananas. Tea is never served with bananas in that culture. Her serving them together is a signal that the marriage is not approved. In this way, the woman's mother does not have to insult the man's mother by openly saying "no." The transgression of polite convention signals her disapproval.

In this scenario, both parties understand the message because they share cultural norms. Their communications are encoded in ways that both understand. Needless to say, not all of us would have understood the meaning of tea served with bananas. Though the cultural diversity of our society brings us many benefits—new perspectives, attitudes, values, and modes of creativity—it can also create complications and barriers to communication. People communicate differently, depending on a variety of factors, including culture.

Even within a single culture, communicative norms that apply in one context—for example, the social sphere—may not apply in a different context, such as business. It is wrong to assume that everyone from a particular ethnocultural group will behave in a certain manner. We cannot safely speak of "fixed" cultural traits; culture is dynamic and ever-changing.

The communication problems between people from different cultures have less to do with language than with lack of knowledge about cultural variations among communicative norms and rules. And these problems can arise even between people from the same culture, since communicative norms and conventions vary between families, workplaces, and professions.

Communication and Interaction

Communication involves more than the input and output of information from one person to another. It involves making meaning through the interpretation of information. These meanings, in turn, influence how we respond to the information. Different meanings, as we discussed in Chapter 4, are produced from different cognitive schemas or maps that help us to organize complex information and make sense of it (Sargent, Picard, & Jull, 2011, p. 352). The whole process of communication takes place in social contexts, which influence how we perceive and respond to others, and they to us.

Regardless of their social or cultural context, all messages contain meanings that involve at least two elements: substantive content and emotion. To understand a message fully, we must uncover and apprehend these two elements. Messages also contain information about the nature of the relationship between the individuals who are communicating—in other words, information about how the speaker perceives his or her relationship with the listener. For example, if a person speaks in a rude or abrupt tone to her co-worker, she may be sending an implicit (or explicit) message about how she views the other person in relation to herself. Alternatively, she could be revealing that she is having a difficult day, which has made her lose her patience. The co-worker's response may be affected more by the message's implicit meanings, which are conveyed by its tone, than by its actual content (Stone, Patten, & Heen, 1999).

Stone, Patton, and Heen (1999, p. 7) expand on this idea. They suggest that in all difficult communicative exchanges (and such exchanges are inevitable, in conflict situations), our thoughts and feelings can be organized into three categories, or "conversations." These conversations are as follows:

1. the "What Happened?" conversation,
2. the "Feelings" conversation, and
3. the "Identity" conversation.

In the communications about conflict that typically occur in mediation, the "What Happened?" conversation refers to the disputants' struggle to get to the "truth" about what happened. In conflict—as in many life experiences—subjective perceptions count. There is no one truth; instead, truth is in the eye of the beholder. This means that, in mediation, the focus is not on who is right (as in rights-based processes and adjudication) but on ensuring that all "truths" are identified and understood.

The "Feelings" conversation is about emotional messages. Sometimes, this conversation is loud and clear within a person; at other times, it may be muffled or even silenced. Retzinger and Scheff (2000, pp. 76–77) say that the suppression or denial of deep-rooted emotions like shame, hurt, and fear—that is, when such emotions are "hidden from self and others"—can be a leading cause of intractable conflict. Likewise, the emotional messages that people convey to each other, often non-verbally, are sometimes clear, but sometimes they are confusing or misleading. When someone is crying, for example, we conclude that they are hurt or sad. But this may not be the case. When someone is speaking loudly and behaving in an angry or agitated manner, we may have no idea of the feelings of insecurity or fear that may be motivating this. Understanding and responding to the parties' "Feelings" conversations are essential to good conflict communication.

The "Identity" conversation is about how we see ourselves in the conflict and how the conflict affects our self-image and self-esteem. It is the conversation we have with ourselves about whether we are competent or incompetent, good or bad, strong or weak, and how we are perceived by the other party. When our sense of self is shaken by conflict, it affects our emotions, communications, and decisions in ways that may be difficult to understand and predict, even for us.

"Feelings" conversations and "Identity" conversations are often hidden; they are difficult to discern and respond to in direct, explicit ways. That is why mediators need to develop indirect, intuitive, and artful ways of discovering and communicating about these sources of conflict.

Gordon (1977, p. 50) said the following: "People don't get down to the real problem until after they have first ventilated a feeling or some opening message." By "opening message," Gordon was referring to statements such as "I knew I should have stayed home today" or "I'm not sure what I am even doing here, the situation is impossible!" Explosive statements like these are common in the opening stage of the mediation process. Communicating what is important—so that the other person really understands it—is not easy, especially in situations of heightened emotion. There are a number of reasons why this is so difficult. They are as follows:

1. *We hear through filters.* Filters include factors such as our background and ethnicity, our life experience and our world views, as well as our education, gender, and social class. We are usually unaware of filters, yet they play a major role in interpreting what someone says or means. Our personal filters allow us to generalize, distort, and delete information. Some sociologists claim that there is no *objective* reality or knowledge, that in fact all reality is *subjective* or *interpretive*, due to cultural influences (Gergen, 1999; Burr, 1995). Lakoff and Johnson (1980, p. 159) also reject the long-standing notion of objective or absolute truth, affirming that "truth is always relative to a conceptual system that is defined in part by metaphors that have evolved in our culture over a long period or are imposed by people in power." Narrative theories are based on this idea—that we generate individual stories to make sense of ourselves in the world and that we are influenced by the dominant stories of the society in which we live (Winslade & Monk, 2000). These stories create meaning for us, and they set the context for the messages we "hear." So, we often hear what we *expect* others to say, not what they *actually* say.
2. *Actions speak louder than words.* We "hear" as much with our eyes as with our ears. If someone tells us something but doesn't look as if she means it, we do not believe her.
3. *Non-verbal cues.* Non-verbal cues have different meanings in different cultures at different times. Take eye contact, for example. For many Canadians, direct and sustained eye contact sends the message that we are being truthful and honest. Social mores teach us to look a person in the eye if we want to be believed. However, for some of Canada's First Nations' peoples, sustained and direct eye contact may—depending on the social setting—be considered disrespectful or a sign of dishonesty or trickery.
4. *Listening is a two-way process.* As speakers, we become more effective when we show interest in listening to others. Covey's (1989, pp. 236–241) principle comes to mind: Use empathic listening to seek to understand before you speak to be understood. Nichols (1995, p. 64) says something similar: "Most people won't really listen or pay attention to your point of view until they become convinced that you've heard and appreciated theirs."
5. *Misunderstanding.* Misunderstanding can exist and we may not even know it, because a speaker's intent and a listener's impression may never be completely disclosed.
6. *Emotions are not easily shared.* This is the case because disputants are often not fully aware of their own emotions, or they may not have words to express them. They also may not feel safe in talking about what really matters.

7. *Listening is hard.* Research suggests that our average listening efficiency is about 25 percent (Katz & Lawyer, 1994, p. 15). We may be distracted by what is going on around us, by our own internal strains and stresses, or we may be too busy thinking about what we are going to say next. Listening is also hard because thinking is much faster than speaking; as one person speaks, the listener has time to tune out information or fill in the other's story in ways that may not be relevant.
8. *Listening is a skill that is not often taught.* Listening is not formally taught in school or in everyday life. But good mediators must be good listeners. The majority of a mediator's time is spent listening, really listening, to the hopes and concerns of the individuals he or she is trying to help. This takes immense concentration; the mediator must listen for both facts and feelings, must ensure that the message he is hearing is correct, and must withhold judgment about what is said.

While good communication cannot guarantee that conflict will be resolved, poor communication surely increases the likelihood that it will be made worse. Parties in conflict are often unable to engage in effective communication on their own because each side strongly believes that it is right and the other is wrong. Each party believes the other must be made to change its view. This gives rise to the "attack–defend" pattern of communication. The intervention of a mediator can overcome such patterns, open channels of blocked communication, and restore effective communication.

Communication Blockers

When people are in conflict, their ability to perceive, understand, and communicate about the conflict in a fully productive way is limited by a number of factors, collectively known as communication blockers. We will consider three types:

1. responses that block communication;
2. limiting assumptions; and
3. conflict emotions.

Responses That Block Communication

Certain ways of responding to other people's communications discourage these people from sharing their thoughts and feelings. These blocking responses get in the way of building trust and rapport, and they create barriers to ongoing and deep conversation.

Communication blockers are responses that make a person who has tried to communicate feel judged, blamed, considered incompetent, or not listened to. The message received, whether intended or not, is that the person is in the wrong and should change his or her mind or behaviour or not feel as he or she does. Not feeling accepted for who we are leaves us less willing to disclose our real needs and feelings. It increases our defensiveness and resistance to new ideas. Blockers close off communication or, at best, keep it at a superficial level. This prevents the exploration of important underlying issues in a conflict, such as human needs, goals, values, fears, and expectations, as well as religious, political, or social beliefs.

It is not usually our intention to cool conversation—to put up communication blockers. Such responses are often unconscious habits we have learned over time, without our being aware of their effect. For communication to work well, Cornelius and Faire (1989, p. 41) tell us that we must do the following:

- Respect an individual's right to her opinion by not manipulating her into seeing it our way.
- Regard the person as our equal by not dominating her.
- Value her decisions by not undermining her.

That certain kinds of responses block communication will be obvious to you. That others do so may be more surprising, because they frequently are accompanied by good intentions. Communication blockers fall into three broad categories: (1) being judgmental, (2) giving advice, and (3) minimizing.

Being Judgmental

Criticizing, moralizing, diagnosing, disagreeing, and analyzing all fall into the judging category. When people feel judged, their common reaction is to defend themselves, which, in turn, makes them appear aggressive and uncooperative. Criticizing focuses on the negative aspects of the situation—or of the other party. It induces guilt and lowers self-esteem. Moralizing involves backing up our viewpoint with social, religious, or moral authority. Diagnosing and analyzing, which involve playing detective by probing for hidden agendas and motives, can threaten and undermine an individual's self-confidence. Disagreeing places that party in a superior position, leaving the other party feeling inferior and belittled.

Giving Advice

The category "giving advice" includes ordering, threatening, using too many "shoulds," and providing solutions. You might ask what is wrong with giving advice, especially when a person solicits it. Here are four things to consider:

1. Often the person asking for the advice has not had a chance to explore what really matters about the issue. As a result, the adviser can only comment on the problem being presented, not the underlying—and more important—problem.
2. Giving advice sends the message that you believe the person unable to solve her own problems. Inviting her to talk through the problem with you—

rather than telling her what to do—demonstrates respect for, and confidence in, her ideas and feelings.
3. Each of us is different, and what works for one person may not work for another person.
4. When we give advice, ownership of the problem shifts from the person to us. If the advice does not work, we are likely to be blamed.

Minimizing

Minimizing responses include name-calling, reassuring, diverting, focusing exclusively on logic and fact, and praising in order to manipulate. People respond negatively to having their ideas minimized through name-calling and sarcasm, and they often feel resentment and frustration when this happens. Reassuring a person by telling him that everything will be all right overlooks his feelings and suggests that he should not feel the way he does. Trying to smooth things over in this way is not empathetic; it may also be overly optimistic. Diverting attention from the listener's problem to your own message says that you are more important than the listener. Using logical arguments and focusing on the factual aspects of the situation tends to minimize the listener's emotions. This can be infuriating; it says that feelings are not important, and the listener should not have them. Using praise to entice a person to do something that she does not want to do—or to change her behaviour—is manipulative. Even when the praise is sincere, it often is not heard.

The minimizing category of responses is perhaps the least obvious one, because these responses are frequently intended to be helpful and to show empathy. Regardless of the speaker's intent, however, if the listener does not feel valued and respected, he or she is not likely to want to discuss what really matters to them.

Limiting Assumptions

There are a number of assumptions that all people, including mediators, sometimes make that limit their ability to communicate about a conflict in a fully productive way. Some are things we learned early in our development and tend to accept reflexively. Among these unconsidered assumptions are the following:

- Conflict emotions such as anger, resentment, jealousy, and hatred are bad and should not be displayed or expressed.
- It is wrong to confront and talk about conflict because doing so will cause it to escalate.
- People who confront conflict and express their conflict emotions openly are difficult people—"troublemakers."

These assumptions serve us fairly well in many social situations. Used as guidelines, they enable us to get along with most people and to maintain amicable relations with family, friends, and others. However, by leading us to avoid conflict or tiptoe around it, these assumptions will significantly limit our ability to communicate effectively in conflict, whether as a party to the dispute or as a mediator.

Conflict Emotions

In Chapter 4, we examined in some detail how emotion affects a person in conflict. We looked at how powerful emotions such as anger, suspicion, fear, and disgust strongly influence a disputant's perceptions of his or her adversary, as well as his or her general interpretation of the conflict situation. Emotion shapes or, in many cases, distorts a person's narrative of the conflict. For most people, then, conflict emotion limits the parties' ability to have the full and effective communication they need to have in order to resolve their conflict.

Because people lack the ability to express their emotions constructively, they suppress them. When this happens, the emotion does not simply go away; there is usually some non-verbal communication of it. Owing to this process, attempts to avoid conflict will sometimes backfire, as the non-verbal communication, unintentionally expressed, ends up offending the other party and making things worse.

Non-Verbal Communication

Forms of non-verbal communication include the following:

- *Visual non-verbal expression*. Before and during conversations, people exhibit various facial expressions, gestures, body postures, and body movements, according to a system known as "kinesics" or "body language."
- *Auditory non-verbal expression*. Each person's voice has a certain quality based on tone, pitch, timbre, texture, inflection, loudness, and rhythm. The signals conveyed by this means are called a "paralanguage."
- *Proxemics*. This form of non-verbal communication relates to how people use the space between them and the interpretations they derive from that.
- *Chronemics*. This refers to how people use the time they have and the significance they derive from that.
- *Appearance and artifacts*. A person's clothes and grooming, and other aspects of his or her physical appearance, convey many messages, intended or unintended.

As mediators, we need to be aware of all aspects of non-verbal and emotional communication. It is also important that we understand our own interpretive tendencies and be conscious that others may not share them. We need to understand that, in any conflict interaction, much is being communicated that is unintended and even unconscious. We also need to recognize—as discussed in the High-Context

BOX 5.2 » Scenario: Performance Review

Let's consider the non-verbal communication that might occur in the following situation. Sara is Joe's boss and they are meeting in Sara's office to discuss Joe's six-month performance review.

They start the meeting with a minute or two of pleasant, non-business conversation. Then Sara, with a friendly yet professional expression and tone of voice, summarizes some of the key aspects of the written performance review that she had given to Joe a few days before. As she proceeds, she stops after each item to give Joe an opportunity to respond, inviting him to express his point of view and any feelings or concerns he may have. Joe doesn't say too much, but when he does, he speaks calmly and professionally.

At one point in their meeting, Joe says: "I think things have been going very well in our section." Sara responds with: "That's great—I feel the same way."

When Joe said this, he avoided referring to things that had happened in the section and things that Sara had done that had annoyed and upset him. Some of Sara's decisions that Joe had disagreed with had caused him unnecessary difficulty in his job. But he had never expressed this to Sara, and did not do so in this meeting.

They finish by agreeing on what each of them will do to ensure that their working relationship is even more effective over the next six months.

Non-verbal communication has cognitive and interpretive effects, as well as emotional ones. Let's consider the non-verbal communication and its effects at the point where Joe says to Sara, "I think things have been going very well in our section."

What emotion or emotional meaning does Joe intend to convey to Sara by this statement? In saying this, Joe intends to convey to Sara that he is happy working with her in this section, that things are going well, and that he is confident and content with his job. We can assume that he intuitively believes that Sara will regard him favourably if she perceives him as a contented, optimistic, and confident employee in her section.

What emotion or emotional meaning is Joe conscious of that he intends not to convey (in other words, to conceal)? There were things that happened in the section and things that Sara herself did that annoyed and upset Joe. When Sara made certain decisions that Joe disagreed with and that caused him unnecessary difficulty in his job, he did not say anything to her, suppressing his dissatisfaction.

What emotion might be occurring within Joe that he is not conscious of? In Joe's conscious mind, the things about Sara that annoy him are minor grievances, not worth mentioning. Whenever he thinks of them, he says to himself: "It's no big deal—forget about it." In general, he feels optimistic and confident; he feels good about his future prospects with the organization. On the other hand, Joe may not be conscious of his underlying emotions of fear and mistrust toward Sara. If he thought about it, he might realize that his decision not to speak to Sara about his minor irritations and grievances is motivated by fear of what she might think and do if he criticized her. He might realize that he doesn't trust her to respond positively to such feedback, even if it is true and potentially useful to the workplace.

To what extent is Joe's unconscious emotion communicated to Sara? Some of Joe's underlying emotion is likely to be communicated to Sara despite his being unaware of it or unwilling to share it. This emotional communication is conveyed to Sara by Joe's body language and paralanguage. She senses that he is not as happy or as confident as he says he is. This causes her to feel a bit tense and wary toward Joe.

The underlying emotion that Joe may be experiencing is probably not the same emotion that Sara perceives or that she herself feels. In fact, much of Joe's emotional communication is likely to be distorted. In this example, what is being communicated could trigger various emotional reactions from Sara, including any number of the following: doubt, confusion, ambiguity, anxiety, worry, pressure, coercion, insecurity, apprehension, fear, mistrust, suspicion, irritation, anger, dislike, and so forth.

Most of Sara's emotional reaction will be unconscious. Her conscious feeling could be merely confusion ("There's something about him that I can't put my finger on"), or it could be mild aversion ("There's something about this guy that bothers me"). Her emotional reaction to Joe is different from whatever emotion is occurring unconsciously within Joe, and the emotion that Sara attributes to Joe is not the one actually occurring within him. Sara is not likely to know from this conversation that Joe feels some irritation toward her.

The situation would be very different if Joe were to display his feelings openly to Sara. For example, with an angry expression and tone of voice, Joe could say to Sara: "It's impossible for me to do a good job when you keep changing your mind. You say one thing one day and then two days later, you want something else. Are you really trying to make my life so difficult?"

This emotional communication is clearer. If Joe said this, she would know that he is angry and frustrated with her. The problem, of course, is that such a statement is likely to trigger feelings of anger and hostility within Sara. It could also trigger any number of other underlying emotions in her, including fear, intimidation, insecurity, hurt, weakness, vulnerability, vindictiveness, or alienation. For the most part, these underlying emotions may be unconscious. Yet they are very powerful and will have a strong influence on how Sara thinks and acts toward Joe.

Communications scenario (Box 5.1)—that some messages will not be understood and may not even be noticed. In short, we need to develop communication skills adequate to address all challenges we will face in mediating interpersonal conflict. In particular, we need skills for helping parties discover both their underlying emotions and the perceptions, assumptions, and interpretations that are influencing their interaction.

The Communication Skills of a Mediator

In this chapter, we cover basic communication skills that all mediators need. In subsequent chapters, we consider other skills and strategies that mediators need depending on the nature of the conflict and the mediator's goal for the mediation. The basic communication skills that a mediator needs fall into four broad categories:

1. reflective listening skills,
2. productive questioning skills,
3. connecting skills, and
4. non-blaming and non-defensive response skills

The Skill of Reflective Listening

In *The Lost Art of Listening*, Nichols (1995, p. 64) set out a definition of "genuine listening":

> Genuine listening means suspending memory, desire, and judgment—and, for a few moments at least, existing for the other person.

The notion of active listening or, as we call it, *reflective listening* (because the listener is reflecting what he or she has heard) was first popularized by Thomas Gordon in his 1970 best-seller *Parent Effectiveness Training* and then again in his later books: *Teacher Effectiveness Training* (1974) and *Leader Effectiveness Training* (1977). Gordon's influential training books and programs have taught parents, teachers, and administrators, as well as leaders in organizations of every type, the skill of how to listen so that others will talk. The discussion that follows is rooted in Gordon's ideas about effective listening, as well as in ideas from Cheryl Picard's *Mediating Interpersonal and Small Group Conflict* (2002). These ideas are supplemented by our own experience in the practice of mediation.

The skill of reflective listening is used, to some extent, in all models of mediation, but it is not just for mediators. It is a life skill for anyone involved in or helping with conflict. It serves a number of purposes: to demonstrate interest, to help people feel understood, to ensure correct understanding, to let a speaker think about what he or she has said, to encourage the speaker to explain further, to enable a person to express strong emotion, and to perceive the unintended meanings conveyed through non-verbal expression.

Reflective listening involves gathering information, processing and decoding the information, interpreting what the speaker meant, and checking that your interpretation of what was meant is correct. (It is this last step that makes communication reflective.)

Remember that reflective listening involves paying respectful attention to *both* the content *and* the emotion of a speaker's message. Proficiency in the skill of reflective listening involves three sub-skills:

1. attending,
2. paraphrasing, and
3. identifying emotion.

Attending

Attending involves taking account of non-verbal indicators and watching for congruence between what is said and what is expressed non-verbally. These indicators may include actions such as leaning forward; making eye contact in an open, accepting, and non-judgmental manner; and using hand gestures and body posture to indicate interest.

Paraphrasing

Paraphrasing involves *restating* briefly, in your own words, the verbal and emotional content of what the speaker has said, and suspending judgment on it.

Consider the following hypothetical scenario—the mediation of a workplace conflict between Danny and Teresa. (This dispute is fully described in the Workplace Change scenario in Chapter 8; see Box 8.1). Let us suppose that the mediator asks Danny to describe what he needs to talk about in the mediation. This is Danny's response:

> Until Teresa started with us, everything was going fine. We had a good little group going. We had our nose to the wheel and did our work. Our organization has gone through a lot of change in the past five years and we've managed to get through it okay. Don't get me wrong, we aren't against improving things. Computers were introduced to the section recently, and that has worked out, except that a couple of people lost their jobs as a result. We were told that would happen, I guess. Then Teresa starts coming up with all these ideas of doing things differently again! Some of us got upset because it's not one idea she has, it's like 150 ideas! But we said okay, we'll give her ideas a try. The reality is that these ideas have really disrupted our lives, and to make matters worse she doesn't seem to be interested in the changes that, in our view, don't work. Sure, she talks to some of the others in the department, but they're afraid to speak out; I'm not. I've been around for 15 years. I know what I'm doing. These are tough times for all of us and we need to stick together. She can't just go around saying that everything we do here is wrong and that we have to change or perish. Some of us like it the way it is now. I've got 10 years left, and I don't want to die before I retire. There are just so many changes people can take at one time!

The mediator ensures that she fully understands Danny by restating, non-judgmentally, the content of what she has heard. In other words, she uses paraphrase:

> Over the past five years, you've seen lots of changes in your organization. The introduction of computers was one thing. This went okay, although some staff did lose their jobs. Recently, Teresa has approached your group with a number of new ideas, some of which you have given a try. However, you find them disruptive, and you have not found Teresa to be open to hearing about ideas that are not working. While some of the staff are afraid to speak out about how they feel, you are not. You have worked here a long time and it is important to you to continue to have a good working environment, because you hope to work here until you retire.

Danny, after listening to this paraphrase, will let the mediator know whether she has heard his message correctly.

Identifying Emotion

Reflecting emotion involves listening for and naming or responding to the other person's emotion, without appearing negative or judgmental. This skill often requires that you first figure out what those emotions are, since people do not readily share their emotions. Returning to the Workplace Change scenario introduced above, imagine that Danny responds to the mediator's paraphrase by adding more information:

> Well, change leads to people losing their jobs and people being hurt. Take Joe, for example. He is trying to do this new thing suggested by Teresa. But he doesn't know how to do it, and there is no time allotted for people to learn new stuff. Teresa is too busy coming up with ideas to help Joe out. It is embarrassing for him and makes us look incompetent.

The mediator responds by *reflecting* back the emotion that has been exchanged through this new dialogue:

> It is clear, Danny, that you and other colleagues are feeling overwhelmed by the number of changes that are being suggested by Teresa. Not being able to do them has been embarrassing, especially for Joe, and many of you are worried about possible job losses. It seems to you that she is saying nothing you do is right and this is hurtful.

Once again, Danny will tell the mediator whether she has in fact correctly understood his message.

We can't emphasize the following enough: reflective listening, like all skills, has to be learned and practised for it to be effective (see Box 5.3). It is a life skill that can be used by all of us in our everyday lives.

Reflective listening skills are not unique to mediators. Human resource professionals, business people, counsellors, parents, teachers, and others who want to understand what an individual is truly saying use these skills. When you first try to practise reflective listening, it may feel insincere and somewhat artificial. To reduce this sense of artificiality, keep the following in mind:

- Focus on key points rather than trying to get all the details.
- Use your own words—parroting is not appreciated.
- Avoid using lead-ins, such as "So, if I am hearing you correctly ..." or "If I understand what you are saying ..." or "What I think you are saying is ... ." Lead-ins are cumbersome and unnatural.
- Avoid sounding too tentative and unsure. Don't worry, the person will correct you if you are wrong and will appreciate that you are trying to understand them. Good listeners demonstrate close attention.
- Be transparent and honest. If you don't understand, say so—ask for clarification.

BOX 5.3 » Tips for Reflective Listening

- Do not agree or disagree with what has been said.
- Do not take sides.
- Respond to non-verbal clues.
- Shut out distractions and concentrate on what is being said.
- Show understanding through non-verbal gestures such as eye contact, tone of voice, nodding the head, and hand gestures.
- Be sure to *restate* the content (facts) and *reflect* emotion (feelings).
- Be brief and to the point—you do not want to talk for as long as the person you have been listening to.
- Try to put yourself in the other person's shoes and get a sense of what they might be experiencing.
- Avoid interrupting, finishing sentences, or offering suggestions.
- Do not bring up similar problems or feelings from your experience.

Reflective Listening Tools

When you are learning to listen reflectively (actively), you will find it helpful to think in terms of having a job to do that requires a number of different tools. Each of these tools is designed to achieve a particular outcome in specific circumstances. As with any tool, knowing when and how to use it takes knowledge and considerable practice.

Here are six tools that can help a mediator become a reflective listener:

1. *Encouragement.* Encourage the conversation.
2. *Clarification.* Clarify your confusion.
3. *Restatement.* Restate the facts.
4. *Reflection.* Reflect the feelings.
5. *Summarization.* Summarize the major ideas.
6. *Validation.* Validate the effort.

Encourage the Conversation

Showing interest in what the speaker is saying encourages the person to continue talking. It involves the use of both verbal and non-verbal messages.

Gesturing for the person to continue speaking, moving forward in your seat to show you are listening intently, making eye contact, and nodding your head all demonstrate interest. So do short statements, such as "Please go on" or "Say more about that." More pointed statements, such as "I am happy to listen while you talk," "I am interested in hearing more about the changes," and "Talking about our fears often lessens them," provide assurance that you want to listen.

Clarify Your Confusion

When you are no longer able to follow the story, it is hard to continue listening, and the process of gathering information comes to an end. Therefore, it is important to dispel your confusion, even though it may require interrupting the speaker and asking him or her to elaborate on something already said.

Here are examples of two clarifying interventions that a mediator might use in the Danny–Teresa workplace mediation (see Box 8.1, Chapter 8):

> Teresa, I don't understand the acronyms you are using. It would help me if you would explain what is meant by "NLHRS."
>
> Danny, you keep mentioning your little group. Who is it that you are referring to when you speak of this group?

Restate the Facts

You may use this tool to prove that you are listening and to check that you have correctly heard and understood the content of the speaker's message. All messages contain *content* and *emotion*, and restating is a way of confirming that you have correctly understood the former. If you have not, restating provides the speaker with an opportunity to correct your misunderstanding. Do not be afraid if you get the message wrong or leave out important parts. Speakers will let you know if you missed something important, and they will appreciate that you are trying to understand them.

Use your own words when restating. Here is an example of a restatement the mediator might use in the Danny–Teresa workplace mediation:

> One of the things you've mentioned, Danny, is that the group takes exception to the lack of discussion with Teresa about the ideas she has that do not work.

Reflect the Feelings

Reflecting is the tool you use to check out the emotional part of the speaker's message—to confirm your impression of how the person is feeling, based on what he or she said. It requires the listener (you) to use "feeling" words. Sometimes we are fortunate, and speakers will explicitly tell us, in words, how they are feeling. More often, feelings are hidden, and we have to guess at them. We can never know exactly what a person is experiencing because we cannot get inside of them. A person's physical posture, tone of voice, and facial expression are often good clues as to their feelings. An example of a reflecting statement that the mediator might direct at Danny would be the following: "Not being asked for your opinion is frustrating for you and for the group, leaving all of you feeling undervalued."

Many people first learning to mediate find it difficult to find the right feeling word, so here are some of the more common words that reflect both negative and positive emotions.

afraid
annoyed
anxious
appreciated
apprehensive
betrayed
cared for
comfortable
concerned
confident
depressed
disappointed
displeased
eager
embarrassed
excited
excluded
frightened
frustrated
glad
happy
helpless
humiliated
hurt
impatient
irritated
insulted
let down
manipulated
miserable
neglected
nervous
offended
ostracized
pained
perplexed
powerless
provoked
puzzled
rejected
sad
satisfied
scared
secure
shocked
slighted
stressed
supported
surprised
suspicious
trapped
troubled
undecided
undervalued
uneasy
unnerved
unsure
upset
wary
worried

Summarize the Major Ideas

Summarizing involves restating in a condensed form the understandings or perceptions that have been expressed. You can use this tool to review progress, link important ideas, and establish a basis for ongoing discussion. It is also a useful tool when the conversation seems to be going in circles and you want to refocus on key issues. Here is an example of a summarizing statement, once again based on Danny and Teresa's workplace conflict.

> Danny, you and your co-workers are worried about how to implement the changes that Teresa is suggesting, especially since no time has been allotted for retraining. You have not told her about your concerns because you are not sure how tight she is with management, so you would feel vulnerable confessing to her that you are not able to use the new computer system. Teresa, you indicated that learning to use the new system could be done in less than a day. In fact, you could provide this training yourself, and there would be no need for management to be involved. You have not offered to do this before because no one has let you know that they need help. Let's talk more about training.

Validate the Effort

Validating is an important and often underused listening tool. It involves acknowledging and showing appreciation for one party's efforts or actions. In the Workplace Change scenario (Box 8.1, Chapter 8), for example, here is one way the mediator might validate Teresa:

> Teresa, you clearly wanted to jump in when Danny was talking, and I asked you to hang on until he was finished. I appreciate that you allowed him to

finish his point. It is not always easy to refrain from interrupting a person when you have a different point of view. Please tell us what you wanted to say.

Productive Questioning Skills

Since the mediator is there to help parties discover the underlying issues and gain insight into the root of the conflict, he or she must be able to ask useful, productive, and sometimes difficult questions. Questions designed to elicit insights are non-judgmental and do not put parties on the defensive. Rather, they help the parties articulate their values and concerns. Parties trying to negotiate on their own also need to be able to ask open, non-accusatory questions. Cloke (2001) believes mediators should refrain from taking the easy route to a quick compromise. For him, the central task is to help the parties create choices for themselves. This means exploring what sometimes might be dangerous terrain, to help parties get to the heart of the matter. Asking deeply honest questions that elicit the parties' values and concerns, and doing so with empathy, in an environment where the parties feel safe—this is what collaborative problem solving and mediation are all about, in our view.

Mediators use questions to gather information, understand experiences, learn about perspectives, explore issues, discover interests, develop options, and find solutions. The questions asked reflect the mediator's understanding of the goal of mediation and his or her role in it. They shape relations within the mediation and they set the tone. A skilled mediator asks questions that are both purposeful and strategic; a less experienced mediator has a tendency to ask questions that are either too broad and unfocused or too narrow and limiting. The answers to these inexpert questions tend to be vague and noncommittal, making the mediator's job still harder. Asking effective questions, like listening effectively, is a skill that takes considerable practice.

Types of Questions

Basically, there are two types of questions: open-ended and closed-ended. Closed-ended questions yield "yes" or "no" answers. They are useful when we want an individual simply to affirm or deny a statement. They are often used in a courtroom context. But they are not useful when we are trying to discuss something fully or to gather new information. Here are a few examples of closed-ended questions:

> Will it be okay if Danny seeks you out over coffee breaks to discuss his ideas?
>
> Will you give Teresa feedback on her ideas, if she approaches you directly instead of at staff meetings?

Open-ended questions are elicitive; that is, they draw a person out. They invite him or her to go beyond what is already known. They generally start with the words "what," "when," "where," "who," or "how." Occasionally they start with "why," but "why" can be problematic; it often causes a person to feel judged and to become defensive because it shifts the emphasis, from the issue to that person. Open-ended questions (or probing questions, as they are also called) elicit information by encouraging a speaker to provide new information, to expand further on something he or she has said, and to go more deeply into issues and concerns. Here are some examples of very broad open questions:

> What else can you tell me about the situation?
>
> Who else is part of the group?
>
> When were you hoping this would happen?
>
> Where did you plan to take the training?
>
> How would you prefer that Teresa presented new ideas?
>
> Why is this issue so important to you?

Open-ended questions can be used for various purposes. Ten of these purposes are listed below, along with sample questions for each.

1. *To clarify*: "What do you mean when you say that she is pushy?"
2. *To explain*: "What makes you think that he should replace the missing computer?"
3. *To challenge*: "What will happen if the two of you are not able to settle this matter here today?"
4. *To brainstorm*: "What are all the possibilities that you can think of to solve this problem?"
5. *To identify interests*: "What do you fear will happen if she is given access to the files?"
6. *To fact-find*: "How long will it take for you to be able to offer the training?"
7. *To seek opinion*: "What do you think about the idea of meeting during breaks to discuss the group's views?"
8. *To test consequences*: "How do you think he will react to hearing about this decision?"
9. *To problem-solve*: "How have you tried to resolve this problem, and what is preventing you from resolving it now?"
10. *To empower*: "Think back to a time when someone told you that they appreciated your assistance to help work through a tough situation? What did you learn about your capacities through their appreciation, and how might these capacities help you now?"

Broadening and Deepening Questions

Another way to decide what kinds of questions to ask in mediation is to consider whether you want to *broaden* your knowledge about the situation or to *deepen* your understanding of what was said. Broadening questions are "curious" questions designed to expand the information that you and the parties have about the situation. They tend to be general, or non-specific. "What is the problem?" "What brought you here today?" "What is the background to this incident?" Such questions are often fact-finding in nature, seeking to elicit information about what may have helped give rise to the conflict situation.

Deepening questions, on the other hand, go more deeply into information already known. They arise out of the answers given to the broadening questions. They help to peel back the onion, metaphorically speaking. The following short dialogue, in which a broad question is followed by deepening ones, will help you see the difference.

> *Broadening question*: "What is it that you want to talk about here today, Teresa?"
>
> *Response*: "I want to get this problem with Danny settled once and for all! I've had it with him and his little group!"
>
> *Deepening question*: "What is it about Danny's behaviour that is causing you to feel so annoyed and frustrated?"
>
> *Response*: "Well, I keep asking him to tell me if he has problems with my ideas, before we go into meetings, but he never does. Instead, at staff meetings, when I bring forward my ideas for improving the Documents Section, he just says, "No, that would never work here." Then he refuses to discuss why. It is so maddening—even embarrassing at times."
>
> *Deepening question*: "Danny's behaviour is clearly a problem for you. How is it that you find it embarrassing?"
>
> *Response*: "Well, isn't it obvious? I am trying to do a good job by coming up with suggestions that respond to what the staff have been telling me is not working. Danny's constant blocking of my ideas must leave the staff thinking I am either not listening to their concerns or that I don't care. Both of these are so untrue!"

Having obtained insight into Teresa's difficulty with Danny, the mediator now tries to expand her understanding by asking a broadening question.

> *Broadening question*: "Clearly, you want to be seen as doing a good job and this means having the opportunity to present your ideas at staff meetings. How do the others at your meetings respond when Danny rejects your ideas without explanation?"

Remember, the way a question is worded—and the tone in which it is asked—will greatly affect the answer obtained, along with the willingness of a party to continue the discussion. You need to stay curious and avoid judging or problem solving, knowing there is no single truth. Your goal is to seek insight into the meaning of the conflict situation for each of the parties involved.

Connecting Skills

Some communication responses demonstrate "connecting skills." Such responses purposefully link what a mediator has heard or seen with a related question or statement. We discuss three kinds of connecting skills below: bridging, immediacy, and confronting discrepancy.

Bridging

Bridging requires the mediator to do two things: first, determine the meaning of the speaker's statement by paraphrasing what she (the mediator) has heard; and, second, ask a deepening question or make a statement that will lead the speaker to further explore the interests, intent, or assumptions behind the statement. In one of our examples above, based on the Danny–Teresa Workplace Change scenario (Box 8.1, Chapter 8), the mediator offered a paraphrase of one of Danny's statements. Here's an excerpt of that paraphrase, followed by an example of a bridging statement.

> *Paraphrase*: Recently, Teresa has approached your group with a number of new ideas, some of which you have given a try. However, they are disruptive, and you have not found Teresa to be open to hearing about ideas that are not working. … You have worked here a long time and it is important to you to continue to have a good working environment, as you hope to work here until you retire.
>
> *Bridge*: It may help the two of you understand each other better if you would give an example of how Teresa's ideas have been disruptive to the staff and to you, Danny. It would also be helpful if you could tell Teresa why the staff believe she is not open to hearing about ideas they believe will not work.

Here is one more illustration of bridging. The mediator uses a reflecting statement to let Danny know that she heard the emotion behind his statement. This time, however, she follows with a bridge that is in the form of a deepening question.

> *Reflecting statement*: It is clear, Danny, that you and others are feeling overwhelmed by the number of changes that are being suggested by Teresa. Not being able to do them has been embarrassing, especially for Joe, and many of you are concerned about possible job losses. Furthermore, it seems to you that she is saying nothing you do is right and this challenges your sense of professional competence and is hurtful.
>
> *Bridge*: Where is the concern about job loss by the staff coming from, Danny?

A bridging statement or question can also be used to return to information that was discussed previously, or to take the conversation in a new direction. The mediator's bridge might be as follows, for example:

> Danny, earlier you mentioned that in the past the department had done some downsizing. When did this take place and how did it come about?

In general, a mediator uses bridging to take the discussion to a place where, because of what the parties have already said, she believes it needs to go to move towards resolution.

Immediacy

The second connecting skill that we are highlighting here is immediacy. Mediators use this response to deal with what is happening in the moment. It is a skill related to attentiveness and noticing. Focusing on the here and now may require the mediator to interrupt the general direction of the conversation and to attend to strong verbal or non-verbal messages. Through immediacy, the mediator keeps emotions from escalating; she attends to them as they emerge. Immediacy requires proficiency as well as courage. Proficiency enables the mediator to be alert to what is going on between one party and the other, within one or both parties, and within the process itself. Courage enables the mediator to share his or her feelings and thoughts directly and respectfully. The following two examples show the mediator practising the skill of immediacy in the workplace dispute between Danny and Teresa:

> *Example 1*: Teresa, when Danny just told you why he and the staff are concerned about job loss, you shook your head and crossed your arms, which looked to me like an expression of exasperation. What was that all about?
>
> *Example 2*: Danny, when I look at you right now, you appear to be discouraged. Perhaps you are wondering if there is any point in continuing with these discussions. It would be very helpful if you could tell us what you wanted to happen that has not happened—and why you are feeling this way.

Confronting Discrepancy

This connecting skill has three elements: observing, describing, and questioning. Mediators use it to point to discrepancies in words or actions, as well as to point out discrepancies between a person's goals and the actions he or she has taken to achieve them.

Mediators need to use this communication response sparingly and with sensitivity. The parties are capable of hearing it as judgmental, even when this is not the mediator's intention. Tone of voice is critical when a mediator is confronting discrepancy;

use of this skill should convey curiosity rather than blame. Following is an example of the mediator applying this skill to the Danny–Teresa workplace dispute.

> Danny, you have told us a few times now that you want to know what Teresa's job really is. Yet every time she tries to explain her job, you tend to dismiss her explanation. It is hard for Teresa to explain her job when she is cut off and criticized. Could you restate what you have heard her say, thus far, about her job—and why you find this inconsistent with her behavior? Then, Teresa, perhaps you would add what else you would like Danny to understand about your job and what you are trying to achieve.

Non-Blaming and Non-Defensive Response Skills

Non-blaming and non-defensive response skills are part of *assertive communication.* The difference between aggressive communication and assertive communication is not clear to everyone. It is a crucial distinction, however. Assertive communication is a key element in principled negotiation.

Fisher and Ury (1991) clearly distinguish principled negotiation from both "hard bargaining" and "soft bargaining." A hard bargainer, engaged in strong positional negotiation, will typically use aggressive communication that attacks, accuses, or intimidates the other party. Aggressive communication tends to elicit adversarial behaviour and adversarial relations between the parties. In contrast, a so-called soft bargainer will typically use passive communication to avoid confrontation.

A person engaged in principled negotiation uses assertive communication, clearly conveying his or her experiences, feelings, and needs with respect to the conflict interaction. This person uses non-blaming and non-defensive responses. Assertive communication, practised effectively, tends to elicit collaborative behaviour and collaborative relations between the parties.

The aim of assertive communication is twofold:

1. to enable us to say how we feel in a non-accusatory way; and
2. to break the communication pattern of "attack and defend" that prevails when parties feel accused and defensive.

As mediators, we use and encourage these skills of assertive communication when we see that parties are feeling unfairly judged or attacked, and we need to break this pattern.

Non-Blaming Statements

Non-blaming statements are a form of assertive communication known as "I" messages. They contrast with "you" messages, which blame, accuse, threaten, and cause people to feel guilty and to respond defensively. "I" messages tell another person what you perceive, what you feel, why you feel that way, and what you need when you feel that way. Mediators have various purposes when they use this communication tool themselves, including: (1) to let a party know the effect of his or her behaviour on the mediator; and (2) to educate parties in how to improve their pattern of communication.

"I" messages have three basic elements, which can be combined in any order.

- *"I feel"*: This is a statement of your feeling(s), and uses a feeling word.
- *"When"*: This is an objective description of the problem behaviour or situation that causes the feeling.
- *"Because"*: This is an explanation of why the behaviour or situation affects you as it does.

Don't be fooled. The formula may look easy, but in our experience it is difficult to follow, mainly because it is so easy to send disguised "you" messages, unintentionally causing a person to feel negatively judged. The objective is to be clear about how a specific behaviour or action is affecting you rather than assuming the other person is intentionally behaving in a certain way.

To illustrate a non-blaming "I" statement, let's assume that the mediator is speaking, but that Danny starts to speak before the mediator has finished. The mediator intervenes and says the following:

> Danny, a couple of times now, you have started to speak before I finished. When that happens, I feel cut off and that makes it difficult for me to listen to what you clearly want me to hear. What you want me to know is important to me too, so as soon as I finish my thought I will listen to you.

As this example demonstrates, "I" statements need to be clear and appropriately assertive. But remember, "I" messages, even well-intended ones, may result in a person feeling criticized and defensive. It is very important then to notice how the message has been received before carrying on the conversation.

Non-Defensive Responses

The aim of a non-defensive response is to neutralize a verbal attack and break the cycle of attack and defend. To make a non-defensive response, the person being attacked asks for clarification instead of defending his or her position. Asking for clarification involves using an open-ended, inquiring question, such as "What have I done to annoy you?" Non-defensive responses are intended not to give the combative party any further basis from which to attack the speaker. They also try to avoid putting the combative party on the defensive. Like non-blaming statements, the non-defensive response is a skill that takes practice. It also takes patience; often a series of questions is needed before the speaker calms down enough to engage in constructive conversation about the problem. Tone of voice and expression are critical to applying this skill successfully.

Fisher and Ury (1991, p. 108) refer to this type of response as "negotiation jujitsu"—a way to counteract one party's adversarial statements or actions:

> If the other side announces a firm position, you may be tempted to criticize and reject it. If they criticize your proposal, you may be tempted to defend it and dig yourself in. If they attack you, you may be tempted to defend yourself and counterattack. In short, if they push you hard, you will tend to push back. Yet if you do, you will end up playing the positional bargaining game. Rejecting their position only locks them in. Defending your proposal only locks you in. And defending yourself sidetracks the negotiation into a clash of personalities. You will find yourself in a vicious cycle of attack and defense, and you will waste a lot of time and energy in useless pushing and pulling.
>
> If pushing back does not work, what does? How can you prevent the cycle of action and reaction? Do not push back. When they assert their position, do not reject them. When they attack your ideas, don't defend them. When they attack you, don't counterattack. Break the vicious cycle by refusing to react. Instead of pushing back, sidestep their attack and deflect it against the problem. As in the ... martial arts of judo and jujitsu, avoid pitting your strength against theirs directly; instead, use your skill to step aside and turn their strength to your ends. Rather than resisting their force, channel it into exploring interests, inventing options for mutual gain, and searching for independent standards.

To illustrate this communication skill, let's return to the Workplace Change scenario we've been discussing (see Box 8.1, Chapter 8). Suppose that Teresa says the following to Danny:

> Frankly, Danny, I have had just about as much of your dismissive and disgruntled attitude as I can take! You belong with a one-man crew, not here!

Danny wants to understand Teresa's frustration, so he responds non-defensively by asking,

> Teresa, what am I doing that seems so dismissive to you?

However, Teresa is not so easily defused, and she retorts,

> It doesn't matter what I say or do, you trash every idea I bring forward at our meetings.

This time, the mediator intervenes with a non-defensive response:

> Teresa, you are clearly upset. What is it that Danny does that seems so unreasonable and dismissive of your ideas?

Teresa hears that both Danny and the mediator are interested in her frustration, so she begins to offer more useful information:

> Well, for one thing, I brought new proposals to the last two staff meetings. Even before I explained the details, Danny said, "It is too soon for the team to consider new changes." He doesn't even know what my ideas are before he starts rejecting them. It is just not fair or professional.

As a final point, some words and phrases tend to inflame, no matter how benign or generous the intention behind them. Phrases such as "I know how you feel" are presumptuous. We are all separate beings, and our individuality should be respected; we can never truly know how another feels. A better way of expressing empathy might be, "I can understand how you might be feeling about this." People speak from their own experience, so the words we use should describe, not judge. Also, avoid global statements such as "You always" and "You never"; they are dismissive and cause people to feel defensive.

Summary

In this chapter, we have introduced communication skills that are essential to being a competent mediator. These skills include the ability to listen reflectively, to ask questions in a way that elicits information that goes to the root of the problem, and to interact with disputing parties in ways that are encouraging and non-judgmental. Learning to communicate effectively and to promote effective communication is essential to good mediation.

As with any ability, being a competent mediator starts with knowledge, analysis, understanding, and a great deal of practice. These are what lead you to achieve a level of fluency and unconscious competence. In other words, you reach a level where you have integrated theory and practice and can apply them in a holistic and organic way.

DISCUSSION QUESTIONS AND EXERCISES

1. Discuss in small groups how each of you typically talks when you find yourself in conflict with someone at home, at school, or at work. How effective is this way of talking? How do others react to it? How able are you to get your point across? How able are they to get their point across to you? After reading this chapter, how might you talk differently the next time you are in conflict?
2. Why is giving your friend advice about how to deal with a conflict she is having with her friend, even when she solicits this advice from you, a communication blocker?
3. What is emotional communication and how may it affect a conflict interaction? What are some ways to respond effectively to these challenges?
4. Identify some communication blockers that you have or use. For example, do you find yourself giving advice to friends or siblings as a way of trying to be helpful? Have you ever tried to reassure a co-worker when he encountered a

problem, thinking you were being supportive? Over the next few days, prepare an account of the communication blockers you may have created by your behaviours, emotions, or assumptions. In preparing this journal, you may want to answer some of the questions below:

a. Have you ever been aware of your own communication blockers?
b. Which one or ones have occurred most often? In what situations did they occur?
c. What are some of your limiting assumptions?
d. What impact did these blockers have on your communications and on your relations with the people involved?
e. When they occurred, how were you feeling (for example, impatient, bored, preoccupied, rushed)?
f. What could you do differently to improve your communications in these situations?

5. Reread this chapter's Performance Review scenario (Box 5.2).
   a. Based only on what Joe and Sara said to each other, what would be your impression of the state of their working relationship? Taking into account Joe's suppressed dissatisfaction, what would you say are the consequences of this latent conflict for their ongoing working relationship?
   b. How might this affect Joe's ongoing work and future advancement in this organization?
   c. How might Joe communicate his dissatisfaction and conflict emotions to Sara more effectively, in a way that would be beneficial for both of them?

FURTHER READING

Gudykunst, W.B. (1991). *Bridging differences: Effective intergroup communication.* Newbury Park, CA: Sage.

LeBaron, M. (2002). *Bridging troubled waters: Conflict resolution from the heart.* San Francisco: Jossey-Bass.

Nichols, M. (1995). *The lost art of listening.* New York: Guilford Press.

Picard, C.A. (2002). *Mediating interpersonal and small group conflict.* Ottawa: Golden Dog Press.

Rosenberg, M.B. (2003). *Nonviolent communication: A language of life.* Encinitas, CA: Puddle Dancer Press.

Stone, D. & Heen, S. (2014). *Thanks for the feedback: The science and art of receiving feedback well.* New York: Viking.

Stone, D., Patton, B., & Heen, S. (1999). *Difficult conversations: How to discuss what matters most.* New York: Penguin.

Winslade, J. & Monk. G. (2000). *Narrative mediation: A new approach to conflict resolution.* San Francisco: Jossey-Bass.

Websites

Communication and Conflict: http://www.communicationandconflict.com

This website offers information, support, and resources to individuals and groups experiencing conflict and to conflict resolution and mediation specialists. Some of the features posted on this website include: principles of effective interpersonal communication; underlying philosophies of mediation; and communication skills to be effective communicators.

Conflict Resolution Network (CRN): http://www.crnhq.org

Conflict Resolution Network offers communication and conflict resolution skills to build stronger organizations and more rewarding relationships. It provides books, trainers' manuals, audio and video tapes, DVDs, and posters. These materials enhance communication skills that are relevant for such focus areas as management, facilitation, gender, negotiation, mediation, training support, and more.

REFERENCES

Burr, V. (1995). *An introduction to social constructionism.* New York: Routledge.

Cloke, K. (2001). *Mediating dangerously: The frontiers of conflict resolution.* San Francisco: Jossey-Bass.

Cornelius, H., & Faire, S. (1989). *Everyone can win: How to resolve conflict.* East Brookvale, NSW: Simon & Schuster.

Covey, S.R. (1989). *The seven habits of highly successful people.* New York: Freeside.

Fisher, R., & Ury, W. (1991). *Getting to yes: Negotiating agreement without giving in* (2nd ed.). New York: Penguin Books. Copyright © 1981, 1991 by Roger Fisher and William Ury. Reprinted by permission of Houghton Mifflin Company. All rights reserved.

Folger, J., & Jones, T. (Eds.). (1994). *New directions in mediation: Communication research and perspectives.* Thousand Oaks, CA: Sage.

Gergen, K.J. (1999). *An invitation to social constructionism.* Thousand Oaks, CA: Sage.

Gordon, T. (1970, 1975, 2000). *Parent effectiveness training: The proven program for raising responsible children.* New York: Three Rivers Press.

Gordon, T. (1974). *Teacher effectiveness training.* New York: Three Rivers Press.

Gordon, T. (1977). *Leader effectiveness training.* Toronto: Bantam.

Gudykunst, W.B. (1991). *Bridging differences: Effective intergroup communication.* Newbury Park, CA: Sage.

Gulliver, P. (1979). *Disputes and negotiations: A cross-cultural perspective.* New York: Academic Press.

Hofstede, G., Hofstede, G.J., & Minkov, M. (2010). *Cultures and organizations: Software of the mind.* (3rd ed.). New York: McGraw-Hill.

Katz, N.H., & Lawyer, J.W. (1994). *Resolving conflict successfully: Needed knowledge and skills.* Thousand Oaks, CA: Corwin Press.

Lakoff, G., & Johnson, M. (1980). *Metaphors we live by*. Chicago: University of Chicago Press.

Nichols, M. (1995). *The lost art of listening*. New York: Guilford Press.

Picard, C.A. (2002). *Mediating interpersonal and small group conflict* (2nd ed.). Ottawa: Golden Dog Press.

Retzinger, S., & Scheff, T. (2000). Emotion, alienation and narratives: Resolving intractable conflict. *Mediation Quarterly*, *18*, 71–85.

Sargent N., Picard, C., & Jull, M. (2011). Rethinking conflict: Perspectives from the insight approach. *Negotiation Journal*, *27*(8), 343–366.

Stone, D., Patton, B., & Heen, S. (1999). *Difficult conversations: How to discuss what matters most*. New York: Penguin.

Winslade, J., & Monk, G. (2000). *Narrative mediation*. San Francisco: Jossey-Bass.

CHAPTER 6

Convening and Preparing for a Mediation

LEARNING OBJECTIVES

After reading this chapter, you will be able to:

- Understand the convening process and how it works
- Understand how to prepare parties for mediation
- Identify the three phases of convening and explain the activities involved in each phase
- Explain the four criteria used to determine the suitability of mediation
- Understand the considerations involved in selecting a mediator
- Identify the benefits of co-mediation

CHAPTER OUTLINE

Introduction 155
What Is Convening? 155
What Does Convening Entail? 158
The Convening Process 162
How Convening Varies in Different Situations 164
A Framework for Convening 165
Mediator Selection 178
Pre-Mediation: Preparing for Mediation 182
Summary 185

Spectacular achievement is always preceded by unspectacular preparation.

Robert H. Schuller

Introduction

In this chapter, we examine the process of **convening** and screening candidates for mediation. Our examination considers what makes a conflict situation generally suitable for mediation, and we set out the basic elements of convening: the objectives and goals of the process, a framework for conducting convening interviews, and the criteria for assessing whether the parties should pursue mediation. This chapter also includes a discussion of pre-mediation—the stage at which the mediator works with the parties to prepare them for mediation.

What Is Convening?

Convening is the process by which an impartial person—that is, the convenor—helps the parties determine whether and how mediation might help them resolve their conflict issues. In some cases, the same person is both convenor and mediator.

In others, the convenor begins the process, then passes it on to the person who will be mediating the case.

Mediation is not a guaranteed fix for every conflict. In some cases, it is not the appropriate process. Mediation would not be appropriate where

- the issues are not negotiable, as with some human rights violations;
- the power differential between disputants is too great for uninhibited conversation; or
- one or both parties have no interest in resolving the issues, as when one party plans to remove himself from the relationship of conflict.

Advocates of mediation favour an assessment to determine whether mediation is suitable for a particular case. This is a primary aim of convening. Again, mediation is sometimes not appropriate. For example, family conflicts where there has been a history of domestic violence or where there are unequal power relations between the marriage partners may not be well served by mediation—one spouse may feel threatened by the other and may be, in consequence, susceptible to being intimidated into agreeing to terms that are not in her interest. Some critics suggest that, in such cases, family mediation outcomes are often unfair to the party with less power—usually the women involved (see Benjamin & Irving, 1992, pp. 133, 143–147; Astor, 1995; Kolb & Putnam, 2005). To prevent the misuse of mediation, family mediation networks have developed a screening tool to determine whether domestic violence and abuse are an element in the conflict in question. Using this tool is compulsory if one is a certified member of a family mediation network such as Family Mediation Canada or the Ontario Association for Family Mediation (see the websites for these organizations at the end of the chapter).

Who Convenes?

Many community-based mediation programs use paid case-development officers to conduct the convening process, and volunteer mediators to facilitate the actual mediation sessions. Most federal government departments and agencies now have in-house mediation programs that use coordinators or directors to perform intake and convening tasks, while staff or external mediators perform the mediation services.

While it is common for mediation programs, whether based in the community or in the workplace, to have a person formally dedicated to the function of convening, this is not always the case. A modified convening process can be undertaken by people in human resources, by those in the labour relations field, by union executive members, by representatives from equity and human rights advisory groups, and by staff in supervisory positions. This modified process entails learning about the conflict situation and ascertaining, at least at a superficial level, which dispute resolution methods would best address the situation.

In court-connected mediation programs, most of the convening function falls to the mediator; he or she will determine whether mediation can help the parties. In many workplaces, the human resources professional trying to address conflict among employees may not have the knowledge to make such determinations. However, he or she may refer the case to a mediator. In these cases, the mediator retained will determine whether mediation is appropriate, and will provide the parties with some basic information about the process.

In other contexts, the convenor may also take on the role of mediator, should the parties go forward with mediation. This commonly occurs in private practice, where there is only one person performing convening and mediation activities. It also occurs in programs that are staffed by a single mediator, such as a program manager. In international mediation processes, convenors may be former heads of state or eminent persons, expected both to convene and to lead the mediation. They often have staff who meet members from the different sides and prepare parties for negotiations. When the convenor represents a state, he or she may have a stake or interest in the mediation outcome and may not be perceived as entirely neutral. For example, in 2014, US Secretary of State John Kerry attempted to bring Israel and Palestine to the table for peace negotiations. It is difficult to imagine the US as "neutral" in these dialogues, since the US government consistently remarks that Israel is and will remain an unconditional ally. No such remarks are ever made in favour of Palestine, nor is the Palestinian Authority offered the same opportunities as Israel to purchase American weapons.

Convenors as Mediators

There are benefits to having the convenor also serve as the mediator:

- the convenor has already developed a relationship of trust with all parties;
- he or she has gained a solid understanding of the issues in advance; and
- he or she is familiar with the parties' communication and negotiating styles.

All of these factors contribute to the effectiveness and efficiency of the mediation. In fact, we have noted that many parties prefer to use the convenor as their mediator; they like the fact that, when the mediation process begins, they have an established relationship of trust with the person conducting the process. This is particularly true when the disputants are from cultural groups in which mediators are normally people well known to the disputants, such as respected elders or religious or community leaders.

Some commentators have expressed doubt about whether one person should perform both roles. Their concern is that a convenor may form conclusions about the conflict that make him or her less curious and open-minded in the mediation phase. Such an individual may base his or her strategy for the mediation on misleading or incomplete information.

On the other hand, mediators must learn to approach all conflicts in an open-minded, non-judgmental manner. An experienced, competent mediator—one who remains curious and open-minded throughout the process—should have no problem doing the convening, the pre-mediation, and the mediation. In all three of these phases, the third-party intervenor is working with the disputants to prepare them for the joint session dialogue and to make them more receptive to one another's conflict narrative. Being curious and open-minded is the key to success for any intervenor, whether convenor or mediator.

It is common for the mediator to do most, if not all, of the convening and pre-mediation work with the parties in the following kinds of disputes:

- family,
- court-connected,
- commercial,
- environmental, and
- other public disputes.

In this chapter, we refer to the person who carries out the tasks of first contact, intake, and assessment as the convenor, with the understanding that any or all of these tasks may be completed by a mediator.

What Does Convening Entail?

Convening consists of three phases:

1. It begins with the "first contact"—that is, when someone connected to the situation, either one of the disputants or a referral agent, gets in touch with the convenor to explore whether mediation is suitable for the conflict.
2. The second phase is commonly known as "intake and assessment." During this phase, the convenor begins to collect information about the conflict, as well as to provide the party or parties with information about mediation, its principles, and what they can reasonably expect of the process. The convenor and parties then assess whether mediation is appropriate and determine what other information, research, and preparation the parties may require before deciding whether to use mediation.
3. If the parties do decide to use mediation, they move on to the third and final phase of the convening process: selecting a mediator.

The convenor may undertake another task—namely, helping the parties become ready, willing, and able to use mediation. However, this function is generally fulfilled by the mediator before the first joint mediation session.

After the parties have decided to use mediation and have selected a mediator, the next phase begins. This is the pre-mediation phase, during which the mediator works with the parties to prepare them for mediation. This preparation may include

- coaching parties in their communication;
- discussing their needs with regard to collecting information such as collective agreement points, legal requirements, and policy details, in order to be fully informed in the mediation process;
- providing parties with the orientation they need to engage in dialogue within the mediation process; and
- asking questions that constitute a reality check, so that the parties have a clear understanding of their alternatives to mediation and the implications, financial or otherwise, of not resolving the situation.

The pre-mediation process varies depending on the type of mediation and the particular situation. Family/community conferencing and victim–offender mediation, for example, are distinct types of mediation, and their pre-mediation processes are distinct. The pre-mediation process is distinct, too, in a case where the disputants are groups, represented by agents or select members. In cases involving multiple parties or large groups on one side or the other—for example, land-use or environmental disputes or peace mediation—the convening and pre-mediation phases usually require more time and consultation than they do with other types of mediation. Pre-mediation is discussed in greater detail later in this chapter.

Convening requires a good deal of knowledge not only about the potential of mediation, but also about its limitations. The scenario described in Box 6.1 is a typical neighbourhood conflict, and it illustrates some of the complexity involved in helping people choose the best possible process for their situation.

BOX 6.1 » Scenario: Not in My Backyard

Mr. Morgan is a professor of law at the University of Wisdom. He lives in Yogaville, next door to the Ozmans, a recently arrived immigrant family of seven. His wife runs her own catering business in an upscale neighbourhood. Mrs. Ozman is a single parent of six children, who range in age from 4 to 16. She lost her husband and eldest child in the war that has been waging in her native country. It was her fear of losing other family members to the war that brought her to Canada. (She also has a cousin who lives close by with his family.)

Recently, Mr. Morgan and Mrs. Ozman stopped speaking to one another. The event that brought about this tension occurred the previous week, when Mr. Morgan saw Mrs. Ozman's son starting to chop down the beautiful old maple tree in the Ozman's back yard. Though it grows in the Ozman's yard, the branches of the tree extend into the Morgans' yard. Mr. Morgan began yelling at the boy that he was desecrating a heritage tree and that he had better stop, or Mr. Morgan would call the municipality and the police. The Ozman boy was stunned. He did not know, nor did his mother, that he could be told what to do on his own property! He began arguing with and swearing at Mr. Morgan, who nearly hit him.

The tree does extend into the Morgan's yard and forms a quite lovely shaded area for the summer garden parties that the Morgans like to have. Mr. Morgan believes that it will destroy the ambience of his backyard; moreover, he doesn't want to see such a beautiful tree destroyed.

For the Ozmans, who had no idea their new country could get so cold in winter, the tree could provide weeks of firewood to heat their home more effectively than does the electric heating they currently rely on. On his own initiative, the Ozman boy thought that he would help out his mother and his family by making firewood.

Mr. Morgan has approached Community Mediation Services (CMS), a four-year-old organization devoted to resolving neighbourhood disputes in Yogaville, to settle his conflict with Mrs. Ozman. CMS has been funded by the municipality, and it offers a free service to residents in the community.

CMS has agreed to mediate this dispute and has appointed Ruth Callaghan, a strong volunteer mediator who has been with CMS for its entire existence. Ruth is now retired, but she worked for many years for a municipal court judge. It's not unusual to find volunteers like Ruth at CMS, where many white-collar professionals seeking career changes test whether mediation might be a new career. Ruth would eventually like to mediate in the court-mandated program in Yogaville. She has also just taken a two-day course in diversity and believes that she will be sensitive to the cultural needs of Mrs. Ozman.

Some Questions for the Convening Stage

The Ozman–Morgan case demonstrates the challenge of convening and how complicated it can be to decide about going to mediation. Following are three of the many questions that arise in this case:

1. *What is the law concerning cutting down maple trees on private property?*
   This question is useful and probably necessary to both parties' perspectives, but the conflict is not likely to be resolved by answering it. The convenor will need to know more about the relationship between the neighbours, about other misunderstandings they may have had in the past, and—most likely—the role that cultural values may play in the conflict.
2. *How balanced is the power dynamic in this particular situation?*
   Certainly, Mr. Morgan has an advantage over the Ozmans in this regard. As a law professor, he would be familiar with the legal parameters of the case, and quite knowledgeable about rights and entitlements. Mrs. Ozman and her family, as newcomers to Canada, will likely not have such extensive knowledge of these matters. Moreover, the fact that the Ozmans will be speaking English as a second language might also place them at a disadvantage. A skilled mediator or co-mediation team would be aware of socio-economic,

linguistic, and other power inequities that could affect the balance in mediation. A cultural interpreter might also help the process along.

3. *Who should mediate this case?*
   While there is no doubt that Ruth Callaghan, the volunteer mediator with CMS, has a certain type of experience, it is not certain that she would be the best candidate to mediate the Ozman–Morgan case. First impressions lead us to think that she may come from the same background as the Morgans and may share their values. One might consider using a mediator who has knowledge and experience with cross-cultural conflict, someone who can relate to the Ozmans and to their experience. Perhaps a co-mediation team, with balanced values and experiences that are more representative of all parties, would be the best alternative.

Here are some other questions to consider in the convening stage of the prospective Ozman–Morgan mediation:

- What do the parties themselves—the Ozmans and the Morgans—really think is causing this conflict?
- Before this conflict arose, what was the relationship between the families?
- If they had the opportunity to replay the conflict, what would they have done differently?
- How has this conflict affected them?
- What does the conflict mean?
- For the Morgans, what is the most important thing that the Ozmans need to understand?
- For the Ozmans, what is the most important thing that the Morgans need to understand?
- What does each side believe has caused the conflict?
- What kind of relationship would each side like to have with their neighbours?
- What would they need to get there?
- What options do they have available to them to resolve this conflict?
- What process is most likely to assist them in reaching their goals?
- What form of mediation and style of mediator would be most helpful in this case?
- How comfortable would the Morgans and Ozmans be in mediation?
- What accommodations, if any, would they be seeking?
- Are there negotiable issues to mediate?

This list of questions is by no means exhaustive. However, it does give you a sense of the convenor's work and of the importance of collecting necessary information. Convening a mediation is a time-consuming and complex undertaking. Let's now look more closely at the actual process of convening.

The Convening Process

A convenor listens to the parties carefully and actively, summarizes information, and asks pertinent and often difficult questions. The process is not unlike that of the actual mediation, with the convenor exploring the parties' interests, needs, values, anticipated consequences, and perspectives, and trying to ascertain the meaning that each side ascribes to the conflict. The convenor must be a skilled listener and communicator, able to draw upon his well-developed mediation skills and techniques.

By and large, convening, like mediation, is a responsive process. This means that the convenor takes cues from the parties while conversing with them. People's requirements tend to vary. Some people need to speak about their situation before they can really listen to a convenor. In these instances, the convenor begins by listening actively, building trust, and demonstrating understanding. Other people may not be comfortable speaking about their conflict until they have clear information about the mediation process. In this situation, the convenor responds by providing the parties with an overview of the goals, roles, and processes of mediation. Written or visual materials—brochures, information sheets, flyers, or videos of mock mediations—can be very helpful in supplementing this overview. Convening requires both knowledge and intuitive skills, since the convenor tries to "read" the needs of the parties to determine whether mediation is suitable for them and will meet their expectations.

Now that you understand *what* convening is, let us discuss *why* convening is undertaken. First and foremost, convening helps the parties begin to think and speak differently about the situation, a process that will, ideally, continue in the pre-mediation phase. To promote this process, the convenor needs to

1. build trust,
2. have the parties reflect on the situation,
3. determine whether mediation is suitable for the conflict in question,
4. ensure that the parties are making an informed choice, and
5. prepare the parties for mediation.

Let's look at each of these tasks more closely.

Building Trust

Early in the convening process, the convenor works to develop a rapport with the parties, trying to gain their trust and confidence. Doing so encourages frank discussion and full disclosure. This enables the convenor to extract the information necessary to understand the situation and determine whether mediation is suitable.

Encouraging Reflection

One of the convenor's main tasks is to help the parties reflect on the situation—in other words, to help them think about their motivations, about the meaning of the conflict and its effects, about their needs, and about their options for resolving the conflict. This leads to a fuller understanding of the conflict for everyone involved and thereby increases the parties' capacity to make decisions about what they need. This process of reflection is particularly important when the parties are reticent about mediation or firmly believe that they are in the right and have a strong chance of success through formal or legal processes.

Determining Whether Mediation Is Suitable

An important task for both the convenor and the parties is to determine whether mediation is appropriate and likely to be helpful. This enables them to decide whether to proceed with it.

Ensuring Informed Choices

The parties must know the full range of dispute resolution processes available to them—from no action at all to litigation—and which ones are likely to work best for them. Only then can the convenor be sure that the parties are making an informed choice and will in consequence be committed to the process they choose. The convenor's overriding objective is to help the parties choose a process that is most responsive to their needs. While the convenor may not be responsible for providing *detailed* information about options other than mediation, he or she ought to encourage parties to seek out this information.

Preparing the Parties

If the disputants are good candidates for mediation, the convenor may begin to prepare them for it by performing some of the functions usually done by the mediator in the pre-mediation phase. The convenor may, for example, begin encouraging them to think about

- what their values, needs, and interests are;
- how to express themselves;
- how to test the realism of their alternatives; and
- what their overall hopes for the session are.

To prepare the parties, convenors sometimes give them materials to read or activities to complete. A party in the convening stage, trying to decide on a dispute resolution process, may need to collect further data or carry out more research. If the party is an agent of a larger group, he or she may need to consult with members of the group before continuing with the process. All of this ensures the best possible preparation for mediation; it gives the parties a realistic perspective on the process and its potential for success.

Whether parties opt for mediation or decide to pursue another process, they will benefit from the convening phase. We have heard many people say, after going through this process, "You have made me think about things differently. No one ever asked me those kinds of questions."

How Convening Varies in Different Situations

The process of convening will vary depending on the type of conflict involved. One variable concerns who will perform the convening function, and whether the convenor will also act as the mediator should the case go forward, as we have already discussed. In legal disputes where both parties are represented by lawyers, the lawyers often undertake the convening. Many lawyers have experience with mediation and have a good understanding of what occurs and can be achieved in mediation. The lawyers often begin discussing the process with their clients and with each other, and these discussions may culminate in a decision to use mediation.

Convening for Court-Connected Mediation

The convening process for court-connected mediation usually involves lawyers. The mediator, a private practitioner recommended by the parties' lawyers, usually connects with the parties' counsel by phone. The convening process undertaken at this point is truncated, since the mediation will inevitably go forward in the case of mandatory mediation. The mediators are provided with a written statement of facts and issues from each side in the dispute.

Convening for Multi-Party, Environmental, and Other Public Disputes

Multi-party public disputes, such as environmental disputes, also tend to use private practitioners as mediators. The mediator takes on the convening role here, but with a different twist. Public multi-stakeholder disputes, by virtue of the numbers involved, are not conducive to individual interviews.

For an illustration, recall the Sonata Development scenario from the end of Chapter 2 (see Exercise 1). In that scenario, as you may remember, a suburban community group and home developer were in conflict. It would be far too time-consuming for the convenor to interview each and every member of the community group before mediation. In this case, convening would likely take place with either one or several representatives of the community group and with one or several representatives of Haven Homes, the developer. Some convenors might meet with the entire community group in a town-hall session, in order to learn about all the concerns and to help the group develop consensus concerning its needs. In addition, the representative for the city government would be interviewed during the convening process.

Convening for International Disputes

As mentioned above, mediators of international peace processes frequently perform the functions of the convenor, with the assistance of staff and associates. Many international mediations involve group efforts. The convening process here would therefore be similar to the one for public multi-party disputes, with various meetings taking place between the convenor and the representatives of the different factions. The mediator's staff and associates would help in this process, eliciting the information required from the large and diverse groups.

Convening for Community-Based Mediation and Restorative Justice Programs

Most community-based mediation and neighbourhood justice programs have separate people working as mediators and convenors. Staff, often the program directors or case developers, undertake convening, while volunteer mediators are used for the mediation sessions themselves. The use of volunteers to mediate disputes is also found in victim–offender and other restorative justice programs, although these processes tend to have much stiffer screening criteria and lengthier preparation than other types of community-based disputes.

Convening for Workplace Mediation

Increasing numbers of organizations and large businesses have in-house mediation programs. Employees in dispute meet with the mediation program coordinator or director for a convening process. The coordinator may or may not mediate the case herself, if it proceeds to mediation. Workplaces without in-house programs retain private mediators to conduct both convening and mediation sessions.

A Framework for Convening

Whatever the particular form it takes, convening always needs to address certain issues. Below, we provide a model for convening.

This framework, or model, for convening consists of three stages. (See Figure 6.1.) Any convenor, regardless of his or her particular style, will need to go through these stages at some point, and some convenors may revisit certain stages several times during the process. In general, the three stages can include anything from one meeting or telephone conversation to several meetings with each party, before mediation begins. (Remember that some parties may opt for a dispute resolution process other than mediation, once they understand the principles of mediation.)

The three-stage framework outlined in Figure 6.1 is usually the model for convening when the conflict issues are interpersonal and the group is not large. As we suggested above, public multi-stakeholder disputes, by virtue of the numbers involved, are not conducive to individual interviews with everyone. In these cases, convenors

Figure 6.1 The Three Stages of Convening

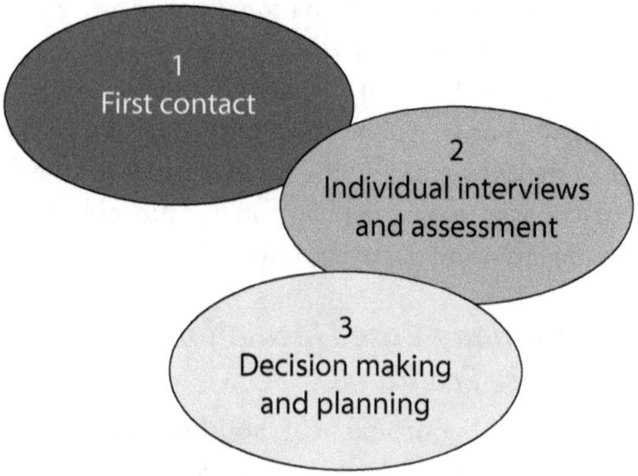

often interview spokespersons, or representatives. Convenors must be sure to contact these representatives and discuss with them the mediation and everyone's roles within it, so that the parties have realistic expectations of the process.

Stage 1 in the convening process (first contact) is when the convenor or mediator comes to know about the conflict. In Stage 2 (individual interviews and assessment), the convenor, either in person or by phone, contacts all those involved to elicit information about the situation, about the parties' needs, and about the viability of mediation. The convenor will educate each party about mediation, assess whether mediation is suitable, and consider, with the parties, how any limitations they perceive may be overcome, and how any concerns they have may be accommodated. In Stage 3 (decision making and planning), the convenor, in collaboration with the parties, concludes the convening process with the following steps: deciding whether to use mediation; determining what measures need to be taken, if any, to accommodate the parties; selecting a mediator; and making plans for the mediation process.

Stage 1: First Contact

People come to mediation for many reasons. People involved in any of the following may initiate contact with a convenor: public disputes; environmental conflicts; divorce and separation, as well as custody and access issues; collective bargaining and union grievances; and disputes requiring a mandatory mediation process. In any of these instances, legal counsel is often the first to propose mediation to the disputant. When parties contact a mediation service directly, they have often already tried other dispute resolution processes and found them wanting.

In workplaces, contact with a convenor may be initiated by a third party—someone who knows one or both parties, yet is not directly involved in the conflict. This third party might be

- a supervisor,
- a union representative,
- a lawyer,
- a co-worker,
- a representative of another dispute resolution office,
- personnel from the ombudsman's office,
- human resources personnel, or
- a human rights or employment equity adviser.

This third party, checking out the viability of mediation for the situation at hand, is considered to be the referral agent. The referral agent usually seeks information about the use of mediation to resolve the conflict and about his or her role in such a process. A supervisor, for example, may contact mediation services after becoming frustrated in her efforts to deal with two employees who cannot get along. In a situation where harassment is alleged and a formal complaint process has not yet been chosen, a human rights adviser might recommend mediation. Supervisors and human rights advisers are the most common referral agents for mediation services offered within organizations. When mediation services are provided to an organization by external mediators on a contractual basis, the referral most frequently comes from a human resources department.

In the case of international conflicts, mediators are usually selected and solicited by concerned third parties, such as the United Nations (UN) or a regional governmental organization such as the African Union. In these situations, the concerned third party can set up meetings between the prospective mediator and all parties to the dispute, so that the mediator can meet them and begin discussions about a dialogue process. International mediations that are established through the UN usually involve a "group of friends." These are representatives of countries that have an interest in or commitment to resolving the conflict and that provide resources—financial, human, and other—to support the convening work of the UN, as well as the dialogues themselves once they are underway. The UN also now has a Mediation Support Unit, staffed by skilled mediators who have expertise in a variety of contexts such as natural resources, gender, security sector reform, and constitution making (Whitfield, 2010; UN Department of Political Affairs, 2014).

For victim–offender reconciliation programs, a spiritual adviser, lawyer, or someone within the criminal justice or corrections system, such as the police department, the Crown attorney's office, or the probation service, refers the offender to the process. In many instances, community-based disputes arrive at mediation services through the recommendation of social service or health departments, or of municipal housing offices.

In many dispute situations, lawyers are required to inform clients about the possibility of mediation, and may contact a service themselves to explore its suitability. Because of the heavy reliance on referrals to mediation, it is necessary that private practice mediators and mediation programs within organizations develop strong relationships with referral agents.

Another possibility is for one of the parties involved in the conflict to contact a convenor, to explore whether mediation might be constructive in his or her situation. In interpersonal disputes, the party may be uncomfortable about making first contact: he or she may believe that it is a weakness not to be able to resolve conflicts on one's own or may find it difficult to discuss personal issues with a stranger. A party who contacts a convenor in this way is likely seeking information about mediation, and looking for assistance and support in resolving the situation. Approaches of this kind occur most frequently in community-based mediation programs or in the conflict resolution services found in some workplaces.

Asking a community leader, religious leader, or elder for assistance in resolving a conflict is very common in close-knit, homogeneous communities, where disputes are traditionally resolved by this means. Community-based dispute resolution takes place all over the world, every day—whenever someone approaches a wise member of his or her community for assistance with a problem. Sometimes the process works the other way around: community leaders, on their own initiative, may approach the parties who are involved in a conflict that is disrupting the community harmony.

Less commonly, all the parties involved in the conflict will approach a convenor. In this instance, parties have already agreed that mediation can help them solve their conflict. Public and environmental disputes might use this approach. Divorcing couples, too, may arrive at mediation by this route. For the convenor, this situation is ideal, because the parties themselves have some understanding of mediation and have selected it as the first option to resolve their conflict.

Another way that disputes come to mediation is through the convenor or through the mediator. He or she might hear about a conflict situation and seek to contact either the parties involved or a referral agent, to offer the services of mediation. These are known as "cold contacts"—where the convenor enters a conflict situation without any invitation.

These kinds of contacts usually occur with public conflicts, possibly ones that are getting media attention. In such cases, the convenor is simply ensuring that those who are involved in the conflict have an awareness of mediation. In the case of the Sonata Development scenario set out at the end of Chapter 2, for example, the convenor might contact both the community group's chairperson and the manager of the Haven Homes development. In such situations, convenors must act with a great deal of sensitivity and compassion because the parties are likely to be surprised at being approached and may become defensive.

In all cases of first contact, the convenor's first duty is to put the party at ease through skilled listening and empathy. When meeting with the disputants, the convenor needs to collect information from the parties about certain matters and discuss other aspects of the mediation process with them: confidentiality requirements; the information needs of the superior, the union representative, or other people who have been or should be informed; information about rights or entitlements, and about the law; and information concerning other dispute resolution methods the parties should explore before proceeding. There may also be some discussion of the following: the party's concerns about mediation and how to address them; the consequences of not addressing the conflict or of addressing it through another process; and what people, if any, the parties would like to have present for support, expertise, or comfort in a mediated process. Usually, the convenor also discusses with each party the best way to approach the others involved.

Stage 2: Individual Interviews and Assessment

Here, the convenor and parties in conflict gather and sift through information, determining whether mediation is a good way to resolve the conflict. In our opinion, preparation is essential, and this stage constitutes the core of convening.

Individual meetings help the convenor gain a general understanding of various matters: the issues; the parties' needs, particularly with respect to support, accommodation, or adaptations in mediation; the appropriateness of mediation; and the strengths and characteristics required of mediators. Without individual meetings, key information can go missing.

When contact has been initiated through a referral agent or through a phone message left by a party, the convenor should get in touch with the parties as soon as possible, ideally within 24 hours. Delays can diminish the chances of a successful mediation. As it is, people in conflict tend to wait too long to contact mediation services. This tendency toward lateness becomes more acute when organizations request the services of an external mediator. Often, by the time a mediator in private practice receives a request for services, the dispute in question has already been dealt with by the organization's human resources department, or unions have become involved, or perhaps an adversarial process (such as a grievance, a harassment complaint, or even a legal suit) has commenced. The longer a situation festers, the greater the likelihood that people will entrench their positions, lash out at the other party, escalate the conflict, and harden their stance toward adversarial options (Folger, Poole, & Stutman, 1993, pp. 10–11).

Individual interviews can take place in person or by phone. The average time spent in such interviews is about an hour or so for each person. However, they can take considerably longer, depending upon the complexity of the disputes and parties, as well as on the cultural norms for relationship building and communication.

In our experience, it is best to conduct convening face to face. When convening is done over the phone, the convenor is more likely to miss subtle cues from the parties and opportunities for trust building with them. There are other reasons to favour in-person interviews. If one of the parties is elderly, has a disability, or is from a minority cultural group, in-person interviews will make communication clearer for both the party and the convenor. If there is a language barrier, it is much more beneficial to meet in person and use an interpreter, if necessary. If the case involves some complicated issues, in-person meetings will provide fuller understanding. Sometimes the party is not free to speak over the phone owing to a lack of privacy in his or her environment; in this case, a face-to-face interview enables a free flow of information. And in a situation where the party is particularly anxious about the conflict and about resolving it, the convenor can provide more support in person.

Exchanging information can be time-consuming and complex. It is a process well suited to individual interviews, which offer the benefit of not usually being linear. Given the importance of building rapport and legitimacy throughout this second stage, convenors need to be flexible and responsive. This will enable them to understand the conflict from the perspective of the parties being interviewed, so they can help them decide how to proceed. To demonstrate the complexity of this interview stage of convening, we have broken it down into five tasks:

1. setting a comfortable climate,
2. exploring the conflict,
3. educating the parties,
4. coaching and motivating the parties, and
5. determining suitability for mediation.

Task 1: Setting a Comfortable Climate

Early in an interview, the convenor is building trust and rapport, encouraging the party to talk about the situation and reflect on it. Umbreit (1995) underscores the importance of relationship building in individual interviews. Satir (1988) does the same, emphasizing authentic human connection as essential to change processes.

The convenor begins by introducing herself and explaining the meeting's purpose and how mediation services came to be involved. She then informs the party of the meeting's purpose and parameters, as well as any limitations on confidentiality (see Boulle & Kelly, 1998, pp. 300–314). If the contact is by phone, the convenor determines whether it is a good time to talk, then clarifies that he or she would like to meet in person. Finally, the convenor outlines an agenda for the conversation. In the Not in My Backyard scenario (see Box 6.1), the convenor might use the following script:

> Hello, Mrs. Ozman. My name is … and I am calling from the Yogaville Mediation Centre. Mr. Morgan has contacted me regarding the situation he and your family are involved in, and he is hoping that you will consider mediation to resolve it. I would like to hear your perspective on events, find out what your concerns are, and what you would like to see happen in this situation. You might find it useful to hear what we do at the Mediation Centre and how

we might be able to assist you. I also want to let you know that what you say here is confidential. Please let me know if now is a good time for you to speak. It is? Great. So, how would you like to proceed?

Task 2: Exploring the Conflict

Listening intently and with empathy is critical when the convenor is exploring the conflict during the interview phase. The convenor must connect with the party by demonstrating that he or she understands and acknowledges the emotional impacts the party has sustained. To do this, the convenor should adopt an open and attending posture, using reflective listening skills and an appropriate tone of voice to convey respect and openness. During the interview, the convenor should be asking questions and recording whatever the party identifies in the way of facts, issues, values, interests, relations, and goals. To illustrate what some of the convenor's questions might be, let's return to the Not in My Backyard scenario described in Box 6.1. In this instance, assume the convenor is interviewing the Ozman son who clashed with Mr. Morgan while cutting down the tree. The convenor's questions, organized topically, might be as follows:

1. What is the conflict about?
   a. *How did this situation between you and the Morgans come about?*
   b. *When did things start going wrong between the two of you?*
   c. *How long has this situation been bothering you?*
2. What are the party's values, needs, and interests?
   a. *What were you hoping to gain by cutting down the tree?*
   b. *What concerns you about Mr. Morgan's reaction?*
   c. *What was so important about the tree?*
   d. *How were you expecting him to react? What do you think is causing him to act so differently from what you expected?*
3. Who is involved in the conflict?
   a. *Who would need to participate in a discussion about events?*
   b. *Who else has strong opinions about these issues?*
   c. *What has been the impact on those close to you?*
4. Is it an interpersonal or group dispute?
   a. *How has your family been affected by the conflict? How are others involved in this? How have other families in the neighbourhood been affected?*
5. What is the problem to be resolved?
   a. *So, how can your families coexist peacefully? It also sounds as though you would like the Morgans to understand how difficult this winter's been for you.*
   b. *What would need to happen for this to end for you?*
   c. *What sort of resolution would make you happy?*

6. What was the relationship like before the conflict, and what is it like now?
   a. *How did the two of you get along before this happened?*
   b. *What kind of relationship did you previously have with the Morgans?*
   c. *What is your relationship like now?*

Task 3: Educating the Parties About Mediation

The convenor needs to ensure that the party has sufficient information about options that he or she can make an informed decision—the best decision possible—about how to proceed. To complete this task, the convenor describes mediation, detailing what will happen during the process and the roles of the parties and the mediator. The convenor then discusses confidentiality and its constraints, and invites questions from the party about the process. In the case of the Morgan–Ozman dispute, the mediator might say the following to the Ozmans:

> Mediation is a process that will enable your family and the Morgans to hear about events from one another's perspectives; to have the opportunity to talk about what the situation has been like; to have the Morgan family gain insights into your experience while you gain insights into theirs; and to come up with practical ways to live together in the future. A mediator will assist you in this conversation, by asking questions, listening intently, and guiding you toward a resolution of your choosing, one that will meet your needs.
>
> The mediator has no obligation to report to anyone and will keep confidential anything she hears in mediation. Only your two families need to know what happens.

In the Not in My Backyard scenario (Box 6.1), the community-based mediation service has no reporting requirements, particularly because the referral came from one of the parties (Mr. Morgan). In other situations, such as some of those discussed earlier in the chapter involving union, human-resource, or human-rights-adviser referrals, there may be a need to get back to the referral agent, and there may be some limits to confidentiality. The mediator must be upfront about reporting requirements with all concerned. Another thing the convenor may do to educate the parties about mediation is to provide them with accounts of how mediation has been helpful in situations similar to their own. The convenor will also, certainly, elicit and respond to the party's fears and anxieties about the process. In the case of the Morgan–Ozman dispute, for example, the mediator might say the following to the Ozman son:

> You're worried that Mr. Morgan will dominate or overpower the discussion. … Let me tell you how that will be addressed in mediation.
>
> What other things concern you about going to mediation?
>
> Do you have any other questions about the process?

At this stage, the convenor and the party will determine whether the latter needs to bring to the mediation a representative or someone to offer support or assistance. There are certain cases where supporters and lawyers are present: workplace conflicts involving legal or policy grievances; human rights complaints; unlawful dismissal cases; and many litigation claims. In cases where one or more parties have cognitive disabilities, it is quite normal to have supporters present in mediation. Spouses who have experienced domestic abuse will often bring a representative with them to mediation. With most commercial or court-connected mediations, the party's counsel is included in the sessions.

Task 4: Coaching and Motivating the Parties

Quite often, the convenor will find that, though he or she believes that mediation is the appropriate process for the parties' dispute, one of the parties is reluctant to use it. In such cases, the convenor's role is

- to help the party see the conflict in a different light and consider the implications of a variety of outcomes,
- to respond to any concerns or questions the party may have about the mediation process,
- to assist the party to focus on his or her real concerns, and
- to find the best possible way to address those concerns.

Here, the convenor is listening for anxieties and fears, as well as misperceptions about mediation. To the end of eliciting these fears and misperceptions, the convenor might pose the following questions:

> How might mediation help the situation?
>
> How do you see mediation making things worse?

The convenor needs to have the party reflect on how best to resolve the conflict, as well as on the best possible, worst possible, and most likely outcomes if the conflict is (1) left unaddressed, (2) addressed through a rights-based process, or (3) addressed through mediation. Fisher and Ury refer to these as BATNAs (best alternatives to negotiated agreements). (To review BATNAs, see Chapter 2.) Fisher and Ury assert that a mediated solution should provide no less than its best alternative, or BATNA, provides; otherwise, there is little incentive for a party to participate in mediation (1991, pp. 99–106).

It is not unusual for a party to have an "inflated" BATNA—in other words, an exaggerated notion of how well he or she will be served by a formal procedure such as a court or a tribunal. This can happen when a party consults an expert (such as a lawyer, a human rights officer, or a union president or executive) and that expert hears only his or her side of the conflict. Hearing only one side, these experts may adopt and encourage an exaggerated view of the strength of the party's case. With parties who have been advised by such experts and who believe, in consequence, that their BATNA is stronger than it is, convenors need sometimes to act as reality testers and to encourage these parties to see mediation as being in their interest. In the course of coaching and motivating the Ozman party with respect to mediation, the convenor might ask the following questions:

> What do you think is likely to happen if you don't address the issue?
>
> What is the worst thing that could happen if you and the Morgans come together in mediation to try to talk about this?
>
> What is likely to happen if you take this to court?

The convenor needs to discuss with the parties the advantages, disadvantages, and limitations of each process alternative, especially adjudication or any other formal process option. (See the discussion of the benefits and limitations of mediation in Chapter 3). The parties need to have enough information about their process alternatives that they can compare them in terms of cost, time, effect on their relationship, likely and possible outcomes, consequences of success and failure, and other factors.

For example, in a case where litigation is the main alternative process, parties need to know that the litigation process could take several years, could entail legal fees of $30,000 or more (in some cases, the legal costs for one party alone, even *before* trial, could be $100,000 or more), and will be an adversarial process that will damage or destroy whatever relationship the parties may have. They also need to be told (although many people in conflict don't seem to hear or believe this until they actually go to court) that no matter how strong their legal case may seem to be, there is always a significant risk of an unfavourable or unsatisfactory outcome.

Finally, the convenor should acknowledge that the party's agreeing to discuss the dispute is in itself a positive step. It is not easy to speak with a stranger about a situation that we do not believe we have handled well. Doing so often makes us feel inadequate and vulnerable. The convenor should recognize and reward risk-taking behaviour, which will be needed if the case goes to mediation. Here are examples of some encouraging statements the mediator might make in the Morgan–Ozman case:

> You are showing a strong commitment to resolve this issue today.
>
> You are demonstrating just how important it is for you to fix this relationship.
>
> You have really taken a big step forward in coming here today, and I know it wasn't easy for you.

It is worth noting, in conclusion, that what we have identified here as the fourth task in the interview–assessment stage of convening will in some cases be carried out by the mediator in the pre-mediation phase, discussed at the end of this chapter.

Task 5: Determining Suitability for Mediation

The fifth task in the interview–assessment stage of convening is to ascertain whether the dispute is suitable for mediation. This involves posing four important questions:

1. Do all participants, including the mediator, have a reasonable assurance of safety?
2. Are the parties able to negotiate freely and competently?
3. Is there an invisible party, not present at the table, who could be adversely affected by the outcome of the mediation? Is this a public or a private dispute? Are there systemic problems that would be better addressed in other forums?
4. Do the parties possess the will to address the dispute?

The first question is about security. If any party's security cannot reasonably be assured throughout the process, or if a mediator cannot maintain a safe and non-threatening environment for the parties, or if the mediator's own safety could be compromised, the process should not go ahead. If there is a significant risk of violence, or a situation in which a party has concerns about safety, or cannot speak openly without fear of reprisals or intimidation, mediation may not be suitable. An alternative is for the mediator to adapt the mediation process to the situation by implementing certain safety measures. If such measures satisfy the parties and provide reasonable assurance of security for all participants, then mediation may proceed. In some instances, security concerns may prevent mediation from going forward at all.

Family mediators must consider and respond to security concerns whenever one spouse has been the victim of physical or psychological violence. Among the measures a mediator might take in such circumstances are the following:

- using "shuttle" mediation, whereby the parties do not meet face to face;
- having the at-risk spouse attend all mediation sessions with a support person or advocate (for example, a lawyer);
- having staggered arrival and departure times for the parties; and
- having legal conditions (for example, a restraining order) in place to control the party of concern.

Where peace agreements are being mediated, ceasefires are usually brokered before parties meet for negotiations. Clearly, though these negotiations are about ending violence, they themselves are always shadowed by the threat of violence. And yet the prospect of peace overrides this threat for the participants and for the mediator, and the process goes forward.

The second question the convenor needs to ask, when trying to determine the parties' suitability for mediation, is about their motivation and competency to participate fully in the mediation. The convenor needs to manage this without the benefit—in most cases—of being a trained psychologist. Some parties are too emotionally invested in a dispute to hear the other party's perspective at all. Other parties may not have the competencies to negotiate, because of an inability to express or understand emotions, values, needs, interests, or consequences (Crawford, Dabney, Filner, & Maida, 2003).

Many disputes in the areas of public housing, disability accommodation, workplace, human rights, and guardianship involve parties with cognitive or emotional disabilities, and these disabilities may hamper the parties' capacity to understand the process and the options under discussion and to give voluntary and informed consent to any agreement reached (Crawford et al., 2003). In other situations, an imbalance of power between the parties may restrict one side's ability to freely negotiate; he or she may fear the consequences of "talking back" to a boss or spouse. Another possible obstacle to mediation is a party's not having the authority to settle. If these obstacles cannot be removed or the mediation process adapted to overcome them, mediation is not recommended.

Sometimes, to accommodate those who are not ready or able to go through mediation, the convenor can delay the process. A cooling-off period or a period of personal counselling might help a party prepare for a session. In these instances, a convenor may give homework to the parties to help them develop skills for mediation. In peace negotiations, each faction might receive training in negotiation skills. In all cases, the convenor needs to ensure that people with the proper authority to make decisions are present or available.

Both convenors and mediators tend to focus on what they can do to encourage parties to participate in a mediation. This requires setting the threshold of party competence as low as reasonably possible, provided the convenors and mediators are able to accommodate any deficiencies in capacity or power imbalances between the parties. Accommodating measures they might take in this area include the following:

- ensuring that the less powerful voice is heard and responded to in the process;
- having a support person or advocate attend with the at-risk party;
- using shuttle mediation, whereby the parties do not meet face to face;
- providing for a cooling-off period of a day or two between the time the decisions are made during mediation and the time that the final, binding agreements are made.

In a case where a party with cognitive or emotional disabilities is accompanied to a mediation by a support person or advocate, the latter will help the party to communicate clearly and to develop the competencies needed to negotiate effectively. The advocate or support person can also be responsible for ensuring that the party understands what is going on in mediation and is capable of offering his or her assent to various agreements.

The third question the convenor needs to ask, when trying to determine the dispute's suitability for mediation, is whether it is a private or a public dispute. A common criticism levelled at mediation is that it privatizes public disputes (Goundry et al., 1998). It may not be wise to use mediation alone to address conflicts of a systemic or structural nature, especially those involving public or collective rights. In other words, where the protection of rights (granted through collective agreements, employment law, the *Canadian Charter of Rights and Freedoms*, or other legislation/policy) is the issue of contention, a rights-based process may address the party's concerns better than mediation can. A case involving collective interests (for example, a harassment-free workplace) should not be diverted to mediation alone, particularly if the application of existing policy requires that a process other than mediation be undertaken.

This does not mean that interpersonal conflicts should not go to mediation simply because they involve systemic elements or fundamental rights. Consider a situation where a female soldier feels discriminated against by her superior. The collective interest might be to address a poisoned work environment where gender equity does not appear to be present. Responding to the collective interest may require the training of all staff, the implementation or application of a policy on human rights, or even disciplinary action against an employee who does not follow organizational policy. However, the female soldier may still wish to work in that particular unit. Her individual interest is in improving her relationship with her supervisor. In this case, it is possible to address both needs, if the convenor works closely with other dispute resolution advisers in the organization to address different aspects of the conflict. Organizations should, as a matter of policy, adopt integrated systems that include rights-, power-, and interest-based or value-based processes for responding to organizational conflicts. Systemic problems cannot usually be addressed through interpersonal approaches alone.

The final assessment question the convenor needs to ask is an important one. It concerns each party's openness to the process of mediation—to new ideas and to the possibility of changing one's viewpoint. Some parties are not open in this way. When this is the case—when a party does not appear to have any stake in resolving the situation—a convenor might introduce this individual to the idea of trying to see the conflict differently and to trying to recognize his or her role in the situation. If the convenor's approach is unsuccessful, mediation probably should not proceed. If the party will not participate in good faith, a successful process is unlikely. Some mediators have remarked that parties who feel no empathy for others are poor candidates for mediation. The same is true for parties who will not be honest in the mediation. Agreements cannot be based on manipulation and lies.

Stage 3: Decision Making and Planning

The disputants alone cannot voluntarily decide to go forward with mediation. The convenor must also agree that mediation is the best option. Mediation is not a panacea; it is not right for every conflict situation. The convenor must feel reasonably sure that participation in mediation will not harm the parties. In workplace disputes, when the convenor is a fellow employee, she has an added responsibility; she has to consider both the well-being of individuals and his or her responsibility to improve the organization. This dual responsibility provides strong incentive for a responsible and extensive screening process. In all cases, the criteria for assessing the suitability of mediation should always be applied.

A convenor who has determined that mediation is suitable for a certain conflict needs to help the parties themselves make the same determination. Resistance to the mediation process is common; many people need to be encouraged to try it. Much of that resistance comes from preconceived notions about what is likely to happen in mediation. For example, some people think that mediation is a "touchy-feely" process in which they will be expected to express emotions and to hear the emotions of the other party. Others believe that mediation is not a serious process for resolving disputes. There are also those who cannot imagine that speaking with the other party could be helpful, given the amount of animosity between them. The convenor needs to devote a good deal of time to addressing these misconceptions and educating parties about mediation.

If a party needs time before making a decision about mediation, the convenor usually sets a date and often takes responsibility for follow-up, because she or he knows how easy it is for a party to procrastinate. Most people involved in conflict hope the problem will just go away, although few actually believe that it will.

When Parties Decide Not to Use Mediation

In referred situations, when the parties and/or the convenor decide not to proceed with mediation, the convenor may need to inform the referring party of this decision. When doing so, the convenor needs to respect confidentiality with respect to the parties. A convenor would never say, "A mediation will not be going ahead because Jack didn't want to." This statement could be used against Jack in future proceedings.

Mediator Selection

A convenor who has facilitated the information-gathering and assessment stages of a prospective mediation will acquire a sense of which skills, strengths, and other characteristics the mediator will require. These qualifying characteristics might have to do with, among other features, the mediator's experience, gender, age, language, ethnicity, or status. The convenor also gets a sense of how the process will need to be adapted to accommodate the parties' needs. These adaptations might involve co-mediation, support, interpreters, or separate sessions with each party. Familiar with the conflict situation and with the parties, the convenor plays an important role in making recommendations as to who should mediate the case. This principle only applies, of course, to mediation programs where the mediating and convening functions are kept separate. If the convening and mediating responsibilities are assumed by one person, she needs to reflect on her own capacity to take on the mediation. Will her style work for the parties? Can she act impartially? Does the situation require, and she possess, substantive knowledge of the issues to be mediated? Would she be more effective with a co-mediator?

In family mediation, for example, some mediators specialize in child custody and access disputes, whereas others confine themselves to property and financial issues. A "property and financial" family mediator who has been working with the parties during the convening process may discover that child custody is a significant issue between the parties. In that case, the convening mediator may refer the parties to a child custody mediator or may suggest co-mediation (see below), a process in which the convening mediator would work with the child custody mediator throughout the mediation process.

What a Mediator Needs to Know

How much knowledge does a mediator need about the substantive issues in dispute—and the context in which the conflict takes place? To mediate divorce settlements, mediators do need to know family law. Custody and access issues are usually mediated by someone with experience and knowledge in child development and family systems. Workplace mediators are required to have an understanding of workplace culture and systems, as well as knowledge about workplace policies, collective agreements, labour laws, and any other relevant legislation that could have an impact on the issues in contention. For complex disputes in contract law, construction, business, environment, and public policy, a mediator with knowledge and experience of the area is likely to follow discussions more effectively. Mediators with substantive knowledge and experience of the conflict area must be careful, however, not to impose their own judgments about the issues, particularly if the parties are not seeking an evaluative process.

Returning to the Not in My Backyard scenario set out in Box 6.1, it is clear that the mediator for the Ozman–Morgan conflict should have an understanding or experience of being in a new culture, as well as some sensitivity to difficulties arising from cross-cultural communication. He or she should also possess enough charismatic power to balance some of Mr. Morgan's. Parties from a particular ethnic group, though they don't necessarily require a mediator of their own ethnicity, may need peer mediators when particular issues in conflict centre on cultural norms and traditions. (For more on peer mediators, see below.) In other situations, the ethnicity of the party may create an opposite pressure; one party may consider the dispute too personal to be witnessed by a member of his or her peer group. A co-mediation team or a cultural interpreter can sometimes help to increase understanding of the different cultural positions. The convenor needs to ask the parties themselves what they are comfortable with in these regards.

When Should the Convenor Become the Mediator?

Should the convenor become the mediator? To have a mediator who is distinct from the convenor is typically not an option in many private practices. However, it is sometimes an option for internally funded conflict resolution services or community-based programs. In private practice, mediators who have acted as convenors and who realize they are not the best person for a particular dispute usually refer their cases to other mediators. Sometimes, if the convenor has spent a lot of time with one of the disputants and not the other, it is best for him or her to refer the case to another mediator. On the other hand, it *is* appropriate for a convenor to mediate when she has developed a strong rapport with the parties in conflict and believes that she can mediate impartially.

After considering all these issues, the convenor needs to recommend a mediator who meets the requirements and with whom the parties will be comfortable. Another possibility is that the convenor may conclude that the situation calls for co-mediation, with two mediators rather than just one.

Co-Mediation

Co-mediation is a popular and effective means of doing the following:

- apprenticing less experienced mediators;
- balancing the mediators' characteristics with those of the parties to maximize perceptions of impartiality and understanding; and
- ensuring that the mediators are sufficiently knowledgeable about complex legal, psychological, economic, or environmental matters.

Love and Stulberg (1996, p. 180) emphasize that "for co-mediation to be effective, the mediators must match themselves with compatible partners and must make a plan for effective teamwork, or they will lose the potential benefits." Co-mediation offers both advantages and disadvantages.

Advantages of Co-Mediation

Co-mediation offers a variety of benefits. Mediation can be intense—physically, intellectually, and emotionally draining. Having another mediator working alongside you can lighten your load. It is also easier for a mediator to listen and observe when the role is shared; the sharing creates more space to listen, since the pressure is not on a single mediator to catch every word or gesture. In some cases, the co-mediator may serve to reflect the gender, ethnicity, or other attributes of the parties. For a party from another culture, having someone in the mediator role who "looks the same" may help that party feel at ease—although it should not be assumed that this is always the case.

Other advantages of co-mediation are that it can provide invaluable training for inexperienced mediators, demonstrate cooperative teamwork in action, and provide mediators with the opportunity to debrief and obtain peer review and feedback on their mediation approach and skills (Picard, 2002).

With co-mediation, the mediators can join forces in analyzing and reflecting on conflict dynamics during breaks in the mediation process. A good team will use these breaks to modify and improve their strategies. Having the opportunity to debrief together is one of the special advantages of co-mediation. Being able to analyze with another person the mediation's strengths and weaknesses is helpful both for less experienced and for senior mediators. Debriefing can improve teamwork and provide the opportunity for peer review and reflective practice.

The Process of Co-Mediation

Co-mediation involves more than just having another mediator in the room. The process requires forethought, experience, and compatibility if its potential is to be maximized. First and foremost, co-mediators need to have similar visions of their role and compatible styles of mediation. Having different understandings of fundamental goals is likely to result in the mediators working against one other. Furthermore, they should complement each other's strengths and weaknesses and know how to support each other. Preparation is key. How will the responsibilities be divided, especially in the opening stage of the mediation? We think it is best for co-mediators to share the task of communicating preliminary information to the parties, and to do so in a natural and balanced way. Having both mediators speak early in the session allows each of them to establish legitimacy in the parties' eyes with respect to communication, and it models cooperation and teamwork.

It is a good idea for the co-mediators to decide in advance which of them will begin the session, which will record notes on the whiteboard or flip chart, which will write the agreement, and so forth. Determining how a caucus will be handled is another matter for them to decide. In our view, it is essential that both mediators should together caucus with each party, rather than conducting separate caucuses individually. This will ensure that each co-mediator has a similar understanding of issues and interests and that there is no possibility of either party driving a wedge between them. Ideally, co-mediators will have some way of signalling to each other, within the session, when they would like the other to take the lead—when, for example, one of them is unsure of how to deal with the situation at hand or where to go next. Being able to send such signals in a natural manner and at appropriate times is important. One co-mediator should avoid interrupting a conversation and taking it in a different direction when the other is following a hunch and doing some deepening work. Co-mediators don't need equal air time. Flexibility, cooperation, and teamwork are what they need.

When it comes to seating, we suggest that co-mediators position themselves so that they can see one another easily and pick up one another's non-verbal signals. One mediator might want to tell the other, for example, that it is a good time for the other to become more active and take over the lead. In the matter of positioning, we suggest, more specifically, that the parties sit across from each other. However, other seating arrangements may be more appropriate depending on the situation. Love and Stulberg (1996, p. 183) say that having the mediators sitting beside each other helps unify the focus of the conversation and "contributes to balancing and harmonizing the room." Once again, the point is to be thoughtful and purposeful about how best to convene the mediation session.

Pre-Mediation: Preparing for Mediation

After the parties have decided to proceed with mediation and have selected a mediator, the next step is for the mediator to have pre-mediation meetings (in person or by telephone) with each party. It is important to keep in mind that, even after parties have decided to use mediation, either one of them may at any time, during pre-mediation or during the mediation process itself, decide to terminate the process.

There are a number of items the mediator will want to discuss with the parties, even if the convenor has already mentioned them. First, if the mediator is in private practice, he or she needs to discuss the fees for the mediation. Fee structures range broadly, depending on the area of practice, the mediator's educational background, and sliding scales. If the parties themselves are paying for the mediation, the cost is usually divided evenly between them. If an organization is paying the mediator's fee, the mediator will have made payment arrangements directly with the convenor or organizational representative during the convening process.

Second, the mediator may introduce an Agreement to Mediate form (see Appendix A). This is usually a one- or two-page document that outlines the principles of mediation, the role of the mediator, the parties' roles, the rules regarding confidentiality, and clauses preventing the mediator from being called as a witness to a formal dispute resolution process in the event that the mediation is not successful. It is common practice for parties to take away this form, so they can consider the information and share it with their significant others or—in cases where they represent an organization—with members of the organization they represent. It is then brought back to be signed by everyone at the beginning of the first joint mediated session.

Reporting Requirements

When a case has been referred to mediation by someone not directly involved in the dispute (such as an organizational convenor, supervisor, or union representative), the mediator needs to discuss what communication he or she will have with that person. Many mediators have standard processes for handling referred cases. This issue is critical when the referral comes from an office that requires written confirmation about case outcomes. For example, a human rights officer may refer a complainant to mediation and require written correspondence to prove that the case has been closed. Courts with mandatory mediation programs also require correspondence confirming that the mediation has occurred and indicating whether the case was settled. Divorce and child custody agreements reached in mediation are often filed with the court, so do not remain fully confidential. If the referral agent does require additional information about the mediation process or wishes to be privy to mediation documents, this is discussed or negotiated with the parties in advance of mediation.

When the parties determine that the referral agent should be involved or advised, it is often the parties' responsibility to request that he or she become involved or to decide what they would like to say in a report back to the referral agent. At the behest of the parties, a mediator can take on the task of informing the referral agent of further steps—or can request that she or he be present. When a conflict is referred, the mediator respects confidentiality. Upon conclusion of the mediation, he or she may be asked to report back to the person who made the referral, informing that person of the outcome without divulging details about any agreement reached, unless disclosing such details is a legal requirement.

Homework

As part of pre-mediation, the mediator, or in some cases the convenor, may send parties off with "homework" to help them prepare for mediation. This homework might include the following: a series of questions to ponder; the research compiled by the convenor concerning their situation (for example, relevant organizational policies applicable to their case, or information about their best and worst options if this case is pursued in a different dispute resolution process); or exercises for honing the communication skills that will be needed in the mediation.

In a divorce mediation, for example, the mediator will probably ask the parties to obtain complete information about their property, financial assets, debts, income, and expenses. The mediator may request from each party, or help them to complete, a comprehensive property and financial information form. When mediation occurs between community members who have been in conflict, homework might consist of asking each side to come up with questions they would like to ask of the other side. After the conflict in the Balkans, for example, Bosnian and Serb neighbours were asked to come up with seven questions they would like to ask each other.

Communication

The conflict experience may have produced strong emotions in the parties. During pre-mediation, the mediator may need to assist each party individually in communicating emotion, so that he or she can be more readily heard and understood during the upcoming mediation. The mediator can help the party to frame these strong emotions in a constructive way. This is often accomplished through "owning" one's feelings, rather than projecting them on the other.

A mediator will help parties "own" their emotions by asking questions like the following:

> What has the experience been like for you?
>
> How has it affected you?
>
> How do you think Mr. Morgan will react if he hears you say that? How could you express it differently?

The mediator may also encourage a party to focus on his or her values and interests and to speak from needs, not demands. As well, the mediator needs to develop an awareness of previous communication patterns. He can also discuss with the parties what kind of relationship would be ideal for them in the future. These various tasks may involve questions such as the following:

> How do you need to relate to one another in order to be good neighbours?
>
> What is important to you in your relationship with your neighbours?

During pre-mediation, the mediator should speak with the parties' lawyers and other representatives or supporters, to clarify the role these associates will take in the session and to plan for their participation, if required. Lawyers, representatives, and support persons can exacerbate conflict if they adopt an adversarial approach in mediation. The mediator needs to discuss with these people in advance the goals and the process of mediation, to provide them with guidance to determine what each side hopes to achieve. Most lawyers are very helpful when they have a clear understanding of the mediator's role. They usually wish to help their clients achieve goals that go beyond the upholding of rights and entitlements—for example, maintaining relationships and fulfilling other intangible needs that cannot be met through an adversarial process. Other advocates, supporters, and representatives are likely to be similarly supportive.

Collecting Information

The mediator should also determine during pre-mediation whether the party requires information from advocacy or other process experts and, if possible, refer the party to other agencies to collect that information. This is also the point in the process where gaps are identified in the information parties require and a discussion is held with the parties about how to fill these data needs.

Moore (1996, pp. 116–117) also suggests that data be collected from direct observation and site visits, and from secondary sources such as financial records, government and annual reports, minutes of meetings, newspaper articles, and any research on the issue. This is particularly important in the case of public policy disputes, environmental conflicts, multi-party conflicts, and any situation requiring thorough understanding of complex data. An organization's policies relevant to the issues and any correspondence between the disputants may also be needed. A mediator may also need to know about the following: collective agreements in a unionized workplace; policies on human rights complaints, harassment, and abuse of power; the documentation needs from referring agencies; mediation agreement forms; and agreement-to-mediate forms. Knowledge about the history of a region or of the relations between the peoples within a region may be helpful in multi-party and international disputes.

Scheduling the Mediation

During pre-mediation, the mediator also needs to consider and discuss with the parties the location and set-up for the upcoming mediation. Usually, this will be a private, neutral location that has sufficient space to caucus and is equipped with paper and pens, a flip chart or whiteboard, water, and tissues. Depending on the mediator's assessment and the parties' preferences, rooms may be set up formally, with a board table and upright chairs, or more informally, with a low coffee table and more informal seating. The first joint session should be scheduled as soon as possible after the pre-mediation has been completed.

Summary

Convening is not easy work, either for the convenor or for the parties in conflict. Yet, if it follows the process outlined in this chapter, convening can transform the parties in a beneficial way. In a safe and trusting environment, the parties' perspectives are challenged by the convenor, who attempts to open up interpretive possibilities that will be followed through in mediation. Like a mediator, a convenor needs to prepare for his or her work, devoting maximum energy and attention to the tasks at hand. When it is conducted by an artful guide, convening, like mediation, can be a magical process that leaves the parties with new insights.

Convening a mediation demands full use of a person's senses and skills. The process is composed of stages similar to those of mediation, and the communication skills employed are precisely those needed by mediators. The convenor must follow the parties' lead, flowing and bending with the process. At the same time, she must ask the necessary questions—the questions that will elicit the information needed to give her a coherent understanding of the issues, values, needs, interests, and goals of the parties, and enable her to assess the suitability of mediation for the situation at hand. The convenor should not feel pressured to have every case go through mediation. If the situation would be better addressed through other dispute resolution avenues, the convenor should encourage the parties to take them. This principle—that the convenor's role is only to assist the parties in making an informed and appropriate choice about what path to follow—is of paramount importance.

DISCUSSION QUESTIONS AND EXERCISES

1. Why is it very important for an organizational mediation program to have an effective convening process? What is required to achieve that?
2. Imagine that you are the convenor in the Not in My Backyard scenario, described in Box 6.1.
   a. What concerns would you have in this case?
   b. In the convening phase, what additional information do you need to obtain from the Ozmans? What additional information do you need to obtain from the Morgans?
   c. Would you recommend that this case go to mediation? Why or why not?
3. Consider the ideal attributes of a convenor, with reference to the following:
   a. Think about a conflict situation in which you have been involved recently. If you spoke with a third party about it and found him or her supportive and helpful, list the reasons you found that person supportive.
   b. In the event you found no one helpful to speak to about the situation, consider what attributes you would have found helpful and supportive. What actions and behaviours were not, or would not have been, helpful?
4. Imagine yourself in the following scenarios:
   a. You are the coordinator of a peer mediation program in a school and have been asked to set up a mediation between two 12-year-olds, one of whom alleges that she is being harassed and bullied by the other. The young woman being bullied says she does not even feel safe being in the same room with the other student, who, she alleges, has pushed and punched her in the past. Should this dispute go forward to mediation? Why or why not? How could the mediation process be adapted to address the young woman's concern?
   b. You are a mediator in private practice who has been approached by two lawyers representing two siblings in an estate dispute. The siblings have not been in contact or communication for over 15 years and intensely dislike one another. In fact, they are certain they cannot even be in the same room together. Should their dispute go forward to mediation? Why or why not? What, if anything, could you do to make mediation feasible by accommodating their disinclination to be in the same room together?

c. You are a convenor at a community-based mediation program and have been asked by the police to mediate a dispute involving two brothers who have been damaging property and vandalizing businesses in the neighbourhood over the past two years. They have now been accused of something further: tormenting the pets of residents in the neighbourhood. Should this problem go forward to mediation? Why or why not? What, if anything, could you do to accommodate this conflict in mediation?

FURTHER READING

Crawford, S.H., Dabney, L.M., Filner, J.M., & Maida, P.R. (2003). From determining capacity to facilitating competencies: A new mediation framework. *Conflict Resolution Quarterly, 20*(4), 385–401.

Kolb, D., & Putnam, L.L. (2005). Negotiation through a gender lens. In R. Bordone & M. Moffitt (Eds.), *Handbook of dispute resolution*. San Francisco: Jossey-Bass.

Moore, C.W. (2003). *The mediation process: Practical strategies for resolving conflict* (3rd ed.). San Francisco: Jossey-Bass.

Picard, C.A. (2002). *Mediating interpersonal and small group conflict*. Ottawa: Golden Dog Press.

Umbreit, M. (1995). *Mediating interpersonal conflicts: A pathway to peace*. West Concord, MN: CPI Publishing.

Whitfield, T. (2010). *Working with groups of friends*. Washington, DC: US Institute of Peace Press.

Websites

Family Mediation Canada: Practice, Certification and Training Standards: http://fmc.ca/sites/default/files/sites/all/themes/fmc/images-user/CertificationStandards.pdf

MIT–Harvard Public Disputes Program: http://web.mit.edu/publicdisputes

Ontario Association of Family Mediators. (2013). Policy on abuse—Mediation in domestic violence cases: https://www.oafm.on.ca/membership/policies/abuse-policy

St. Stephen's Community House: Conflict Resolution & Training: http://www.sschto.ca/conflict-resolution

UN Department of Political Affairs: Mediation Support: https://www.un.org/wcm/content/site/undpa/mediation_support

Winnipeg Mediation Services: http://www.mediationserviceswpg.ca

REFERENCES

Astor, H. (1995). The weight of silence: Talking about violence in family mediation. In M. Thornton (Ed.), *Public and private: Feminist legal debates* (pp. 174–196). Melbourne: Oxford University Press.

Benjamin, M., & Irving, H.H. (1992). Toward a feminist-informed model of therapeutic family mediation. *Mediation Quarterly, 10*(2), 129–153.

Boulle, L., & Kelly, K.J. (1998). *Mediation: Principles, process, practice*. Toronto: Butterworths.

Crawford, S.H., Dabney, L.M., Filner, J.M., & Maida, P.R. (2003). From determining capacity to facilitating competencies: A new mediation framework. *Conflict Resolution Quarterly, 20*(4), 385–401.

Family Mediation Canada. (2003). *Practice, certification and training standards*. http://fmc.ca/sites/default/files/sites/all/themes/fmc/images-user/CertificationStandards.pdf.

Fisher, R., & Ury, W. (1991). *Getting to yes: Negotiating agreement without giving in* (2nd ed.). New York: Penguin.

Folger, J.P., Poole, M.S., & Stutman, R.K. (1993). *Working through conflict* (2nd ed.). New York: Harper Collins College Publisher.

Goundry, S., Peters, Y., Currie, R., & Equity Matters Consulting. (1998). *Family mediation in Canada: Implications for women's equality*. Ottawa: Office of the Status of Women Canada.

Kolb, D.M., & Putnam, L.L. (2005). Negotiation through a gender lens. In M. Moffit & R.C. Bordone (Eds.), *The handbook of dispute resolution* (pp. 135–149). San Francisco: Jossey-Bass and Program on Negotiation, Harvard Law School.

Love, L., & Stulberg, J. (1996). Practice guidelines for co-mediation: Making certain that two heads are better than one. *Mediation Quarterly, 13*, 179–189.

Moore, C.W. (1996). *The mediation process: Practical strategies for resolving conflict* (2nd ed.). San Francisco: Jossey-Bass.

Picard, C.A. (2002). *Mediating interpersonal and small group conflict* (2nd ed.). Ottawa: Golden Dog Press.

Satir, V. (1988). *The new peoplemaking*. Palo Alto, CA: Science and Behavior Books.

Umbreit, M. (1995). *Mediating interpersonal conflicts: A pathway to peace*. West Concord, MN: CPI Publishing.

UN Department of Political Affairs. (2014). Mediation support. https://www.un.org/wcm/content/site/undpa/mediation_support.

Whitfield, T. (2010). *Working with groups of friends*. Washington, DC: US Institute of Peace Press.

CHAPTER 7

Cultivating Constructive Dialogue in Mediation

LEARNING OBJECTIVES

After reading this chapter, you will be able to:

- Understand some of the reasons why constructive dialogue and collaboration in mediation are challenging for mediators and parties
- Identify ways that mediators cultivate dialogue, both before and during mediation
- Explain a number of strategies mediators use to overcome adversarial emotions and behaviours and to cultivate constructive dialogue in mediation
- Understand the role that lawyers and other advisers can play in mediation and how they can contribute or detract from the process

CHAPTER OUTLINE

Introduction 189
Understanding the Sources of Conflict 190
Cooperative Behaviour 194
How Mediators Cultivate Dialogue 197
The Parties' Conflicting Perspectives 200
Beginning the Mediation 201
Exploring the Parties' Narratives 205
Strategies for Transforming Adversarial Dialogue 207
Participation of Parties' Advisers in Mediation 217
Summary 220

If there is any great secret of success in life, it lies in the ability to put yourself in the other person's place and to see things from his point of view—as well as your own.

Henry Ford

Introduction

Recall the five-stage framework for a generic mediation process discussed in Chapter 1:

1. pre-mediation,
2. cultivating dialogue,
3. getting to the heart of the conflict,
4. reaching decisions and completing the mediation process, and
5. post-mediation.

In Chapter 6, we considered the first stage, pre-mediation. In this chapter and in the following two chapters, we examine what happens in the remaining four stages of the mediation process, from the opening dialogue through to resolution and post-mediation.

This chapter will focus primarily on the second stage, cultivating dialogue. The opening dialogue between the mediator and the disputants lays the foundation for constructive conversations about two matters: the issues that brought the parties to mediation; and their perspectives on one another and on the conflict. Mediators can help the parties interpret their conflict in a new way, introducing them to differences in perspective. This can lead to a visible shift in the ways that parties interact, a change that exemplifies what some have called the magic of mediation. We will say more about this process in Chapter 8, when we discuss Stage 3.

Mediators cannot always explain this "magical" transformation. However, we do know that there are ways in which we, as mediators, can help to bring it about. We also know some of the barriers to successfully resolving conflict and some strategies for overcoming them. Understanding the sources of conflict is a key to determining the best approaches and strategies in mediation.

Understanding the Sources of Conflict

Causes of conflict are a much discussed subject in many fields of study. Specialists in the field of international relations have examined the causes of war and violent conflict. Psychologists have studied intrapersonal, interpersonal, intragroup, and intergroup conflict. Researchers in sociology and political science, among other disciplines, have sought to understand why conflict occurs. The mediation field has drawn its theoretical understandings of conflict and its causes from all of these areas of study.

Christopher Moore (2003), a mediator and scholar, has examined the basic causes of conflict in order to help mediators determine the best strategies for response. Through this research, he has produced a useful typology. Conflicts, according to him, usually belong to one or more of the following five categories:

1. *Data conflicts* occur when one or both parties lack essential information or when they interpret the information they do possess differently from each other, or when one party withholds information from the other. Sometimes a data conflict involves all three of these sources.
2. *Value conflicts* refer to the clash of beliefs among or between parties with regard to how one should behave, how one should live one's life, or how one should evaluate actions or goals. Value conflicts are subjective and deeply rooted expectations of oneself and others.

3. *Relationship conflicts* result from poor communication, strong emotional reactions, stereotyping, and repetitive negative patterns of interaction.
4. *Structural conflicts* occur when there exist systemic inequities such as unequal patterns in control, power, ownership, or authority.
5. *Interest conflicts* arise when there are actual or perceived differences in how decisions should be made (procedural), when there is an actual or perceived scarcity in resources such as land, money, or other tangible assets (substantive), or when there are actual or perceived emotional or relational issues between the parties (psychological).

All of these sources of conflict involve some form of incompatibility between parties. In some cases, parties in conflict may want the same thing—for example, the corner office in the building where they work. They will struggle against each other and jockey for position to attain this goal, bringing their colleagues into the dispute as supporters. They perceive the situation as one in which there is not enough to go around (there is only one corner office). In this particular situation, each party sees her goal as incompatible with the other's, since they both want exactly the same thing and there is only one of these things. In other cases, people have different goals—for example, two friends who want to see different movies at the theatre. They too will struggle over incompatibility. In both these cases—the corner office and the movie—there is a conflict over who gets to decide and perhaps over what criteria should be used to make the decision. Other factors could be complicating these disputes. For example, there might be poor communication between the two office mates jockeying for the corner office. The disagreement between the two friends may be, in part, a data conflict if, for example, neither of them actually knows what the movies are about.

How Understanding Conflict Sources Influences Mediator Strategies

We believe that there is space in the mediation field for a wide variety of practices and approaches and that parties' goals and needs should determine the strategies adopted by mediators. If we return to Moore's sources of conflict, it is clear that a data conflict would be handled quite differently from a conflict that arises out of relationship issues.

With a data conflict, Moore advises that parties first need to agree on what data is important and then jointly determine criteria for evaluating that data. With mediator assistance, parties might then agree on a process to collect data or they might invite third-party experts to provide an assessment of the data or information. For purely data-driven conflicts, there is usually little need for the mediator to address emotional factors or focus on relationship issues.

Figure 7.1 Circle of Conflict: Causes and Interventions

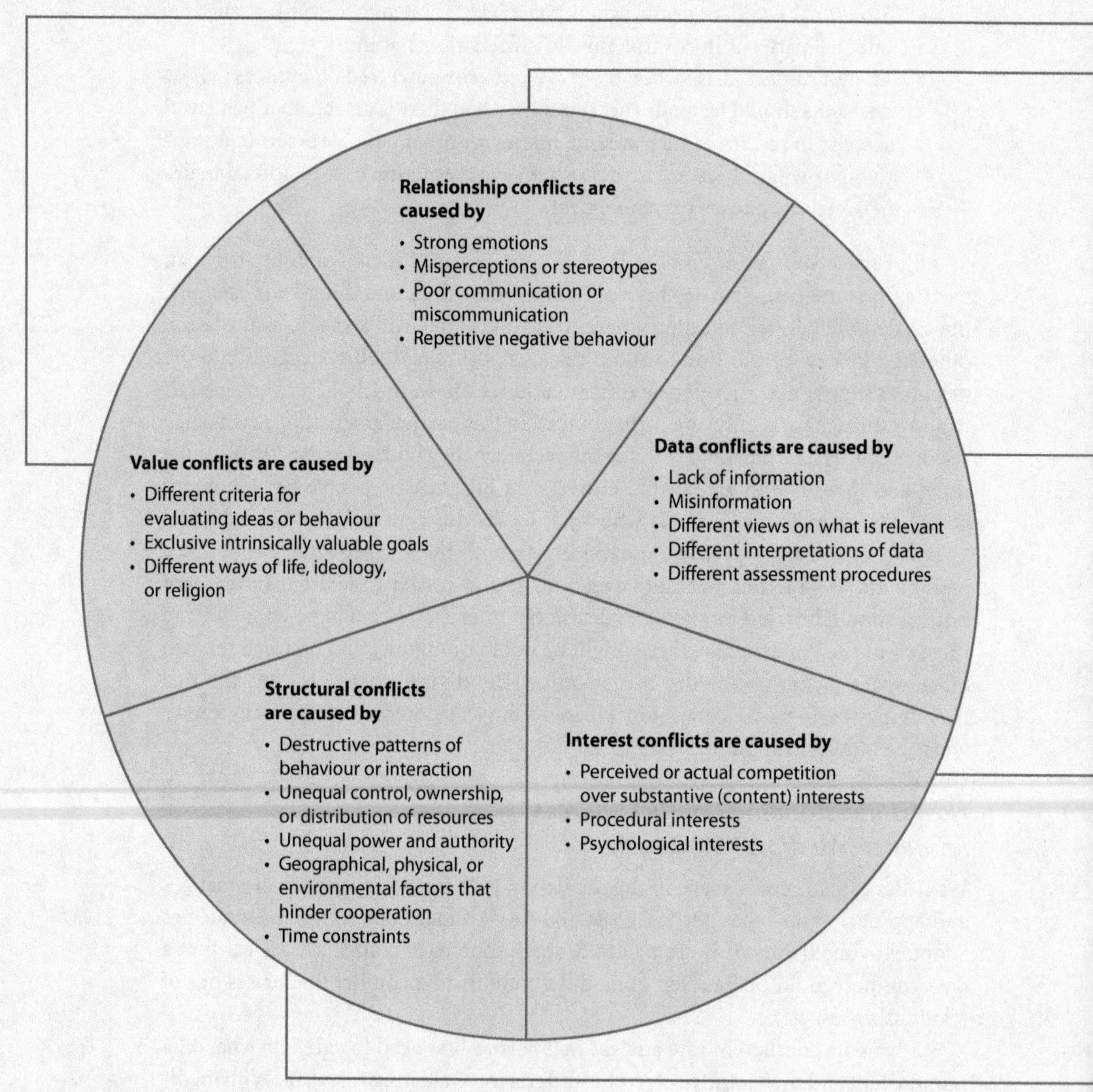

Source: Moore (2003, p. 64). Reprinted by permission.

Possible Value-Related Interventions

- Avoid defining problem in terms of value
- Allow parties to agree and to disagree
- Create spheres of influence in which one set of values dominates
- Search for superordinate goal that all parties share

Possible Relationship Interventions

- Control expression of emotions through procedure, ground rules, caucuses, and so forth
- Promote expression of emotions by legitimizing feelings and providing a process
- Clarify perceptions and build positive perceptions
- Improve quality and quantity of communication
- Block negative repetitive behaviour by changing structure
- Encourage positive problem-solving attitudes

Possible Data Interventions

- Reach agreement on what data are important
- Agree on process to collect data
- Develop common criteria to assess data
- Use third-party experts to gain outside opinion or break deadlocks

Possible Interest-Based Interventions

- Focus on interests, not positions
- Look for objective standards and criteria to guide solution development
- Develop integrative solutions that address needs of all parties
- Search for ways to expand options or resources
- Develop trade-offs to satisfy interests of different strengths

Possible Structural Interventions

- Clearly define and change roles
- Replace destructive behaviour patterns
- Reallocate ownership or control of resources
- Establish a fair and mutually acceptable decision-making process
- Change negotiation process from positional to interest-based bargaining
- Modify means of influence used by parties (less coercion, more persuasion)
- Change physical and environmental relationship of parties (closeness and distance)
- Modify external pressures on parties
- Change time constraints (more or less time)

For example, consider Jack and Marella, who are separating after 15 years of marriage. They have no children, and their parting has been mutual and amicable. Marella is asking that Jack pay her an equalization payment of $200,000 on the grounds that Jack's assets, including his pension and income property, are worth $600,000 whereas her assets are worth only $200,000. Jack disputes this, taking the position that his assets are worth only $300,000, so he should only have to pay Marella $50,000. The mediator for this dispute helps Jack and Marella find the resources they need to properly value these assets, and they subsequently determine that a fair and reasonable equalization payment would be $90,000. With a data conflict of this kind the mediator did not need to devote a lot of time and effort to addressing the parties' conflict emotions or relationship issues, especially since Jack and Marella addressed the issues rationally and non-emotionally and were not going to have any continuing relationship.

On the other hand, in a conflict over relationship issues, responding to emotions will be the key to resolving the conflict. Moore suggests that the mediator in this case needs to focus on the negative perceptions each party has regarding the other and to help the parties transform those perspectives through empathy and increased understanding. This is obviously a very different process than the one needed for a data conflict.

Now revisit the spousal separation dispute between Paul and Jo-Anne, described in the first exercise at the end of Chapter 3. There is data conflict involved in this dispute, as in most disputes. However, in this case, where custody is a central issue, the main sources of conflict are what Moore refers to as relationship and interest conflicts. As a result, the mediator will have to put in significant time and effort addressing the strong conflict emotions and relationship issues between these two parties. This is especially necessary given that Paul and Jo-Anne, as the parents of two young children, will have to interact with each other for many years to come.

Most disputes involve several sources of conflict. Mediators must try to attend to all sources and help the parties develop the best strategies to resolve each area or issue in dispute.

Cooperative Behaviour

Early theorists of international relations viewed conflict as a win–lose struggle over values and over claims to status, power, and resources, which were in short supply (Deutsch, 1973). In this struggle, according to Mack and Snyder (1973, p. 36), parties behaved in ways "to destroy, injure, thwart or otherwise control another party or parties" and could "gain (relatively) only at each other's expense." Contemporary theories from the social sciences view conflict as emerging from the interdependence of parties, in that each party is necessarily affected by the actions or perceptions of other participants. This explains why parties in conflict are often concerned about the behaviour of other parties, even when that behaviour does not appear to affect them directly. When conflict is perceived as emerging out of relations of mutual interdependence, each person's choices have an impact on the other. Conflict occurs when one party perceives the other as acting in such a way as to block him from achieving his goals. For this reason, mediators focus on helping parties overcome their antagonism or competitive feelings toward each other; they encourage the parties to adopt instead cooperative approaches to solving their issues.

Before considering strategies for helping parties engage in collaboration rather than competition, you need to have some understanding of the theory of cooperative behaviour. Without such understanding, it is hard to imagine how parties engaged in intense conflict ever learn to cooperate. As we know from our discussion of the "negotiator's dilemma" (see Chapter 2), parties need to have some measure of trust in each other in order to collaborate. How do they acquire such trust?

There is a strong association between trust and cooperative behaviour. Trust is learned, or earned, through cooperation, rather than the other way around. The experience of cooperative behaviour induces trust, especially when parties learn that cooperation can result in individual and collective benefits that cannot be achieved through competition. In many different types of human social interactions, cooperation and competition coexist; they are not mutually exclusive patterns of behaviour.

This is not to say that we are naturally cooperative or sensitive toward others. The point is that we are social actors; at work, in our families, on the road, and even in the sphere of international relations, we live in conditions of *interdependence* with the people around us. This creates occasions for both cooperation and conflict.

Given this condition of interdependency, the basic question for many conflict resolution practitioners and mediators is how to increase the possibilities for productive, cooperative behaviour between parties who may have a long history of conflict and are now in the midst of it. If the parties can be helped to understand the benefits of cooperation, the conditions that have given rise to conflict are likely to be diminished, along with the conflict's destructive effects.

The Theory of Cooperative Behaviour

The theory of cooperative behaviour that underpins mediation posits that cooperation is a learned human behavioural strategy, a strategy that we use to achieve both individual and collective goals. Humans are social actors with both individual and collective needs. To meet our needs, we learn how to live in groups—in families, at school, at work, in church, and in other such communities. At work, for example, we help others by going beyond the limits of what our job description may require us to do. Even day-to-day driving on city streets involves a great deal of learned cooperative behavior. We give way, allowing other drivers to enter our lane of traffic or to back out of a tight parking spot. Some drivers are more cooperative than others; however, the traffic interactions that we experience daily involve far more cooperative behaviour, generally speaking, than they would if everyone drove strictly according to the rules of the road.

You can see this element of learned cooperative behaviour in our political process, too. Every three or four years, people vote for the candidates they want to represent them, whether in a local school board election, a municipal election, a provincial election, or a federal election. It is presented as an organized competition between competing candidates or political parties, but it is also, fundamentally, a process founded on cooperative behaviour and trust. The winners, for example, are expected to take into account the interests of those voters who did not vote for them. A considerable degree of learned cooperative behaviour is required, then, even within a competitive democratic political process.

These examples are intended to point out the obvious: cooperation exists in the midst of competition. Cooperation and competition are not mutually exclusive. There may be considerable opportunity for cooperation even in situations of intense conflict. As Schelling (1960, pp. 4–5) points out, situations of pure conflict, in which the contending or conflicting parties share no common interests, are very rare. Consider the Cold War between the United States and the USSR, from the 1950s to the 1980s. Even in this context, there were significant areas of cooperation between the two superpowers. They developed certain norms of cooperation. Even the strategy of mutually assured destruction, whereby each side was convinced that both sides would be destroyed in the event of a nuclear attack by one side, was an instance of cooperative behaviour. There were also arms control negotiations, and the tacit principle of non-interference in each other's geopolitical spheres of influence.

One of the best-known theorists of conflict and cooperation is Morton Deutsch, who developed what he calls "Deutsch's crude law of social relations" (Deutsch, 1973, p. 365). With this law, Deutsch posits that the conditions that promote cooperation are learned and tend to be self-reinforcing. *Destructive* conflict emerges when these conditions, which may exist even in the midst of conflict, have broken down. Conflict is considered constructive when the opposite conditions prevail—that is, when conditions favouring cooperation are strengthened or improved. This strengthening and improving can occur even in the throes of conflict.

One of the mediator's most important functions is to foster the conditions that promote cooperation. This is something he or she can begin doing in the early stages of mediation—by setting up the room; by securing the parties' agreement to mediation guidelines; and by modelling good communication practices such as turn-taking, reflective listening, and asking non-judgmental questions. These practices help establish a climate of cooperation which will, in turn, help parties to move from a competitive standpoint to a more collaborative one as the mediation proceeds.

There are various strategies and techniques that mediators can use to help parties overcome their adversarial orientations and thereby increase their ability to engage in collaborative interactions and dialogue. This is what we mean by the phrase "cultivating dialogue."

How Mediators Cultivate Dialogue

In this section, we discuss a number of strategies that mediators use to enable parties to engage in collaborative dialogue. Mediators may perform these actions differently, depending on their practice area and their training. The strategies that we will be discussing include the following:

1. establishing and managing the process,
2. educating the parties,
3. assessing parties' collaborating knowledge and skills, and
4. facilitating communication and collaboration.

Establishing and Managing the Process

The mediator supports or, in some cases, takes the lead in establishing and overseeing the mediation process. He or she, in collaboration with the parties, determines the elements of the process, including who should attend, the roles of participants and the mediator, and process and communication guidelines. That said, the mediator does not simply impose a rigid, standardized process on the parties; instead, she elicits the parties' input in how the process will proceed. This emerges from a consideration of the needs and abilities of the disputants, recognizing that the parties often rely on the mediator's experience and expertise. The mediator assists the parties in reaching a decision on how they will interact in the mediation. Ideally, this involves committing to respectful, collaborative interaction and seeking to fully understand the perspectives, goals, interests, and values of the other party. Parties generally agree to this because they genuinely believe it is in their best interests to do so and some good will come of it, not because the mediator suggests it.

The mediator is responsible for ensuring process integrity. An essential element of managing the process is ensuring that both parties' experience of the process will be what they agreed to undertake.

The mediator must ensure that the mediation process is fair to all parties. That will mean different things to different people. Indeed, the concept of "fair" has various philosophical and cultural formulations. One definition of process fairness is that (1) each party is able to fully express his or her views, concerns, needs, feelings, interests, and values so they are understood by all other participants; (2) all of these are adequately explored, clarified, and addressed; and (3) the process for formulating a resolution is equally responsive to all parties. Whether a fair process will necessarily result in a fair outcome may be a matter for debate. Some say that the outcome of a fair process is, by definition, a fair outcome.

Eliciting the parties' input into the structure of the mediation helps to ensure that the process is responsive to all parties' needs. This ensures, in turn, that they will perceive and experience it as a fair and beneficial process. When this happens, the parties will be much more ready, willing, and able to participate in a collaborative way.

Educating the Parties

There are times when the mediator may need to act as a coach or tutor, so that each party has the communication skills necessary to undertake a collaborative process. Or, the mediator may need to educate the parties on the nature of collaborative interaction, their role and responsibilities, and what they can expect of the mediator. This may include helping them appreciate and overcome some of the difficulties and challenges of collaborating. Each party needs to understand and accept that the other party has different perceptions, interpretations, behaviours, emotions, and goals that are legitimate. We tell parties that "understanding does not mean agreement." With that knowledge, both parties must be willing to try to understand the other party's perspectives, even though they may disagree with them. Finally, both parties must be willing, at some level, to work at overcoming their barriers to collaborating—and must want to try to find a resolution that will serve their own interests and those of the other parties. The mediator's objective is to help each party come to understand the advantages to them of collaborative interaction—and a willingness to commit to such a process. This education—through behaviour, direct instruction, or other means—starts in the convening stage and continues throughout the mediation.

Assessing Parties' Collaborating Knowledge and Skills

The mediator needs to ensure that the parties have a genuine willingness to entertain the idea they may not understand each other's viewpoints, and that by doing so the possibility of collaboration may emerge. The mediator also needs to determine if the disputants have things to learn—or obstacles and "disabilities" to overcome—before the joint mediation sessions begin. In addition, the mediator must feel assured that the parties are able to communicate with each other honestly and openly. If this is not feasible, the mediator may need to undertake steps to ensure open communication. For example, a translator or advocate may need to be brought into the sessions.

Factors That Influence Collaboration

As depicted in Figure 7.2, there are positive and negative influences that affect the degree of collaboration in a given conflict situation. Positive influences include goodwill, motivation, trust, and respect between the parties. Negotiation skills, willingness, and confidence are also significant. Likewise, there are factors that inhibit

Figure 7.2 Factors For and Against Collaboration

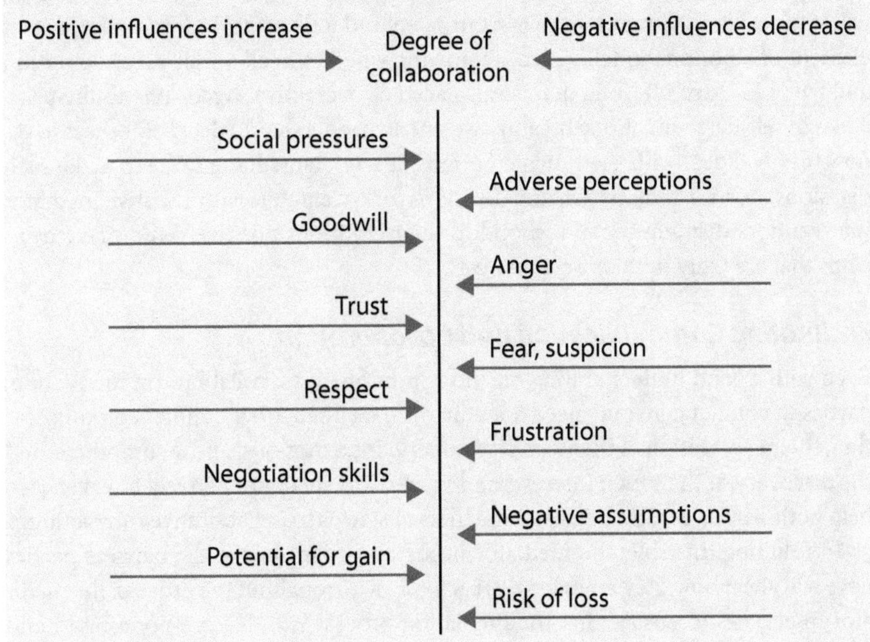

collaboration or escalate conflict, including misperception of each other, strong emotions such as anger, fear, or frustration, and negative attribution errors of willful harm. Without some form of intervention, negative assumptions and emotions increase as the conflict unfolds, causing the interaction to become more adversarial and destructive. Negative influences can overpower the goodwill, respect, and human connection interfering with productive interaction. Mediator interventions that reduce negative forces will allow the positive forces to take effect and increase the degree of collaboration.

Collaborative interaction will not be achieved by having people suppress or ignore their adversarial emotions, perceptions, and inclinations. Nor will it be achieved by asking or trying to persuade people in conflict to be civil or "nice" to each other. It will definitely not be achieved by a mediator simply establishing a process with ground rules that require people to be civil and respectful, although such a process, if consistently applied, can certainly help. What is essential is that mediators recognize and deal with the negative influences. If they are addressed, the parties will have an opportunity to deal with them beneficially. If they are ignored, they will wreak havoc.

It is important to distinguish when emotion is being destructive from when emotion is being protective. All emotions, including fear, suspicion, mistrust, and anger, will at times play an important role in our safety and well-being. Indeed, an important element of emotional intelligence is knowing when to heed a well-placed emotion and when to "turn off" one that is misplaced or overactive. According to the principles of self-determination and empowerment, people should decide for themselves how they will deal with their own emotions. It is not a mediator's role to make such decisions, nor, for that matter, any decisions for others. But with effective mediator intervention, disputants can respond to their emotions positively and make decisions that are truly in their best interests.

Facilitating Communication and Collaboration

Even with a good understanding of, and commitment to, collaborative interaction, parties in conflict generally need a mediator to facilitate their conflict communication, their exploration of their conflict perceptions, emotions, and assumptions, and the discovery of their own interests and values. The mediator actively intervenes to help both parties resolve or overcome their obstacles to collaborative interaction.

In fulfilling this role, the mediator needs to recognize that the barriers parties have will affect how they interact with each other. Throughout the process, the mediator intervenes to ensure that the mediation process is indeed responding to and fulfilling each party's needs.

The Parties' Conflicting Perspectives

Mediators enable parties to engage in collaborative dialogue about their differences by encouraging them to be respectful, open, and cooperative. Think for a moment about two people in a dispute who have never experienced mediation and know very little about it. What might they be thinking and feeling about the situation and about each other? Let's return to the Car Repair Blues scenario from Chapter 1, and the two parties, Dale and Chris (see Box 1.1).

Before mediation, Dale might perceive Chris as a cheat and an arrogant chauvinist who would gladly gouge her for an extra $1,000. She feels anger and resentment and generally has a strongly negative attitude toward him. Dale feels strongly that she has been victimized by Chris and that, as soon as the mediator gets the whole story, he will help her get her car back and resolve the dispute fairly. This is Dale's conflict narrative.

Chris, for his part, perceives Dale as a pushy, inconsiderate, supercilious person who expects him to drop whatever he's doing and jump when she calls. He may well believe that he bent over backward to provide Dale with fast, excellent service, and that he makes essential repairs at fair rates. Therefore, he is offended at Dale's attempt to get something for nothing, by twisting and manipulating the situation. Chris has agreed to mediation because he is certain that any fair-minded person will see Dale for the kind of person she is and will set her straight. As in most conflicts, Chris's conflict narrative is very different from his adversary's.

Chris and Dale have strong *adversarial* perceptions, emotions, and assumptions toward each other—and these will obviously influence how they interact in mediation. As well, their understanding of mediation, of the mediator's role, and of their own role in the process may be very limited. So, in the convening phase and in the early stages of the mediation, the mediator must address these adversarial attitudes, the parties' expectations of the mediator's role, and their own role in the mediation.

The mediator can help the parties move from an adversarial to a collaborative interaction, if each party understands what is required and takes individual responsibility to achieve that—but only if they both want to. The mediator *cannot* do that, only the parties can. Parties often need a lot of assistance from the mediator, but, no matter how much they rely on the mediator's skill, presence, and wisdom, they will successfully collaborate only by their own efforts, insights, and understanding.

Self-motivated collaboration is fundamental to the role of a mediator. Genuine collaboration between parties in conflict occurs only when each party really understands what collaboration means and requires, and truly wants to engage in a collaborative process. However, in most conflict situations, such understanding and motivation rarely exist at the start of the mediation process. Yes, the mediator explains the process and may try to persuade each party of the benefits of a collaborative approach, but this requires much more than a rational, analytical understanding. Mediators need to recognize that, if collaboration is to be achieved, party understanding and motivation must develop through the mediation process, as each party gains experience and insights of genuine collaborative interaction—in other words, as parties learn more about themselves and others. Mediators sometimes work wonders to help parties get to the point where they can fully engage and interact with each other as collaborative negotiators.

Beginning the Mediation

As we discussed in Chapter 6, the mediator or mediation convenor, before the mediation process starts, has discussions and preparation with each of the parties. All parties are informed of the various features of the process, and agreement to proceed is obtained. The issues discussed and agreed to beforehand include who will attend, confidentiality, impact on possible future proceedings, the basic elements of the process and its objectives, communication and interaction guidelines, the roles of the mediator and the parties, as well as logistical information and requirements. In cases with complex substantive or legal issues, preparation means collecting and becoming familiar with data relevant to those issues.

For parties to make fully informed decisions, they need to be educated about the mediation process, their role, and the role of the mediator. Since imposing a set of rigid terms and conditions would be contrary to the principle of self-determination, the mediator will elicit each party's opinions and input on various process decisions and then, if necessary, suggest other protocols for ensuring a safe and fair process. The mediator then confirms that all parties understand and commit to this process. In a case in which the dispute involves the parties' rights and obligations (that is, one that could proceed to adjudication if not resolved), the mediator should have the parties sign an Agreement to Mediate before or at the beginning of the joint session (see Appendix A).

The final task before the first joint session is to determine how best to conduct the mediation. This question involves when and where to hold the mediation, what physical arrangements are needed to accommodate disabilities, the seating pattern to use, the use and shape of a table, and the need for and availability of private caucus rooms. It also includes considering who will participate, in terms of parties, their legal, union, or other representatives, and secondary parties such as friends, constituents, or the media. Furthermore, consideration is given to whether co-mediation, or even panel mediation, would work better than a sole-mediator model.

Preparing for Dialogue

To illustrate what might happen at the beginning of the first joint mediation session, let's listen in on the discussion the mediator has at this stage with the parties in the Car Repair Blues dispute (see Box 1.1 in Chapter 1).

> *Mediator*: Hello, Dale and Chris. I am pleased you both came today, because I know it takes effort to talk face to face about issues that you do not agree on and that you feel strongly about. I want you to know that while mediation may not be easy, in my experience it is often useful and successful.
>
> As you recall, I met with each of you separately to explain what would happen here today and to confirm that mediation is appropriate for your dispute. Let me begin by reviewing some of what we talked about.
>
> My role is to help you discuss the issues in dispute so you learn things about each other that will help you resolve this conflict.
>
> I will not judge who is right or wrong, nor will I be telling you what you should do to resolve your dispute. That will be for you to decide. If you reach an agreement and want to put it into written form, I can help you do that.
>
> Now I want to discuss how each of you will participate in this mediation. In particular, we need to discuss how you will communicate with each other. In that regard, I would like to know the following:
>
> - How do you want the other person to speak to you?
> - What do you want the other person to do while you are speaking?
>
> *Dale*: I hope that Chris will be … civil and … respectful.
>
> *Mediator*: Chris, how do you want Dale to speak to you?
>
> *Chris*: I want the same thing. I want our discussion to be respectful.

> *Mediator*: Chris, what could Dale do when you are speaking that would show respect?
>
> *Chris*: Well, I want her to listen.
>
> *Mediator*: You want Dale to listen to you and to try to understand what you are saying? Dale, is that what you want?
>
> *Dale*: Yes, it is.
>
> *Mediator*: The key is that you express yourself in a way that the other person can really hear and understand you? As your mediator, I will do everything I can to help you understand each other.
>
> Is there anything else that either of you would like to add to ensure a productive and safe discussion today?

As this discussion demonstrates, the mediator begins by eliciting the parties' input and ensures that there is agreement on how the parties will interact. This confirms that the parties take responsibility for their own dialogue process, both of them deciding and agreeing that they want a respectful discussion in which each will strive to understand the other. This explicit agreement is very useful to the mediator; during the mediation, when the parties stray from this ideal of respectfulness (as they usually do), the mediator might remind them of their earlier agreement and why they wanted those terms of agreement.

The mediator's next step, as the following exchange illustrates, is to address the matter of confidentiality:

> *Mediator*: I want to assure you that what I hear today will remain confidential. I will not be discussing outside the room what is said here, nor am I required to report on what the two of you discuss. Usually mediation is a private, confidential process. What expectations does each of you have regarding confidentiality?
>
> *Dale*: It doesn't matter much to me. If he wants it to be confidential, that's okay with me.
>
> *Chris*: Yes, I do prefer that what we discuss today will not be shared with others outside this room.
>
> *Mediator*: OK, so each of you agrees that everything discussed during the mediation will be confidential?
>
> *Parties*: Yes.

Since this is a private dispute between these two parties, the confidentiality question is straightforward. Neither party has a constituency or a higher authority they need to report to. If either party needs to consult a lawyer, then these communications with their lawyer could and should be an exception to the confidentiality requirement. The same would be the case if one or both of the parties are representing a group and have requirements to report back.

The mediator will also confirm with the parties that disclosures in mediation will not be admissible in court, should the dispute end up there. The mediator's statement in this regard might be as follows:

> *Mediator*: Because this is a legal dispute—one that could go to small claims court if you don't reach an agreement in mediation—I have prepared a written Agreement to Mediate containing some of the terms we talked about in our pre-mediation discussion. After I review this agreement and before we start, I will ask each of you to sign this agreement. The first point I would like to go over is a legal term known as "without prejudice."
>
> Paragraph X of this agreement states that all oral and written communications in this mediation process will be "without prejudice." This term applies if you do not reach agreement in mediation and one of you takes the issue to court. In that event, this term means that nothing either of you says during the mediation can be used by the other party as evidence in a court proceeding. The other point in this paragraph is that I, as your mediator, can never be required to come to court and to give evidence about what you discussed during the mediation. Dale and Chris, are you each clear about this term?
>
> *Parties*: Yes.

In a case like this one, which could move to a legal process if the parties do not reach agreement in mediation, this "without prejudice" term is very important. It removes a significant concern for each party; it allows them to speak freely during the mediation knowing that whatever they say cannot be used against them in some future legal proceeding.

Another matter the mediator commonly addresses, in preparing the parties for dialogue, is that of private caucusing between the individual parties and the mediator. It is important for parties to know that they can speak privately with the mediator if they have to. For many people, this "safety valve" can help to increase their trust in the process and their ability to engage in the process fully and confidently. So the mediator might say the following to the parties:

> *Mediator*: At any time, you can ask to meet with me privately. I may also feel the need to talk with each of you privately, in a caucus, and will let you know if I do. Our discussions in any of these caucus meetings will be private and confidential. I will not share anything we discuss with the other party unless you specifically give me permission to do so.

The mediator will also want to determine in the joint session whether the parties have the authority to resolve the dispute. The mediator in the Car Repair Blues scenario, for example, might ask a question like the following:

> *Mediator*: I also want to find out if each of you has the authority to settle this dispute today. Dale or Chris, do either of you need to consult anyone before making final decisions on the issues between you?
>
> *Parties*: No.
>
> *Mediator*: Do either of you have any questions or want to add anything? Are you both ready and willing to proceed with the mediation?
>
> *Dale*: I have no questions. Yes, I am ready.
>
> *Chris*: Yes, I am ready to go.

In this opening phase of the mediation, the mediator will review all aspects of the mediation process, answer any questions, and get verbal confirmation of each party's understanding and commitment to participate. Even when these process issues were discussed and agreed to by the parties before the first joint session, it is important to discuss them again in joint session so that each party will know that the other party has the same understanding and commitment toward the process.

This introductory phase of mediation gives the mediator a chance to establish a relationship with the parties and set a tone of warmth, trust, and competence. It also provides the first opportunity for the mediator to demonstrate his or her promise to listen and to respond to the parties' concerns. Mediators who employ alternative strategies might begin this stage with a ritual—the smoking of sweet grass, an exercise to release physical tension, or other creative strategies.

One of the mediator's objectives during the initial phase of mediation is to explore the parties' conflict narratives. We will now examine in some detail how a mediator might initiate this part of the process.

Exploring the Parties' Narratives

After reviewing the mediation process and obtaining verbal confirmation of each party's understanding and commitment to the process, the mediator begins to elicit each party's conflict narrative. From these narratives, she infers the key issues that need to be addressed during the process. How these stories are elicited varies according to the mediator's style, training, and the nature of the case, as well as to the party's goals and needs.

Eliciting the parties' stories begins with the mediator's asking each of them for a brief opening statement about the problem or the issues to be discussed. The mediator's request for an opening statement in the Car Repair Blues scenario from Chapter 1 (see Box 1.1) might go something like this:

> Dale and Chris, I would like each of you to give me a brief statement about what it is that you have come to talk to each other about today. This will give us an overall sense of the problem and some of the issues to be discussed in

> this mediation from each of your perspectives. Please be assured that you will have ample time to go into the details of the situation as we proceed. At this point, I would very much like you to provide only a general sense of the problem needing to be discussed. Which one of you would like to begin?

Mediators often have to give parties time to think about the question of who should begin. If neither party offers, the mediator needs to find an impartial way to ask one party to start. A common practice is to begin with the party who is the complainant or with the party who first requested the mediation. In the Car Repair Blues scenario, this party would be Chris, and the opening statement of his narrative might sound like the following:

> *Chris*: She came in that morning without an appointment, expecting me to drop everything and work on her car right away. She seemed pushy, almost rude. But, I figured she was in a hurry and really needed her car back as soon as possible. So I decided to give her the benefit of the doubt. I decided I would do whatever I could to get her car back to her the same day.
>
> *Mediator*: Why was that important to you?
>
> *Chris*: I've had this garage for 18 years. I have always done everything I can to provide excellent customer service. I have built up a loyal clientele by giving people what they need for a fair price. I really go out of my way to do that.
>
> *Mediator*: So, what happened?
>
> *Chris*: When I inspected her car, I found that her radiator was almost shot. It was clear to me that it had to be replaced, if not right away, then very soon. If I could get her a good rebuilt radiator and put it in right away, I figured she would be much better off than waiting and having to come back in a month or two, to be without her car for one or two days or more, and perhaps have to pay a lot more. In fact, I was able to locate a good rebuilt radiator for $350, instead of the $400 or even $450 I have to pay sometimes. Even though I didn't have her express authorization, I went ahead, confident that it was what she would want me to do.
>
> When she came in at the end of the day, I gave her the bill and was starting to explain the work I did on her car when she took a fit and refused to pay my bill. She said: "What is this, a licence to print money?" Then I told her she wasn't going to get her car until she paid me.
>
> *Mediator*: How did you feel when Dale reacted the way she did?
>
> *Chris*: I was steamed—especially when she made that crack about my place being a "licence to print money?" She might as well have called me a crook! I bend over backward to do everything she needs right away, and what do I get in return? She expects me to do all that for next to nothing, and slaps me with insults at the same time. Forget it!

After responding further to Chris, the mediator would invite Dale to provide her opening statement. This is what she might say:

> *Dale*: When I took my car to Arco, I thought it was pretty straightforward. Could he do the routine six-month service that my car needed and get it back to me at the end of the day? He said he could. I didn't ask him to do any major repairs. So, when I came in at the end of the day and he gave me a bill for $1,200, I was floored. What kind of sucker does he think I am? His bill is ten times more than what it was supposed to be and he expects me to just suck it up, pay it, and walk away! I don't think so.

Strategies for Transforming Adversarial Dialogue

As both Dale and Chris did in the Car Repair Blues scenario, parties in mediation often express adversarial conflict narratives in their discussions early in the mediation. In this section, we will examine various strategies and techniques a mediator may employ to respond to these narratives. In doing so, we need to consider two preliminary points.

First, we need to recognize that a party's conflict narrative always contains and is influenced by his or her strong conflict emotions. As we discussed in Chapters 4 and 5, some of these emotions, such as the anger expressed by both Chris and Dale, are visible. Other emotions, such as the fear, insecurity, suspicion, and/or mistrust that parties often experience in conflict, are less evident. If there is considerable antagonism between the parties, a mediator needs to be mindful of, and seek to discover, these conflict emotions, especially the underlying ones, and respond appropriately to them. It is only by responding effectively to the emotions impeding cooperation that the mediator can help parties to overcome their adversarial attitudes and behaviours and start to interact more collaboratively.

Second, to deal effectively with a person's conflict emotions and behaviour, a mediator needs to establish a relationship of trust. Indeed, in many cases, it is the party's personal connection with the mediator that helps shift that person's attitude from adversarial to collaborative. When the mediator develops such a connection with both parties, he or she becomes a bridge or channel between them. Whatever the mediator achieves with one party gets transmitted to the other. In mediating the conflict between Dale and Chris, the mediator's understanding, validation, empathy, and respect for Dale helps Chris to experience the same toward Dale, in some measure. By seeking and eliciting what is positive and good in each party, the mediator enables the disputants to connect those qualities with each other. When the mediator helps to reduce the negative forces that decrease collaboration, the positive forces that are already present will tend to move parties toward increased collaboration.

Mediators use a number of strategies and techniques to respond to and transform negative influences in conflict situations. Elsewhere in this text, we discuss certain skills and techniques that the mediator can use to manage the strong emotions that can adversely affect a mediation process: connecting skills, non-blaming statements, and non-defensive responses. We discussed these in Chapter 5. (See also Chapter 8, under the heading "The Creative Communicator.") Now we will examine the following strategies:

- educating,
- acknowledging,
- affirming,
- normalizing,
- asking for suggestions,
- inviting expression,
- exploring consequences,
- naming conflict perceptions, assumptions, and behaviours,
- inviting response,
- reframing, and
- intervening creatively.

We will also discuss further the use of *caucusing*, a process whereby the mediator meets privately with each party.

Educating

Educating a party for collaborative interaction begins with the first contact between the mediator and the party, likely in the pre-mediation phase. For example, a mediator will often discuss the benefits of mutually respectful communication and help the party to gain a genuine appreciation of how this is in his or her best interests. Then, during the mediation process, if a party becomes overly disruptive, the mediator can refer to those earlier discussions and help the party become aware of how such behaviour is contrary to his or her own interests. In this way, the mediator is not educating through "telling" the party what to do; rather, he or she is assisting the party to develop awareness and make decisions based on that awareness. Such a conversation, before mediation, might go like this:

> *Mediator*: Dale, what kind of communication do you hope to have with Chris in the mediation? How do you hope he will speak to you? What do you hope that Chris will feel toward you during the mediation?

During the mediation, it might go like this:

> *Mediator*: Dale, I really don't know if such allegations by you against Chris are going to foster the open communication and mutual understanding that you both want to create. How might you express to Chris your feelings and experience of the situation so that he can hear what is important to you?

In addition to pointing out communication patterns, mediators can educate the parties about their non-verbal interactions, including gestures and tone of voice, which might be negatively influencing their abilities to resolve their conflict.

Acknowledging

Listening for and verbally acknowledging peoples' negative emotions is an essential first step to helping them move beyond them. Letting a party know that you recognize the emotion, and are not judging it, is a very powerful acknowledgment of his or her experience. Such acknowledgment helps parties to move beyond those strong feelings, once they have been recognized and accepted. It can also help the other person better understand that person's experience of the conflict. The following examples demonstrate *reflecting* (discussed in Chapter 5) being used to respond to strong emotions.

> Chris, I can tell you are angry and hurt over how Dale reacted to the work you did for her on her car.
>
> You are upset, and that tells me that this issue is important to you.
>
> So Dale, you were surprised, even shocked, when Chris presented his bill for $1,200 and you reacted strongly to that because you expected something quite different.
>
> After this conflict arose, both of you had considerable difficulty trying to discuss this situation and that's why you decided to use mediation.

Affirming

Acknowledging and affirming parties' efforts, ideas, or intentions may achieve a great deal in helping them resolve their conflict. Positive feedback has a tendency to open up possibilities in a mediation session. When a party's actions or intentions are appreciated, she or he often becomes more generous in the mediation. This can result in a party accepting the other's good intentions, considering an option that she or he might otherwise have dismissed, or owning up to a moment when his or her intentions were not so honourable—all of which provide opportunities for positive or constructive discussion.

> *Mediator*: Dale, when you went back the next day to speak to Chris, even though it didn't go well and tempers flared, it certainly sounds like your intentions were good. You wanted to discuss the situation and try to sort things out. Indeed, in choosing mediation, you both have shown that you want to try to work this out amicably.

Normalizing

Mediators are often able to recognize when the emotions, perceptions, and behaviours that parties are experiencing are normal for people in similar situations. Saying this can help a person accept difficult or negative feelings and behaviours, enabling them to deal with them more constructively. Normalizing can also help to humanize the parties' experience of each other and thereby help them to move forward. The following examples show a mediator engaged in normalizing:

> *Mediator*: In my experience, it is quite common for this kind of thing to happen when people have been feuding for a long time.
>
> *Mediator*: It's pretty normal to feel that way when the well-being of your own child is involved.
>
> *Mediator*: It is certainly understandable that someone in your situation would feel (or act) that way.
>
> *Mediator*: In my experience, people in difficult conflict situations such as yours often feel frustrated and discouraged at this stage.
>
> *Mediator*: Dale, I know you are anxious to jump in and say how you see the situation. People in mediation often feel and act that way when they have to sit and listen to the other person tell their story, especially when they disagree with it. I want you to know that you will have ample opportunity in a few minutes to say everything you need to say. For now, I would encourage you to take this opportunity, difficult as it may be, to really hear and understand Chris's view of the situation.

Asking for Suggestions

Having identified counterproductive behaviour, it is often useful for the mediator to ask one or both parties for suggestions regarding how they might behave or interact more productively, rather than to advise them what to do. This is part of the education process. Mediators often ask the parties for suggestions on how to proceed when things seem blocked or resistance is strong. This gives the parties an opportunity to take responsibility for their own actions and for their mediation process. When done well, it can be empowering.

> *Mediator*: You have been arguing and criticizing each other for a couple of minutes. This has happened a few times during the mediation, and I don't think it's accomplishing very much. I'm wondering if either of you has any suggestions for how to deal with this in a more productive way?
>
> *Mediator*: It seems to me that this discussion is going around in circles. What do you need to address to break this cycle?

Inviting Expression

Inviting a party to express his or her feelings about—or experience of—a difficult situation may sometimes be the key to enabling him or her to move forward. As a mediator, you should use this strategy only when a party is comfortable enough in the session to discuss his or her private thoughts and feelings. Again, this can be a very powerful experience for parties who feel that someone (the mediator) is connecting with them for the first time in the conflict situation.

> *Mediator*: Chris, you seem upset about what Dale has been talking about. My impression is that this situation has been very difficult for you. It might help if you were to talk about your feelings and experience of the situation.

Exploring Consequences

It is also helpful to invite one or both of the parties to consider the possible consequences of continuing a certain type of behaviour or interaction. Questions that invite the exploration of consequences can assist the mediator and the parties in refocusing the discussion more constructively. Following are two examples of a mediator exploring consequences with the parties:

> *Mediator*: It's happened a few times now that when this issue comes up, you end up arguing over who was supposed to do what. I don't think either of you is achieving much by doing that. What do you think? Chris? Dale? Do you want to talk about the consequences of continuing to take that approach?

> *Mediator*: Dale, you have said that if Chris doesn't agree to what you have asked, you will speak to the Better Business Bureau. I wonder if you could say more about what really concerns you about this situation and what you would hope to achieve by speaking to the Better Business Bureau.

Naming Conflict Perceptions, Assumptions, and Behaviour

Here, the mediator's objective is to be openly curious about unspoken perceptions and assumptions that each party might have toward the other—and give each of them an opportunity to express them. The basic premise of this approach is that unstated negative perceptions and assumptions often fuel aggressive feelings, attitudes, and behaviours. If they remain unstated, they continue to adversely influence the discussion's dynamics. However, when such perceptions and assumptions are honestly expressed and named, everyone can better understand this source of aggression and deal with it. This naming process is shown in the following exchange:

> *Dale*: I can't believe he did that. He knew I only wanted routine service that would cost $150. Then he just goes ahead and runs up a bill for $1,200 as if it's nothing at all.

> *Mediator*: From what you said, it seems you assume that Chris didn't care how much your bill would be—that he didn't think it would matter to you how much the bill was.

> *Dale*: Yes, exactly.

For such an intervention to succeed, the mediator must first establish an environment in the mediation that will allow these perceptions and assumptions to be discussed safely. In the above example, this would mean that

- Dale may express her assumption without fear of its being criticized or attacked; and
- Chris, in hearing this, is able to appreciate that this is her honest belief and how she has been experiencing their interaction, regardless of what his thoughts and intentions actually have been. Chris is able to hear this without feeling and reacting in an excessively defensive way.

Provided that it is done appropriately and in a way that respects the interests of both parties, an intervention whereby the mediator names a party's perception or assumption can be helpful for both parties. By ensuring that perceptions and assumptions are openly acknowledged and, if appropriate, normalized, the parties will be able to resolve or move beyond them. This strategy often leads to discovering that prevalent assumptions are false and thus can be de-linked from the conflict interaction. (See Chapter 8, under the heading "Linking and De-Linking.")

In addition to naming assumptions and perceptions, it can be helpful to describe in specific, concrete terms the conflict behaviour of each party and its effects on the other as a way to help them understand their different perceptions. Getting these underlying issues on the table gives parties the information they need to generate new ideas about how to deal with their conflict constructively.

Inviting a Response

A powerful strategy for the mediator is to invite one party to respond to what the other party has been saying. This is a potentially high-risk intervention that should be used only when parties have moved, at least to some extent, beyond their adversarial attitudes and behaviours. To invite a person who is feeling hostile or defensive to respond to another is to invite escalation of the conflict. Therefore, this technique should be used only when the mediator has good reason to believe that the party invited to respond will do so constructively. The following example illustrates this technique:

> *Mediator*: Chris, Dale said she could not imagine what you could have done to come up with a bill for $1,200. What would you like to say to Dale about your bill that might help her to understand what you did?

Another variation of this strategy is to invite a party to restate what he or she just heard the other party say. This ensures that what one party is saying has been accurately heard by the other, and demonstrates that he or she has been listening. If what has been heard is not accurate, it can be corrected. This strategy can be perceived as a paternalistic or condescending approach, so the mediator should have a strong rapport with the parties before attempting it.

Reframing

Reframing is a process used to convert an interaction from adversarial to collaborative. It is a "process" because it usually takes two or more steps to achieve. Reframing may take different forms and be used in different ways in many different situations. Picard (2002, p. 83) describes it this way:

> Reframing is the process of changing how a person defines or conceptualizes a particular situation or event. In resolving conflicts, it is important to remember that our perception and emotional response to a particular event is based on the frame of reference within which it is viewed. It is possible to change the meaning of an event by changing this frame of reference. If this happens, our attitude and our response to the situation can also change.

Reframing can be used to shift positions to interests, statements to issues, or negative orientations to more positive ones. Let's look at an example:

> *Chris*: When she came in that morning, she was very pushy, expecting me to drop everything and take her car right away.

Instead of focusing on the blaming, the mediator focuses on Chris's experience of Dale, his feelings, and his perceptions of her.

> *Mediator*: Chris, it seems your first meeting with Dale was difficult, which made it challenging for you to get off on the right foot with her.

The mediator has acknowledged Chris's feelings. In making this statement about Chris's experience interacting with Dale, the mediator has shifted the focus away from Chris's judgment of Dale's "negative" behaviour, which Chris has characterized as "pushy." In attending to the speaker, to Chris, and to his feelings and experience, the mediator essentially prompts him to say more about his experience, which provides more information and insight for the mediator to work with. The following exchange reflects this process:

> *Chris*: That's for sure! She wanted her car fixed that day and she wasn't going to take "No" for an answer.
>
> *Mediator*: So, you felt that you had to get everything done on her car that day no matter what, is that right?
>
> *Chris*: Yes, I knew that she would not be happy unless I did everything that needed to be done to her car that day.

Mediator: So, it was important for you to get all of the work on Dale's car done that day so she would be a happy customer.

Chris: Yes, it was.

Mediator: And, having happy customers is important to your business.

Chris: Yes, it is.

The mediator has completed the reframing process. At the beginning, the focus was Chris's negative and value-laden evaluation of Dale's behavior—his perception that she was "pushy," demanding, and impatient. After the reframing, the discussion has been redirected to a key insight about the pressure of running a small business and keeping the customer happy as an explanation for Chris going ahead with the work on Dale's car that same day, even if he wasn't able to consult her. This is a step in the right direction. Provided Dale can hear Chris non-defensively, she will be able to get a much better understanding of why he went ahead that day and did all of this work on her car. She will be able to see him in a new way. She will have a new understanding of his motivation.

Reframing is one of the more difficult tools for the mediator. The process requires the mediator to find and open the right door so that parties can move from a negative frame of mind to a more positive, constructive, or even creative attitude. The intervention usually requires a number of steps, with appropriate timing or pacing from step to step. Let's dissect a typical reframing process and analyze the component steps:

1. Focus on the speaker's experience, perceptions, emotions, and needs.
2. Be open and curious.
3. Respond empathically to the speaker.
4. Acknowledge the speaker's perceptions, concerns, and emotions.
5. Ask for the speaker's confirmation.
6. Verbalize the speaker's key interest.
7. Frame the speaker's interest in such a way that satisfying it will be mutually beneficial for all parties.

Intervening Creatively

Many of the techniques and strategies outlined above can be considered "scientific" interventions. By and large, they are based on communications and psychological theories. A whole other set of interventions follow more creative "out of the box" ways of thinking that ask parties to shift their perspectives from "left brain" logic into the more creative "right brain." For example, a mediator might ask parties, either in the mediation session or in preparing for a session, to draw, write about, or mime what they are experiencing, thinking, or feeling. A lot can be "said" without the use of words and for some individuals, especially children, this way of communicating can be very informative. The point to be stressed here is that mediation is not formulaic; it needs to be flexible and creative.

Mediators may also ask parties to physically move—to switch seats or to get up to stretch and walk around. The intent here is to change the somatic effects of the moment. Since people carry their emotions in their bodies, asking them to transform their physical state can release some of their tension.

In addition to art work, music can also help parties break destructive patterns. Doing so tends to release parties from the moment of tension, and disputants often end up laughing at their drawings, lightening the mood. A word of caution: not all people are comfortable being asked to create a piece of art or music. A mediator needs to recognize when the time is appropriate for these sorts of interventions.

Caucusing

Recall that a caucus is a separate or private meeting that a mediator has with one party (or others, such as counsel who might be attending the mediation with the party) to discuss some matter in private. With such a variety of mediation models, there are also many ways and reasons to caucus.

Reasons for Caucusing

Caucusing with a party should be in the best interests of all parties and the process. Here are six instances where this is the case:

1. *To deal with strong emotion or "difficult" behaviour*. Sometimes, there is an underlying source of conflict that a party has not revealed in joint session and that is causing him or her to continue to exhibit adversarial or disruptive behaviour. A private caucus will allow the mediator to explore whatever may be causing such disruptive behaviour. A mediator might say something like the following in a caucus discussion:

   > *Mediator*: Jean, I can tell you're still very upset about the situation and seem very angry with Alex and his counsel. I thought you might like a chance to talk about it privately. If there is something specific that is bothering you, it could help to get it off your chest.

2. *To bring out information or interests*. The mediator may believe that one of the parties is reluctant to communicate significant information or reveal his or her concerns or interests. A caucus may help to determine why.
3. *To educate or empower the parties*. Generally, the mediator will have taken steps to educate and empower each party in joint session—to help them interact in a constructive, beneficial manner. However, if the mediator notices that a party is doing something on an ongoing basis that seems to

be interfering with or undermining his or her ability to engage in productive negotiations, the mediator may choose to deal with that in caucus.

4. *To encourage or re-energize a party.* If it becomes apparent in joint session that a party's enthusiasm or motivation for the process has declined, a private caucus discussion with that party may be helpful. It can give him or her an opportunity to open up, express any difficulties or frustrations, let off steam, take a break, or otherwise do whatever is needed to refocus and re-energize and come back ready, mentally and emotionally, to continue with the process.
5. *To explore or develop possible settlement options.* In some circumstances, some of the techniques for the resolution phase, outlined below, may work best in caucus. A party may be reluctant to respond positively to such mediator suggestions or interventions in the presence of the other party. If there is a significant risk that a party may react negatively or positionally to a particular mediator suggestion or intervention, the mediator may decide to try it out in caucus—to "run it up the flag pole"—where any negative reaction can be managed with less adverse fallout.
6. *To overcome impasse.* Reality checks, exploring best alternatives, or other techniques for overcoming impasse can be employed in caucus. In an impasse situation, a party may be reluctant to fully discuss his or her analysis or assessment of the situation in the presence of the other party for fear that it could put them at some disadvantage or expose them to some risk. Having this type of discussion in caucus allows parties to *save face.*

Guidelines for Caucusing

Here are some guidelines for caucusing:

- Don't caucus too soon.
- Ensure that everyone understands that either party or the mediator may request a caucus.
- Ensure that everyone is clear on the rules of confidentiality for caucusing.
- Caucus for a specific reason, and tell the parties what that reason is.
- *Always* caucus with both sides. The mediator may have a different reason for caucusing with each party.
- Keep the caucus brief and to the point.
- After caucusing with both parties, return to joint session and summarize in general terms the results of the caucus, respecting caucus confidentiality, of course.

The mediator's overriding purpose in caucusing is to positively influence the dynamic between the parties. If the parties' interaction has been adversarial and non-productive, the mediator hopes that by breaking the interaction with brief and purposeful caucus sessions, the dynamic will change and both parties will be able to re-engage with a different and hopefully more positive mindset.

Despite the potential benefits of caucusing, we urge mediators not to caucus prematurely. Private meetings can undermine the trust between the parties, and even their perception of the mediator. A party might wonder what the mediator is doing with the other party while she waits for his or her return. It is our experience that some mediators use caucus for interventions that could just as easily be undertaken in joint sessions. For example, if strong emotion is difficult for mediators, instead of hiding it away in a caucus, we suggest that mediators acknowledge it and work with it in joint session. This not only normalizes emotion in negotiations, but also ensures that important, albeit difficult, communication is taking place between the people who really matter—the parties themselves.

Participation of Parties' Advisers in Mediation

For many disputes that proceed to mediation, parties may have lawyers or other advisers who participate in the mediation: union representatives, accountants, staff relations advisers, professional agents, or other experts in the substantive areas under dispute. Usually, these advisers have been trained and are experienced in adversarial approaches to dispute resolution, but may have little training in collaborative processes like mediation. This raises particular challenges for them. While most of the discussion in this section will be about the role of lawyers in counselling their clients in mediation, much of what is covered also applies to other types of advisers.

Certainly there is no reason, in principle, why participating lawyers should undermine the mediation and prevent it from being a collaborative process. Indeed, the participation of lawyers who understand and are skilled at principled negotiation may significantly enhance the collaborative process and contribute to the success of mediation. In some cases, a lawyer who understands the potential benefits of collaborative negotiation—and knows how to pursue such an approach assertively and effectively—may enable his or her client to pursue collaborative interaction, particularly in a case where, without such assistance, the client would be unable to do so.

In legal disputes, parties and their lawyers often tend to have an adversarial mindset and pursue an adversarial approach, even if the lawyer is skilled at principled negotiation. Below are various reasons why that may happen:

- The lawyer and the client may believe that the opposing party and his or her lawyer or representative will be aggressive or will use adversarial tactics such as intimidation or stonewalling.
- The lawyer may be concerned that if the client openly reveals his or her wishes, preferences, and intentions, the other party may use that to advantage in negotiation.

- The lawyer may be concerned that if the client provides all the evidence and information he or she has of the situation, the opposing party (and lawyer) may acquire a tactical advantage by being able to find other evidence, information, or arguments to refute it.
- The lawyer may believe that the other party and lawyer are deceitful and manipulative—that, after appearing to collaborate, they will simply lead them and the mediator "down the garden path."
- There has been so much animosity and bad blood between the parties that, even if their intellect tells them to collaborate, their hearts will say "no."

Mediators need to recognize the psychological, relational, and systemic reasons why parties and their lawyers or other advisers may be inclined not to engage in collaborative interaction.

The Role of Lawyers in Mediation

One role that lawyers play is to inform and educate their clients about the timely and effective use of mediation. This should be done at an early stage of the lawyer's involvement in the dispute. In Ontario, rule 2.02(3) of the *Rules of Professional Conduct* of the Law Society of Upper Canada states the following: "The lawyer shall consider the use of alternative dispute resolution (ADR) for every dispute, and, if appropriate, the lawyer shall inform the client of ADR options and, if so instructed, take steps to pursue those options."

To meet this professional responsibility, lawyers must be knowledgeable about the possible merits of using mediation—and understand how mediation can be used effectively in their clients' circumstances. That includes knowing how to achieve maximum success from a mediation, while at the same time ensuring that their clients' legal rights are protected.

Counsel must also provide legal advice to their clients throughout the mediation and in relation to any mediated agreements or settlements. Lawyers also help their clients select a mediator. Some factors to be considered are the mediator's orientation, objectives, and style; training and experience; ability to be impartial; gender, cultural background, or ethnicity; and fees and availability of the mediator.

One of the more difficult role changes for lawyers may be allowing parties to speak for themselves and to participate fully in the mediation process. In some cases, this may mean the lawyers take a back seat in the joint session and provide their input and advice in caucus. While some mediators may discuss the lawyers' role during the convening process and at the beginning of the mediation, legal counsel must understand and respect the importance of allowing their clients to be the primary voice in the mediation and the primary decision maker. Being successful in the adversarial legal process generally means achieving the best possible legal result, which in large measure is determined by the lawyer as the legal expert. In the interest-based mediation process, in contrast, being successful means achieving an outcome that satisfies the client's interests—personal, social, and emotional, as well as professional, vocational, and economic. In other words, the scope for successful outcomes in the interest-based process is much broader than in the legal, rights-based process. Lawyers must recognize this fundamental difference and ensure that their clients are given ample opportunity and support to fully engage in mediation in a way that will satisfy their interests as much as possible. For many lawyers, this requires them to transfer significant control and responsibility for the process to their clients.

Skills and Competencies as a Mediation Adviser

To help achieve their clients' best interests, lawyers need to understand what mediation is, the different approaches that can be taken, and the different types of mediators (discussed in Chapter 3). Lawyers will also need to help their clients decide whether mediation is a suitable process for their clients' dispute. As with various legal processes, lawyers play a pivotal role in helping their clients prepare for mediation. This includes advising them of the strengths and weaknesses of their own legal case and of the other party's case. The lawyer should be familiar with the mediator and the mediator's approach to mediation. To prepare their client to fully and properly engage in the mediation process, lawyers need to

- clarify the issues and identify the client's interests and the emotions underlying his or her position;
- identify the range of possible options to meet the client's interests;
- consider and analyze what the other party's positions, interests, and meaningful outcomes are likely to be;
- discuss the types of strategies and behaviours that might be expected from the other party or lawyer—and how they might respond to these strategies constructively;
- gather and organize information, and prepare documents or summaries to be used at the mediation;
- clarify issues of confidentiality, the use of agreements to mediate, and written agreements, and ensure that communications within the mediation may occur "without prejudice" to the client's legal rights and position;
- formulate and analyze the client's BATNA (see Chapter 2), including the strengths, weaknesses, costs, and risks of proceeding with legal action for *both* parties;
- deal with logistics, including location, timing, who attends, and other matters determined during the convening process; and

- advise the client about options other than court or mediation that could be used to resolve the dispute, such as arbitration, mediation-arbitration, or, in some cases, fact-finding or investigation.

A basic goal of collaborative processes is to create value. As explained by Lax and Sebenius (1986, pp. 29–41) and by Mnookin, Peppet, and Tulumello (2000, pp. 11–43), in most negotiating situations there is a fundamental tension between creating and claiming, presented as the "negotiator's dilemma" (see Chapter 2). In cases in which parties have formulated their positions in terms of their legal claims and rights, the negotiator's dilemma is ever-present. The traditional legal approach, in which lawyers are trained, is the adversarial method. To the extent that parties and their lawyers pursue the adversarial method, they will forcefully advocate their claims, argue the merits of their position, minimize any contrary views, and undermine the positions and opinions of the opposition. Clearly, such an approach will elicit claiming and defensive strategies from the other side and will stifle any potential for collaborative interaction.

This, then, is the challenge for the lawyer who wants to provide effective legal representation and, at the same time, to serve the client's best interests. This is what we call the lawyer's dilemma. To meet this challenge, the lawyer needs to develop an approach that assertively presents the client's legal position in an articulate and clear way, while simultaneously enabling the client to pursue an effective, principled negotiation approach through the mediation process. To succeed, the lawyer will need to know how to apply the elements of principled negotiation in the mediation process, and what the roles of the parties, lawyers, and mediator will be in such a process. The lawyer will need to have a sufficient understanding of those roles and expectations so that the participants, especially the lawyers and mediator, are complementing each other and not working at cross-purposes.

In some cases, a party and his or her lawyer may anticipate that the other party and/or the other lawyer may be aggressive, intimidating, or abusive. In a case where a party client may feel threatened or overpowered by the other party, the lawyer should give particular thought and care to what he or she can do to ensure that the client can participate in mediation safely and securely—and in a way that serves the client's best interests.

Summary

Cultivating dialogue in mediation is a critical first step in setting the stage for further dialogue. Yet, for various reasons, people in conflict think, say, and do things that adversely influence the conflict interaction. Mediators help parties change their negative ways of interacting, thus creating the potential for constructive dialogue and negotiation. This is not as difficult as it might sound given that it is human nature to want to understand those with whom we are in conflict. We are continually trying to make sense of our environment, and that search includes making sense of our everyday interactions.

The mediator's role is to help the parties feel safe enough to engage in dialogue that allows them to move through their conflict productively. In this chapter, we discussed a number of the key strategies and techniques that a mediator may use to help people in conflict overcome the barriers that limit their dialogue and that inhibit their reaching a resolution that addresses their interests, needs, and values. The mediator needs to be artful as well as strategic in his or her role as a conflict bridge. Both of these abilities require that the mediator be theoretically knowledgeable, experientially confident, flexible, and creative.

The rewards are great for the parties who overcome the inclination to disengage from the other or to strike back at them, and who instead pursue a path of understanding and insight. The mediator's role is to help them choose this path.

DISCUSSION QUESTIONS AND EXERCISES

1. How would you apply the philosophies of Mahatma Ghandi or Martin Luther King Jr. in the context of this chapter?
2. What is the significance of the negotiator's dilemma in mediation? What can a mediator do, before and during mediation, to overcome the negotiator's dilemma and cultivate collaboration?
3. Think of a conflict situation you have experienced in relation to a group project at school or at work. (It may be the same conflict you considered in answering discussion question 3 at the end of Chapter 4). What different types of conflict (data, value, relationship, structural, and interest) were present in that case? How may your understanding of these different sources of conflict influence the way you approach and resolve this conflict?
4. How much room is there for cooperation in the midst of conflict? Can you think of any situations in which parties might still be cooperating while competing with each other?
5. Refer to Exercise 1 at the end of Chapter 3. Imagine that you are mediating the divorce dispute described there, between Paul and Jo-Anne. Consider some additional facts about the dispute that are provided below.

   For years, Paul and Jo-Anne argued frequently about finances, home and family activities, and their children. They have very different ideas about how to raise children. Although they got angry with each other during their marriage, neither one ever behaved in a violent or abusive manner. Since deciding to separate, they have disagreed on various issues. They own a three-bedroom single family home worth about $400,000 that has a mortgage of $260,000, with payments of $1,200 per month. Paul has his government pension and an RRSP account of about $15,000. Jo-Anne has a smaller pension and no other savings or RRSPs. Paul's employment income is $90,000 per year and Jo-Anne's is $50,000 per year.

Jo-Anne wants full custody of both children. She wants Paul to transfer his interest in the home and all the furniture to her so she can continue to live there with the children. She wants Paul to pay child support of $1,250 per month (the Child Support Guidelines say $1,280 per month). Jo-Anne believes that getting Paul's $70,000 share of the equity in the home is the minimum she should receive in settlement of her claims for division of property spousal support.

Paul sees things very differently. He feels strongly that the house should be sold and the proceeds divided so they can each get a smaller place. His position is that if he pays Jo-Anne $30,000 from his share of the proceeds of sale of the home (that is, if she gets a total of $100,000 and he gets $40,000), that would be a very fair and reasonable settlement of all claims she may have for property and spousal support. Paul wants joint and shared custody, with the children spending roughly equal time with each parent. He thinks that he should pay Jo-Anne only $400 per month for child support. Jo-Anne is strongly opposed to shared custody.

a. In terms of Moore's circle of conflict framework, presented at the beginning of this chapter (Figure 7.1), what are the main sources of conflict between Jo-Anne and Paul? If you were mediating this dispute, how would your analysis of these sources of conflict help you?
b. What are some of the emotions that each party will likely display or experience during the mediation? As mediator, what are some ways that you may respond effectively to these emotions?
c. As mediator, what are some ways you can cultivate collaboration between Jo-Anne and Paul during this mediation? Consider which of the strategies and techniques described in this chapter you could apply, and how you might do it.

FURTHER READING

Axelrod, R. (1984). *The evolution of cooperation*. New York: Basic Books.

Axelrod, R. (1997). *The complexity of cooperation*. Princeton, NJ: Princeton University Press.

Boulle, L., & Kelly, K.J. (1998). *Mediation: Principles, process, practice*. Toronto: Butterworths.

Cloke, K.K. (2001). *Mediating dangerously: The frontiers of conflict resolution*. San Francisco: Jossey-Bass.

Moore, C.W. (2003). *The mediation process: Practical strategies for resolving conflict* (3rd ed.). San Francisco: Jossey-Bass.

Websites

Kenneth Cloke's Center for Dispute Resolution: http://www.kennethcloke.com
This site has a number of articles, references, and links related to the subject matter of this chapter.

Social Psychology Network—Morton Deutsch: http://deutsch.socialpsychology.org
This site provides access to the work of Morton Deutsch, founder of the International Center for Cooperation and Conflict Resolution (ICCCR) at the Teachers College, Columbia University. Deutsch has done work on cooperation and competition, intergroup relations, conflict resolution, social conformity, and the social psychology of justice.

Institute for the Study of Conflict Transformation:
http://www.transformativemediation.org
This site has information, videos, bibliographies, and links related to the transformative approach to responding to conflict.

REFERENCES

Deutsch, M. (1973). *The resolution of conflict*. New Haven, CT: Yale University Press.

Lax, D., & Sebenius, J.K. (1986). *The manager as negotiator*. New York: Free Press.

Mack, R.M., & Snyder, R.C. (1973). The analysis of social conflict—Toward an overview and synthesis. In F.E. Jandt (Ed.), *Conflict resolution through communication* (pp. 25–87). New York: Harper & Row.

Mnookin, R., Peppet, S., & Tulumello, A. (2000). *Beyond winning: Negotiating to create value in deals and disputes*. Cambridge, MA: Belknap Press.

Moore, C.W. (2003). *The mediation process: Practical strategies for resolving conflict* (3rd ed.). San Francisco: Jossey-Bass.

Picard, C.A. (2002). *Mediating interpersonal and small group conflict* (2nd ed.). Ottawa: Golden Dog Press.

Schelling, T.C. (1960). *The strategy of conflict*. Cambridge, MA: Harvard University Press.

CHAPTER 8
Getting to the Heart of Conflict

LEARNING OBJECTIVES

After reading this chapter, you will be able to:

- Understand the logic of the mediation process and its stages
- Identify a variety of strategies for eliciting insights and enabling parties to arrive at a new and deeper understanding of their conflict
- Identify a number of creative communication strategies that can be used to get to the heart of conflict
- Explain some specific strategies and skills that can be used to mediate or to respond to conflict effectively

CHAPTER OUTLINE

Introduction 225
The Logic of the Mediation Process 225
Strategies for Getting to the Heart of the Problem 229
What Makes a Mediation Work? 230
Expanding Parties' Ways of Understanding 232
The Creative Communicator 239
Summary 248

Relationships are all there is. Everything in the universe only exists because it is in relationship to everything else. Nothing exists in isolation.

Margaret Wheatley

Introduction

In Chapter 7, we discussed how mediators respond to adversarial narratives and strong emotions. In this chapter, we build on that, focusing on the logic of the mediation process and on skills and methods that mediators can use to enable the parties to get to the heart of their conflict and resolve it.

The Logic of the Mediation Process

Every mediation session has a structure and a style. Some may be loose, spontaneous, and unstructured; others may be very structured, following a logical sequence of pre-patterned steps. As discussed in Chapter 1, the goals that the parties bring to mediation help shape the process. For example, mediation between business partners who simply wish to dissolve their relationship and to divvy up their capital and business may require a mediator who can focus on the interests behind the partners' desires and help them to bargain over some of the issues in dispute. A dispute between an insurance company and a person injured in a car accident may require that the mediator, in order to close the file, devote some time not only to the financial issues but to the emotions of loss the injured party has experienced. In a family dispute, the mediator may need to help parties navigate complex emotional and relational family dynamics.

Most mediations, whatever the particular approach being used, follow the general pattern of progression or logic that we presented in Chapter 1. Many mediators structure their mediation process in several stages that follow a pattern of storytelling, exploration of issues, interests and values, option generation, and closure. In such mediations, each stage has certain objectives and a strategic purpose. Mediators need to know what types of activities and communications occur in each stage of the approach they are using, and why parties should engage in each of these activities and at that specific time.

By way of illustration, if our goal is to have a beautiful garden that will delight the eye and calm the soul, one of our objectives will be to start with a deep garden bed of rich, fertile soil. We will have to invest hours of time and effort in digging out and carting away the useless rocks and dirt that are 4 inches below the surface, and in bringing in many loads of super soil, mushroom compost, and other smelly stuff that plants love. Our objective of having 18 to 24 inches of fertile, aerated, and well-drained organic material in the entire garden bed is a key requirement for achieving our goal of a beautiful garden. It is one of our strategic objectives. This is our metaphor for the initial stage of the mediation process we discussed in Chapter 7, when the mediator helps to cultivate a foundation for collaborative dialogue between the parties.

After establishing the basis for a more collaborative interaction, as we discuss in this chapter, the mediator will help the parties get to the heart of their conflict. According to this logic of the mediation process, before parties will be able to productively discuss possible options for resolving the issues, the mediator needs to help them reach a deeper understanding of each other's interests and values that are connected to the issues. This is based on the fundamental principle that the more the parties know about themselves individually and collectively, the greater will be their ability to generate a broad range of creative and mutually acceptable options. If the parties go directly to discussing options and negotiating their final agreement before they have gained a deeper understanding of each other, they will be confined to a narrower range of options. This may result in agreements that fail to last, or at best serve as Band-Aid solutions, rather than in ones that are more likely to be long-term and stable. Furthermore, parties will fail to discover and appreciate potential benefits they could have realized from their negotiation.

In Chapter 1, we presented a five-stage framework for a generic mediation process that is typical of that used by most mediators. In Chapter 6, we considered the first stage—pre-mediation; and in Chapter 7, we examined the second stage—cultivating dialogue. In this chapter, we focus on the third stage of our framework—getting to the heart of the conflict.

As we discussed in Chapter 1, the mediator's primary goal in this stage is to help all participants—the parties and the mediator—get a deeper understanding of the conflict problem and of the underlying interests, needs, and values of the parties. We will now discuss a useful strategy for moving into this third stage of the mediation process, a strategy known as *framing the problem*.

Framing the Problem

One of the key tasks for a mediator in transitioning from Stage 2 to Stage 3 is to articulate or frame the problem and the resulting issues to be addressed. It is important that the mediator do this in a way that is impartial and non-judgmental, and in a way that will promote collaboration rather than competition between the parties.

In a mediation context, this framing process may be very different from its equivalent in an adversarial court proceeding. For example, if a lawyer rather than a mediator were dealing with the divorce dispute between Jo-Anne and Paul (described in Exercise 1, at the end of Chapter 3), he or she would describe the issues as follows:

- division of property,
- spousal support,
- custody and access of the children, and
- child support.

The lawyer's framing of these issues, especially the last two, would give the impression that one of the parties will win custody and get the kids, while the other will lose out.

A mediator might frame these issues in a more integrative way, with less emphasis on win–lose. With the issues of custody and child support, for example, the mediator might say the following:

> You also need to address and decide the issue of the children's living arrangements and your parenting responsibilities for them, including their financial needs, now and in the future.

By framing these issues in this way, the mediator does not portray the children as a prize to be won. Rather, she emphasizes the parties' responsibilities to their children and the various arrangements and decisions that the parties must make in the children's best interests.

During the early part of the mediation, the mediator is trying to understand the main problem that has given rise to this dispute—that is, the "presenting problem." After each party's opening statement, the mediator seeks to broaden the story line through comments such as the following:

> It would be good to get some background to this situation and how it became a problem for the two of you.

In the case of the Car Repair Blues scenario (see Box 1.1 in Chapter 1), the mediator might say the following:

> Dale, please tell me more about how you came to be at Chris's garage.

It may take a while to bring all the issues to the surface, especially in the case of multi-issue disputes. At this stage, the mediator is only trying to get a snapshot of the problem and of the issues that need to be discussed in the mediation. The stages are quite fluid, however, as we discussed above; during this phase of the mediation, the parties may begin to provide information about their interests or to provide details about why they hold the perspectives they do. A mediator may provide a summary of the parties' perspectives and issues before he or she begins to explore underlying values, interests, or needs.

At the end of Stage 2, as a transition to Stage 3, the mediator may provide a statement summarizing the main issues to be addressed in the mediation. Following is an example of such an issue (or problem) statement, this one from the hypothetical mediation in the Car Repair Blues scenario:

> Dale, a few days ago you left your car at Chris's garage for a tune-up because it was running rough. You needed your car, so you asked Chris if he could have it ready by the end of the day. Chris, you agreed to try and move things around to accommodate Dale's request to have her car fixed in one day. After inspecting the car, you found that the radiator was almost shot. You tried to reach Dale, and when you could not you went ahead and did the work. Dale, when you came to pick the car up you were shocked by the amount you were being charged, which angered you to the point that you left the garage without your car. It seems that you need to talk more about the repairs to the car and the costs, how the situation has affected each of you, and how to deal with the car, which is still in the garage.

Notice how this statement of the problem contains information both about what happened and about what the parties are concerned about or need to discuss further—for example, Dale's anger about the bill she was presented with when she went to pick up her car from the garage. The issue statement does not contain any blaming statements. This is important. Both parties have to feel that their issues are represented in the problem statement. If either party feels blamed or judged by the statement, he or she is likely to become defensive and to reject it. There is another reason, too, for the mediator to craft a non-judgmental issue statement: it is a way of modelling good communication skills in mediation, and it helps the parties move toward further dialogue.

Strategies for Getting to the Heart of the Problem

This third stage is central to the mediation process. In it, the mediator seeks information about the parties' interests, needs, values, and emotions—information that enables the parties to learn about each other's perspectives and about why each holds his or her own so dear. This is the stage where the "magic" occurs, according to some mediators. It is the stage where the mediator, after identifying the problem in Stage 2, attempts to "peel back the onion" to find what underlies the issues—what is at the core of the problem. It is quite common for parties to be reluctant to talk about the underlying problem, because it may be private and risky. They may not even be fully aware of what lies beneath their feelings and positions.

Strategically, the mediator tries to broaden the discussion and uncover information by asking broadening questions such as the following:

> What happened when you found the radiator faulty, Chris?
>
> What made you decide to go ahead and replace it?
>
> Dale, how did you feel when you saw how much you were being charged for the work on your car?

After broadening the story, the mediator will explore more fully, asking deepening and layered questions generated from answers to the broadening questions. (Broadening and deepening questions are explained in Chapter 5.) The mediator's objective is to help the parties learn what is important to them about the issues, to hear and learn what is important to the other person, as well as to learn what is motivating each of them, and why. The mediator then links each of these interests to the issues in dispute. For this stage, a mediator takes on the role of a *curious* guide embarking on a path of *discovery* with the parties, to help them gain *insights* into their separate needs as well as their shared ones. These insights are what help parties collaborate on the construction of a plan that satisfactorily resolves their issues.

During this part of the mediation, a mediator asks lots of questions to draw out interests. Interests are the motives underlying a person's demands. Some of these are what we call CHEAP BFV questions. The acronym stands for the following:

- Concerns
- Hopes
- Expectations
- Assumptions
- Priorities
- Beliefs
- Fears
- Values

Here are some CHEAP BFV questions the mediator might ask in the Car Repair Blues scenario:

> What are some of your concerns regarding the cost of repairs?
>
> What did you hope Chris would do upon finding problems with the car?
>
> What were your expectations of what you should do after finding problems with Dale's car?
>
> It seems you made some assumptions about how the repairs were carried out. What were some of those assumptions, Dale?
>
> Getting your car back without having to incur a large debt is a priority for you, isn't it, Dale? It might be helpful to tell us more about why that is.
>
> What has been your biggest fear through all of this?
>
> Chris, you talked about how you place a high value on quality work at your garage. How did this influence the actions you took with Dale's car?

What Makes a Mediation Work?

Connected ways of knowing are essential for seeing conflicts as part of relational systems. These connections emerge from the links we have with others and from acknowledging and understanding the influence of those ties that bind us to one another. Like Benjamin (1995a, 1995b), LeBaron (2002) recognizes the need for resourcefulness and flexibility in mediation; she affirms that mediators draw knowledge from the experience of the mediation itself, and this knowledge complements the more traditional analytic ways of understanding. We believe that creative tools are essential for fully knowing and expressing the human conflict experience.

As trainers in the field of mediation, we often speak of analytical skills, intuitive skills, and communications skills as the fundamentals for any practitioner. Because we believe that the system (relationship) is in conflict, we must make changes within it. This is largely accomplished when the parties are able to shift their perspectives on one another and reframe the situation, establishing a different and shared understanding of events and needs. There are some conflicts, however—for example, data conflicts, structural conflicts, and some interest-based conflicts—where the relationship is not a key element of the dispute. In these cases, the mediator will work to help parties understand their differences and assist them with raising and considering a variety of options to resolve their dispute.

While there are many names for the process of shifting or creating new understandings of the links between parties, being strategic about this process is most critical for creating success in mediation—because the mediator is *not* the one who needs to open up his or her understanding of the conflict. Rather, it is the parties who need to cooperate to become joint problem solvers, who need to collaborate in resolving their conflict. The key is to shift the parties' ways of knowing, as well as their ways of communicating, to help them find a more holistic approach to resolving their own conflicts.

Being strategic means that the mediator *intentionally* employs a skill or tactic because he or she is aware of its purpose and has learned that it will evoke a certain response. The mediator knows the skill or tactic is appropriate, based on theoretical knowledge, intuitive knowledge, or experience. Of course, not everything turns out as expected, and the unanticipated response may require a different strategy. Flexibility is important in strategic practice—if something is clearly not working, then do not persist with it. Try something else.

The point is that knowledge and skills are used with intent—sometimes consciously and other times not. Knowing what works can be derived from sources other than traditional, intellectual knowledge. It is not unusual for a skilled mediator to describe the source of particular interventions as coming from what he feels. A good mediator cannot rely on technique alone. Mediators must use both their heads and their hearts.

Where Does a Mediator Begin?

First, mediators must listen carefully to each party's story—to the connections and assumptions one party has made about the other. Chapter 5 outlines *how* to listen. Now we want to indicate what to listen for and to discuss the importance of being intentional and strategic.

Although mediation is often described as non-directive, the mediator is far from inactive. A good mediator must be assertive and confident, using strong leadership skills to guide parties through the process. The mediator must be a strategist. Using her analytical skills, the mediator sifts through information received in the session, developing hypotheses about what she is hearing, and relying on intuitive and learned knowledge about the parties and about their relationships to one another. The mediator develops hypotheses based on her theoretical understandings of conflict, communication, and negotiation, and on her knowledge of social and psychological theories about human behaviour and interaction. The mediator uses this collective knowledge, experiential and learned, to respond in intentional and informed ways.

How a mediator responds to a surprising statement, an unanticipated action, a moment of uncertainty, or a particular roadblock is determined through a process of *awareness*—then *reflection* and *hypothesizing*—before she undertakes any action or makes any statement. To an experienced mediator, this process is often so rapid that it is reflexive. For a new mediator, processing information tends to take more time.

When the process of awareness, reflection, hypothesizing, and responding takes place without pause in the mediator's actions, this is what is known as "artistry" in mediation (see Figure 8.1). For a discussion of artistry in professions, see Lang and Taylor (2000).

Figure 8.1 Artistry in Mediation

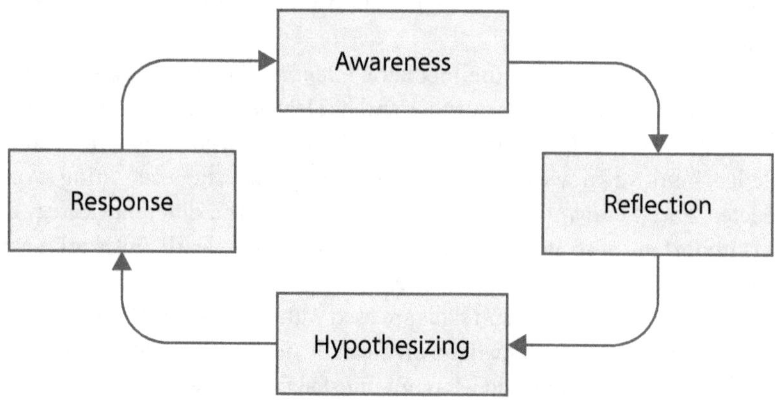

Strategizing should not be undertaken like a recipe, but rather as a situational response that takes the entire context into consideration. It requires that mediators observe the individuals in conflict at the same time that they are attentive to the relationships and interactions of those same individuals. Mediators are continually processing and reflecting upon the information they receive (verbally and non-verbally). Their actions are based on theoretical knowledge about human behaviour and interaction, as well as knowledge drawn from more intuitive sources, such as somatic, imaginative, or connective intelligence, as outlined by LeBaron (2002).

To illustrate this process in action, let's consider the workplace conflict between Teresa and Danny, described in the Workplace Change scenario (see Box 8.1).

The mediator's internal process, shown at the end of Box 8.1, spells out what would actually be a micro-moment in a mediation, culminating in an intervention—a point where the mediator is required to draw upon her various areas of knowledge concerning how people behave in conflict and why, and how communication works and why. This knowledge would inform her emotional fluency, her ability to understand emotions and read actions, and her somatic intelligence, which tells her body how to move empathetically. While the mediator is not likely to be able to tell us where all the knowledge came from for that particular intervention, she is probably able to tell us that she had an intuitive sense about what was needed.

Expanding Parties' Ways of Understanding

Few mediators would deny the importance of mediation's potential to educate. The process of mediation itself can be one of learning (Picard, 2003; Melchin & Picard, 2008). The education extends to the mediator, who is engaged in a process of discovery similar to that of the parties, who are learning about themselves and the

BOX 8.1 » Scenario: Workplace Change

Danny is a long-time employee of the Library working in the Documents Section. Teresa, an employee for less than two years, has been given the task of modernizing the library, especially the Documents Section. At every turn, Teresa meets resistance and opposition to her ideas from Danny and his small group of co-workers. Totally frustrated and confused by their resistance, she seeks help from an in-house mediator to see if there is any way to change this dynamic. She needs the support of this group to determine the merits and drawbacks of the changes she is suggesting, and she will need their support if they are to be implemented. Teresa is fed up with Danny's resistance, because it appears to be calculated to personally undermine her. Teresa believes that bringing about change in a collaborative fashion is the most effective and efficient way to do her job.

Danny and his co-workers, on the other hand, find it extremely difficult to continually adapt to change. They are more comfortable with routine, which is why they chose to work in the Documents Section in the first place. They are slow to pick up the new ways of working, especially cataloguing by computer, and they are threatened by the possibility that they might lose their jobs if cataloging becomes computerized. Even if jobs are not lost, they worry that change will make their jobs less interesting and fulfilling. Teresa's presence is threatening because it seems to imply that the work they have been doing is no longer considered to be of value to management. Their attitude is, "If it ain't broke, why fix it?"

At one point in this mediation, Teresa moves her chair back a few inches and states the following:

> You think that asking me to join your group at this late stage is going to solve my problem? Well, think again!

She leans back in her chair and crosses her arms over her chest. The mediator, observing this, goes through the following stages of perception and active response:

> Teresa has physically moved out of our dialogue circle and is strongly rejecting the option suggested by Danny. [*Awareness/Observation: What is happening in the moment?*]
>
> She is withdrawing because we haven't understood her perspective on this, and she is becoming more frustrated at not being heard. This is evident in her physical withdrawal and the locking of her arms in front of her body. Moreover, she has broken eye contact with both Danny and me. [*Reflection/Analysis/Intuition: Why is this happening?*]
>
> Based on what I know about human behaviour, communication, and interaction, I need to better understand her and why this option doesn't

work for her. I also need to let her know that I have seen her frustration. Once she knows that I understand some of what she is experiencing, she may begin to trust me and will thus be more willing to provide information about what she needs to move forward. [*Hypothesizing: What response is required and why?*]

I move forward in my chair as though reaching out to Teresa. "You're feeling progressively more isolated here. It's clear we haven't understood what is really important to you. What's missing for you in Danny's suggestion?" [*Response: Acting on what is hypothesized.*]

others involved in the conflict. When parties learn, the nature of the conflict can change (Picard, 2003, p. 478).

The objective of expanding parties' awareness of their assumptions and relationships is present in almost all styles of mediation. For example, Winslade and Monk (2000) direct the mediator to create, with the parties in conflict, an alternative contextual understanding of events and behaviours, embedding them in new narratives. Bush and Folger (1994) believe that the mediator's task is to assist the parties in enhancing their connectedness, first by understanding themselves better (empowerment), and subsequently by linking emotionally to the other through recognition. Bodtker and Jameson (1997) discuss the mediator's role in sharing his or her interpretation of events with the parties. They view reframing as a process of creating new and shared interpretations among the parties and the mediator. Melchin and Picard (2008) tell us that an insight mediator believes that parties' relationships are altered when new insights are developed about one another's beliefs, feelings, and behaviours. Relationship transformation occurs when one party's cares and concerns are "de-linked" from the other party's fears and threats through the process of gaining insights.

Eliciting Insights

From the very start of the mediation session, mediators are in a process of discovery and learning—they are working to gain insights and to understand the nature of the conflict situation and the dynamic of the parties. They need these insights to listen for and hear discrepancies that might lead parties to new insights. Mediators seek insights by listening. They are curious. They wonder. They question underlying motives, concerns, and needs. They notice. They get hunches. They listen for discrepancy. They probe intent. They acknowledge and validate. They restate, to open new horizons and shift horizons. They search for ways that parties can save face and negotiate away from their positional "corner." Being curious promotes individual viewpoints coming together to create a "bigger picture." Listening for discrepancies leads to changing the angle from which the problem is being viewed. Making links between the past, present, and future leads to a reformulation of original positions. The mediator then verifies, with the parties, if the insights she has gained are correct.

Linking and De-Linking

An important strategy in the insight approach is *linking* and *de-linking*. This strategy involves discovering how present actions and feelings are linked to past experiences and expectations of dire futures. It helps mediators discover what is behind the parties' emotions, what really matters to them, and why. Very often, this process reveals that the assumptions and fears creating barriers to dialogue are misplaced and can be de-linked. This opens up new opportunities for learning. The parties may learn, for example, that there are links between what one party cares about and what the other party finds threatening; and they may learn, in the process, how this link is affecting the conflict situation.

Finding how one party's cares are linked to what threatens the other is done intentionally. Insight mediators often ask parties this very question. Throughout the mediation, from beginning to end, they are listening carefully to each party's story—in particular, they are listening for discrepancies in what each of the parties is describing. They are listening for information on how past histories are linked to current emotions. Has something similar happened in the past, and how is that affecting a party now? How is that event linked to his or her current position on the issues in dispute, and how is it linked to his or her behaviour in the conflict? They also listen for and ask about how present behaviours are linked to anticipated outcomes—and how parties' experiences are currently affecting their relationship with one another. Accomplishing this task may require the mediator to employ creative and intuitive knowledge and skills, as well as linear logic tools.

Once the parties and the mediator get insight into the interests and values that lie behind both parties' positions, the mediator attempts to discover whether what one party cares about actually needs to be a threat to the other party's cares. If not, the mediator works to de-link these connections. De-linking incorrect links is an insight that results from the mediator listening for discrepancy and from his or her continued curiosity. It involves separating the parties as objects of conflict, identifying incorrect assumptions, and separating past experiences and anticipated outcomes from present feelings. This opens up space for parties to be curious and circumstances for them to care about each other.

Discovering how what one party cares about is linked to what threatens the other party is not as difficult as it sounds. To do it, mediators often ask parties very direct questions. In the Workplace Change scenario (see Box 8.1, above), the mediator in search of links might ask Danny the following: "So what is the link between what's been happening between you and Teresa, some staff being laid off a few years ago, and the ideas that Teresa has been bringing forward?"

Listening for Discrepancy and Understanding

Mediators also listen carefully for discrepancies between what one party is saying and the other is hearing. One way to discover this is for a mediator to ask one party what he or she heard the other party say. Mediators also listen for information about how past histories may be linked to current feelings. They are curious to find out whether something similar has happened in the past and how that affects a party's attitude and behaviour in the present. They also want to learn how the past is linked to a party's current position on the issues in dispute. If we return to the scenario with Danny and Teresa, we might discover that Danny does not trust Teresa. This is because, in the past, when new people came into the organization with ideas for change, they appeared to be more concerned about looking good to their bosses and getting promoted than about making a difference in the working conditions of the front-line staff. Because Teresa is also new and responsible for upgrading systems, she was labelled as having the same motives. But Teresa has no knowledge of this past history, and therefore no understanding of why Danny feels so threatened by her ideas. She strongly believes that collaborative approaches to organizational change are best and, when used, will produce the most efficient and effective change. She perceives Danny as being "old school"—his behaviour is getting in the way of change happening.

Mediators also ask consequential questions and listen very closely for how a party's position may be linked to anticipated outcomes. Returning to our scenario, Danny knows that, in the past, when change happened, people lost their jobs. He expects that Teresa's ideas for modernization will end up in job cuts or, at the very least, people being put into new positions that they will not like. The link here is that Teresa's ideas mean problems for Danny; thus, what she cares about (being collaborative and instituting change) is a threat to Danny (fear of job loss and being seen as incompetent). As for Teresa, she thinks Danny is outdated because he will not collaborate on her ideas for change, which makes him a threat to her being able to do a good job. Figure 8.2 sets out how present behaviours are linked to past and future expectations. We also use these linkages to show the conflict between Danny and Teresa.

Understanding Conflict

Why do one person's cares pose a threat to what is important to the other party? Threats usually get constructed via the following process: as the conflict escalates, the respective parties construct mutually contradictory understandings of it. This leaves them fighting not only about the issues in dispute but about the meaning and causes of the conflict itself. The parties have not yet understood, or perhaps even identified, each other's interests. Once these interests are discovered, the parties start gaining insight into whether there is actually a link between what one party cares

Figure 8.2 Possible Linkages

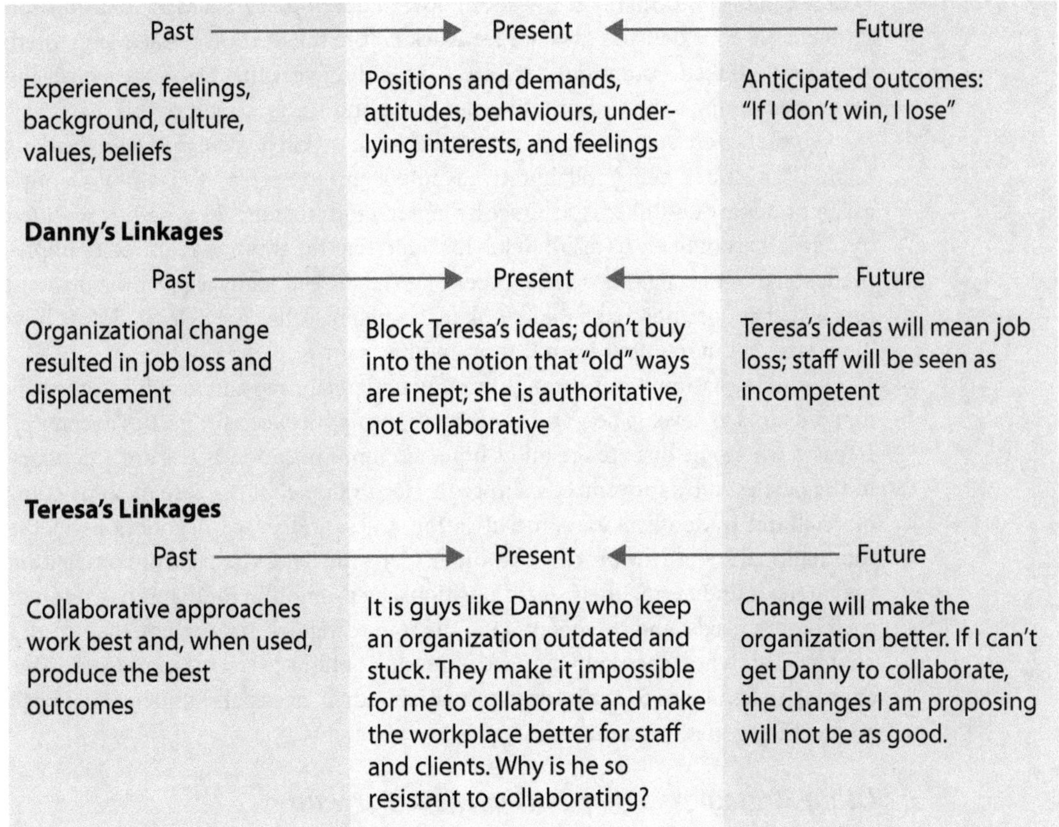

about and what the other party is threatened by. If the assumption of a link is incorrect, the job of the mediator becomes one of de-linking.

Here, it is helpful to remember that parties in conflict are interdependent and that their conflict often reflects the different ways they perceive each other to be interfering with what each of them wants. Danny perceives Teresa to be interfering with the team's ability to feel secure in their jobs, and Teresa, for her part, believes that Danny is obstructing her efforts to improve the workplace. In some cases, these perceptions will be discovered to be incorrect. In others, they will be found to be justified; one party's actions, intentionally or not, may indeed be interfering with the fulfillment of the other's goals.

In our scenario, Danny can only become interested in, or curious about, what is important to Teresa when he starts to feel that what is important to her might not be a threat to him. The same is true for Teresa. When she hears that Danny is not resisting the ideas she is proposing but the speed at which they are being developed, she and Danny can begin to share ideas—about how to develop new ideas so that staff can understand, consider, and give her feedback before the next proposal is presented. Another de-linked assumption for Teresa is her discovery that Danny perceives the work she is doing to be authoritative, not collaborative; as a result of this discovery, the two parties are able to discuss what collaboration will involve for Danny and his team. (Remember, being collaborative is important to Teresa.) Certain of Danny's assumptions are de-linked, too. Once he understands that the ideas being presented by Teresa are not likely to result in job loss, and that the training required to implement some of the changes can be undertaken at a speed manageable by staff—and in a way that does not make them look incompetent—they are able to discuss how Teresa can get more input from Danny and his team.

De-linking assumptions through gaining understanding and insights is one way for mediators to develop new and better relationships between the parties in conflict. In cases where the dispute's relationship and communication issues are secondary to the parties' substantive needs and goals (for example, in the case of some commercial and trade disputes, some litigation cases, and peace negotiations in the international arena), the process may differ. Here, mediators help parties by eliciting the interests underlying their stated positions, by promoting mutual recognition of each other's needs, and by encouraging them to recognize areas where they do not conflict. This is how they help the parties develop options to resolve their issues. This approach often leads to the parties' prioritizing their needs and undertaking back and forth negotiations in order to arrive at agreements.

Using Strategies to Help Parties Move Forward

Once each party's key issues have been identified and the interests, needs, and values behind them understood, the mediator works with the parties to prioritize these issues through the process of generating, building, testing, and accepting or rejecting hypotheses. The mediator may do this by determining the level of importance of each issue for each party, or by identifying the most likely areas for movement at the time. Large concerns may be broken into smaller ones; negative concerns or perceptions may be reframed. If appropriate, the mediator may write the issues or interests, or both, on a flip chart, chalkboard, or easel.

Another strategy some mediators use is to identify what both parties agree on and what they have in common. Often, parties have the perception that they do not agree on anything, making them feel less than hopeful about finding a collaborative solution. Other activities in this stage can include highlighting areas of progress, reframing indirect or negative interests, and working to achieve and maintain a climate of productive interaction. These tasks require the mediator to use effective communication skills, such as reflective listening, broadening and deepening questions, bridging, immediacy, normalizing, and confronting discrepancy. Mediators are also transparent about their intentions, and they share the responsibility for the mediation with the parties. They avoid premature assessments, act as an agent of reality in joint sessions and in caucus, help parties to focus on objective criteria, and continuously remind parties of their progress, emphasizing areas of agreement and common ground.

The Creative Communicator

To this point, we have taken a fairly traditional approach in looking at communication processes, strategies, and skills. In *Bridging Troubled Waters* (2002), LeBaron reminds us that conflict resolution work needs to come from the heart. This means that, as mediators, we need to be flexible and creative and operate outside the box. We need to be authentic, imaginative, and aware. We need to remember that conflict is a relational activity and that helping others to resolve conflict requires us to have an open mind to diverse ways of knowing. LeBaron says this well: "It asks us to notice not only issues and relationships that befall each other but the deeper levels of symbol and meaning that fuel the collisions" (2002, p. 181).

To encourage you to explore your creative mind and heart, here are some artful communication tools—the use of metaphor, storytelling, and other creative methods.

Using Metaphor

LeBaron (2002) depicts metaphors as windows into our worlds; Lakoff and Johnson (1980) link metaphors to how people organize and give meaning to events in their lives; Hocker and Wilmot (1995) use metaphors as tools for analysis in conflict intervention. All of these authors are reminding us that we can learn much about peoples' lived experience by listening for, or asking for, images that connote how parties position themselves in relation to others. Metaphorical concepts that are culturally and experientially created govern everyday functioning, down to the most mundane details (Lakoff & Johnson, 1980, p. 3).

In "Symbol in Mediation," Fisher (2000, p. 88) says the following:

> There appears to be a groundswell of sentiment that "rational discussion and logic are not sufficient to effect the changes in perspective required by disputing parties for conflicts to be settled" [Benjamin, 1995a, p. 3]. The emotional and spiritual dimensions of every conflict escape rational expression. When eloquence deserts us or words seem inadequate, we need a more universal language. "When we use words it's more difficult to dip into your soul. With symbol there's something that goes on at an entirely different level," says mediator Nancy Good Sider (interview, Nov. 20, 1997).

In this quotation, the term "words" means attempting to describe an experience in a rational or scientific way, and "symbol" refers to ritual, visual art, metaphor, and story.

When people use metaphors and other comparisons and images, they often make explicit their assumptions, judgments, and views about the world. Metaphors manifest cultural differences and perceptions, and they tell us much about one's approach to conflict. Proverbs, like metaphors, provide a window into how different cultures define and respond to conflict. Lederach (1995, p. 78) points out that "this is especially true in societies with oral traditions where drawing on wisdom and oratory skills is both a revered art and a conflict resolution tool." Besides mediation, metaphors are also used as process design tools in conflict dialogues by groups such as Common Ground, Public Conversations Project, and the Institute for Multitrack Diplomacy. This dialogue includes naming and sharing metaphors, unpacking their dimensions, comparing them, generating inclusive metaphors, and designing a process that invites participation (LeBaron, 2002, p. 216).

When coupled with visualization techniques, metaphors can be extremely powerful in assisting the parties to shift their perspectives. Imagine being asked to describe your ideal workplace in a metaphor. It would likely lead to a rich description of your future ideal, and it could also lighten the mood—you would probably laugh as you try to explain how your metaphor works practically. Metaphors can be effectively employed in cross-cultural conflicts, where linear-logic models of knowing often fall short.

Fisher (2000, pp. 88–89) makes another very interesting observation about how parties in conflict may use metaphor:

> Metaphor presents the most profound opportunity for an "I" message available. Searching for their own metaphor encourages people to own their feelings, values, and assumptions in a conflict rather than focus solely on the shortcomings of their opponent. They may connect with previously unrecognized desired outcomes or needs, which refocus their approach in the mediation.

To further explore how much information is contained in a metaphor, look at some of the phrases, below, that people link to conflict. For each, consider the speaker's values, feelings, expectations, and relationships, as well as experiences, judgments, and assumptions.

Shape up or ship out

We are embroiled in a battle

She has a real short fuse

We are now clearly at war

Your behaviour is indefensible

I need to let off some steam

We must attack or be attacked

Our office is like a war zone

I keep getting caught in the cross-fire

Negotiating with her is an uphill battle

He did an end run on me

They dropped a real bombshell

I'm at the end of my rope

You hit the nail on the head

Put a lid on it	*Talking to him is like talking to a brick wall*
She blew up at me	*I think the odds are in my favour on this one*
Time is money	*Better half a loaf than no loaf at all*
Let's cross that bridge when we come to it	*I can't dig any deeper into my pocket*
Let's bat around some ideas	*Kill your enemies with kindness*
Scratch my back and I'll scratch yours	*He certainly knows how to push my buttons*

When we asked mediators what metaphors they would use to describe their work, they responded in various and sometimes surprising ways: peacemaker, conduit, bridge builder, guide, assistant, marathon runner, yogi, trickster, firefighter, orchestra conductor, cabinet maker, chef, interior designer, meandering river, referee. These different metaphors vividly reflect the very different notions these individual mediators have of their role.

LeBaron (2002, p. 187) finds metaphors useful because they "invite us into imaginative conversation" and because they "offer shorthand ways to enter other worlds of meaning, bridging difficult conflict and deeply divided communities." She also reminds us of the danger of interpreting the meaning of the metaphor incorrectly. It is always wise to check out the meaning of messages by restating and reflecting. Remember that metaphors are culturally, socially, and gender-based.

Properly interpreted, metaphors reveal a person's inner emotions and fundamental perceptions. Consider the following exchange, based on the Car Repair Blues scenario from Chapter 1 (Box 1.1), and consider how you as a mediator might respond.

> *Dale*: He's a sly fox, that one. He saw me coming a mile away. Then, as if it was no big deal, he slams me over the head with his bill.

What do these metaphors reveal about Dale's emotions and interpretation of the conflict situation? Take a few minutes to consider your answer to this question.

As mediator, you need to be aware of these metaphors and to reflect on and respond to their underlying meaning. When Dale says that Chris is a "sly fox" and that he "saw me coming a mile away," it tells us clearly that, in Dale's conflict narrative, Chris was deceitful and manipulative and intended to take advantage of her as much as he possibly could. The ensuing exchange between the mediator and Dale might be as follows:

> *Mediator*: When you say that Chris was a sly fox and that he saw you coming a mile away, you seem to be saying that, in your mind, his intentions were not honourable.
>
> *Dale*: Right. He probably took me for the little woman who knows nothing about cars and who will accept whatever he does, and whatever he charges, without question.

> *Mediator*: So, Dale, you have some questions and concerns about what Chris did on your car and what he charged that you need to pursue further with Chris.
>
> *Dale*: Yes, definitely.

Dale used another metaphor, too, in saying that Chris "slammed me over the head with his bill." This metaphor tells us that, as Dale sees it, Chris assaulted or attacked her with his unexpected bill for $1,200. We know, then, that the interaction left Dale feeling hurt, fear, intimidation, and/or resentment. This metaphor also reveals Dale's assumptions about what Chris himself was thinking and feeling; she attributes aggression to him. This also is something that the mediator needs to explore. She might do so in the following terms:

> *Mediator*: In addition, you said that Chris "slammed you over the head with his bill." What did you think and feel when you got Chris's bill for $1,200?
>
> *Dale*: I was floored … and stunned. It really was as if he had hit me over the head with one of his tire irons. I thought: "How could you do this? What could you possibly do that would be worth $1,200 and why would you ever do that without first consulting me?"
>
> *Mediator*: This bill for $1,200 is a real financial burden for you and, it seems, you wanted and expected Chris to be more aware of that—is that right?
>
> *Dale*: Yes, exactly. I think he should have been a lot more mindful and considerate of his customer's situation.

This mediator's intervention helps to unpack the underlying emotions and meaning of Dale's metaphors, and it should help Chris get a better appreciation of Dale's experience of their conflict interaction and why she reacted as she did.

Using Stories

LeBaron (2002, p. 223) suggests five reasons why third-party intervenors (mediators) might want to use stories as part of their conflict resolution work. She says they can

1. engage our attention,
2. stimulate empathy,
3. provide contextual information,
4. convey messages indirectly to save face and preserve harmony, and
5. engage us in deep listening.

Stories convey more than just facts; they also contain important information about cultural norms, personal motivations, and expectations. They build connection, invite us to listen with our minds and our hearts, and engage our imaginations.

Stories are often used to provide clues for change and ways to break down resistance. The brainstorming process in mediation provides a concrete example of how mediators use stories. In this stage, disputants are asked to visualize then share scenarios for positive change. These stories can form the basis for more detailed discussion of possible options and final solutions.

Lederach (1995, p. 82) also advocates the use of stories in conflict resolution work. He says that using stories—once we get past the point of associating stories with playtime—"propels us toward the view that stories create a holistic approach to thinking and understanding in which people are invited to mingle with the characters as a device of interacting with their own realities." Therapists have long known the value of using stories and fables in their work with children and families. Increasingly, mediators have found the concept of "stories" to be useful in their efforts to elicit insights and frame conflict stories.

As discussed in Chapter 3, narrative mediators deliberately work to engage parties in the co-creation of an alternative story (to the problem story) as the means of helping the parties resolve their differences. Narrative mediators pay particular attention to cultural and historical stories, as they believe them to be windows to both understanding the dispute and resolving it. As a side note, Cobb and Rifkin (1991) point out that the order in which a person is asked to tell his or her story in mediation is significant, and that the person is doing more than just taking his or her turn. Using social constructionist theory and basing their contention on the analysis of over 30 videotaped mediation sessions, these authors tell us that it is the first party's story that gets played out in the actual mediation. That story becomes the primary narrative; the second party's story becomes the subplot. Several authors emphasize the importance of creating an alternate story that re-positions both parties in more positive ways.

Stories can help us both illustrate our own point of view and understand others'.

Using Strategies from the Narrative Approach

We have now considered how stories can be tools in the mediation process. Mediators can make use of narratives strategically in order to motivate the parties to communicate and to effectively move forward in the mediation process. For instance, mediators trained in the narrative approach use a strategy known as externalizing the conversation to form questions that will shape the conversation in a constructive way.

Externalizing the Conversation

In narrative mediation, the strategy of "externalizing the conversation" relates to one of Fisher and Ury's (1981) principles of negotiation: separate the people from the problem. Using this skill, a mediator often talks about the conflict as if it were a third party. Winslade and Monk (2000, pp. 144–145) report that this way of speaking opens up possibilities for new ways of thinking and—an important benefit—prevents parties from feeling blamed. Here are some examples they give of mediator questions that reflect this skill:

- How did this argument catch the two of you in its clutches?
- How does what happened invite you to feel?
- To what extent is blame stopping you from resolving your differences?
- What did the argument make you think about the other person?
- The conflict has made you feel a very strong emotion like hatred. How did it manage to take over your feelings in such a strong way?

Portraying the conflict itself as a third party allows mediators to "make sense of phenomena in the world in human terms—terms we can understand on the basis of our own motivations, goals, actions, and characteristics" (Lakoff & Johnson, 1980, p. 34). Viewing conflict in this way provides explanatory power that often leads to action. This is why mediators do the following: focus on the problem, not the person; externalize the conversation; and use metaphors to help parties define their everyday realities.

Types of Questions Used by Narrative Mediators

Winslade and Monk (2000, pp. 87–89) outline five types of questions used by narrative mediators:

1. the unique outcome question,
2. the unique account question,
3. the unique redescription question,
4. the unique possibility question, and
5. the unique circulation question.

The *unique outcome question* is designed to "invite people to identify actions and intentions that stand apart from the problem story" (2000, p. 87). One example Winslade and Monk give is the following: "Why did hurt feelings and blame not stop you from cancelling this meeting?" (2000, p. 87). The second type of question that narrative mediators use is the *unique account question*, which "asks a person to make sense of an event that is an exception to the conflict story it represents"—an exception that the party may not have registered (2000, p. 87). Winslade and Monk provide two examples of this kind of question:

> How do you explain that you were able to be more in charge of blame, humiliation, hurt feelings, or injustice than you initially thought? (2000, p. 87).
>
> What do you think it means that you are agreeing about that issue? (2000, p. 88)

The third type of question used by narrative mediators is the *unique redescription question*. This invites people to reflect on themselves and on their relations with the other party, so they can develop a fuller articulation of who they would like to be. The following is an example of this type of question: "What does this tell you about yourself that you would not otherwise have known?" (2000, p. 88). The *unique possibility question* is the fourth type of question. It moves the focus toward the future and "encourages people to speculate about the implications of what has been talked about in the mediation and to project it forward." The example provided by Winslade and Monk (2000, p. 88) is the following:

> Given your present understanding and your desire to heal the wounding effects of blame, what might be your next step?

The final type of question that narrative mediators use is the *unique circulation question*, designed to "anchor the newly developing more-preferred story through the provision of an audience, as stories are not always the property of those at the center of a dispute" (2000, p. 89). Here are two of the examples provided by Winslade and Monk (2000, p. 89):

> Who will be most likely to support the continuation of these developments?
>
> If your children were witness to these discussions, who would be most excited about this change in direction?

Winslade and Monk give many examples of each of these questions and go into much fuller descriptions than we have room to provide here.

Using Visualization

The positive effect of asking disputants to visualize a less conflict-filled relationship or ideal future is also well documented. (See, for example, LeBaron, 2002, pp. 111–117.) Visualizing an image orients parties to work from that image; it becomes, effectively, their guiding light. The power of visualizing lies in its ability to shift perspectives and transform antagonistic parties into collaborating allies.

Imagine that the mediator asks the parties to describe the conflict situation; she is likely to receive negative reports from both of them on the relationship and on the other party's actions. If, instead, she asks the parties to describe their ideal vision of the relationship—and then has them focus on how to get there—they are likely to shift into more productive dialogue, working from current strengths or advantages in the relationship to ways of enhancing those positive attributes.

Visualizing and imaging in this way do require a level of readiness on the part of those in conflict. Some mediators may begin their sessions by requesting that the parties visualize the ideal future. Other mediators prefer to wait until the parties have had the opportunity to discuss past hurts and disappointments, and to resolve these as far as possible, before asking them to look ahead.

Establishing Connection Through Ritual

The sharing of rituals between opposing parties has been demonstrated to be effective in creating bridges. Practitioners involved in international disputes, such as the Israeli–Palestinian conflict and others, have noted the positive impact on both sides when they share meals and social time during lengthy negotiations. Strong advocacy roles are dropped during social rituals. Then, the parties can begin to learn about one another as husbands and wives, mothers and fathers, sisters and brothers, professionals, sports players, and other identities. In essence, they become human to one another and are less likely to see one another as "the faceless other." Connecting through rituals—whether meals, social events, religious or spiritual ceremonies—promotes relationship building, a prerequisite to seeking resolutions of mutual benefit.

Ritual is also about what is commonly done before, during, and at the end of the mediation—bringing symbolic meaning for the people involved. Ritual is a patterned set of actions through which we communicate meaning, build community, and remind people that they are connected to each other. During the negotiations, some mediators incorporate the ritual of sharing food and drink. Others start with a statement of wisdom, a prayer or blessing, a song, or gestures such as the shaking of hands, to communicate respect, cooperation, hope, or other important messages.

In Canada, ritual is often used in mediations involving First Nations people. Here, rituals are considered necessary to a productive negotiation process. First Nations peoples' common and important rituals include the use of prayer before and/or after the session, a teaching by an elder, the smoking of sweet grass, and the use of a talking feather or stick to indicate whose turn it is to speak.

Winslade and Monk (2000) also talk about the importance of ritual, pointing out that, for many Maori in New Zealand, the absence of rituals for engagement (negotiation) would likely lead to the failure of the mediation. Our experience working with immigrants from Africa and Asia has also taught us the importance of allowing storytelling (no matter how long it takes) to be part of the mediation process. The setting of a protocol for the mediation session can also be seen as a ritual, to ensure respectful and safe discussions. What happens before the mediation—during the convening stage—can also be seen as ritualistic.

Doing the Unexpected

A mediator might surprise the parties by asking them to physically draw their conflict, perhaps on a flip chart, in the hope of eliciting more emotional, holistic, and creative ways of discussing the situation. Other mediators might ask the parties to physically move, in order to shake off their rational perspective and tap into other sources of knowledge. Others might begin a mediation with music, in order to establish a peaceful environment or an emotional orientation to the session.

Effective mediation requires creativity and flexibility. In fact, LeBaron sees creativity as a core competency for a mediator (2002, p. 205). Being creative allows us to do something different from the way others do it or the way it has always been done. Here are some other creative tools: ask parties to draw their conflict on paper; ask children to act out their conflict; ask disputants to use imagery, visualizing, free association, and mimetics to describe difficult events; and, of course, use metaphors, fables, and stories—to learn from the past and highlight emotion and experience.

Using the Mind, Heart, Body, and Spirit

Mediators must use all of their capacities in a session—the communication skills that they've been taught through training, their ability to analyze and process the information they are receiving, and their intuitive ways of understanding and acting. Often, introductory training workshops focus exclusively on the acquisition of communication skills, which is why new mediators often lack confidence in their ability to conduct mediations. Mediators-in-training are not taught what to do with information about how each party defines his or her connections to the other. If this is the crux of understanding for mediators and the key to why mediation works, it should be the area of greatest focus in training. Mediators need to learn how to tap into their resources and develop a capacity to work with metaphors, symbols, imagery, narratives, and rituals.

Successful mediators are keen listeners. They pay attention not just to the parties but to the various systems of knowledge that emanate from their analytical, emotional, somatic, and intuitive intelligence. Mediation requires attention from one's whole self—and conflict must be seen as a whole system requiring a transformation. This may not be reassuring to the new mediator who wonders how he or she will ever get there. Lang and Taylor (2000) describe the process of becoming a mediator as one of developing artistry. We begin as novices, move to apprentices, work as practitioners, and finally become artists. The process repeats itself in every mediation, for it is a circle that forms a system of learning (see Figure 8.3).

LeBaron (2002) urges us to develop our non-intellectual capacities so that we are better able to serve our mediation clients. Kydd (1996, p. 368) encourages us to return to the elemental sources of language—nature, family, love, and relations. He asks us to deepen our language, "exalt[ing] feeling, being and relation"; "green" our metaphors, using analogies that express relations that exist in nature—viewing the whole over the parts; and "culture" our language, adopting words of relation and feeling that come from other languages with richer and fuller understandings.

Figure 8.3 The Dynamic Four-Stage Model of Professional Development

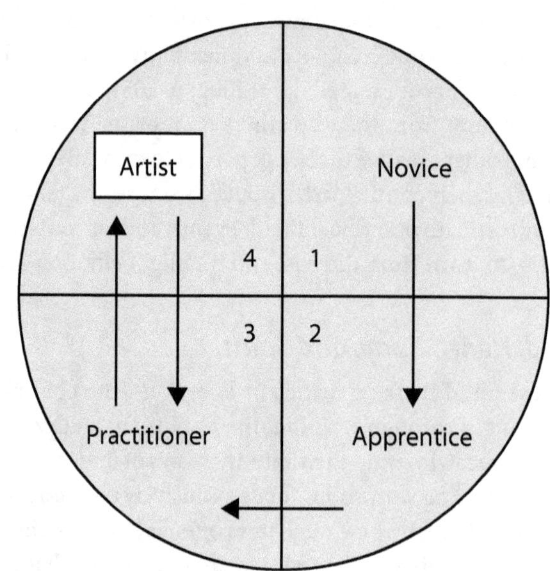

Source: Lang & Taylor (2000, p. 12). Reprinted by permission.

Summary

In this chapter, we have considered how mediators help parties get to the core of the dispute—the heart of the matter—through gaining understanding of the interests, assumptions, cares, and threats that are driving the conflict and making it difficult for parties to collaboratively resolve their conflict.

The effectiveness of mediation is largely a result of its holistic approach to understanding conflict and to helping parties transform their relationship. A holistic approach seeks knowledge through an understanding of relationships and the interconnectedness of systems (see Chapter 3). Logic and rational discussion alone are not sufficient to generate understanding of the subjective experience of parties in conflict. In their efforts to promote relational change, mediators today use not only the traditional scientific methods of analysis and strategic planning, but also the holistic procedures of the new science—that is, somatic, emotional, intuitive-imaginative, and "connected" ways of understanding. These procedures involve the heart, mind, body, and spirit.

DISCUSSION QUESTIONS AND EXERCISES

1. What is the logical progression of a typical mediation? Discuss this in as much detail as you can.
2. What are some strategies that you would use as a mediator to help parties arrive at a new and deeper understanding of their conflict?
3. Why do mediators need to be creative communicators? How can you develop your abilities as a creative communicator?
4. Refer to the Divorcing Spouses scenario involving Paul and Jo-Anne, described in the Exercises section at the end of Chapter 3. Again, imagine that you are mediating this divorce dispute.
   a. What are some adversarial perceptions and assumptions that each of these parties may have of the other that are a source of conflict between them? What useful insights might the parties gain during the mediation in relation to these perceptions or assumptions?
   b. What are some of the mediator strategies or techniques you could use in this case to help Paul and Jo-Anne gain insight and understanding into their conflict?
   c. In particular, what are some of the questions you would use as you proceed through this phase of the mediation? Imagine what each party might say in responding to your questions, and think of further questions or strategies you might use to deepen and enhance the mediation dialogue.
5. Sit back, close your eyes, and think for a moment about common metaphors that you have heard in relation to conflict. Jot these metaphors down on a piece of paper. Reflect on the amount of information you learn about a person's experiences and viewpoints from his or her use of these short phrases.
6. Refer to Box 8.1 of this chapter—the Workplace Change scenario. Imagine that you are mediating this conflict between Teresa and Danny. Consider the following exchange, which occurs during the mediation:

> *Mediator*: And so what have you interpreted or assumed when people haven't come and asked for help?
>
> *Teresa*: Oh yeah, well, of course I've just assumed that they are comfortable and know what is going on. It's not like I'm not approachable. I might be busy but I am generally available.
>
> *Danny*: That's the problem.
>
> *Mediator*: What's the problem?
>
> *Danny*: The problem is assuming things. Assuming things like change is good for everybody or we need to grow, and it's assuming that this doesn't affect people. Isn't it a surprise that nobody has told you anything? Like you did the talking and people do the listening. Isn't it a surprise to you that no one except for me, you know, has actually come up to you and said, "This

won't work." And any time I do that, there is no point in interrupting you because I know you don't listen anyway. Isn't it a surprise that I'm the only one! Is it just me? I'm not a dinosaur, you know. I know what I'm doing.

Teresa: Well I don't find your interruptions very helpful. I find them stifling, and I don't get any constructive feedback from you on where to go next. All I get is "No change!", "Say no to everything!" "Everything is comfortable, keep everything the same way. We don't want to see anything happen." It's very stifling. It's like you're killing growth before it's even happened.

Danny: Well, go somewhere else. You know this is the way it is. This is the way things work here. This is Records.

It's like, there are certain ways of doing things, and when it comes to Records in the Library, it's pretty simple. A book's got to be where it's supposed to be—correctly filed. There aren't 150 ways of doing that. There are certain jobs that are stable, and people pick them for that reason, and now we have this big whirlwind coming in and trying to change everything around. And I know where this is going, too. Teresa is looking for a promotion. That is the way they work. These young ones, they come in and start using these big words like *process re-engineering*, and, you know, people lose their jobs, and next thing you know they are running the place.

Mediator: And you get left where?

Danny: I get left … . My life has been completely disrupted. I have to pick up the pieces when the young ones get through changing everything around, and then they take off, you know. And the rest of us have to pick up the pieces, and we just get it right and then somebody else come along and does it all over again. That's the way the way it goes. It's sort of like that everywhere.

Mediator: Right, right, and so part of your being closed to or objecting to Teresa's new ideas is saying, "Look, I don't want to have to pick up the pieces, I don't want to have to go through this again."

Danny: Exactly. I know where it's going. I know where it's leading. So it's, like, cut it off before it becomes a big mess.

Teresa: Can I just ask something? What do you mean when you talk about "picking up the pieces"? I don't understand that.

Danny: Well, when you get your promotion and move on, and all these new ideas you're now trying to introduce don't work, we still have to … . I mean, we're still doing our real jobs while we're trying to implement these new ideas of yours. And now we have to sort out all the disruption these new ideas cause, and all the embarrassment that people feel because of them. It takes a while for people to get that out of their system. And meanwhile, you know, we just end up going back to doing things the way they've always been done. There is a procedure that has been in place for 10-15 years now. It works, everybody is happy with it. We go back to that and smooth things out. Right now, things aren't smooth. That's what I'm talking about. It's like breaking into pieces. That's the way it is. That's what I mean by picking up the pieces.

a. What are some of the metaphors that Danny uses in this portion of the mediation? What do they reveal to you about the underlying emotions, cares, and assumptions he has regarding his conflict with Teresa?
b. How might you respond to these metaphors? What are some questions you might ask? What could you say and do to unpack the underlying meaning of Danny's metaphors?
c. What insight and new understanding could Teresa get from Danny's metaphors?

FURTHER READING

Melchin, K., & Picard, C. (2008). *Transforming conflict through insight.* Toronto: University of Toronto Press.

Mezirow, J. (1991). *Transformative dimensions of adult learning.* San Francisco: Jossey-Bass.

Picard, C. (2003). Learning about learning: The value of "insight." *Conflict Resolution Quarterly, 20*(4), 477–484.

Picard, C., & Melchin, K. (2007). Insight mediation: A learning-centered mediation model, *Negotiation Journal, 23*(1), 35–54.

Smith, T.H. (2004). Using disputant's metaphors in mediation. Available at Social Science Research Network (SSRN): papers.ssrn.com/sol3/papers.cfm?abstract_id=536243.

Winslade, J., & Monk, G. (2000). *Narrative mediation: A new approach to conflict resolution.* San Francisco: Jossey-Bass.

Winslade, J., & Monk, G. (2008). *Practicing narrative mediation: Loosening the grip of conflict.* San Francisco: Jossey-Bass.

Websites

Centre for Conflict Education and Research, Carleton University: http://www.carleton.ca/ccer

The Narrative Centre: http://www.thenarrativecentre.com.au
This is an Australian website of narrative practitioners. You will find information and research material on the narrative approach.

Center for Narrative & Conflict Resolution: http://cncr.gmu.edu
CNCR is a learning center at the School for Conflict Analysis and Resolution, George Mason University, Virginia, USA.

Insight Conflict Resolution Program: http://www.insightconflictresolution.org
The Insight Conflict Resolution Program (ICRP) is a learning center at the School for Conflict Analysis and Resolution, George Mason University, Virginia, USA. ICRP's mission is to advance research, practice, and training in the Insight approach to conflict analysis and resolution.

B.C. Council on International Cooperation/Deliberative Dialogues:
http://bccic.ca/deliberative-dialogues
This is an interesting website, which has a video of a deliberative dialogue and links to a number of resources on this process for addressing public disputes and issues.

REFERENCES

Benjamin, R. (1995a). The constructive uses of deception: Skills, strategies, and techniques of the folkloric trickster figure and their application by mediators. *Mediation Quarterly, 13*, 3–18.

Benjamin, R. (1995b). The mediator as trickster: The folkloric figure as professional role model. *Mediation Quarterly, 13*, 131–149.

Bodtker, A.M., & Jameson, J.K. (1997). Mediation as mutual influence: Reexamining the use of framing and reframing. *Mediation Quarterly, 13*, 237–249.

Bush, R.A.B., & Folger, J.P. (1994). *The promise of mediation*. San Francisco: Jossey-Bass.

Cobb, S., & Rifkin, J. (1991). Neutrality as discursive practice: The construction and transformation of narratives in community mediation. *Studies in Law, Politics and Society, 11*, 69–91.

Fisher, J. (2000). Symbol in mediation. *Mediation Quarterly, 18*, 87–107.

Fisher, R., & Ury, W. (1981). *Getting to yes: Negotiating agreement without giving in*. Boston: Houghton Mifflin.

Hocker, J., & Wilmot, W. (1995). *Interpersonal conflict* (4th ed.). Madison, WI: WCB Brown and Benchmark.

Kydd, J. (1996). Language and family: The poverty of English. *Family and Conciliation Courts Review, 34*, 351–372.

Lakoff, G., & Johnson, M. (1980). *Metaphors we live by*. Chicago: University of Chicago Press.

Lang, M., & Taylor, A. (2000). *The making of a mediator*. San Francisco: Jossey-Bass.

LeBaron, M. (2002). *Bridging troubled waters: Conflict resolution from the heart*. San Francisco: Jossey-Bass.

Lederach, J.P. (1995). *Preparing for peace: Conflict transformation across cultures*. Syracuse, NY: Syracuse University Press.

Melchin, K., & Picard, C. (2008). *Transforming conflict through insight*. Toronto: University of Toronto Press.

Moore, C.W. (2003). *The mediation process: Practical strategies for resolving conflict* (3rd ed.). San Francisco: Jossey-Bass.

Picard, C.A. (2003). Learning about learning: Value of insight. *Conflict Resolution Quarterly, 20*, 477–484.

Winslade, J., & Monk, G. (2000). *Narrative mediation*. San Francisco: Jossey-Bass.

CHAPTER 9

Reaching Decisions and Completing the Mediation Process

LEARNING OBJECTIVES

After reading this chapter, you will be able to:

- Understand the role of the mediator in the final stage of the mediation process
- Identify a number of factors that limit collaboration and make it hard for some parties in conflict to accept a resolution that also benefits the other party
- Explain a number of strategies a mediator may use to help the parties generate and develop options, and move toward agreement
- Recognize the difference between a final agreement that is intended to have legal consequences for the parties and a memorandum of understanding that outlines party agreements without legal consequences
- Understand the responsibilities a mediator has for finalizing agreements and completing the mediation process.

CHAPTER OUTLINE

Introduction 253

Generating Options to Resolve the Problem 254

Strategies for the Resolution Phase 263

Reaching a Final Decision or Resolution 270

Stage 5: Post-Mediation Action 280

Summary 283

I must have a prodigious amount of mind; it takes me as much as a week, sometimes, to make it up!

Mark Twain, *The Innocents Abroad*

Introduction

In this chapter, we consider Stage 4, the final stage of the actual mediation process, which involves generating options to resolve the problem and then reaching agreement or deciding on a resolution. Generally speaking, this chapter focuses on how mediation enables parties in conflict to make decisions. These decisions may either move them along the path toward resolution or resolve their dispute entirely. We will consider obstacles to effective decision making and how these obstacles can be understood, addressed, and overcome. We will discuss ways of expanding the range of resolution possibilities and increasing the parties' openness to these possibilities. We examine how mediators can help parties to reach final decisions and incorporate these decisions into a written memorandum or agreement. Finally, we discuss what is involved in implementing the decisions and agreements made in mediation—in other words, what happens at the conclusion of the five-stage mediation process.

Typically, in the Stage 4 resolution phase, the mediator facilitates a process whereby the parties generate, consider, and assess various options for resolving their dispute. In the course of this, they move through a process of negotiation and collaboration. How the resolution phase proceeds varies depending on the nature and the context of the dispute. These two factors always affect the role played by the mediator and the nature of the parties' decisions.

The resolution and decision-making phase of mediation is largely determined by the parties' goals—both the goals they established before the mediation began, which may have shifted through the mediation process, and the new goals developed through mediation. If their primary goal is restoring relationships, the parties might prefer not to express in formal, written terms the agreement or decisions they have reached; they might prefer to let their future relationship shape itself in a more informal way. In other cases, the parties may wish to express their agreement in legally binding terms, terms that they can refer to in the event of future disagreement.

Take, for example, two parties who co-own a business and have decided to part ways. They might engage in mediation in order to terminate their business relationship and to decide on a reasonable price at which one party might buy out the other. If a misunderstanding between the two has led to troubled relations, it is possible that mediation will clarify these misunderstandings and repair the relations between the parties. However—assuming they are still intending to part ways—the parties will need to settle tangible financial questions. In this case, the mediation will focus on developing criteria for evaluating the business and on standards for fairness, so that they can agree on a purchase price.

Generating Options to Resolve the Problem

In the early part of Stage 4, the mediators continue to work with the parties toward resolution. A number of factors affect this part of the process, determining how it leads to the resolution at the end of the mediation. In this phase of the process, mediators should be aware of the following three considerations:

1. All the parties' decisions should be made voluntarily and based on complete information.
2. The parties need to be ready for the final movement toward concluding mediation and agreeing on a resolution.
3. Many factors can limit collaboration.

Decisions: Voluntary and Fully Informed

Central to mediation is the principle that the parties' decisions should be voluntary and based on complete information. The parties should not feel unduly pressured to reach a decision or to settle their dispute. In making their decision, they need to be aware of their alternatives and freely choose the one they perceive as best for them. Even when mediation is mandatory for the parties, as with a court-connected mediation program, they must determine for themselves what issues they will or will not resolve in mediation.

The principle of self-determination is a foundational principle of mediation. A mediator's goal is to enable all parties to make voluntary and well-informed decisions that are free of coercion, manipulation, or deception, after they have considered all of the alternatives for themselves. Section 3 of the ADR Institute of Canada's Code of Conduct for Mediators enshrines this principle of self-determination:

> PRINCIPLE OF SELF-DETERMINATION
>
> 3.1 It is the right of parties to a Mediation to make their own voluntary and non-coerced decisions regarding the possible resolution of any issue in dispute. Every Mediator shall respect and encourage this fundamental principle of Mediation.
>
> 3.2 The Mediator shall provide the parties at or before the first Mediation session with information about the Mediator's role in the Mediation. The Mediator shall discuss the fact that authority for decision-making rests with the parties, not the Mediator.
>
> 3.3 The Mediator shall not provide legal or professional advice to the parties. The Mediator may express views or opinions on the matters at issue, and may identify evaluative approaches, and where the Mediator does so it shall not be construed as either advocacy on behalf of a party or as legal or professional advice to a party.
>
> 3.4 The Mediator shall, where appropriate, advise unrepresented parties to obtain independent legal advice. The Mediator shall also, where appropriate, advise parties of the need to consult with other professionals to help parties make informed decisions.

For the full text of this Code of Conduct for Mediators, see Appendix C.

The mediator may provide information, including legal opinions, about the issue in dispute without violating the principle of self-determination—that is, the principle of free and autonomous decision-making by the parties. By going further—by taking on an advisory role or seeking to persuade or pressure a party to settle the dispute in a certain way—the mediator would be contravening the principle of self-determination and the ADR Institute's Code of Conduct.

As we discussed in Chapter 6, all parties, to be eligible for mediation, must in the mediator's view have the capacity to make informed decisions and voluntary choices. Such a capacity means that (1) the party has the cognitive capacity to make intelligent, informed decisions that are in his or her best interests, and (2) the party has the ability to make autonomous choices, free of any unfair coercion or manipulation by the other party. In most cases, the mediator will make a determination of this capacity in the pre-mediation phase, but he or she needs to continue to monitor it throughout the mediation process, ensuring that each party is indeed able to function as a competent, autonomous decision-maker.

If, at any time, it appears a party does not have the capacity or ability to make free, autonomous decisions, it becomes the mediator's responsibility to consider ways to equip the party in this regard. Women and children from certain cultures or cultural contexts, for instance, may not be used to making decisions on their own. If a mediation involves a woman from such a cultural context, the mediator may need to address the power imbalance that results from her lack of familiarity with decision making, so that she has a voice throughout the mediation, and decisions are not unduly influenced by the opposing party's assertiveness. Among the strategies the mediator might use to accomplish this are the following:

- suggesting that the party be accompanied in mediation by a support person—a friend, advocate, or family member;
- separating the parties and speaking to them individually for some or all of the mediation process; and
- ensuring that both parties have one or two days to consider any final decisions and the opportunity, if appropriate, to consult a lawyer or other adviser before any agreement is considered final and binding.

For the parties to have informed choice, they must undertake a full examination of the dispute resolution alternatives to negotiation or mediation. As we discussed in Chapter 2 (under the heading "Negotiating Power: BATNA"), each party needs to know his or her BATNA (the acronym for *best alternative to a negotiated agreement*) (Fisher & Ury, 1991, p. 97). In other words, what is his or her best course of action if the parties do not settle their dispute or reach agreement on the issues between them? In many cases, the best alternative will be to proceed to adjudication and a judge's or an arbitrator's decision. The challenge for each party and for his or her legal counsel is to make a reasonably accurate assessment of what might happen if the dispute proceeds in that way. What might the judge's or arbitrator's decision be, and how much time, effort, and cost will be involved in getting it? What is the risk of an unfavourable decision?

As discussed below (under the heading "Judgmental Overconfidence"), parties and their counsel, deluded by partisan perceptions, often have an overly optimistic view of the decision a judge or arbitrator might render. In such a case, what is the mediator's role in helping to ensure that parties (and their counsel) have a realistic assessment of their BATNA? Different mediators approach this problem in different ways.

Some mediators are very hands-off when it comes to educating parties about their BATNA; they leave it to the parties and to their counsel to discuss and decide on their own. Other mediators take on the responsibility of ensuring that each party is very aware of the time, effort, costs, and risks of proceeding with litigation or with another formal dispute resolution method. Some evaluative mediators take on the role of assessing the evidentiary and legal merits of each party's legal case and expressing an opinion on the possible or likely judicial outcome if the case goes to court. Some would say that this is not really mediation; it is something called "neutral evaluation." However, in some cases the lines between neutral evaluation and mediation are fuzzy.

Some institutionalized mediation services allow a limited amount of time to resolve a dispute. While time pressures can sometimes help parties reach an agreement, the agreement they reach may not be the best or the most durable or the most meaningful one. Open-ended discussion is almost always a benefit when it comes to resolving conflict, whether the issues involved be substantive, relational, or symbolic ones.

Ensuring That Parties Are Ready to Proceed to Resolution

Mediators-in-training often ask us the following question: "When is it time to start generating options for resolution?" Parties might begin to offer solutions quite early in the mediation. The mediator will note these suggestions, but is unlikely to pursue them until the parties have sufficiently dealt with past concerns and grievances and are ready to look to the future. Groundwork for devising solutions will be easier if parties are aware that multiple perspectives exist on the conflict issues and if they recognize the need for multiple options to resolve these issues. Finally, as we discussed in Chapters 7 and 8, parties need to be ready and able to collaborate with one another in generating possible solutions.

As a general guideline, the mediator will take cues from the parties that they are ready to consider different options for resolving their conflict. Parties should enter into the decision-making stage of mediation only when they have a full understanding of all the issues that need to be addressed. Sometimes, a party may be ready to decide on an issue, only to discover during the dialogue that another issue has surfaced and needs to be discussed before anything can be decided. Mediation is not a linear process that moves progressively through one stage to another. The parties' perceptions of the conflict and of its issues may change and develop through mediation.

In reality, parties often move back and forth among the stages, particularly the three in the middle—exploring the narratives, getting to the heart of the problem, and generating options. This is normal and to be expected. However, the parties do need to uncover, with the mediator's help, what is motivating them in the conflict—

the interests, needs, and values that are at play. Unless they do so, the parties will find it very difficult to devise options for settlement other than ones that are zero-sum. Consequently, parties will be ready to consider options only when sufficient information has emerged about the issues—that is, after they have discussed what really matters to them.

New mediators often rush to the consideration of options without sufficiently exploring what drives the issues and why they are so important to the parties. Helping the parties become aware of their respective values, goals, interests, and needs is critical to helping them know when to cooperate or when to stand firm on their position. To the extent that the mediator has been successful in this regard, the parties will be able to engage in a collaborative negotiation process. A collaborative negotiation will be one with a broader and deeper range of resolution possibilities. It will be one in which the parties and the mediator are able to "expand the pie"—that is, to generate multiple options for resolving the dispute, options that satisfy the needs and interests of all parties.

According to Moore (2003, p. 269), the mediator needs to ensure that the parties are aware of the need to consider multiple options. The mediator can start to do this early in the process, even during pre-mediation. Usually, parties to a dispute have a narrow, adversarial focus. They each believe in the inherent rightness of their position and in the solution they initially develop—one that satisfies their wants, but largely ignores or rejects the needs of the other party. By being open-minded and curious—at once encouraging and exemplifying that way of thinking during the mediation process—the mediator can help each party see that there are different perspectives and approaches to the subject matter of the dispute. For example, the mediator can use expressions and pose questions such as the following:

- "That's one way of looking at it."
- "What do you think B's expectations of that were?"
- "How do you think B considers that?"

By legitimizing different points of view without accepting any one of them, the mediator helps each party recognize that there are a variety of legitimate perspectives on the issues in dispute, and that each of these various perspectives involves its own approach or option for resolution. Moore also asserts that the mediator needs to do whatever he or she can to detach parties from positions (that is, demands) that are unacceptable to the opposing party (2003, p. 271).

Factors That May Limit Collaboration

Fisher and Ury (1991, pp. 57–59) caution against certain factors that may limit collaboration: premature judgment, searching for the single answer, the assumption of a fixed pie, and thinking that "solving their problem is their problem." These factors inhibit creative problem-solving, interfere with the brainstorming of possibilities, and result in limited options that are unlikely to address the myriad interests of both parties.

Other researchers, too, have identified psychological factors that inhibit collaborative decision making. These factors cause parties to act in ways that are contrary to their own best interests, often preventing them from recognizing the benefits of a collaborative outcome. These factors include the following:

- partisan perceptions,
- tunnel vision,
- zero-sum thinking,
- attribution errors,
- anchoring assumptions,
- loss aversion,
- reactive devaluation, and
- judgmental overconfidence.

Partisan Perceptions

Partisan perceptions refer to the tendency to view the conflict through a self-referential or self-interested lens (Mnookin, Peppet, & Tulumello, 2000, p. 157). Parties in conflict usually have differing perspectives about what has happened, what the conflict is about, who is to blame, and what needs to be done to resolve the conflict. Each party typically believes that his or her own perspective on the conflict is objectively true, and that any fair-minded observer would see the conflict this way. That is why parties sometimes have such difficulty hearing the other side's view of the conflict; this view often differs radically from their own. By giving all parties the opportunity to tell their side of the story, mediators provide them with the opportunity to hear the other side's conflict perspective, often for the first time. Meeting in joint session can therefore be very important. For this reason, we recommend that mediators use caucusing only when they believe it to be absolutely necessary (see Chapter 7, under the heading "Reasons for Caucusing").

Tunnel Vision

Neglecting the other side's viewpoint or being exclusively focused on one's own view of the problem leads to tunnel vision. A party with tunnel vision is unable to imagine any view of the problem except his or her own and lacks the capacity for peripheral vision. The ability to focus all our attention on one issue and to exclude non-essential information is an important human survival strategy. Tunnel vision becomes dysfunctional when it causes a person to ignore helpful information. In the case of conflict resolution, helpful information is information that could help the person see the conflict, or the other parties engaged in the conflict, in a different way.

Tunnel vision can be problematic not just for the parties in dispute, but for mediators. As we discussed in Chapter 6, mediation is a responsive process whereby the mediator takes his or her cues from the parties; he or she must remain open to new information about the parties' subjective perceptions, needs, interests, and values as these matters emerge in the course of the mediation. The mediator otherwise risks imposing his or her own perception of the conflict onto the parties. By remaining open to and curious about information that emerges from the parties during mediation, the mediator models for them an attitude of "responsive intentionality." This can help them overcome their own tunnel vision and expand their horizon of expectations concerning ways of resolving the conflict.

Zero-Sum Thinking

Zero-sum thinking is the mindset that, where a dispute is concerned, any outcome that is beneficial for one party must necessarily come at the expense of the other. Imagine two children at the dinner table, each wanting a slice of pie. Most of the pie is gone; there is enough for the children to have one small piece each if what is left is cut in half. If the pie is cut so that one child gets more than half, the other will get less than 50 percent. A gain for one child is a loss for the other. This image and images like it condition our thinking when it comes to disputes. With respect to mediation, if one party believes that the conflict is structured in zero-sum terms, he or she is likely to be suspicious of any proposal that involves gain for the other party.

Zero-sum thinking often occurs in conflict situations where there has been a history of escalated conflict between the parties. In such cases, mistrust prevails; neither side is prepared to consider a solution in which the other side benefits, for fear that this may involve a loss for himself.

Imagine a conflict between two divorcing spouses who have children. One of them cannot agree to any parenting arrangements proposed because he is locked into a pattern of zero-sum thinking about custody and access. This way of thinking prevents him from seeing that the children's interests and needs, as well as his wife's and his own, would benefit, now and in the future, from a more collaborative approach. Mediators can play an important role in showing such a party that what he or she perceives to be a zero-sum conflict is not necessarily so. A party is more apt to accept this from the mediator than from the other party, especially if the mediator has built a relationship of trust with the party during the course of the mediation.

Attribution Errors

Attribution errors occur when a conflicting party unconsciously attributes hostile motives or intentions to the other party, and then adjusts his own behaviour accordingly. In the classic instance, one party justifies her competitive behaviour as a response to the competitive attitude the other party has shown toward her. This often occurs when there has been a history of conflict and distrust between the parties.

Each blames the other for escalating the conflict. Neither is prepared to make the collaborative overture that might end their entrenched pattern of competitive interaction. The mediator can help such a situation by making the parties less certain about the motivations they attribute to each other.

Remember that cooperative behaviour is learned. If one party experiences its benefits, even in a small matter, he or she may be prepared to try it elsewhere. Experienced mediators know that cooperative behaviour over small issues can lead to the same behaviour over larger ones. Having the parties try to cooperate on small issues is a useful start to having them try to collaborate on the dispute's main issues: if the attempt fails, there is still room to try again, and the uncooperative party gradually learns the benefits of cooperative behaviour. This is the basis for the "tit-for-tat" bargaining model developed by negotiation researchers such as Robert Axelrod (1984). Their experiments showed that, even where the parties mistrusted each other, they learned by trial and error, through simulated bargaining sessions, the benefits of cooperation and the costs of not reciprocating. These research subjects tended to become more efficient over time when it came to cooperative decision making.

Anchoring Assumptions

Anchoring one's assumptions can negatively affect decision making. What does this mean? To anchor your assumptions is to make a single issue or condition, consciously or unconsciously, the basis for considering any possible change. Take, for instance, a workplace grievance complaint concerning the denial of a promotion. The employee who has been denied promotion and has lodged the complaint may be convinced that, if the grievance is upheld, he will automatically get the promotion. This anchoring assumption is likely to affect his willingness to try mediation or to consider any outcomes to the conflict that do not involve getting what he assumes he is entitled to. However, it may be that, even if the unpromoted employee's grievance is upheld, the arbitrator will not overturn the decision but send the issue back to be decided again within the organization, with appropriate procedures. In other words, the complainant's expectations, based on his or her anchoring assumption about what an arbitrator will decide, might turn out to be wrong.

A party with an anchoring assumption is unlikely to consider any other possible options for resolving the conflict until the anchoring assumption is questioned or made uncertain. To be effective, this questioning may need to come from the mediator, not from the opposing party. The mediator may be able to function as an agent of reality; she may recommend that the parties obtain more information about the matter in dispute, perhaps by obtaining independent legal advice, before attempting to reach decisions through mediation. The mediator's questioning of the party's anchoring assumption may loosen it enough to cause the party to consider other options.

Loss Aversion

Behavioural psychologists have shown that parties in conflict tend to attach greater weight to prospective losses than to potential gains. According to this research, the fear of losing—of being "beaten" by the other party—outweighs the motivation to pursue collaborative gains. In a series of experiments, psychologists Tversky and Kahneman (1981) showed that negotiators' response to a proposed decision is influenced by how the decision is framed. Parties who are concerned about protecting themselves tend to be very cautious in their decision making and unwilling to consider options that might result in mutual gains for all sides. Mediators need to be aware of this psychological tendency. When they are, they can help the parties who are in the decision-making stage of mediation present options for consideration that do not appear to involve risk of loss.

Reactive Devaluation

How a party responds to an option in the decision-making stage of mediation depends on several factors. One of them, as we noted above, is how the proposal is presented. Another factor, as researchers have shown, is *who* makes the proposal. Where there is an absence of trust between the parties, an offer or proposal from one party may be reflexively devalued by the other party, regardless of the proposal's content. The same proposal from a trusted person may get a much more positive response (Mnookin, Peppet, & Tulumello, 2000, p. 165). This is why mediators need to establish a climate of trust in mediation, and to encourage the parties to engage in cooperative behaviour whenever possible, even in small areas of the mediation process—for example, by taking turns in speaking, and by being respectful with each other.

Even where the issues are slight, reciprocal cooperation and respect between the parties help break down the mistrustful attitudes with which they often enter the mediation room; the parties become more open to the options presented by the other side, and reactive devaluation is neutralized. Given this possibility, you can see why the decision-making stage of mediation needs to wait until after the parties have had sufficient opportunity to explore what matters to them, and to begin to understand the other party's point of view.

Judgmental Overconfidence

Researchers have also shown that parties to a negotiation have a tendency to overestimate the strength of their own position and to underestimate both the validity of the other side's arguments and the other side's willingness to defend its position under pressure (Mnookin, Peppet, & Tulumello, 2000, p. 159). A mediator, as an impartial third party who has built a relationship of trust with both sides, is often able to correct such misperceptions—to introduce each party in turn to the other side's perspective and to demonstrate the legitimacy and potential merit of the opposing points of view. This can help reduce the factor of judgmental overconfidence.

Strategies for the Resolution Phase

In Chapter 3, we discussed various types of mediators and what bearing a mediator's particular approach may have on how actively he or she intervenes in the mediation process. A social network mediator (see Chapter 3, under the heading "Social Network Mediator"), for example, is often selected by the parties for her reputation in the community and her familiarity with the community's norms and values. The parties expect this type of mediator, whose decisions carry a considerable degree of informal authority within the community, to play an active role in the decision-making process, sometimes even to function as a kind of community arbitrator, rather than as a mediator. This mediation style is practised all over the world in communities that have traditional dispute resolution structures. The style of mediation used in these cases is very different from the style taught in North American mediation programs, which emphasize a professional, third-party, neutral style of mediation (see Chapter 3, under the heading "Independent Mediator").

The nature of the dispute can also influence how actively a mediator intervenes in the decision-making process. In a labour–management dispute over the terms of a new collective agreement, for example, the parties may wish the mediator to play an active role; they may look to her to try to narrow the differences between the parties, and, in some cases, even to propose terms of settlement. This would be an example of a mediator adopting a very directive role in the decision-making process.

In some institutional mediation programs (for example, the mediation program of the Canadian Transportation Agency or of a human rights commission), the mediator may also function as a subject matter expert, providing the parties with information about certain technical aspects of the dispute and helping them appreciate what may or may not be a feasible resolution in that case.

In the case of a mediated peace agreement for an international conflict, a mediator may shuttle between the two sides, carrying proposals for each to consider and helping each side evaluate the proposed terms of settlement.

Involvement of Non-Participating Parties

A mediator also has to ensure that parties have the authority to enter into agreements, and that the needs of all parties likely to be affected by the outcome are considered in the decision-making process. For instance, in a divorce mediation, the two parties most involved in the mediation are the separating or divorcing spouses. But the issues often include parenting arrangements, along with custody and access decisions. Children who are legally still minors (under the age of 18) are too young in the eyes of the law to be included as parties in the mediation or litigation process.

The mediator, then, must take into account the children's needs, as well as the parents' needs. In Canada, those who mediate child custody and access issues usually have knowledge of family systems and act to ensure that the child's or children's interests are fully considered.

There are other situations where the issues being mediated may have an impact on absent parties or external constituencies. Mediation used for urban planning requires that all the stakeholders—community residents, local politicians, developers, and construction companies, as well as private businesses that will be affected by the plans—be represented by agents (if not by themselves) during negotiations. Failure to consider any of these third-party audiences and their interests and needs is likely to make any decision reached in mediation less durable, less satisfying, and ultimately less effective.

In some cases, the parties in the mediation are representing wider constituencies whose support is required for any agreement to take effect. Both the parties and the mediator need to be aware of this. As we have discussed, mediation entails a learning process for the parties, as they come to understand more about one another's conflict perspectives and one another's interests, needs, values, and fears. However, this understanding within the mediation room may not extend outside it, to the wider constituencies the parties represent. There is a risk that these outside constituencies will remain locked in an adversarial or competitive stance toward each other and will not support any agreement reached. It is important for both the parties and the mediator to be aware of this dynamic, and to try to generate creative ways of extending their own learning process to the external constituencies. For this to occur, the parties may need to develop an educational or awareness-building strategy among their respective memberships. They may need the press or the media to help them with this task.

Parties Not at the Table

An ethical question arises for mediators when decisions are being made that will affect parties not at the table. Who represents the absent parties' interests? Should the mediator do so? This question arises with divorcing parents, as we noted above. How are the children's interests to be represented? Should mediators take this responsibility? If they do, can they still maintain their role as impartial mediators? This ethical question also arises when the agreement will affect parties that are not yet born. For example, all mining or resource-extraction planning should consider not only the interests of those at the table—business interests, for example, intent on the short-term benefits of extracting the resource—but on the environmental interests of future generations—human, plant, and animal. Menin (2000, p. 285) tells us that "a mediator has a right and a responsibility to bring to the table issues or perspectives that may not have been identified or addressed by either party but that affect an absent party."

Mediators advocating for the public interest need to be concerned about impartiality. The ethical dilemma is how to advocate for reasonable agreements while remaining impartial. Some family mediators ensure that the children have an advocate to speak on their behalf. In cases where the children are old enough and their presence is appropriate, they are invited into the negotiations.

Social network mediators—those mediators who, in diverse societies around the world, perform traditional community dispute resolution—are expected to hold community interests above the needs of individuals within the community. The community accepts this role and function for its mediators; the latter are expected to be impartial only to the extent of treating the parties in mediation fairly and without bias. But they are not expected to be value-free. It is assumed that they will intervene to protect community interests.

Methods for Generating, Discussing, and Assessing Options

A mediator can use various strategies to help parties generate options and move toward agreement.

Joint Problem Statement

Chris Moore (2003) recommends that the mediator incorporate the interests of both parties into what he calls a "joint problem statement." A joint problem statement, in Moore's words (2003, p. 265), "enables negotiators to commit to work on a common problem because they believe that their needs will be respected (if not met) by the solutions that will be developed." The statement is crafted from the knowledge gained through uncovering interests, values, and needs, and it is typically framed as a goal.

In the Car Repair Blues mediation (see Box 1.1 in Chapter 1), for example, the mediator may present the following joint problem statement before inviting the parties to present their ideas for possible resolution options:

> What are the elements of a final agreement that will meet the following needs?
>
> - Dale's need to know that she is paying a fair and reasonable amount for necessary repairs to her car; and
> - Chris's interest in being recognized, by Dale and by the community, as an honest, reliable, and fair auto mechanic who provides good value for money.

Brainstorming

Moore (2003, p. 283) has described brainstorming as "a procedure in which two or more people generate a variety of ideas or options for consideration." The notion of *consideration* is crucial; the mediator needs to make it clear to the parties that, in suggesting any idea or option, the person is not committing to it. It is merely one possible component of a possible agreement. The mediator also needs to emphasize that the brainstorming process works best when everyone agrees not to judge or criticize any idea.

The purpose of brainstorming is to generate as many ideas and options as possible. After it is finished and all of the ideas have been written down, the mediator leads the parties through a separate process of considering and assessing all of these ideas and boiling them down to a short list of options that, according to all parties, *could* be included in a final agreement.

During the brainstorming process, the mediator should prompt the parties, helping them to see the problem from different perspectives and to consider a variety of options. Some mediators will resist contributing their own ideas; others will be quite pointed in prompting the parties to consider options they may not have considered. For example, in the case of the Car Repair Blues scenario, the mediator may need to prompt Chris to consider offering Dale a voucher or gift certificate for future service (for example, an oil change) as one component of the final agreement.

Moore lists a number of specific procedures for generating options to settle disputes. Settlement options may address either specific issues or general principles. If the parties are already in an established relationship, they may decide to specify which elements of their current relationship they would like to continue in the future. The parties may develop their own objective standards to evaluate options or they may consider settlement agreements from similar disputes and find their standards there. The parties may try hypothetical modelling, a process whereby each party ranks a number of different hypothetical settlements in terms of his or her satisfaction with each. The parties may identify linked issues and explore the possibility of trade-offs. Alternatively, they might consider different package settlements that address all issues. To develop a comprehensive package, they may draft and redraft a single settlement proposal until it meets all of their essential needs.

When the conflict involves groups or when a single party represents a larger constituency, the parties may generate options through more than one procedure. As well as having an open discussion during the mediation, they may brainstorm solutions outside of the mediation, in structured sessions with their constituencies. Mediators may play a role in these structured brainstorming sessions, which may involve consulting outside experts who can further broaden the parties' perspectives on the dispute and on the range of possible solutions.

Flip Chart or Whiteboard

Using a flip chart or whiteboard to develop options or proposals can be a powerful tool for integrating parties' ideas and proposals to bring about collaboration. In this respect, it is much like the "one text" method discussed below (under the heading "One-Text Procedure"). In a two-sided mediation, parties tend to have a competitive, "us versus them" mentality. The mediator represents the "third side" (Ury, 2000), whose role is to create an integrative place—a common ground—where both parties can go to find or develop a resolution that belongs to both of them. The mediator represents the "neutral space." However, even with the mediator, mediation discussions usually have parties facing each other across a table, which underscores that the two sides are opposed. When the mediator uses a flip chart or whiteboard, it can become a physical manifestation of the common ground where parties can collaborate rather than compete. When the mediator writes on the flip chart, parties face in the same direction and gain a sense of working together on a common problem.

Back to the Future

During the option-generating stage, parties should be focusing on the future—what they need to do now and tomorrow to resolve the issues. If a party continues to talk about the past, the problems suffered, and the other party's actions or failures, more work probably needs to be done to uncover interests, needs, and values. Another strategy for the mediator to try is to invite the parties to consider a ground rule that brings them "back to the future." This is a particularly useful strategy when parties are pressed for time and must settle their dispute. It is preferable for parties to take the time they need to get to this stage, but unlimited time is not always possible.

"In Principle"

A party may be reluctant to discuss an option suggested by the other, even though it may have potential benefit. Specific concerns or risks may lead one party to reject such an option. By asking parties if they will consider the idea in principle, the mediator is asking them to acknowledge the potential merit of the idea and their willingness to discuss and develop it further. Such a statement might sound like the following:

> I know you have concerns about how this might work, and that a number of details would have to be worked out. I assure you that you will have the time to talk about that. For the moment, however, would you be willing to consider in principle the idea of reinstating your contractual relationship?

"What Would It Take?"

Asking the parties what it would take for an option to work can also reveal new information that helps parties move forward in the resolution phase. A mediator might ask the following questions:

> You seem to have reservations about that offer. What would it take to make it work for you?
>
> What would it take to make that proposal into something you could accept?
>
> What do you think it would take to make that proposal into something the other side could accept?

Role Reversal

A variation on the what-would-it-take strategy is to ask one of the parties to put himself in the other party's shoes. The following questions exemplify this strategy:

> If you were Alex, why do you think your proposal may not be acceptable?
>
> Put yourself in her shoes and imagine the arguments or objections you would have to this proposal. What options can you suggest for overcoming those objections?

Trading on Differences

As explained by Lax and Sebenius (1986, pp. 92–106) and by Mnookin, Peppet, and Tulumello (2000, p. 14), the differences between the parties provide opportunities to find or to create value, to the mutual benefit of the parties. Trading on differences is central to most negotiation. Mnookin, Peppet, and Tulumello identify the following five types of differences.

1. *Different resources.* These can include goods, services, money, knowledge, know-how, opportunities, education, natural resources, and land.
2. *Different relative valuations.* Each party values actions or resources differently. Think about the Fruit Exchange scenario from Chapter 2 (see Box 2.2). By creating an unusual trading scheme, everyone wins.
3. *Different forecasts.* Parties have different knowledge or beliefs about what the future will hold. Michelle may be confident that there will be high future demand for a particular product she has invented. Mario may feel less optimistic. Therefore, Michelle may be happy to agree that a substantial component of her compensation will be based on a percentage of net income, if Mario markets and sells the product.
4. *Different risk preferences.* A party's capacity to take on risk depends on the party's nature. For example, the capacity of the insurance industry or of an insurance company is very different from that of an individual policyholder.
5. *Different time preferences.* One party may be more concerned with what happens in the short term; the other may only be concerned about the longer term. If one party is going to pay money to the other, often there are differences as to when it is ideal for that to happen. In some cases, the benefit to the payer in being able to pay the amount over an extended period of time may be substantially greater than the burden to the payee of waiting for full payment. In other cases, receiving cash sooner than later may be important to the payee, in which case the payee may be happy to receive a lower amount than he or she otherwise might be entitled to.

"What If?"

The mediator or either party may introduce a "what if" idea as a hypothetical option. This is a relatively non-threatening and non-forcing way of exploring an idea that may itself become a term of a settlement agreement, or may open the door to other settlement ideas. Any such idea may be introduced in an exploratory way, by asking about the consequences of a particular decision or action. The following is an example of such a question:

> What if, during specified daylight hours, the railway did what Karim has suggested and carried out all of its shunting operations in one particular corner of the yard?

Exploring the consequences of an action enables the parties to deal with, and potentially resolve, concerns that may have prevented one, or even both, of the parties from presenting it as a settlement option earlier.

Often accompanying "what if" ideas are suggestions such as the following, which involve trial periods:

> What if you tried Karim's idea of using one corner of the yard for shunting, strictly as a trial for two or three months, without any commitment to continue beyond that time? A few weeks before the end of the trial period, the two of you could confer to discuss what, if anything, would continue to happen after that time.

"Some People"

There are times when it may be appropriate for the mediator to suggest an option or idea as something that "some people" in such circumstances have found to be useful. Here is an example of such a suggestion:

> In similar situations to yours, people have developed communication protocols that are instituted on a trial basis for one or two months. What do you think about exploring something similar?

Assuming Ownership

A party may have an option to propose, but she believes there could be some disadvantage or risk in proposing it. Nonetheless, the party would like to know whether it might be acceptable to the other party. The mediator may *assume ownership* of the idea and test the water by putting it forward as a "what if" to the other party. An option or idea generated by the mediator may avoid reactive devaluation by one party.

Reaching a Final Decision or Resolution

Having generated a range of resolution options, the parties must consider those options and reach an agreement. Sometimes, a solution may be obvious, and the parties readily accept it. At other times, a mediator will need to work with the parties to assess and negotiate the options they have identified. He or she will help them arrive at the best solution, one that meets the needs of all parties.

There are three types of agreements that can be reached:

1. full agreement, with all the parties resolving all the issues between them;
2. a partial agreement, with some issues resolved and others left outstanding; and
3. an agreement in principle, whereby neither party requires a formal, detailed record of what they have decided, but are comfortable proceeding toward future actions.

Agreements in principle are vital to cease-fire agreements in international negotiations, according to Crocker, Hampson, and Aall (2004). They claim that a framework for negotiations or a statement of principles is the building block from which a binding set of principles for ending conflict can launch more detailed, formal negotiations on how that will occur. In any event, the type of agreement reached will depend on the issues in contention, the relationship between or among the parties, the authority of parties to make decisions, and whether or not all issues were resolved in mediation.

Assisting Parties with Final Negotiations

Assisting in final negotiations can be a lengthy process for the mediator, since the negotiations must expand on the comfort level achieved by the parties through the mediation to that point. Every final negotiation presents the mediator with unique challenges. The following are some tactics a mediator may employ:

- working the settlement range,
- applying objective criteria,
- "one text procedure,"
- reality checks,
- reflection on progress,
- breaks,
- deadlines,
- incremental convergence,
- leap to agreement,
- procedural methods of reaching agreements, and
- the human dimension.

Working the Settlement Range

For disputes in which the primary issue is how much one party will pay the other, the mediator may employ a procedure Moore refers to as the "settlement range" (2003, p. 298). A party's settlement range spans the range between his "target point" and his "resistance point." The target point is the optimal outcome for the party; the resistance point is the point at which the outcome is either too costly or insufficiently beneficial—that is to say, below the party's BATNA. The resistance point is a party's bottom line, or maximum concession. When the disputing parties' settlement ranges overlap, there will be a number of acceptable options. Interest-based mediation will seek the solution that provides maximum mutual benefits.

Sometimes, there seems to be no overlap in the parties' settlement ranges; it is difficult or impossible for the parties to find any mutually acceptable settlement. In such cases, the mediator may try to encourage the parties to adjust their target or resistance points. Mediators can help the parties to identify and understand their settlement ranges, as well as to perform a reality check on inflated expectations the parties may have.

With respect to settlement ranges, the mediator should not always take what parties or their counsel say at face value. Parties often say "This is my bottom line" or "I won't accept a penny less" only to accept a substantially lower amount later in the mediation. Even seemingly intractable parties—insurance companies, for example—sometimes say "This is all we can offer," only to agree later to a significantly higher settlement.

Apply Objective Criteria

Fisher and Ury insist that, wherever possible, agreements should be based on objective standards that measure fairness and stability (1991, p. 81). In fact, mediators should have the parties negotiate these standards before discussing the agreement's details and figures.

Fairness comes in different forms: *equality*, with each side receiving the same amount; *equity*, with each side receiving more or less what they deserve based on their contributions (time, money, or energy committed); or *need*, with each side's needs determining what they receive.

Disagreements over applicable standards are often an important part of the dispute. For example, in a wrongful dismissal dispute, the main issue may be the amount of severance pay that the employer should give the dismissed employee. In most legal disputes, the parties disagree on the correct interpretation of the legal standards or principles that apply in that case. In such cases, if each party recognizes that the other is negotiating in good faith, they have a reasonable prospect of successfully negotiating their differences. On the other hand, one party may perceive that the other is acting in bad faith—in other words, professing a position or legal interpretation that he or she does not actually believe is correct. If one party believes the other is doing this, the mediator will need to address it. Such a suspicion can be an insurmountable barrier to resolution.

In the Car Repair Blues scenario, for example (see Box 1.1 in Chapter 1), Dale may not only believe that Chris did unnecessary work and charged her too much; she may also believe that Chris knew the work was unnecessary and deliberately overcharged for it. If Dale believes this, the mediator will need to address her belief.

There are many valid ways to determine fairness, and it is important not to forget the intangibles in negotiations. Benefits such as gaining recognition or appearing in a favourable light (for example, if someone is representing a constituency) can be included in fairness considerations. Some tips for setting fairness standards include the following:

- looking at what other organizations or businesses have done in similar instances (for example, in developing employee policies);
- checking out "market" standards (in the case of determining fair salaries or product/service pricing);
- using pre-existing evaluation standards (if considering criteria to evaluate candidates for a particular job), and
- using third-party experts (a scientist, for example, might be used in the case of an environmental dispute).

One-Text Procedure

Fisher and Ury (1991, pp. 112–116) propose that the mediator use a "one-text procedure" throughout the mediation process. The "one text" is composed of interests and needs as identified by the parties and drafted into agreement terms to be refined and reshaped by the parties; it is edited and adapted by the parties during the mediation. The mediator writes up a first draft and asks the parties to criticize it. The same process is followed for subsequent drafts until the document reflects those of the parties' key priorities and interests that can best be accommodated. At the final point (perhaps after as many as five or six iterations), the parties are asked to either accept or reject the agreement. Because, after several drafts, the text reflects the key needs of each party, it is likely to be accepted. In September 1978, when US President Carter hosted dialogues between Egypt and Israel at Camp David, the one-text procedure was used effectively to get agreement (Fisher & Ury, 1991, p. 116).

Reality Check

A "reality check" occurs when the mediator asks parties to examine their expectations, and helps them ensure that they are realistic. Cognitive factors, such as partisan perceptions, judgmental overconfidence, and attribution effects, often cause people in conflict to have unrealistic expectations. One important aspect of a reality check is to examine the consequences of not reaching agreement in mediation. This may involve a detailed consideration of the potential benefits, costs, and risks to a party of pursuing their best alternative course of action—that is, their BATNA. A cost-benefit analysis of a party's BATNA can be done in caucus if necessary, in which case the mediator may walk through the exercise with each party separately.

When helping parties examine their BATNAs and expectations, the mediator does not need to be evaluative or to express an opinion about what would likely happen if parties pursued alternative courses of action. In helping them to do a reality check and to examine carefully the potential benefits, costs, and risks of their alternative action, the mediator is helping parties form their own opinions and make their own fully informed choices. When done in a way that satisfies and promotes the principle of self-determination, the mediator is truly helping parties decide on a course of action that is in their best interests.

Reflect on Progress

To help the parties maintain a positive attitude and to encourage them to continue the dialogue, mediators may summarize the progress the parties have made, especially accomplishments related to the process itself—for example, the accomplishments of entering into mediation in the first place and of improved communication, cooperative interaction, and increased understanding. Any area of progress, no matter how small it may seem, is worth mentioning. When the going gets tough and people get discouraged, awareness of what they have achieved, and the time and effort they have invested to do so, may be the incentive they need to push forward to a successful conclusion.

Take a Break

During a break, pressures and emotions may ease off, enabling people to step back and get a broader perspective. They can then come back to the table, refreshed and renewed with the insight, energy, and creativity they need to bring the negotiation to a satisfactory conclusion.

Imposing Deadlines

If parties are not moving forward and seem inflexible, deadlines may help to spur them on to resolution. Deadlines may be internally or externally imposed, actual or artificial, rigid or flexible, with or without consequences, explicit or vague. Mediators can help make the parties aware of existing deadlines or can help them establish deadlines as needed. At the same time, mediators need to be careful not to push deadlines when the result may be bad agreements that will not likely be upheld. Some pressure is helpful, but too much at the wrong time will not assist in producing durable outcomes. Cultural attitudes toward time may also affect the use of deadlines. For example, in the case of the negotiations between the North Vietnamese and the

Americans to end the Vietnam War, which were held in France, the American negotiators booked their hotel for two weeks. The Vietnamese booked their hotel for two months.

Incremental Convergence

Moore (2003, pp. 310–314) has explained the strategy of "incremental convergence." By this process, parties make small concessions, one at a time, until they reach a mutually acceptable compromise. As Moore points out, the mediator can do a number of things to increase the likelihood of succeeding by means of this bargaining process. These include the following:

- helping parties overcome their reluctance to make offers or concessions;
- helping parties view an offer as a sign of strength, not weakness;
- taking ownership of an offer or idea, recognizing that one party may view an idea more favourably if it comes from the mediator rather than from the other party; and
- helping parties save face by helping them understand the rationale for making a new offer or for abandoning an untenable position.

Leap to Agreement

In the leap-to-agreement approach, the parties "leap to" accepting a comprehensive proposal after some very preliminary bargaining. This approach sometimes accompanies the one-text method (see above). The parties first seek agreement on general principles, and then seek to apply those principles to the situation at hand in the agreement-in-principle strategy. This strategy is particularly helpful in preventing impasse and deadlocks.

Procedural Methods of Reaching Decision

When parties are unable to reach a substantive agreement, they may use a procedural method for resolving the issue. Moore (2003, p. 318) defines these methods as follows: "Procedural solutions are process decisions that parties make to resolve disputes without directly deciding the issue." One of these methods involves referring the issue to a third-party decision-maker. For example, in the Car Repair Blues dispute, if the parties are unable to reach agreement on the necessity and value of Chris's work on Dale's car, they may agree to refer the issue to another auto mechanic who will inspect the vehicle and make a binding decision on those matters.

Remember the Human Dimension

Regardless of the size or import or complexity of the mediation—whether it involves two individuals, as in the Car Repair Blues scenario; or a large corporation, such as an insurance company—the mediator must always be mindful of the human dimension.

When the interaction between the parties features honesty and respect, they are much more likely to reach resolution than if their interaction involves significant mistrust or disrespect.

Completing the Agreement

After the parties are satisfied that they have reached agreement, the mediator's task is to ensure that there is no misunderstanding about what they have decided to do. Often, this means preparing a written memorandum of understanding (MOU) or minutes of settlement. A memorandum of understanding (see Appendix B) contains the main terms of the parties' agreement, but usually is not intended to be a legally enforceable contract. On the other hand, when parties (or their participating lawyers) prepare minutes of settlement, this document is a final, legally enforceable settlement of all claims and issues between the parties.

In some cultures, people find that insistence on a written contract is insulting—they interpret the request as a challenge to their honesty and integrity. The mediator needs to be sensitive to situations where written agreements may be unnecessary or even counterproductive.

If the mediated agreement or outcome is not going to be put into written form, the mediator can help the parties develop a clearly understood action plan that includes decisions on implementation, monitoring, and communications by the parties. Mediators should ensure that parties consider the "who, what, where, why, by when, and how" of whatever needs to be done.

Immediate, self-executing agreements, whether written or not, are the easiest to implement. But many agreements require the parties to carry out activities over an extended period of time. Implementation plans will be more successful when they include

- criteria for measuring performance,
- methods for measuring and enforcing compliance,
- general and specific implementation steps,
- regular means of communication between the parties during the agreement implementation, and
- procedures for managing future changes or conflicts.

For example, if the divorce mediation between Jo-Anne and Paul (see Exercise 1 at the end of Chapter 3) results in a final agreement, their written agreement should include provisions concerning what will happen if either party fails to fulfill a term of the agreement or if they disagree on the interpretation of any term. Generally, this provision will state that in the event of future disputes that the parties cannot resolve themselves, they will return to mediation before proceeding with any formal process such as arbitration or court action.

During the agreement-writing stage, everyone needs to be clear about what has been agreed to. A mediator who is helping the parties prepare a written agreement needs to make sure that it specifies, in as much detail as necessary, what each party is promising to do—the who, what, where, how, and when of their agreement. Generally, the terms will be set out in a series of separately numbered paragraphs, which specify what each of the parties has promised to do. The mediator should also ensure that there is some degree of reciprocity and balance to the terms of the agreement. Fisher and Ury (1991) say that a good agreement will be fair, wise, efficient, and stable.

Here are some of the various ways that mediation agreements may be drawn up:

1. The mediator will write out the terms, with input and direction from the parties, who then review and sign the agreement.
2. The parties draft their own agreement.
3. In cases where parties' lawyers are present, the lawyers may draft the agreement.
4. In some cases, it may be appropriate for the mediator or the parties to propose that the basic terms be sent to a lawyer (or lawyers) for drafting of the final agreement.
5. In some cases, it may be appropriate for parties to draft their separate versions of the agreement, which then can be circulated for input from others, with a final document being drafted to include all terms agreed to in the individual versions.

However it is done, it is crucial to recognize that the agreement belongs to the parties, and whatever method suits their needs and interests should be used. Even at this stage, flexibility and creativity continue to be important.

Legal Effect of the Mediated Agreement

No matter what approach is used to finalize Stage 4 of the mediation, it is essential that the mediator and all parties have a clear, common understanding about the legal consequences and enforceability of any agreement or MOU that is prepared. There are three possibilities with respect to enforceability:

1. They intend the written document to be a legally enforceable contract.
2. They intend the written document to be an MOU that will be incorporated (by their lawyers or others) into a legally binding contract, but that, until so incorporated, is not to have legal consequences.
3. They intend the written document to be an MOU that will be a record of their understanding for purposes of future clarity, but without its being legally enforceable or having legal consequences.

When the final agreement is intended as the basis of a legal settlement, the mediator encourages the parties to get legal advice or assistance to finalize the agreement. The mediator also informs the parties that their lawyers may raise certain issues that will require further negotiation or, in some cases, may raise obstacles to final agreement.

One way to think of the decision-making stage is that it creates a plan for the future for the parties. So, a way to know if the plan is working needs to be included. Mediators ask what the parties will do if their agreement fails. Will they return to mediation? Seek other outside help? Pursue other adjudicative methods? If no agreement is reached, mediators generally suggest resources such as counselling, arbitration, or litigation to help them deal with the dispute.

Outcome documents can be made legally binding and subject to judicial oversight. Alternatively, external authority may be brought on board—for example, a supervisor in the case of a conflict between employees—in order to encourage or compel compliance when parties' voluntary compliance is not sufficient.

When a negotiated agreement must be ratified by constituency groups, as in labour disputes, a mediator may help educate the group members about the mediation process and may reassure them that their representatives have negotiated effectively on their behalf. (See the discussion below, under the heading "Disputes with Constituencies.")

Legal Requirements and Implications

When mediation is used to resolve a legal claim, the mediator needs to be aware of certain legal rules relevant to the completion of the mediation process. Unless parties have specifically agreed to the contrary, and subject to the contract principle of "consideration," the parties' negotiation will result in a legally binding contract in either of the following circumstances:

1. Party A has made an offer (for example, a promise to pay) that has been accepted by Party B; or
2. both parties have agreed to a specified set of resolution options.

In the common law of contract, the principle of consideration requires that for one party's promised action (for example, a promise to pay) to be legally binding, the other party must also have provided or promised to provide the first party with something of value. Consider, for example, a case in which Party A has made a claim against Party B for damages suffered in an accident. If Party B offers to pay Party A $20,000 to settle the claim, and Party A accepts that offer, the parties have a legally binding settlement contract. The consideration flowing from Party A to Party B is that Party A, in accepting the offer, has agreed, explicitly or implicitly, to release and forever discharge all claims he may have against Party B relating to the accident.

It is usually (or invariably, when lawyers are involved) the case that when legal claims are settled, one or both parties will be required to sign a full and final release discharging all claims against the other party.

Accordingly, in mediations that involve claims of this kind, the mediator must clarify whether the parties (1) intend the outcome of their negotiation process to be legally binding; or (2) intend that there will not be any legally binding agreement until after the parties have had an opportunity to go away and consider the outcome of the mediation session and, if necessary, consult a lawyer or other adviser concerning it.

In the Car Repair Blues scenario, for example (see Box 1.1 in Chapter 1), Chris may accept a compromise offer from Dale stipulating that she will pay him $800 in four monthly installments of $200. Unless Dale and Chris have previously agreed that their mediated negotiation process will not be legally binding, they will—as soon as Chris accepts Dale's offer, even if he does so only orally—have a legally binding contract requiring Dale to pay these amounts.

Consider the divorce mediation between Paul and Jo-Anne (see Exercise 1 at the end of Chapter 3). Unless both parties have their lawyers at the mediation (and, in this scenario, we have assumed that they do not), the mediator needs to make it clear to Paul and Jo-Anne throughout Stage 4 of the mediation that any agreement they reach will not be legally binding until it has been incorporated into a written separation agreement that has been signed by both parties. Indeed, in Ontario, section 55(1) of the *Family Law Act* requires this in the following terms:

> A domestic contract and an agreement to amend or rescind a domestic contract are unenforceable unless made in writing, signed by the parties and witnessed. [*Note*: In the *Family Law Act*, the phrase "domestic contract" includes a separation agreement.]

To summarize, then, the common practice for a mediation between separating spouses is to produce a memorandum of understanding (MOU) that will not have legal consequences until the parties and their lawyers incorporate the terms into a separation agreement that is signed by both parties and witnessed by their lawyers.

Another legal consideration (one that should be near and dear to the hearts of all mediators) is that of the mediator's own legal liability.

Mediator Liability

There are three situations where a mediator may be vulnerable to liability. The first is where parties believe they could have done substantially better elsewhere. The second is where parties feel aggrieved about the process itself. The third is where one or both of the parties believe they have reached an agreement, but later disagree on what the agreement was or whether agreement was reached at all. Not to minimize the importance of this issue, but we are unaware of any lawsuit against a mediator in Canada.

Boulle and Kelly (1998, p. 262) tell us that mediators can "potentially be liable if they breach the mediation contract between themselves and the parties." Contracts can be written or oral and are commonly used in pre-mediation agreements, where the procedures and expectations of both the mediator and the parties are outlined (see Appendix A). If mediators do not do what they said they would do, they may be held liable for expenses the parties incurred by participating in the mediation, as well as for consequential losses. We can also imagine a breach of contract occurring around issues of confidentiality and conflict of interest. Another area of liability is related to substantive knowledge and expertise or the lack thereof; however, this may be difficult to prove, given the absence of recognized standards.

Other issues that make mediators vulnerable to lawsuits include the following: withholding important information from one party; parties feeling they were coerced into accepting a proposal; communicating with a party secretly; deceiving parties about credentials; revealing confidential information; and withholding information about child abuse, criminal activity, or possible harm to others. A particularly vulnerable area for mediators is trespassing into professional areas in which they are not qualified to practise. In the United States and South Africa, mediators have been successfully sued on the grounds that their mediation practice involved them in the unauthorized practice of law (Boulle & Kelly, 1998, p. 267).

When one or more of the parties at mediation believe they have reached an agreement, the mediator must ensure that all parties have a clear and common understanding about what they have agreed to and its legal implications. Failure to do so certainly exposes the mediator to a potential claim by one or both of the parties. For example, a party to a divorce dispute may believe that the parties have reached a final, legally binding agreement on the issue of disposition of certain items of property, such as their house or car. The other party may believe that they have reached a tentative understanding, but that nothing will be final and binding until their lawyers review all terms of their mediation "understanding" and prepare and finalize a legal, written agreement, often referred to as a separation agreement. Generally, a mediator is not responsible for preparing, and should not be expected to prepare, a legal separation agreement (although some mediators will do this).

Generally, private practice mediators purchase professional liability insurance coverage. Court-connected and other mediation programs often will require evidence of such coverage.

Closing the Mediation

To conclude this final stage, the mediator congratulates each party on his or her hard work in resolving the problem. Some mediators have rituals as part of the closing—handshaking, formal signing procedures, toasts, or other celebratory or culturally appropriate activities. Such rituals are valuable; they can increase the parties' commitment to the agreement. At this stage, the mediator also reminds and reassures the parties about confidentiality, as well as about any post-mediation activities that have been discussed, such as ratification of the memorandum of understanding, consultation with lawyers, or, in some cases, reporting to the court. Formalizing decisions reached through mediation provides an important symbolic end to the conflict. This is true whether the resolution is public or private; or whether it is a written agreement or a verbal promise.

Stage 5: Post-Mediation Action

The work of the mediator often continues after Stage 4. This is the case in circumstances where the mediator is involved in the ratification of an agreement by external parties, such as boards of directors; where the parties in the negotiation are representing groups of people; or where the agreement is to be sanctioned by the court. In other situations, reports might need to be sent to referring parties or program directors, as in the case of community programs that use volunteer or private mediators. These reports generally indicate that the case has been resolved (or not resolved) and are written in such a way that they do not breach confidentiality protocols agreed to in the mediation.

In co-mediation situations, the two mediators generally arrange to debrief. This analysis often takes place immediately following, or soon after, the mediation session. These discussions involve sharing individual experiences and perceptions about the following: what happened in the mediation; emotions that occurred and may still remain as a result of the interactions; self- and peer perceptions of strengths and weaknesses as mediators; and thoughts about how to improve their work as mediators in the future. Where there is only one mediator, some practitioners have mentors with whom they can discuss the events and emotions of the mediation, to further their learning, reflective practice, and development of artistry as mediators.

In some circumstances, mediators may be involved in the following: monitoring the agreement and supervising its implementation; steering it through to the making of a consent order by the court; or holding of funds or documents until the agreement has been completed (Boulle & Kelly, 1998, p. 124).

Many mediators simply find it considerate and respectful to contact the parties after a reasonable period of time, to see how things are going as a result of the mediation. There are circumstances where the parties have requested further mediation but may need time to evaluate their progress, to obtain further information, or to take other action before proceeding with the next session.

Some mediators and some mediation programs have a procedure, in some cases a formal questionnaire, for obtaining feedback from the parties, so they (the mediators) can evaluate the mediation process. We will consider various evaluation methods in Chapter 11.

It is not uncommon for a referring agency, such as a human rights office, a human resources department, or a child protection agency, to request some information about the outcome of the mediation. Generally this will be a report as to whether the dispute referred to mediation has been resolved. As discussed below, for cases in which a formal proceeding was commenced, the parties may need to file a copy of their final settlement agreement with the court, agency, or office in which the proceeding was commenced.

Other follow-up may be necessary when the referral agent's approval is required to implement an agreement. For example, consider a case in which two employees come to an agreement after having been referred to mediation to resolve a conflict they are having over their hours of work. Before they can finalize the agreement, they may need to consult the supervisor who referred their conflict to mediation. They might contact the referring supervisor by phone before they sign their agreement. Or, if the supervisor's pre-approval was not necessary, she could be informed after the mediation is completed.

Implementing Decisions and Agreements of Mediation

Parties may ask a variety of questions at the end of mediation, including the following:

- What happens in the event that one party fails to comply with the terms of any agreement or decision reached?
- What are the potential consequences of non-compliance for the parties if this were to occur?
- What happens if circumstances change for one party after the agreement, or they wish to alter the terms of any agreement or decision reached in mediation?
- Who is responsible for ensuring that the parties comply with their agreements or decisions reached in mediation?
- What is the responsibility of the parties after mediation?

These questions will be answered differently depending on the context of the mediation.

Disputes with Formal Proceedings

Often, mediation is a response to a dispute on account of which one of the parties has already commenced a formal proceeding, such as a civil action in court, a human rights complaint, a workplace grievance, or some other type of complaint or legal claim. In such a case, usually the court, office, or agency will require a post-mediation report from the mediator confirming the following:

- the date the mediation was completed;
- that both parties participated; and
- the result—that is, whether all issues were settled through mediation.

In many (but not all) such cases, the parties or their counsel will file the final settlement agreement with the court, office, or agency in question. In particular, a party who is to receive some future benefit under the agreement will want to file the agreement to ensure compliance. In Ontario, for example, in a spousal separation case where one spouse has agreed to pay child support to the other spouse, that agreement may be filed with the court and then with a provincial government agency called the Family Responsibility Office, to ensure that the support payments are made on a monthly basis.

Legal Disputes Without Formal Proceedings

When mediation has been used to resolve a legal claim for which no formal proceeding has been commenced, there may be no reporting or filing requirement for the mediator or for the parties. In such cases, the parties usually have a formal legal agreement written up that clearly confirms what each party is required to do. In the event that one of the parties fails to comply with the agreement, the other party can then take formal action in court to enforce it.

For example, in the Car Repair Blues scenario, let's say that Dale agreed to pay $800 in four monthly installments of $200 each. If Dale failed to pay one or more of those installments, Chris could issue a Small Claims Court action and file their written agreement so it could then be enforced by the court.

Likewise, if the divorcing couple Paul and Jo-Anne resolved all of their issues in the mediation, they would write that up in a legally binding and enforceable separation agreement. Subsequently, if either of them defaulted on any provision of that agreement, the other could proceed with any of the following steps to enforce that provision: (1) return to mediation; (2) if appropriate and necessary, submit the issue to arbitration; and/or (3) commence a court application, file the separation agreement, and ask the court to enforce it.

Informal Conflicts

In contexts that do not involve legal claims, compliance with what has been decided is left to the parties themselves. In the early years of mediation, there was a concern that this arrangement was too loose; the parties could simply walk away from the agreement without consequences. We have since learned that the odds of compliance with mediation agreements are generally quite high. The reason for this is that mediation agreements are made by the parties themselves. The agreements make sense to them; they have constructed them; and they know they need them to change things for the better. In short, the parties have a vested interest in following through on what they agreed to.

Moreover, as we have emphasized throughout this book, mediation does not take place in a vacuum. Parties are often aware that the costs of not complying with a voluntary mediated agreement are often quite high. They know, for example, that, if they do not comply with the agreement, they are likely to become involved in future conflict whose outcomes will be unpredictable and costly for all sides. They know that a mediated agreement, designed to satisfy the interests of all the parties, offers benefits that other ways of addressing the conflict do not offer. Where the parties are satisfied that the agreement reached in mediation addresses their needs, and is based on fair criteria, compliance is likely to appear far more compelling than non-compliance.

Disputes with Constituencies

Ensuring that all parties affected by the agreement are committed to its terms over time is a more significant concern than non-compliance. We have discussed the problem that sometimes arises when the mediation involves representatives of larger constituency groups: while the parties directly engaged in the mediation process are shifting from an adversarial to a collaborative standpoint, those they represent maintain an adversarial perspective. We refer to this as the problem of learning transfer (See Fisher, 2005, pp. 47–48, 214–216): in other words, the problem of how to ensure that all members of the group affected by the mediation—not just their representatives—perceive the benefits of learned cooperative behaviour.

This is not just a problem with large groups; it can also happen in small groups. A representative might conclude that the terms being considered for agreement are both fair and reasonable for all sides, only to have the party or constituency she represents reject the proposed terms as unreasonable or unacceptable. This rejection may be owing to the represented party's tunnel vision, anchoring assumptions, or overconfidence in the strength of their position.

These psychological obstacles to collaboration may impede the party's willingness to consider any collaborative agreement that also benefits the other party. And these obstacles may resurface after the mediation, leaving that party less willing to comply with the terms of any agreement reached. For this reason, we believe that mediators need to focus not just on helping the parties reach a collaborative resolution, but on teaching them the benefits of cooperative behavior; the parties can apply this learning to any challenges that arise in their relationship following the completion of the mediation process. They can also apply it to any future conflicts they may have.

Summary

This chapter has shown that mediation is, above all, a process that enables people in conflict to make decisions. The mediator's responsibility is to help the parties make wise decisions—decisions that are right for them. To meet this responsibility, a mediator can and should do various things: ensure that the parties have all the information they need; help them to overcome emotional and cognitive barriers to good decision making; and help them communicate in a way that expands their range of resolution possibilities. A skilled, competent mediator can do much to help parties interact better and resolve their differences successfully.

The mediator is also responsible for ensuring that the parties fully appreciate the consequences of their decisions—for example, the risks involved in the future implementation of their settlement agreement. This is especially the case when the parties have not consulted or are not represented by legal counsel.

Mediators also need to remember that not all mediations will result in a final agreement between the parties. In some mediations, a party's best option is to walk away from the mediation and pursue an alternative course of action, such as going to court. Once the mediator has done all he or she can reasonably do to ensure that the parties make a fully informed decision, she needs to let go and respect the individual's decision, regardless of its consequences.

DISCUSSION QUESTIONS AND EXERCISES

1. Think of a situation in which you were a party to a conflict. What were some of the psychological factors that limited *your* ability to fully collaborate in that situation? What limiting assumptions did you have in that case?
2. According to Lax and Sebenius (1986) and to Mnookin, Peppet, and Tulumello (2000), a mediator can discover opportunities for mutual gain by focusing on differences between the parties. What are some specific interpersonal differences in a given mediation that could be used to create value and expand the range of options for the parties? As a mediator, what could you do to tap into that creative potential?
3. Imagine that you are mediating the divorce dispute of Jo-Anne and Paul (see Exercise 1 at the end of Chapter 3).
   a. What goal statement would you provide to the parties at the beginning of the resolution stage of the mediation? How would you frame each of the issues that Paul and Jo-Anne need to negotiate and resolve?
   b. What are some of the challenges you would expect to encounter during the negotiation/resolution phase? What are some strategies or techniques you could use in this case to help Paul and Jo-Anne negotiate the issues they are facing?
   c. Write out some of the options you would expect or hope them to generate with respect to each of the issues you framed in question (a), above.
   d. What are some of the points or terms that would be included in Paul and Jo-Anne's separation agreement, if the mediation is successful?
4. Think of a conflict situation that you have experienced in which one or more of the parties is locked into a pattern of zero-sum thinking about the conflict. What strategies can you think of that might help the party or parties move from

thinking about the conflict in zero-sum terms to adopting a more collaborative approach?

5. Refer to the Unhappy Customer scenario in Chapter 3 (Box 3.1). As a mediator in this case, explain how you would apply some of the strategies and techniques of this chapter in helping these parties negotiate a final resolution of their dispute.
6. Imagine that you are a mediator retained by the parties in the following conflict. Three siblings, Grant, Roberta, and Kate, are in conflict over what living arrangements they should make for their 89-year-old mother. They have agreed to retain you to mediate their dispute. During the mediation, Kate says: "I have looked after our mother for years. I've been living with her for three years now, and the older she gets, the more I have to do for her. And just because I'm single and Grant has a wife and three kids, he thinks it's okay for him to drop in for a little social visit once every few weeks and completely ignore Mother and me the rest of the time."

   Later, Grant says: "Kate, just because you've been living with Mom for the past three years doesn't mean you have the only say in her care and where she will live. I agree we need to make some arrangements for Mom's ongoing care, but there's no way we should put her into a nursing home."

   In response to one of your questions, Roberta says: "I don't know much about what kind of accommodation is available for Mom, but I do know that she is on a very tight budget."

   a. What goal statement might you provide to the parties at the beginning of the resolution stage of the mediation? How would you frame each of the issues that they need to negotiate and resolve?
   b. What are some of the challenges you would expect to encounter during the negotiation/resolution phase? What are some strategies or techniques you could use in this case to help Kate, Roberta, and Grant negotiate the issues they are facing?
   c. What third-party resources might the parties use in this case to further their understanding of the issues and the possible options available to them in this case?

FURTHER READING

Fisher, R., & Ury, W. (1991). *Getting to yes: Negotiating agreement without giving in* (2nd ed.). New York: Penguin Books.

Lax, D., & Sebenius, J.K. (1986). *The Manager as negotiator: Bargaining for cooperation and competitive gain*. New York: The Free Press.

Mnookin, R., Peppet, S., & Tulumello, A. (2000). *Beyond winning: Negotiating to create value in deals and disputes*. Cambridge, MA: Belknap Press.

Moore, C.W. (2003). *The mediation process: Practical strategies for resolving conflict* (3rd ed.). San Francisco: Jossey-Bass.

Websites

ADR Institute of Ontario: http://www.adrontario.ca

Harvard Law School Program on Negotiation: http://www.pon.harvard.edu
This site has a number of online articles and free materials relevant to the subject matter of this chapter.

Mediate.com: http://www.mediate.com
This website is a clearing house of articles on mediation and negotiation.

University of Colorado Conflict Information Consortium: http://conflict.colorado.edu

REFERENCES

Axelrod, R.M. (1984). *The evolution of cooperation*. New York: Basic Books.

Boulle, L., & Kelly, K.J. (1998). *Mediation: Principles, process, practice*. Toronto: Butterworths.

Crocker, C.A., Hampson, F.O., & Aall, P.R. (2004).*Taming intractable conflicts: Mediation in the hardest cases*. Washington, DC: US Institute of Peace Press.

Fisher, R. (2005). Paving the way. Contributions of interactive conflict resolution to peacemaking. Lanham, MD: Lexington Books.

Fisher, R., & Ury, W. (1991). *Getting to yes: Negotiating agreement without giving in* (2nd ed.). New York: Penguin Books. Copyright © 1981, 1991 by Roger Fisher and William Ury. Reprinted by permission of Houghton Mifflin Company. All rights reserved.

Lax, D., & Sebenius, J.K. (1986). *The manager as negotiator*. New York: Free Press.

Menin, B. (2000). The party of the last part: Ethical and process implications for children in divorce mediation. *Mediation Quarterly*, *17*, 281–293.

Mnookin, R., Peppet, S., & Tulumello, A. (2000). *Beyond winning: Negotiating to create value in deals and disputes*. Cambridge, MA: Belknap Press.

Moore, C.W. (2003). *The mediation process: Practical strategies for resolving conflict* (3rd ed.). San Francisco: Jossey-Bass.

Tversky, A., & Kahneman, D. (1981). The framing of decisions and the psychology of choice. *Science*, *40*, 453–463.

Ury, W. (2000). *The third side: Why we fight and how we can stop*. New York: Penguin Books.

CHAPTER 10

Restorative and Reconciliation Processes

LEARNING OBJECTIVES

After reading this chapter, you will be able to:

- Understand four different "stories of justice" and how they inform different processes for dealing with crime, societal rights violations, and mass atrocities during civil war
- Identify the three principles of distributive justice and their relevance to the principle of fairness
- Explain the differences between restorative justice and the traditional retributive justice system
- Understand three different processes for pursuing restorative justice
- Explain how and when victim–offender mediation may be used effectively
- Identify the key elements of restorative circles and sentencing circles.

CHAPTER OUTLINE

Introduction 287
Conflict and the Perception of Justice 288
What Is Justice? 289
Restorative Justice Processes 302
Summary 319

As you press on for justice, be sure to move with dignity and discipline, using only the weapons of love.

Dr. Martin Luther King Jr., "A Testament of Hope"

Introduction

In this chapter, we discuss conflicts in which one party has engaged in some misconduct that has injured or harmed another. In some processes, we call the party injured in these conflicts the *victim*, and the perpetrator the *offender*. In some instances, the actions of the offender may be considered to be criminal behaviour; in others, the offender's actions may be defined as harassment or as some other form of non-criminal conduct. Bullying, in a school or workplace context, is a common example of non-criminal misconduct. We consider the conditions, requirements, and procedures of a variety of the victim–offender mediation processes that are currently applied in both young offender and adult cases. These processes are viewed through different "justice" lenses, which provide key principles upon which these varied procedures are based. This chapter focuses on restorative justice, comparing it with the regular justice system and identifying its key processes—victim–offender mediation, restorative circles, and sentencing circles. Our consideration of restorative and reconciliatory processes will include the transitional processes used in the aftermath of serious, large-scale human rights violations.

Victim–offender cases usually involve individuals or small numbers of people. But they may also be found at the national or international level. Examples of large-scale, systemic injustices that we may view in terms of victim–offender cases are the segregation policies that once prevailed in the United States and South Africa, and the system of residential schools for Aboriginal peoples in Canada. Though these are rarely called "victim–offender" cases, they involve the same elements as such cases, and the efforts to address them typically involve restorative or reconciliatory principles.

In some cases, gross human rights violations are perpetrated by one group against another in the context of civil wars and terror campaigns. We will examine restorative justice processes in connection with these violations, focusing on the period of transitional justice that comes in their wake. Reconciliation processes to promote healing, permit truth telling, and provide some form of justice for victims are often adopted in this context. These processes may accompany formal justice procedures, or they may fill in the "justice gap" while formal justice systems are being re-established.

Perceptions of injustice fuel conflicts. And yet notions of justice vary. We begin this chapter by discussing the connection between injustice and conflict, and then we discuss different notions of justice. How one perceives justice—whether retributive, corrective, distributive, or restorative—will determine what process is chosen to address crime, inequality, and other kinds of harm. We briefly review the diverse perspectives or "stories" of justice before examining in detail the processes of reconciliation and restoration.

Conflict and the Perception of Justice

In the conflict scenarios examined in previous chapters, we have encountered a number of situations where the parties' perceptions of injustice have fuelled the conflict. Both parties felt unfairly treated by the other side, and this reciprocal sense of unfairness helped escalate the conflict and made it harder for the parties to reach a collaborative resolution without a mediator's help. As Deutsch points out (2000, p. 41), a perception of injustice—the feeling that something is just not fair—is a precipitating factor in many conflicts; it tends to cause parties to hold onto their positions or to refuse to consider options that might be in their own best interests. A perception of injustice is more concerned with values than with interests, and conflicts over values are less easily resolved than are conflicts over competing interests. Parties tend to be less willing to make compromises about their values—their beliefs about what is right or wrong—than they are about their interests (Altran & Axelrod, 2008, p. 222).

A mediator thus needs to be attentive to the ways in which an experience of injustice or a history of unresolved grievances may frame the parties' respective conflict narratives. In the Car Repair Blues scenario in Chapter 1 (see Box 1.1), the mediator was able to help the parties move past their sense of unfairness by helping them listen to and understand each other's experience and concerns. This is one of the major benefits of mediation as a conflict resolution process. The process of meeting in joint session, in a non-adversarial environment, and hearing the conflict situation described from someone else's point of view is helpful to parties. It enables them to appreciate that a sense of grievance is not exclusive to them; the other side feels grievance, too, though its basis is different. Both parties, after this experience, are better able to leave their sense of grievance behind and address their conflict interests and goals in a constructive way.

Where one party feels a deep sense of grievance or injustice and the other does not, it may be harder for the first party to set this sense of grievance aside or to move beyond it. This will strongly affect that party's conflict behaviour and goals in the mediation process. In such circumstances, it is important for the mediator to help the parties explore the underlying issues or values that are influencing their perceptions and goals. Otherwise, a continuing sense of grievance is likely to influence the future relationship between the parties and to inhibit their willingness to comply with the terms of any agreement that may be reached in the mediation.

What Is Justice?

Justice means different things to different people, and may mean different things in different contexts. Rather than try to find a single definition of justice, let's examine four different justice stories, each of which emphasizes a different aspect of justice.

The four aspects of justice are as follows:

1. retribution (punishment),
2. correction (restitution),
3. distribution (fairness), and
4. restoration (reconciliation).

Justice as Punishment: The Retributive Justice Story

In many ways, retributive justice is the most powerful, and often the most destructive, justice story that we encounter in our efforts to resolve conflicts peacefully. Fundamentally, the retributive justice story is based on the claim that when people have acted wrongfully, they should suffer the consequences of their wrongful act. The retributive justice story reminds us of the biblical prescription of "an eye for an eye." As Peachey (1989, p. 304) puts it, the primary focus of the retributive justice story is the demand that "the person responsible for creating the injustice suffer in a way that is commensurate with the way the victim has suffered." Only then will the victim have obtained justice.

Justice, when it is conceived of in retributive terms, is equated with punishment; and punishment is understood as the coercive imposition of pain or suffering on the person responsible for the injustice. Punishment may take various forms, but its main purpose, whatever the particular context, is to express the community's condemnation of the wrongdoer's unlawful act. One of the main justifications for retributive punishment is to channel the community's feelings of resentment and anger toward the wrongdoer. The punishment need not be imposed by the person who has suffered the injustice. Indeed, in our modern democratic society, we try to prevent victims of injustice from exacting vengeance for themselves—from "taking the law into their own hands." Instead, we confer the power to punish on a particular authority figure such as a judge, or a parent, or a teacher, and we do so only after an appropriate inquiry has determined that the punishment is justified (Peachey, 1989, p. 304).

In the retributive justice story, there is little concern with whether the wrongdoer consents to his or her punishment. Nor does the punishment require the agreement of the person who actually suffered the harm. With retributive justice, neither of the persons most directly concerned with the actions giving rise to the conflict is given any control over its outcome. In our criminal justice system, an individual who robs a store is considered to have committed a crime against the state, rather than against the person who owns the store. It is up to the government, therefore, not the store owner, to punish the wrongdoer. The store owner is considered to be a third party to the offence, a witness who may be called to give evidence in support of the Crown's case against the accused, and who may also give what is referred to as a *victim impact statement* before the judge pronounces the sentence. But the store owner neither advises nor consents to the punishment handed down by the judge. All too frequently, therefore, retributive justice, at least as practised in our present criminal justice system, does not provide either the victim or the offender with any meaningful sense of participation, satisfaction, or closure (Christie, 1977; Zehr, 1990).

Justice as Restitution: The Corrective Justice Story

Like the retributive justice story, the corrective justice story is concerned with correcting a past injustice. While the goal of retributive justice is to punish the wrongdoer, the objective of the corrective justice story is to provide compensation or restitution to the person who has been injured through the wrongful actions of another (Llewellyn

& Howse, 1998, pp. 29–30; Fletcher, 1996, pp. 87–93). Examples of the corrective justice story would be a civil claim for damages by a patient who has been wrongfully diagnosed and treated by a physician, or a complaint of wrongful dismissal by an employee.

The main focus of the corrective justice story is to determine whether the person who is being asked to make reparations or to pay compensation (known as the "defendant," in legal terms) is actually responsible for the injury suffered by the person claiming compensation. Without proof of the defendant's legal wrongdoing or fault, there is no justification for imposing any legal remedy. (In the law of negligence, this idea is expressed in the phrase "No liability without proof of fault.") The needs of the injured party for financial compensation, or reinstatement, or an apology from the wrongdoer, are always secondary to the primary concern of establishing the wrongdoer's fault. Without sufficient proof of fault, there is no basis for compensating the plaintiff (the injured person).

This is why a person or an organization accused of wrongfully causing injury rarely admits any responsibility for the injury suffered or offers an apology to the claimant. An admission of responsibility is tantamount to an admission of liability.

If the plaintiff is successful in proving his or her claim, the court will order the defendant to compensate the plaintiff for the injury suffered. Normally, this compensation will take the form of an award of financial damages, even in a case of wrongful dismissal. It is assumed that the financial award will fully compensate the injured plaintiff for the injury suffered. Yet, very little attention is paid to the future relationship between the parties. Nor is the defendant ever required to personally admit responsibility for the injury caused. From a corrective justice point of view, once the liability has been determined and any damages awarded have been paid, the legal injustice has been corrected, and the slate is wiped clean for the future.

In the course of a legal proceeding, such as a negligence lawsuit, the defendant often proposes an out-of-court settlement. This is an offer to pay a sum of money to the plaintiff in full satisfaction of all legal claims. Typically, a condition of any such settlement is that the defendant makes no admission of wrongdoing or liability toward the plaintiff. The effect of such an offer, if accepted by the plaintiff, is to bring the legal proceedings to an end, but without any admission of liability or finding of fault. The claimant may get a financial settlement to offset some of the costs of the injury suffered. But the defendant avoids being held legally accountable for the injury suffered by the claimant. This is why many critics of the out-of-court settlement process consider such settlement negotiations to be less than true justice (Fiss, 1984). Instead, the most rational response on the part of a defendant who is accused of negligence or wrongful dismissal is never to admit any wrongdoing—and never to acknowledge any injury caused to the plaintiff. However, this response will certainly inhibit any reconciliation between the parties.

Justice as Fairness: The Distributive Justice Story

Unlike the previous two justice stories, which are both concerned with redressing the wrongs of the past, distributive justice is concerned with prevention of future injustice. Issues of distributive justice pervade all levels of social life, from the most intimate interpersonal relationships to the most complex international disputes. Distributive justice issues arise whenever decisions have to be made about the allocation of scarce resources. Such resources can be economic and tangible, like the size of a pay agreement to be negotiated between management and a union, or the division of territory between two competing states; or they may involve less tangible but equally contested resources, such as access to elected office, to a promotion, to research funds, or to recognition as the discoverer of a new process for smelting metal or protecting crops from certain diseases. In any situation in which there is not enough of the available resource to satisfy every claimant's wants or needs, questions of distributive justice have to be decided.

The distributive justice story is concerned, above all, with two issues: the process used, and the standards relied on, in making allocation decisions that impose costs or benefits on parties. For instance, when the African National Congress and the National Party came together to end apartheid in South Africa, they held discussions to determine what the basis should be for allocating governing power and who should decide this critical question. The disputants may themselves agree on the distributive justice principles that will determine the outcome of the dispute, or they may rely on a third party to assist them in making the distributive decision. If a third party is involved in the distributive process, that party may have an authoritative decision-making role, as does an arbitrator, judge, or parent. Alternatively, the third party may act as a mediator or conciliator whose role is to assist the parties in making their own distributive choice, but with no decision-making authority to impose a decision, even if the parties fail to agree. In South Africa, it was ultimately the third party of citizens—in other words, the electorate—who made the decisions.

Distributive justice theorists such as Deutsch (2000) have identified three broad principles often used in making distributive decisions: the equality principle, the equity principle, and the need principle.

The Equality Principle

The *equality principle* is based on the assumption that a fair outcome requires that all claimants should be treated equally or, as Deutsch puts it (2000, p. 42), that all members of a group of claimants should be entitled to equal benefits; or, in the case of risks, that costs and risks should be distributed equally between all members of a group. Where some members of a group are not treated in the same manner as other members of the same group, the result is likely to be a feeling of injustice or resentment that can often be the basis for future conflict. This may often occur within a family context, if one sibling feels that the parents treated him or her differently than they treated his or her siblings. On a societal level, discriminatory treatment directed against a certain group within society violates the equality principle. For example, under the apartheid system in South Africa, a majority of citizens were not permitted equal access to social and economic goods and were treated differently, solely on the basis of race.

The Equity Principle

Equity as a distributive justice principle is based on the premise that people should receive benefits in accordance with their efforts or contribution (Deutsch, 2000, p. 42; Peachey, 1989, p. 302). For example, if a rock band were to record a hit record, all members of the band would be entitled to a share in the royalties earned as a result of record sales and radio play. But if the lyrics and music to the hit song were created by two of the band members, like Lennon and McCartney of the Beatles, the songwriters would be entitled to additional copyright royalties over and above the money paid to the rest of the band.

Application of the equity principle often involves differentiating between the claims of the various claimants in a way that the equality principle seeks to avoid. Conflicts may often arise if one person in a group feels that his contribution has not been recognized or appreciated. For example, the lead guitarist in the band may have added a catchy guitar riff when the band came to record the song, and feels that she should be entitled to a share in the song-writing credits and copyright royalties. If the other two co-writers do not recognize this contribution, the ensuing conflict may cause division within the band or even cause it to split up.

The Need Principle

The *need* principle—a third approach to resolving distributive conflicts—differs from both the equality principle and the equity principle. According to Deutsch (2000, p. 42), the need principle prescribes that those who need more of a benefit should obtain more than those who need it less. The use of affirmative action policies for candidates from identifiable disadvantaged groups applying for a job or admission to a university or college would be an example of the need principle in operation. The application of the need principle is often seen in situations where there has been a history of unequal treatment between different members of a community. The need principle is then seen as a way of correcting historical injustices.

Case Study: Distributive Justice Principles and Notions of Fairness

Distributive justice conflicts often involve an imbalance of bargaining power between the parties. Take, for example, a dispute over the division of financial assets and custody in a divorce context. (See the Separating Spouses scenario in Box 10.1.)

BOX 10.1 » Scenario: Separating Spouses

During Russell and Hilary's marriage, Russell has been a stay-at-home dad, while Hilary has been working as a lawyer. When they divorce, Hilary refuses to pay Russell half the value of the family assets that she feels she has accumulated through her own hard work; and she threatens to fight Russell for custody of their preschool-age daughter, Tiffany, unless he accepts what she terms a "reasonable" settlement of one-quarter of the value of the assets. As a stay-at-home dad, Russell does not have the financial resources to engage in a lengthy legal battle with Hilary. And he is also concerned that a hostile custody fight would be very distressing to Tiffany and make it harder for her to adjust to the divorce. After considerable heart searching, Russell agrees to Hilary's terms and accepts the house and one-quarter of the other assets, together with no claim to financial support in the future from Hilary.

In Ontario, the statutory rules governing division of financial assets on divorce are based on the equality principle—that both spouses are entitled to an equal share in the value of all family assets accumulated during the marriage. However, provincial family law legislation also permits the parties to contract out of the statutory provisions and reach their own negotiated agreement. (See, for example, part IV of Ontario's *Family Law Act*. Other provinces have broadly similar statutory frameworks. See also Payne & Payne, 2001.)

On the face of it, the agreement reached in the Separating Spouses scenario appears to be a consensual agreement between Hilary and Russell to settle all their financial affairs following the divorce. While it may be consensual, is it just? Viewed from Russell's perspective, Hilary exploited her awareness of his unequal bargaining position to obtain preferential terms, which she would not otherwise have been entitled to under the equality principle (the principle governing division of family assets under most provincial legislation). From Hilary's point of view, there has been no exploitation of a power imbalance. She has legitimately asserted her claim to a larger share of the family assets based on the equity principle. In addition, she asserts that if Russell voluntarily agrees to the arrangement, then there can be no question of injustice.

Part of the difficulty in trying to resolve a complex distributive justice question, such as the one described in Box 10.1, is that there is no single distributive justice principle or standard by which we can evaluate the fairness of the result. Instead, we have at least three competing distributive justice principles to take into account. Under the legislation governing distribution of family assets on divorce, the equality principle trumps Hilary's equity principle. If Russell rejects Hilary's offer and goes to court instead, it is likely that the court would award him half the value of the assets instead of the one-quarter share that Hilary is offering. At the same time, most courts encourage divorcing parties to work out their own financial and custody arrangements after divorce, subject to the need to obtain formal judicial approval in the case of decisions involving children. So, from this point of view, the principle of self-determination, or voluntary consent, may override some inequality in distribution, provided that the parties have first obtained independent legal advice about their rights, and there is no evidence of undue pressure or coercion in reaching an agreement.

The problem is, what constitutes undue pressure? In legal terms, there is nothing to prevent Hilary from going to court to challenge Russell for custody of Tiffany. Does this amount to undue pressure? And Hilary can afford the costs of litigation far more readily than Russell can. Does this amount to undue pressure? Regardless of the outcome of any future litigation, if Russell challenges the terms of the financial settlement he reached with Hilary, Russell's perception of injustice is likely to result in future conflict between the parties. To reiterate a point made earlier: the stability of a negotiated outcome to any conflict is greatly affected by the perception of injustice on the part of any of the signatories to the agreement.

In the context of a family mediation, a mediator may adopt a number of strategies to try to balance the power between the parties. Perhaps most important is to inform the parties of the importance of consulting with an independent legal adviser before reaching any final agreement. This ensures that each party is fully informed about his or her legal rights and entitlements before entering into any mediated agreement that may affect or otherwise alter those rights. The objective is for the parties to make as informed a decision as possible, on the assumption that the more informed the decision, the more likely it is to be a stable decision that both parties consider fair and just.

The presence or absence of independent legal advice is also likely to be a factor in a court's decision about whether to set aside the terms of a separation agreement (or other domestic contract) that appears to differ substantially from what the agreement would be if it were made in strict accordance with the parties' statutory rights. In addressing these kinds of questions, the courts are inevitably involved in a trade-off between competing justice principles of fairness and certainty.

The scenario described in Box 10.1 illustrates that many distributive conflicts involve more than just a struggle over shares in a disputed resource. This scenario asks us to consider what justice principle should govern the allocation decision. With a distributive conflict, a third party can help the disputants decide about the distributive criteria (or justice principles) that should be used in making the allocation decision. If the parties cannot agree in this regard, or if no authoritative process for determining the distributive justice principles is available (such as an arbitrator's decision or an adjudicator's ruling), then the lack of agreement will likely prolong the dispute.

Justice as Reconciliation: The Restorative Justice Story

The final story to consider in examining the many meanings of justice is the idea of justice as reconciliation—the restorative justice story. Dr. Robert Cormier (Allard, 2008, p. 4) has offered the following definition of restorative justice:

> Restorative justice is an approach to justice that focuses on repairing the harm caused by crime while holding the offender responsible for his or her actions, by providing an opportunity for the parties directly affected by the crime—victim(s), offender and community—to identify and address their needs in the aftermath of a crime, and seek a resolution that affords healing, reparation and reintegration, and prevents future harm.

We can elaborate on Cormier's general description and, using the work of leading scholars in the field (Umbreit, 1997; Umbreit, Coates, & Vos, 2004; Zehr, 1990), set out the core principles of restorative justice. These principles are as follows:

- An offence harms relationships among victims, offenders, and the community.
- A restorative approach seeks healing for the victim, the offender, and the community.
- A restorative process focuses on the needs and responsibilities of everyone involved rather than on the legal liability (guilt) of the offender and the legal remedy or sanction (punishment) to be imposed.
- Healing, reconciliation, and justice are achieved through transformative dialogue.
- Successful restorative processes are ones in which everyone is transformed—offenders, victims, and their communities.
- An important part of the healing and transformation that can occur in a restorative process is the development of empathy, understanding, and even compassion between victims and offenders.
- Restorative justice is achieved through peace-making and peace-building rather than through any violent action against an offender or perceived offender.

Restorative Justice Versus Retributive Justice

The restorative justice story challenges the idea of justice as correction, retribution, or punishment (Zehr, 1990; Bianchi, 1994; Van Ness & Strong, 1997; Sharpe, 1998). As we have seen, the retributive justice story derives from the notion of equivalency and from the biblical story of an eye for an eye. Retributive justice demands that pain and suffering be inflicted on the offender in proportion as the offender inflicted them on the victim (Peachey, 1989, p. 304). You will recall from our earlier discussion that the state has primary responsibility for addressing the needs of the victim and the interests of the community through its punishment of the offender.

For many restorative justice theorists, what the retributive justice narrative leaves out is that the offender's wrongful actions are not just committed against the state. An act of violence, or even the robbing of a store, also involves a violation of interpersonal relationships. In significant ways, the harm done is also felt by the victim, by the community, and even by the offender. These harms cannot be repaired by the act of punishment alone. Punishing an offender may serve some justice needs, but it leaves other justice needs unattended to. These needs often remain invisible and unmet, hidden by the dominant narrative structure of the retributive justice story.

Chief among these hidden or unmet justice needs is the need to repair the harm done to the victim. Victims of crime do not just experience a material loss of money or goods or the physical trauma resulting from an act of violence. The victim's psychological loss—loss of trust, feelings of insecurity, a sense that something has been taken from him—may be very difficult to regain. The retributive justice story assumes that the victim's primary justice need is to see the offender punished.

Retributive justice does not give the victim any sense of control over, or even participation in, the process that leads to the arrest, charging, prosecution, and conviction of the offender. The victim may be called as a witness and may be allowed or invited to present an impact statement before the judge hands down a sentence. Otherwise, he or she has little say, or voice, in the process by which "justice" is meted out. Unless the victim is a witness, he or she is not even allowed a formal place in the courtroom, but has to sit in the public gallery with other spectators. Participation and party self-determination are important normative values in conflict resolution. The retributive justice story, by defining crime as an offence against the state and effectively eliminating the victim from the trial process, does not accord with these values (Christie, 1977).

Restorative Justice in Canada

In Canada, the use of a community-based victim–offender mediation process in Elmira, Ontario in 1974 is widely credited as a defining moment in the worldwide development of a restorative justice approach. Two young men from Elmira had pleaded guilty to vandalizing 22 properties. On the recommendation of Mennonite probation officer Mark Yantzi and court worker Dave Worth, who was also Mennonite, Kitchener's Judge McConnell ordered the two young offenders to visit with all 22 victims and make restitution for their vandalism. Through this experience, Russell Kelly, one of the offenders, turned his life around, becoming a restorative justice advocate and practitioner who now volunteers with Community Justice Initiatives in Kitchener, Ontario (Kelly, 2006). What became known as the "Elmira case" is recognized as the world's first victim–offender mediation process (Peachey, 1988; Northey, 2005; see also Dueck, 2010).

Many early restorative programs were established in response to the same dissatisfaction with the criminal justice system that prompted the Elmira experiment.

One of the oldest community mediation services in Canada is Community Justice Initiatives, established in Kitchener, Ontario, in 1978. Like many of the early mediation programs in Canada, it was set up by Mennonite and Quaker communities. The Quakers and Mennonites believed that community mediation was a necessary alternative to the justice system. These faith groups rejected the notion that crime was an aberration or deviance to be controlled and punished, that victims were not relevant to justice, and that retributive measures were the only way to correct behaviour. By the late 1970s, there were court-based victim–offender mediation programs in Halifax, Quebec City, Montreal, Winnipeg, and Regina (Perry, Lajeunesse, & Woods, 1987).

Early mediation proponents believed that crime should be understood as a social problem and that addressing it ought to transform the criminal and to restore the community affected by the crime. A particular conception of *community* was the basis for this approach. This meant that people who commit crimes are to be accountable to their communities and to their individual victims. Whereas the formal system is faceless and anonymous, community processes are very personal. Community members, according to this perspective, need to be responsible for problems within their communities; they need to be empowered to address social inequities causing or contributing to crime; and they need to develop empathy for criminals. Mediation programs make these alternatives possible. They provide empowering and restorative—as opposed to retributive—processes in which communities may participate.

The original programs in restorative justice promoted dialogue among the parties involved in the crime—offenders, victims, and members of the community. They also addressed the community reintegration of people recently released from prison; reconciliation between victims and perpetrators; and the healing and repairing of the community harmed by the crime. In Canada, community mediation has its origins in a social movement rather than a legal one. In this respect, Canada differs from the United States, where the civil rights movement—aimed at gaining legal rights for the disenfranchised—exerted significant influence over the development of early mediation programs.

Justice Needs: Restorative Justice and the Regular Justice System

Many provinces have enacted legislation designed to provide victims of crime with counselling and information about the court process (see Law Commission of Canada, 2003, pp. 22–24). But such victims' rights legislation still does not address the more fundamental issue that the offence is defined as a crime against the state, not against the victim.

A need for many victims, which remains unmet in the regular justice system, is to have the offender acknowledge the harm he or she has inflicted on the victim. Here again, the retributive justice story tends to erase this unmet need from our collective consciousness. If the offender's wrongful action is viewed as a crime against society's laws, it follows that society's public interest in justice will be given priority over the private needs of the victim. Once again, it is assumed that the victim's need for acknowledgment of the harm done will be assuaged if and when the offender is found guilty—and the subsequent public sentencing ritual symbolizes society's denunciation of the wrongful act and its disapprobation of the wrongdoer.

But what if these public and private justice needs are not identical? As mediation theorists and practitioners, we understand the importance of attending to the needs of all the participants in a conflict situation. A party whose needs are unattended to is likely to feel unsatisfied and to feel that the conflict remains unresolved. This is exactly what happens to many victims in our criminal justice system; they experience the justice system as alienating, even when the offender is convicted and sentenced (Zehr, 1990, pp. 30–32).

Moreover, as Zehr observes, victims find this experience alienating even when the offender pleads guilty to the offence charged. The problem, according to Zehr (1990, p. 67), is that in entering a plea of guilty, offenders are not really acknowledging responsibility for the harm done to their victims; they are merely following the advice of their lawyers, who may have reached a plea bargain arrangement with the Crown whereby the offender admits to a lesser charge in return for a reduced sentence or the dropping of more serious charges. Such an arrangement clearly reflects the prime concern of the mainstream justice system—namely, to process as many offenders as possible in the shortest possible time. There is no evident concern to satisfy the human justice needs of the victim, of the offender, or of the community as a whole.

This is why commentators such as Zehr (1990), Braithwaite (1989), and the Church Council on Justice and Corrections (1996) have advocated the introduction of *restorative* justice practices: victim–offender mediation (Umbreit, 1994); sentencing circles (Stuart, 1996, 1997); and family and community group conferencing (Hudson, Morris, Maxwell, & Galaway, 1996; Galaway & Hudson, 1996). These practices redress some of the human justice needs that are left out of the retributive justice story. What animates restorative justice advocates is the ideal of *reconciliation*—"making right" the harm done to shattered relationships, to social trust, and to traumatized victims and offenders alike.

In the wake of conflict, reconciliation processes are very important for both victims and offenders; they lay the foundation for peaceful future coexistence. They are especially important in the case of violent civil conflict. Consider Rwanda, for example, where 800,000 to 1,000,000 Tutsis and moderate Hutus were killed over a period of 100 days in 1994. Mass atrocities were committed during this time. Most perpetrators and victims lived in the same neighbourhoods, so some process of grassroots justice was essential if these neighbours were ever again to cohabit peacefully. This occurred by way of *gacaca* courts, where victims could face the people who had killed or maimed their family members and could describe what had been done, and the devastating effects of these actions. The people responsible confessed to their actions and demonstrated remorse. These *gacaca* courts were not without their shortcomings, but they contributed to raising the profile of the victims' experience and increasing the perpetrators' awareness of that experience. This was an important contribution to the country's reconciliation process.

As Llewellyn and Howse (1998, p. 1) remind us, the restorative justice story is not a new story; it is the basis of many of our central ideas about law and justice, and it has been so in many cultures throughout history. The ideal of restoring social relationships, of reconciliation, and of reintegrating offenders into the community is an ancient one.

Restorative justice can take many forms. There is no single model for the process, nor any agreed-on time-frame in which it must occur. If it occurs after an offender has been sentenced and is serving time in prison, it will be no less meaningful than if it occurs during a pre-trial mediation process aimed at diverting the case from the criminal courts. Victim–offender mediation is not intended to be a substitute for punishment, and sentencing circles are not supposed to substitute for a judge's decision on sentencing after trial (Stuart, 1996). Restorative justice is partly concerned with lessening the offender's sentence and with making restitution in financial or other terms to the victim. But its fundamental goal transcends these particular aims. Its goal is to address the human needs of the people most affected by the crime—namely, the needs for recognition, reconciliation, and social connectedness. These needs are not addressed within the retributive justice story. Figure 10.1 offers a comparison of restorative justice with retributive justice.

The Restorative Justice Approach to Offender Accountability

In his work on reintegrative shaming and restorative justice, Braithwaite (1989, pp. 133–134) looks at restorative justice approaches to shaming offenders. He considers these approaches in relation to a family model of discipline, in which the objective is to teach the offending child to respect the rules governing family behaviour. It is relatively easy to see how restorative justice works within a close-knit family. It is more difficult to see how it applies in the larger community, where crime often occurs between strangers. Imagine, for example, that a store owner is robbed by two youths holding a knife or a gun. In this situation, are there any pre-existing relationships to repair? Is there any need for the state to justify its actions in punishing lawbreakers who steal other people's property and threaten them with violence?

For restorative justice theorists such as Zehr and Braithwaite, it is precisely in these kinds of situations that we need to apply the principles of restorative justice. Zehr (1990, p. 181) observes that even where the store owner and the person robbing the store are not known to one another, the robbery itself creates a relationship between them by harming the victim—a relationship that needs to be made right. The act of robbing the store has, as well, a negative impact on the larger community, impairing its members' sense of safety and trust. Moreover, the state's actions in

Figure 10.1 Restorative Justice and Retributive Justice Stories Compared

Retributive Justice Story	Restorative Justice Story
Crime is defined as a breach of society's laws.	Crime is defined as a violation of relationships or a breach of trust, considered to be a break or tear in our social fabric.
The objective of the process is to establish the offender's guilt.	The objective of the process is to repair harm to the victim and or the community.
The process is adversarial and dictated by professionals.	The process is non-adversarial and encourages dialogue between the participants.
The victim has a limited right to participate in the process.	The victim can initiate the process.
The process encourages the offender to deny guilt.	The process encourages the offender to accept responsibility for the harm caused.
The state has a monopoly over the punishment of the offender.	The participants have more control over the outcome of the process.
Balance is restored by inflicting an equivalent amount of pain on the offender.	Balance is restored by repairing the harm done to the victim and the community.
Shaming is designed to stigmatize the offender.	Shaming is intended to promote reintegration of the offender.

punishing the offender also create a relationship between state and offender. This relationship also needs to be made right, so the offender can be reintegrated into society rather than permanently alienated from the community.

Shaming works best, according to Braithwaite (1989), when it is used positively, to encourage offenders to make recompense for the harm they have caused, and thereby to show themselves worthy of being included once more in the community. One of the key elements of reintegrative shaming is to separate the offence from the offender, to condemn the offence without condemning the offender and thereby enable offenders to acknowledge the wrongfulness of their actions and to repair the harm they have done.

Braithwaite shows that *negative* shaming has the opposite effect. When we stigmatize an offender, we do so in the hope that the offender will be deterred from ever wanting to offend again. To stigmatize is to identify the offender, permanently and inescapably, with the offence. We define offenders by what they have done in the past, not by what they are capable of doing in the future. But stigmatization comes at a price. According to Braithwaite, the offender—the stigmatized "other"—may symbolically reject the legitimacy of the authority by which he is condemned, and thereafter take on a self-imposed identity as an opponent of authority, with little or no respect for the law, increasing the possibility of future social conflict (Braithwaite, 1989).

In this respect, the restorative justice story provides a very different way of responding to the competing justice needs that are raised by the wrongful act of robbing a store. The restorative justice story is not so much concerned with the *quantity of punishment* imposed on the offender as it is with the *quality of justice* meted out to victim, offender, and community alike (Zehr, 1990).

Can it work? Can we envisage a future in which the principles of restorative justice and reintegrative shaming replace our need to punish those who have knowingly violated society's laws? In some respects, this question is unanswerable. We cannot know unless we try. But we do know that our collective vision of social justice is not unchangeable. We do make reforms to our social institutions in the name of social justice. We no longer rely on the death penalty to punish those convicted of murder or treason. We no longer believe that confining inmates within penal institutions—with no opportunities for education or communication with the outside world—is the best way to build social connectedness. We no longer accept, without question, that the best way to teach children math or to internalize our social values is by threatening them with the strap or the cane.

Perhaps the only thing we can say with any certainty is that two wrongs do not make a right. In the end, the restorative justice that we see being practised today—within many victim–offender mediation programs, family group conferencing initiatives, and circle sentencing as an alternative to traditional retributive justice sentencing practices in the criminal justice system—is based on the simple idea that the violation of social relationships caused by an act of wrongdoing or injustice creates many different kinds of justice needs that cannot all be met by punishment alone.

Restorative Justice Processes

In this section, we discuss the following restorative justice processes:

- victim–offender mediation (VOM),
- restorative circles,
- sentencing circles,
- family group conferencing, and
- transitional justice processes.

Restorative Processes Compared with Other Mediation Processes

Restorative processes put the needs of those touched by crime—rather than the institutional needs of the state—at the centre of the process (Zehr, 1990, p. 158; Church Council on Justice and Corrections, 1996, p. 39; Wright & Galaway, 1989, pp. 14–24). The social values underlying a restorative process are clearly related to those we have been discussing in connection with mediation: self-determination, social connectedness, and collaborative decision making. And if we look at restorative justice in relation to the whole array of dispute resolution processes (examined in Chapter 2), we find that transformative, or holistic, mediation comes closest to answering the justice needs identified by the restorative justice story. In a successful victim–offender mediation, for example, the parties will experience emotional and personal transformation, as they do with transformative approaches to mediation. Often this results in a personal and spiritual connection that becomes the basis of an enduring relationship. This occurred in the drunk driving death case that Marty Price mediated in 1994, and it happened in the Cadman–Deas case. (We discuss both these cases below.) Bush (1989) claims that genuine transformative mediation serves the public interest and promotes social justice more than adjudication or the legal system does, but that settlement-type mediation—as it is typically found in civil court-connected mediation—does not.

Restorative justice processes use mediators, but they differ in the following ways from regular dispute mediation processes:

- With restorative justice processes, much of the mediator's work with the parties is done during pre-mediation. In some cases, pre-mediation can be lengthy and involved.
- With restorative justice processes, the mediator has minimal involvement in the joint session dialogue of the parties. During the victim–offender session, parties who have been properly prepared during pre-mediation will engage in an unassisted one-on-one dialogue, with less input from the mediator than is the case with regular dispute mediation processes.
- The primary goal of restorative justice processes is not to reach agreements but to bring about the personal, emotional, and spiritual healing and transformation of the parties. A restorative process—victim–offender mediation, for example—may result in reparation or restitution agreements, but such agreements are very much a secondary goal.

Victim–Offender Mediation

VOM involves a facilitated dialogue between an offender and a victim. It is used in cases where offenders have admitted committing a wrong that could be considered a crime, have accepted responsibility for it, and have expressed remorse. In less serious cases, especially in youth cases, the referral to VOM may be a diversion from the formal criminal justice system, and it may occur either before or after a charge is laid. In other cases, the referral comes after a guilty plea or conviction, and it comes as a possible alternative or complement to sentencing. With VOM, establishing or proving the offender's wrongdoing is not an aim of the mediation process. All participants are in agreement that the offender is guilty. The primary issue to be mediated is what is to be done to restore "right relations" among the offender, the victim, and the community.

Mediation is considered successful to the extent that the following occurs: the offender hears and understands the victim's experience and feelings about the crime; he or she experiences genuine empathy and remorse; and the victim experiences the offender as a person with potential for transformation and growth. VOM is an opportunity for the victim and the offender to have a person-to-person dialogue that will relieve each of them of the psychological burden and pain of the offence. Ideally, transformation and healing occur for both parties. When this happens, the benefits are great for each party. The two case studies provided below exemplify these benefits.

VOM is conversation or dialogue between a victim and an offender that is facilitated by a victim–offender mediator. Usually, VOM occurs within the context of a victim–offender reconciliation program that has been established by a community or by an organization or institution (for example, Correctional Services Canada, or by a school or workplace organization). As we discuss in Chapters 6 and 11, a victim–offender reconciliation program needs a convening process to ensure that a case referred to the VOM program is appropriate for it.

Generally, victim–offender reconciliation programs require that VOM take place only if both parties are ready, willing, and able to proceed. The program convenor must ensure that the victim is well-informed about the VOM process and is willing to enter into dialogue with the offender in a positive and constructive way. A victim who is insufficiently prepared for VOM may be re-victimized by a further encounter with his or her offender.

The convenor must also ensure that the *offender* is a good candidate for VOM. A good candidate is willing to engage in dialogue with the victim, has admitted his or her own wrongdoing, and has accepted responsibility for having offended and harmed the victim. As well, the offender should be capable of expressing genuine remorse for having harmed the victim.

With respect to its timing within the court process, VOM may be used at the following junctures:

- before a charge is laid, often as pre-charge diversion;
- after a charge is laid, but before a plea;
- after a charge is laid, and after a guilty plea, but before a conviction;
- after a conviction, but before sentencing; or
- after conviction and sentencing, sometimes many years after the offender was first imprisoned for his or her crime.

Case Study 1: Victim–Offender Mediation in a Drunk Driving Death Case

In the early years of victim–offender reconciliation programs (from approximately 1975 to 1995), VOM was generally reserved for property offences and for relatively minor crimes of that sort (for example, vandalism, shop-lifting, break and enter, and theft), and it was generally used for young offenders. Many believed it was not appropriate for serious offences or for adult offenders. However, over the past 20 years, VOM has been used with increasing success in cases of violent crime and with other serious crimes, such as impaired driving that causes death, assault with a weapon, and murder. Considerable research and experimentation has been and continues to be done in this area (Roberts, 1995; Umbreit, Vos, Coates, & Brown, 2003; Umbreit, Coates, & Vos, 2004; Urban, Markway, & Crockett, 2011).

The events involved in the following victim–offender case occurred in the states of Washington and Oregon, between April 1993 and 1996.

On April 28, 1993, in Wahkiakum County in Washington State, Elaine Myers was driving home from her night class when a minivan travelling in the opposite direction crossed into her lane, smashed into her vehicle, and killed her instantly. Elaine's family was devastated by her death—her husband, David; her parents, Peter and Kathleen Serrell; and her three sisters Elizabeth Menkin (Betty), Beverly, and Barbara.

Soon after, according to Betty Menkin (1995, p. 1), "Our family's pain was compounded by utter fury when we learned that the driver who had hit Elaine, a young woman named [Susanna], had a blood alcohol level of .20 (twice the legal limit in Washington State)."

Susanna, 25 years old, had a prior conviction for drunk driving. She was a single mother with two children and had never finished high school. Elaine's sister Betty said the following:

> Mingled with my grief was a vengeful rage against the woman who had killed my sister. When I heard that [Susanna] had nearly died in the crash herself, I wanted her to live just so she could suffer horribly. When she pulled through, I wanted someone to gouge out her eyes so she'd never drive again. I was that full of pain.
>
> My family was overcome with grief. My father became withdrawn and depressed. My mother angrily referred to her [Susanna] as, "the human weed that ought to be pulled up." (1995, p. 1)

In June 1993, Elaine's father, Peter Serrell, contacted mediator Marty Price about the possibility of mediation. At this point, Peter was the only member of the victim's family ready or willing to meet the offender in mediation. After recovering from the crash, Susanna went to court with her court-appointed lawyer and pleaded not guilty. In August, Price contacted Susanna's lawyer about the potential benefits of a mediated meeting of the offender and the victims (that is, the family of Elaine Myers). Although the defence lawyer believed this mediation process could be valuable for his client, he also knew she would have to plead guilty before it could occur.

By November 1993, other members of Elaine's family—her mother Kathleen; her sisters Betty (Menkin) and Barbara; and her husband David—joined Peter in agreeing to take part in victim–offender mediation. In November 1993, Susanna pleaded guilty to vehicular homicide, and her sentencing hearing was scheduled for late January 1994. After Susanna pleaded guilty, Price and his fellow mediator, Brenda Inglis, met with Susanna and her lawyer. Finding Susanna repentant and willing to admit her guilt to Elaine's family, they agreed to proceed with the victim–offender reconciliation process.

Preparing for Mediation

Price points to two important considerations prior to mediation:

- A case must "ripen" for mediation. The passing of time will allow for necessary healing and emerging clarity about what the participants want and need from the mediation process. This "ripening" may be encouraged with "homework assignments" that assist the participants in exploring feelings, developing empathy, or getting clear about what they want and need. The mediator must have an ability to sense what is "missing" and craft appropriate tasks.
- A critical factor in the success of this VOM process was that Price did a great deal of case development work. Price knew what he had to do to prepare all parties for their face-to-face encounter, and he knew that he had to assess each participant's readiness for mediation.

The Mediation

The VOM between Susanna and the members of the victim's family took place on January 17, 1994. Marty Price's account (1994, p. 1) of the event is as follows:

> Many tears were shed, many eloquent words were said, and the victims and offender each became allies in the healing of the other. The meeting resulted in a mediation agreement in which Susanna agreed to attend AA meetings and victim impact panels while in prison. She agreed to find ways to work against drunk driving in her community, such as speaking to high school drivers' education classes when she is released. The agreement also included items to help give her the tools to make good on her promises. She will further her education, complete her G.E.D., write at least weekly to each of her children, attend church each week, improve her parenting skills, and give 10 percent of her income to charity. She will write a quarterly letter to Peter [Serrell] to report on her progress on each of these items. The participants consented that the agreement, which would have been confidential otherwise, could be submitted to the prosecutor and the judge for consideration in mitigation of Susanna's sentence.

The Sentencing

The sentencing hearing was held the following week, in late January 1994, and was attended by all of the participants in the mediation. Betty Menkin read from her victim impact statement, written months earlier, speaking of what would be necessary to earn her forgiveness:

> Forgiveness is not something which I believe is my obligation to bestow unilaterally, but it can be earned. The perpetrator must show the five R's: recognition, remorse, repentance, restitution and reform. *Recognition* means admitting that what she did was wrong, and that she is responsible for the wrongdoing and all of the negative consequences that follow from it. (If she is in jail, she recognizes that it is because she drove drunk, not because the prosecutor or the judge was mean or unfair to her. If she is in pain, she recognizes it is because she drove drunk, not blaming it on the lack of pain medicine or a lack of medical science's ability to fix her as good as new.) *Remorse* means that each time she thinks of the wrong she did, she regrets that she did not make a better choice. It is a repeated rehearsal of how she wishes she had done it differently, how she would do it differently if given another chance. *Repentance* is when a deep remorse leads to a firm resolve to do better in the future. *Restitution* cannot be direct in this case—there is no way that she can provide a wife for David or a sister for me. The only restitution she can make is a lifelong commitment to a daily effort toward making the world a better place for her having survived the crash. She is not required to complete the job of repairing the world, but she must not be excused from starting and continually working at the job. *Reform* means that she must create a new form of herself—to emerge as a sober person, a thoughtful and considerate person, a contributor. If she can do all of these, I can forgive. (Price, 1994)

Despite the positive results of the mediation and the prosecutor's submission for a reduced sentence, the judge sentenced Susanna to 34 months in prison because of her previous drunk driving conviction. This was the maximum term that she could receive under the state's mandatory sentencing guidelines.

In his online article (1994), Marty Price summarized some basic principles and guidelines that he gleaned from this case and which he said are equally applicable to the mediation of less serious crimes.

- A violent crime typically impacts many more people than just the immediate victim. The "getting ready" time required for each who could benefit from meeting with the offender will differ. Each victim will move through the stages of grief and loss at a different pace. The case development process must allow for those time differences.
- The mediator must be able to work effectively with, and enlist the cooperation of the defense attorney, as well as prosecutors, judges, probation and corrections officials, and mental health professionals.
- There is a delicate balance to be ascertained between the prerequisites for a successful mediation (such as a certain level of victim empathy on the part of the offender) and the recognition that some level of the same attributes, i.e.,

victim empathy, may need to emerge from the offender as a result of the face-to-face experience of the victim's pain and loss. The importance of protecting victims from the possibility of a re-victimization must be carefully weighed. Sensible, calculated risks may need to be taken, but only with the fully informed consent of the victim.
- A patiently and sensitively shepherded case that is appropriate for mediation will almost certainly produce a positive experience for the participants. If the process of case development is not going well and a positive outcome does not seem likely, it will be essential to slow down and reassess. It may be appropriate to abandon the prospect of mediation and refer participants to other kinds of resources.
- When employed skillfully and in appropriate situations, the power of this process to facilitate healing, closure, reconciliation and rehabilitation is enormous. For many participants, the experience has been life-transforming.

We can learn a great deal from these principles and guidelines and from the very successful VOM process over which Marty Price presided. The following facts about the case, for example, enshrine important principles:

- Mediation, which seemed very unlikely or even impossible in the case of this serious, violent crime, proceeded less than 10 months after the offence was committed.
- The mediation was initiated by Peter Serrell, a member of the victim family, rather than by a referral agent such as a court official or victim services agency.
- This VOM process was truly transformative for all of the parties and for a relationship that was originally marked by deep hostility on one side.
- The members of the victim family moved from extreme anger and hatred to forgiveness, compassion, and connection regarding the offender Susanna. The process enabled all of them to heal from their devastating loss and recover their lives. An important part of that healing came from their being enabled, by the process itself, to enter into a meaningful relationship with Susanna. Susanna was also able to achieve the 5 Rs articulated by Betty Menkin, above. Susanna and the Serrell family remained in regular contact for a number of years, in a unique healing alliance between victims and offender. Susanna remained clean and sober and attended community college, with the Serrell family providing her tuition and books. Susanna continued to tell her story to drunk driving offenders and young driving students.
- This VOM process was successful even though it occurred in the shadow of the court and the criminal justice system. The offender's lawyer played an important role in helping to make the mediation process one that was beneficial for his client and for the other participants.
- In this case, the restorative VOM process was not an alternative to the traditional retributive legal process. Rather, the two proceeded in parallel. The restorative process did not result in judicial leniency for the offender. The

judge gave Susanna the maximum jail sentence she could have received. However, it was owing to the restorative VOM process that Susanna achieved the transformative rehabilitation that she did.

- The personal, emotional, relational, and spiritual benefits of this VOM process were realized by all participants. Such unanimity is typical of the transformative process that VOM brings about, which has to be win–win; it cannot be win–lose. It cannot occur for one party at the expense of the other.

Humanistic Mediation

Mark Umbreit, the Director of the Center for Restorative Justice and Peacemaking at the University of Minnesota, has been a pioneer and leader in the field of restorative justice since the 1970s. Umbreit developed an approach to victim–offender mediation that he called *humanistic mediation* (1997, 2001). This approach differs significantly from the mediation process used in other types of cases, the process outlined in Chapters 7 to 9 of this text. Humanistic mediation is based on the following:

1. the connectedness of all things and our common humanity;
2. the importance of the mediator/worker's presence and connectedness with the involved parties in facilitating effective conflict resolution;
3. the healing power of mediation;
4. the desire of most people to live peacefully;
5. the desire of most people to grow through experience;
6. the capacity of all people to draw upon their inner reservoirs of strength in order to overcome adversity, to grow, and to help others in similar circumstances; and
7. the inherent dignity and self-determination that arise from embracing conflict directly. (Umbreit, 1997, p. 204)

Building on the transformative ideas of Bush and Folger and on the traditional practices of indigenous peoples, Umbreit (1997, p. 205) says that "a number of significant changes in the dominant Western European model of mediation are required" in victim–offender cases to achieve the humanistic approach. Following are some of the key elements distinguishing Umbreit's humanistic approach from other approaches (1997, pp. 205–209):

- *The role of the mediator*. In the humanistic approach, the mediator is seen as a peacemaker who empowers and enables victims and offenders to interact with each other, through dialogue, as "fellow human beings."
- *The importance of pre-mediation*. Much of the mediator's essential work in victim–offender cases is done in the pre-mediation phase. The mediator gathers information, educates and prepares the parties, assesses the conflict and the parties, and helps the latter move from weakness (incapacity) and

alienation toward empowerment and empathetic connection. To accomplish all of this, the mediator has to establish a relationship of trust and rapport with all parties.

- *The depth of the process.* To work with the extreme emotions involved in such conflicts the mediator must connect with the parties in a way that is deeply personal, emotional, and even spiritual (in the sense that indigenous people view all humanity and all creation as part of an interconnected whole). As Umbreit says, "the centering of the mediator throughout the entire process of preparation and mediation … helps the parties in conflict to experience it as a safe, if not sacred, journey toward genuine dialogue and healing" (1997, p. 206).
- *Identifying and tapping into parties' strengths.* The negative and dysfunctional emotions that people in such conflicts often experience tend to overcome and mask the strengths they need to draw on. During pre-mediation and the dialogue process itself, the mediator must discover each of the party's strengths and needs and must then determine how she can empower them to tap into those strengths.
- *Recognizing and using the power of silence.* Umbreit describes this feature of humanistic mediation in the following terms: "By honoring silence and patiently resisting the urge to interrupt silence with guidance or questions … the mediator is more consistently able to assist the involved parties in experiencing mediation as a process of dialogue and mutual aid—a journey of the heart in harmony with the head" (1997, p. 209).

Case Study 2: The Cadman–Deas Case

In October 1992, 16-year-old Jesse Cadman was coming home after a party when he and his friends were accosted by a group of other youths who were drunk, high, and looking for trouble. Jesse was killed by Isaac Deas, who was also 16, and who was later convicted of murder and sentenced to life in prison. Seventeen years later, Deas wanted to reach out to the Cadman family to express his deep remorse and sorrow for his crime. He wrote a letter that found its way to Jesse's sister Jodi Cadman, who was then a 37-year-old mother of three. About six months later, Jodi and Isaac met in a victim–offender mediation with two mediators from the Community Justice Initiatives Association of Langley, BC.

Reporter Cheryl Chan (2010, p. A4) provided the following account of this meeting:

> "In his own words, there was no reason [for the attack]," Jodi says. "He made it very clear that he had no one to blame but himself."
>
> Throughout their initial meeting, Deas said repeatedly that he was sorry. At times, when Jodi spoke harshly, she saw traces of redness creep up his face, she says. At other times, when they talked about her father [former MP Chuck Cadman], the emotions grew raw.

> Finally, sitting across from him, Jodi says she had an unsettling realization: She liked talking to him.
>
> "It's a really strange thing to reconcile in your head," she told him frankly. "Because I'll sit here and have a conversation with you, but you murdered my brother."
>
> He nodded and said he accepted that. After three hours, they stood up to say goodbye. Deas repeated: "Sorry. I'm so sorry."
>
> Jodi said: "You know what, you don't have to say that to me anymore. I forgive you." Caught off guard, Deas managed to thank her.
>
> Thinking back on that moment, Jodi says the words came surprisingly easy.
>
> "In the spirit of everything, it was the right thing to do, and it was just as healing for me." But her forgiveness came with strings.
>
> "I'm not giving it away freely. It's certainly not unconditional," she says. "But if he is doing everything he can possibly do to make things right, then it makes it easier."

Since then, Dona Cadman, mother of Jesse and Jodi, met both Isaac and his mother Supriya Deas, thus completing the circle of forgiveness, healing, and reconciliation. Dona Cadman and Supriya Deas have appeared together in several public presentations to tell their mutual story of the transformative and redemptive power of restorative justice. (See Egan, 2013; Luymes, 2012.)

As we have learned from the victim–offender stories in this chapter, VOM enables an offender to purge his or her wrongdoing, to achieve redemption, and to restore *right relations* with the victim, the victim's family, and the community. This redemptive process, relieving the burden of shame that offenders feel for their misdeeds, is an important step on the offender's path to rehabilitation.

Restitution Agreements in Victim–Offender Processes

Although it is not the primary purpose of the restorative process, restitution—the offender's undertaking to compensate the victim—is an important part of it. It can consist of monetary compensation, service to the victim, community service, or even actions aimed at self-improvement (for example, Susanna's commitment to complete her education in the VOM case above).

In their 2000 research study for Justice Canada, Latimer and Kleinknect (2000, p. 13) summarized their findings on restitution agreements as follows:

- Morris and Maxwell (1998) found that 85% of young offenders in family-group conferences in New Zealand agreed to carry out active penalties (such as community service).
- At four different Canadian restorative program sites, Umbreit, Coates, Kalanj, Lipkin and Petros (1995) found that restitution agreements had been successfully negotiated in 93% of cases.
- In their preliminary findings from an experimental comparison of conference and court cases, Strang, Barnes, Braithwaite and Sherman (1999) indicated that

83% of victims in conference cases versus 8% of victims in court cases, received both reparation and an apology from the offender.

- In Coates and Gehm's (1989) empirical assessment of victim–offender reconciliation programs, they found that 98% of victims and offenders agreed upon restitution. Of these agreements, there was a completion rate of 82% for financial restitution and 90% for service restitution.
- In a national survey of 116 victim–offender mediation programs in the U.S., extensive phone interviews with program staff indicated that in 87% of cases a restitution agreement was reached, with a 99% completion rate (Umbreit, Fercello, & Umbreit, 1998).
- In a comparison of two mediation programs matched with two court sites, Umbreit, Coates and Kalanj (1994) reported a restitution completion rate of 81% for mediated cases and 58% for court cases. When examining the type of restitution agreements reached, the researchers found that 58% were financial in nature, 13% were for personal service to the victim and 29% had a community service component.
- In a preliminary evaluation of victim mediation programs in California, researchers found that of all cases in which an agreement was reached, 97% of the contracts were completed or currently still active. The small number of failures were exclusively from cases dealing with property offences rather than more serious crimes against the person (Niemeyer & Shichor, 1996).

Restorative Circles

Since ancient times, people in different parts of the world have used the circle process as a way to respond to issues or conflicts in the community. The idea of people gathered in a circle has archetypal or universal power, as Baldwin and Linnea (2010, p. 6) describe:

> To understand the power of circle as a collaborative conversation model and the kinds of insights that can pour into this group process, it is helpful to understand that when we circle up in a ring of chairs, we are activating an archetype. Archetypal energy tends to make our dialogue, decisions, and actions take on a sense of significance. … People who have experienced circle often refer to this archetypal energy as the "magic of circle."

In this text, we use the term *restorative circles* to refer to restorative processes that use the circle formation. Other people use the terms *healing circles* or *peacemaking circles*.

The circle symbol conveys certain concepts and values that inform the restorative process. With no beginning or end, the circle is a symbol of eternity; it represents a holistic and creative power that is beyond our human logic. With respect to values, all people in the circle are respected as equals; each contributes to the process and has some responsibility for what the circle produces. The circle promotes the values of mutual concern and respect for all, shared responsibility, consensual decision making, appreciation of differences, and interconnectedness (Greenwood, 2005). Like our most ancient ancestors, we still experience a special sense of community and connection when we gather around a campfire.

The circle facilitator or "keeper" helps all participants to understand and implement the values conveyed by the circle and generally educates them and prepares them for the circle process. By doing so, she helps maintain the circle as a safe and productive space.

The keeper normally structures the circle process in several stages. Each participant has an opportunity (but not an obligation) to speak, and this opportunity moves clockwise around the circle a number of times. The keeper may decide to use something called a talking stick, which is passed from person to person as they speak. The stages of a typical restorative circle process would consist of the following (Baldwin & Linnea, 2010; Greenwood, 2005; Pranis, Stuart, & Wedge, 2003):

- an opening ritual and welcome;
- introduction of the participants and the process, including its purpose;
- establishing values and guidelines for the process, which includes going round the circle and giving people an opportunity to express their core values for the circle;
- storytelling—narratives and issues;
- restorative and reparative responses;
- conclusions; and
- closing ritual.

Sentencing Circles

A sentencing circle is a community-oriented process, conducted in conjunction with the criminal justice system, to generate a sentencing plan for an Aboriginal offender; it addresses the needs of the victim, the community, and the offender. Participants in the circle include the judge, the prosecutor, and the defence lawyer, as well as the offender, the victim, supporters of both victim and offender, as well as leaders, elders, or other representatives of the affected community. The sentencing circle can be thought of as an alternative to the normal sentencing process within the criminal justice system whereby the offender's sentence is left to the judge, after he or she has heard a victim impact statement.

Within the circle, by comparison, all participants have an equal voice, and all are encouraged to do the following: (1) speak from the heart in order to generate a shared understanding of the impact of the offence on the victim, on the community, and on the offender; and (2) identify how to heal all affected parties and to promote the offender's reintegration back into the community. Once the circle has developed a consensus about a proposed sentencing plan, including provisions for implementing and monitoring the offender's compliance with the plan, the plan must be approved by the judge. The judge thus switches roles, from being a participant in, and often keeper of, the sentencing circle, to his or her more traditional role in the criminal justice system.

Sentencing circles were first used in the Canadian criminal justice system in 1992 by Judge Barry Stuart, in the Yukon case of *R v Moses*. They are generally considered to be an Aboriginal approach to justice, one that the federal government supports. In 1996, the *Criminal Code* was amended to promote Aboriginal approaches to justice, including sentencing circles. Section 718.2 provides that "all available sanctions other than imprisonment that are reasonable in the circumstances should be considered for all offenders, with particular attention to the circumstances of aboriginal offenders."

In the case of *R v Gladue* (1999), the Supreme Court of Canada discussed some of the principles and values of a restorative approach to justice, especially in Aboriginal communities. The Court said that the appropriate approach "is largely determined by the needs of the victims, and the community, as well as the offender" (1999, p. 726). According to Justices Cory and Iacobucci (1999, pp. 727–728),

> one of the unique circumstances of aboriginal offenders is that community-based sanctions coincide with the aboriginal concept of sentencing and the needs of aboriginal people and communities. It is often the case that neither aboriginal offenders nor their communities are well served by incarcerating offenders, particularly for less serious or non-violent offences. Where these sanctions are reasonable in the circumstances, they should be implemented. In all instances, it is appropriate to attempt to craft the sentencing process and the sanctions imposed in accordance with the aboriginal perspective.

In her article on the case of Christopher Pauchay, Goldbach (2011, p. 56) summarized the sentencing circle process as follows:

> At a sentencing circle, an inner circle is made of criminal justice participants, including the judge, prosecution, defence counsel, court reporter, the offender, the victim and their respective families. The inner circle may also include probation officers, court workers, youth workers or police officers. Surrounding that circle is an outer circle of friends, relatives, and interested members of the community. The charges are read and brief opening remarks are made by the Crown and defense. Following that, the discussion is opened to other participants, with the procedure facilitated by either a judge or a respected member of the community. The procedure can often be lengthy and calls for high levels of commitment from the victim(s), accused and the community.

Despite the emphasis on alternatives to imprisonment for Aboriginal offenders under section 718.2 of the *Criminal Code*, sentencing circles are not appropriate for all offences committed by Aboriginal offenders. The judge has the ultimate decision-making power as to whether to convene a circle. Criteria for deciding whether to convene a sentencing circle include the consent of the victim, the willing participation of the offender, and whether the affected community has the resources to support both the victim and the offender with their healing processes and reintegration into the community, as well as whether the judge thinks the type of offence is amenable to the sentencing circle process. Where the offender is a habitual offender or where the harm caused to the victim is very serious, to the extent that the victim feels insecure or unsafe, the circle process may not be appropriate. An important concern is that the victim should not feel pressured to participate, either by supporters of the offender or by other community members.

Although the restorative circle process follows the same principles as VOM, there are significant differences between the two processes. VOM is a private, intimate, direct conversation between the victim and the offender. In a restorative circle, by contrast, many others are involved, and all participants speak to the circle.

In some ways, the circle process may be tougher for the offender than VOM is, since it holds him or her accountable not just to the victim but to the community, too. On the other hand, the circle contains some of the offender's supporters and spares him or her having to face the victim one-on-one. Therefore, some offenders may find the circle less daunting than VOM.

The circle process is a tangible and direct manifestation of the community's effort to reintegrate the offender. The tough love, support, and collective wisdom that come from the circle process can contribute greatly to the offender's reintegration.

Family Group Conferencing

Family group conferencing was introduced in New Zealand in 1989, as the primary resolution process for child welfare and young offender cases. It is a restorative circle process that is based on traditional Maori customs, values, beliefs, and practices for responding to child welfare and youth justice cases (Pakura, 2004). Since 1989, family group conferencing has been adopted by many jurisdictions in Canada, the United States, and elsewhere.

In Canada, family group conferencing is often used in child welfare cases, when there is a dispute between a child welfare agency and a child's parents over the care and custody of a child. It is one of the forms of alternative dispute resolution (ADR) that, as of 2006, the Ontario government prescribed in connection with issues related to children and children's welfare.

Emergence of Family Group Conferencing in Ontario: The Legal Context

In 2006, the Ontario *Child and Family Services Act* was amended to require a children's aid society to "consider whether a prescribed method of alternative dispute resolution could assist in resolving any issue related to the child or a plan for the child's care" (section 20.2(1)). Under policy directive CW005-06, issued by the Ontario Ministry of Child and Youth Services in November 2006, children's aid societies are required to use one of the following ADR methods in a child protection case:

- child protection mediation,
- family group conferencing, or
- Aboriginal approaches.

Where the above methods are not available or where another method is deemed more suitable, a children's aid society may wish to prescribe another method of ADR.

The Ontario Association for Family Mediation (OAFM) maintains and manages the Ontario Child Protection Mediation Roster, which lists mediators in Ontario who are qualified as child protection mediators under policy directive CW005-06 (see the OAFM website). They are qualified for all of the above processes except the third one: Aboriginal approaches. (The latter are traditional methods of dispute resolution, including circle processes, that have been established by First Nations communities or Aboriginal organizations for the protection of children; they are presided over by impartial facilitators who do not exercise any decision-making power themselves but are skilled in First Nations traditional methods and help the participants develop a plan that addresses the particular child-protection concerns involved in the case.)

Transitional Justice Processes

Transitional justice encompasses both judicial and non-judicial processes. It is needed in places where there has been a period of systematic human rights abuses—mass atrocities, as in Rwanda, or the forceful suppression of democratic governance, as in certain Latin American countries. Once these abuses have ended, there is an interim period during which, though justice is beginning to emerge, the rule of law and its underlying processes have not yet been fully established.

Transitional justice is based on legal and moral norms, as well as on pragmatic necessity. Legally and morally, victims have the right to hold perpetrators of mass abuses accountable for their crimes and to seek redress for their suffering. The pragmatic bases of transitional justice are also compelling. Leaving mass atrocities and abuses unaddressed can result in ongoing mistrust among members of the population and in highly combustible social divisions; it can hinder institutional reforms and the necessary transition to building or rebuilding democracy and peace. Transitional justice helps countries and peoples come to terms with their past.

Transitional justice falls within the restorative justice paradigm in that it involves the active participation of victims, perpetrators, and affected communities (or societies). These parties engage in processes that heal the past and restore balance and harmony to the social fabric. Reparations from perpetrators and redress for victims may be part of the package of transitional processes. The emphasis is decidedly on the future—what is needed to acknowledge and remember the past and what is required from a society's institutions and individuals so that they can move toward a peaceful future in which violence of the kind recently experienced can never happen again.

Transitional justice can be seen as a tool of transformative social action; it is based on the assumption that a collective remembering of the past will help prevent a future recurrence of violence (du Toit, 2000). The goals of transitional justice are ambitious and numerous, according to Priscilla Hayner (2001, p. 24): to uncover and acknowledge past violations; to respond to the needs of victims; to create a culture of accountability and respect for the rule of law; to delineate institutional responsibility and propose institutional reforms; to further the prospect of reconciliation; and to reduce historical conflict over the past (p. 24).

To date, two different forms of transitional justice have emerged, both in response to massive human rights abuses. The first, exemplified by the South African Truth and Reconciliation Commission, is a highly participatory model, fostering reconciliation through public dialogue and collective acknowledgment of wrongdoing. The other form of transitional justice, exemplified by models found in Guatemala, El Salvador, and East Germany, operates via educational fact-finding bodies; it has the explicit aim of encouraging historical interpretation and of disseminating a new collective memory (Nagy, 2008; Beattie, 2008). Most truth and reconciliation processes conform to one or the other of these two models and promote either memorialization of the conflict (that is, *never forget, so that it will not occur again*) or reconciliation combined with truth telling (that is, *record the past and work actively to heal victims and perpetrators, so they can move forward*).

An important element in most transitional justice processes has been a reliance on traditional forms of societal or community reconciliation, adapted to international legal norms and standards. For example, the *gacaca* courts of Rwanda (from the indigenous word for *grass*; these were "courts held on the grass") were tasked with processing the criminal cases of many perpetrators of the recent genocide. These courts were needed for two reasons. One reason was that there were not enough jails to hold all of those accountable for the genocide. The second reason was that the formal legal system, unlike the *gacaca* courts, did not permit the participation of victims and communities affected by the crimes.

Stability, truth, justice, and healing are the key objectives of any reconciliation process. Reconciliation requires insight, reflection, and self-evaluation on the part of the individuals and of the society as a whole. If violence and insecurity still prevail, reconciliation is impossible. Where there has been a history of conflict and atrocities, perspectives on truth will differ. Nonetheless, most reconciliation processes recognize that a recording of events, a telling of stories, and a public recognition of victims' suffering (as well as perpetrators' suffering) constitute an essential part of the reconciliation process.

Concepts of justice vary, and transitional justice should not only attend to restorative processes. It should also include a distributive element and a retributive one. Retributive forms of justice are often required to ensure that leaders do not perpetrate mass atrocities in the future. Psychosocial support is also necessary, essential for the healing of those who remain after systematic human rights abuses. Restorative justice processes help in this healing process by providing a forum where victims and perpetrators can share their stories, demonstrate their pain and remorse, and—in many cases—reconcile.

Canadian Case Study: Restorative Justice and the Indian Residential Schools

The question of how effective restorative justice processes are in helping communities heal after large-scale systemic injustices is one that has arisen in Canada. There are an estimated 150,000 First Nations, Inuit, and Métis children who, by a policy put in place more than 100 years ago, were forcibly removed from their homes and forced to attend schools that were in some cases hundreds of kilometres from their homes. The express purpose of these government-funded, church-run schools was to remove all Aboriginal influences—spiritual, cultural, and intellectual—from these children. Effectively incarcerated in the schools, the children were not permitted to speak their own languages or interact with their parents, and many were physically and sexually abused. The residential schools finally closed in Canada during the 1990s.

In 2007, the Canadian government established the Indian Residential Schools Adjudication Secretariat (IRSAS), an independent tribunal charged with resolving the many claims of emotional, physical, and sexual abuse made by former students. IRSAS used a claimant-centred process to support healing and redress. The current chief adjudicator, Dan Shapiro (2013), has described the process as follows:

> The IAP provides former students with an opportunity to come forward and speak of their experience at residential schools in an atmosphere of safety and respect. For many claimants, this opportunity is a transformational moment. I feel honoured to have witnessed many powerful examples of intergenerational healing since I began presiding at hearings to resolve claims of abuse.

The Truth and Reconciliation Commission (TRC) of Canada was established in 2008 to address the larger issues raised by the systematic cultural violation of Aboriginal peoples. The TRC was set up to construct a historical account and memorialization of the residential school abuse. It did so in conjunction with the IRSAS, which provided compensation to the victims. The TRC's mission statement (n.d.) includes the following account of its goal and of what achieving this goal will entail:

> Collective efforts from all peoples are necessary to revitalize the relationship between Aboriginal peoples and Canadian society—reconciliation is the goal. It is a goal that will take the commitment of multiple generations but when it is achieved, when we have reconciliation—it will make for a better, stronger Canada.

Summary

In this chapter, we have considered four justice "stories"—retributive, corrective, distributive, and restorative. As we have seen, justice can mean many different things to different people; its meaning varies according to context. We have paid particular attention to restorative justice, which is focused on repairing social relationships between victims, offenders, and others affected by a crime. Restorative justice takes various forms—victim–offender mediation (VOM), restorative circles (for example, family group conferencing and sentencing circles), and transitional justice processes. All of these processes offer particular features and benefits. Principles of restoring harmony and righting relations have had a long history in many human societies and are an important element in the justice ideal. At the same time, holding people accountable for the harm they cause is an equally important part of achieving justice.

DISCUSSION QUESTIONS AND EXERCISES

1. Consider the following list of the different forces that shape our behaviour and lead us to respect rules and the law:
   - values,
   - community norms,
   - fear of social disapproval,
   - fear of legal consequences,
   - peer expectations,
   - sense of belonging and inclusion,
   - desire not to be embarrassed,
   - education,
   - culture,
   - laws, and
   - socioeconomic needs.

   a. Which of these forces are the most important in shaping our behaviour?
   b. Which of these forces are used by the criminal justice system to shape our behaviour? What do you think are the implications of this?
   c. Try to think of forces not mentioned in this list that ought to be included.
2. Imagine that you are mediating the dispute between Russell and Hilary in the Separating Spouses case study (see Box 10.1), and the two parties are discussing the division of property between them. Answer the following questions:
   a. If you were to adopt the principle of equality as your guiding distributive justice principle, how might that influence your mediation with Hilary and Russell?
   b. Would your mediation be different if you adopted the principle of equity? What if you adopted the principle of need? In what ways would your mediation process differ depending on which distributive justice principle you follow?

   c. Now consider the issue of custody and access. How might these same three justice principles be applied if the issue being mediated were how decisions about custody and access should be made with respect to the couple's daughter Tiffany? Do you think these two different types of distributive justice issues—division of property, on one hand, and access to one's child, on the other—should be decided according to the same justice principle? Why? Why not?
3. In your mediation of the dispute between Hilary and Russell, how might you apply some of the concepts and approaches discussed in this chapter? Why would you do that?
4. Why does a restorative process such as victim–offender mediation need to be different from the type of mediation process that would be used in the Car Repair Blues dispute (see Chapter 1, Box 1.1)?
5. Yesterday, after school, a Grade 12 student, Christopher, was beaten up by a group of boys on the soccer field after an important school match had just been played. Christopher's father called the principal of the school shortly after Christopher returned home, beaten and bloody. The principal began investigating and learned that the boy who led the fighting, Jamal, is in the same class as Christopher.
   a. Describe how a retributive justice process would address this situation.
   b. Now describe how a restorative justice process might address the situation.
   c. What do you believe are the advantages and disadvantages of each of these processes in this particular case?
6. Imagine that you are a volunteer mediator at the school described in Exercise 5.
   a. What steps would you take in convening a restorative process to respond to this conflict? For example, how would you determine what process to use and who might be involved?
   b. What are some of the things you would do as circle keeper in conducting a restorative circle process in this case?
7. What will a mediator need to do to prepare both the victim and the offender for mediation in the case of a serious, violent crime?

FURTHER READING

Braithwaite, J. (1989). *Crime, shame and reintegration*. Cambridge: Cambridge University Press.

Gourevitch, Philip. (1998). *We wish to inform you that tomorrow we will be killed with our families: Stories from Rwanda*. New York: Farrar, Straus and Giroux.

Hayner, Priscilla B. (2001) *Unspeakable truths: Transitional justice and the challenge of truth commissions*. New York: Routledge.

Law Commission of Canada. (2003). *Transforming relationships through participatory justice*. Ottawa: Law Commission of Canada.

Minow, Martha. (1998). *Between vengeance and forgiveness: Facing history after genocide and mass violence*. Boston: Beacon Press.

Power, Samantha. (2003). *A problem from hell: America and the age of genocide*. New York: HarperCollins.

Umbreit, M.S. (1994). *Victim meets offender: The impact of restorative justice and mediation*. Monsey, NY: Criminal Justice Press.

Umbreit, M.S. (2013). *Dancing with the energy of conflict and trauma: Letting go—finding peace*. North Charleston, SC: Create Space Independent Book Publishing.

Umbreit, M.S., Blevins, J., & Lewis, T. (2014, accepted for publication in 2015). *The energy of forgiveness: Lessons from former enemies in restorative dialogue*. Eugene, OR: Wipf & Stock Publishers.

Wright, M., & Galaway, B. (Eds.). (1989). *Mediation and criminal justice: Victims, offenders, and community*. London: Sage.

Zehr, H. (1990). *Changing lenses*. Scottdale, PA: Herald Press.

Websites

Beyond Intractability: http://www.beyondintractability.org

Center for Restorative Justice and Peacemaking, University of Minnesota: http://www.cehd.umn.edu/ssw/rjp

Centre for Restorative Justice, Simon Fraser University: http://www.sfu.ca/crj.html

Indian Residential Schools Adjudication Secretariat (IRSAS): http://www.iap-pei.ca/us-nous/us-nous-eng.php

International Center for Transitional Justice: http://www.ictj.org

International Institute for Restorative Practices—IIRP Canada: http://canada.iirp.edu

Ontario Association for Family Mediation—Ontario Child Protection Mediation Roster Program: http://www.oafm-cpmed.ca

Public Safety Canada—A Little Manual of Restorative Justice: http://www.publicsafety.gc.ca/cnt/rsrcs/pblctns/2008-03-lmrj/index-eng.aspx#a0

Restorative Works Learning Network: http://restorativeworks.net
See the video in which Mark Yantzi talks about the first case where offenders met victims: http://restorativeworks.net/2012/03/mark-yantzi-talks-about-first-case-where-offenders-met-victims/.

Truth and Reconciliation Commission of Canada: http://www.trc.ca/websites/reconciliation/index.php?p=312

REFERENCES

Allard, P. (2008). *A little manual of restorative justice*. Public Safety Canada. http://www.publicsafety.gc.ca/cnt/rsrcs/pblctns/2008-03-lmrj/index-eng.aspx#a1.

Altran, S., & Axelrod, R. (2008). Reframing sacred values. *Negotiation Journal, 24*, 221–246.

Baldwin, C., & Linnea, A. (2010). *The circle way: A leader in every chair*. San Francisco: Berrett-Koehler.

Beattie, A.H. (2008). *Playing politics with history—the Bundestag inquiries into East Germany*. Oxford: Berghahn Books.

Bianchi, H. (1994). *Justice as sanctuary: Toward a system of crime control*. Bloomington, IN: Indiana University Press.

Braithwaite, J. (1989). *Crime, shame, and reintegration*. Cambridge: Cambridge University Press.

Bush, R.A.B. (1989). Mediation and adjudication, dispute resolution and ideology: An imaginary conversation. *Journal of Contemporary Legal Issues*, *3*, 1–35.

Chan, C. (2010, October 11). Finding forgiveness, out of the blue. *The Ottawa Citizen*, p. A4. Material reprinted with the express permission of: Postmedia News, a division of Postmedia Network Inc.

Child and Family Services Act. (1990). RSO 1990, c. C.11.

Christie, N. (1977). Conflicts as property. *British Journal of Criminology*, *17*, 1–15.

Church Council on Justice and Corrections. (1996). *Satisfying justice*. Ottawa: Church Council on Justice and Corrections.

Criminal Code. (1985). RSC 1985, c. C-46, as amended.

Deutsch, M. (2000). Justice and conflict. In M. Deutsch & P. Coleman (Eds.), *The handbook of conflict resolution: Theory and practice* (pp. 41–64). San Francisco: Jossey-Bass.

Dueck, J. (2010). Thinking outside the law. *Canadian Mennonite*, *14*(7), 13. http://legacy.canadianmennonite.org/vol14-2010/14-07/14-07small_692_2010-04-05.pdf.

du Toit, André. (2000). The moral foundations of the South African TRC: Truth as acknowledgment and justice as recognition. In R.I. Rotberg & D. Thompson (Eds.), *Truth v. justice: The morality of truth commissions* (pp. 122–140). Princeton, NJ: Princeton University Press.

Egan, K. (2013, November 15). Road to redemption began at opposite ends. *Ottawa Citizen*, p. A1.

Fiss, O.M. (1984). Against settlement. *Yale Law Journal*, *93*, 1073–1091.

Fletcher, G.P. (1996). *Basic concepts of legal thought*. New York: Oxford University Press.

Galaway, B., & Hudson, J. (Eds.). (1996). *Restorative justice: International perspectives*. Monsey, NY: Criminal Justice Press.

Goldbach, T. (2011). Sentencing circles, clashing worldviews, and the case of Christopher Pauchay. *Journal of the Centre for Studies in Religion and Society Graduate Students Association*, *10*(1), 53–76.

Greenwood, J. (2005). The circle process: A path for restorative dialogue. University of Minnesota: Center for Restorative Justice & Peacemaking. http://www.cehd.umn.edu/ssw/RJP/Resources/RJ_Dialogue_Resources/Peacemaking_Healing_Circles/The_Circle_Process.pdf.

Hayner, P.B. (2001). *Unspeakable truths: Transitional justice and the challenge of truth commissions*. New York: Routledge.

Hudson, J., Morris, A., Maxwell, G., & Galaway, B. (Eds.). (1996). *Family group conferences*. Monsey, NY: Criminal Justice Press.

Kelly, R. (2006). *From scoundrel to scholar: The Russ Kelly story*. Kitchener, ON: Russ Kelly.

Latimer, J., & Kleinknect, S. (2000). The effects of restorative justice programming: A review of the empirical. Department of Justice Canada: Research and Statistics Division. http://www.justice.gc.ca/eng/rp-pr/csj-sjc/jsp-sjp/rr00_16/toc-tdm.html.

Law Commission of Canada. (2003). *Transforming relationships through participatory justice*. Ottawa: Law Commission of Canada.

Llewellyn, J.J., & Howse, R. (1998). *Restorative justice—a conceptual framework*. Ottawa: Law Commission of Canada.

Luymes, G. (2012, November 5). "We wanted them to stop hurting": Supriya Deas can divide her life into before and after. *The Province*. http://www.canada.com/story.html?id=99f6a71b-0d30-4171-a2a1-da5bd83e4532.

Menkin, E., with Baker, L.K. (1995, December). I forgave my sister's killer. *Ladies Home Journal*. Also available online at the Victim-Offender Reconciliation Information and Resource Center: http://www.vorp.com/articles/forgave.html.

Nagy, R. (2008). Transitional justice as global project: Critical reflections. *Third World Quarterly*, *29*(2), 275–289.

Northey, W. (2005). Restorative justice vision and spirituality (ARPA Presentation, Langley Canadian Reformed Church, March 5, 2005). http://waynenorthey.com/wp-content/uploads/2014/02/restorative-justice-arpa-march-5-2005.pdf.

Ontario Ministry of Child and Youth Services. (2006, November). Policy directive CW005-06.

Pakura, S. (2004). The family group conference 14-year journey: Celebrating the successes, learning the lessons, embracing the challenges. Paper presented at the American Humane Association's Family Group Decision-Making Conference and Skills-Building Institute, Harrisburg, Pennsylvania, June 2004. http://www.iirp.edu/pdf/au05_pakura.pdf.

Payne, J.D., & Payne, M.A. (2001). *Canadian family law*. Toronto: Irwin Law.

Peachey, D. (1988). Victim/offender mediation: The Kitchener experiment. In M. Wright & B. Galaway (Eds.), *Mediation in criminal justice* (pp. 251–263). London: Sage.

Peachey, D. (1989). What people want from mediation. In K. Kressell & D.G. Pruitt (Eds.), *Mediation research* (pp. 300–321). San Francisco: Jossey-Bass.

Perry, L., Lajeunesse, T., & Woods, A. (1987). Mediation services: An evaluation. Manitoba: Research, Planning, and Evaluation Office of the Attorney General.

Pranis, K., Stuart, B., and Wedge, M. (2003). *Peacemaking circles: From crime to community*. St. Paul, MN: Living Justice Press.

Price, M. (1994). The mediation of a drunk driving death: A case development study. Paper presented at the international conference of the Victim-Offender Mediation Association, Winnipeg, Manitoba. Available online at the Victim-Offender Reconciliation Information and Resource Center: http://www.vorp.com/articles/ddcasest.html.

R v Gladue. (1999). [1999] 1 SCR 688.

R v Moses. (1992). 71 C.C.C. (3d) 347 (Yukon Terr. Ct.).

Roberts, T. (1995). *Evaluation of the victim–offender mediation project, Langley, B.C.: Final report*. Victoria, BC: Focus Consultants.

Shapiro, D. (2013). Message from the chief adjudicator. Who we are and what we do. Indian Residential Schools Adjudication Secretariat. http://www.iap-pei.ca/us-nous/us-nous-eng.php.

Sharpe, S. (1998). *Restorative justice: A vision for healing and change*. Edmonton: Edmonton Victim Offender Mediation Society.

Stuart, B. (1996). Sentencing circles: Turning swords into ploughshares. In B. Galaway & J. Hudson (Eds.), *Restorative justice: International perspectives* (pp. 193–206). Monsey, NY: Criminal Justice Press.

Stuart, B. (1997). Sentencing circles: Making real differences. In J. Macfarlane (Ed.), *Rethinking disputes: The mediation alternative* (pp. 201–232). Toronto: Emond Montgomery.

Truth and Reconciliation Commission of Canada. (n.d.). Reconciliation … towards a new relationship. http://www.trc.ca/websites/reconciliation/index.php?p=312.

Umbreit, M. (1994). *Victim meets offender: The impact of restorative justice and mediation*. Monsey, NY: Criminal Justice Press.

Umbreit, M. (1997). Humanistic mediation: A transformative journey of peacemaking. *Mediation Quarterly*, *14*(3), 201–213.

Umbreit, M. (2001). *The handbook of victim offender mediation*. San Francisco: Jossey-Bass.

Umbreit, M., Coates, R., & Vos, B. (2004). Victim–offender mediation: Three decades of practice and research. *Conflict Resolution Quarterly*, *22*(1–2), 279–303.

Umbreit, M., Vos, B., Coates, R., & Brown, K. (2003). *Facing violence: The path of restorative justice and dialogue*. Monsey, NY: Criminal Justice Press.

Urban, L., Markway, J., & Crockett, K. (2011). Evaluating victim–offender dialogue (VOD) for serious cases using Umbreit's 2001 handbook: A case study. *Conflict Resolution Quarterly*, *29*(1), 3–23.

Van Ness, D., & Strong, K.H. (1997). *Restoring justice*. Cincinnati, OH: Anderson Publishing.

Wright, M., & Galaway, B. (Eds.). (1989). *Mediation and criminal justice: Victims, offenders, and community*. London: Sage.

Zehr, H. (1990). *Changing lenses*. Scottdale, PA: Herald Press.

CHAPTER 11

Using Mediation in Organizations and Communities

LEARNING OBJECTIVES

After reading this chapter, you will be able to:

- Understand the tangible and intangible costs of conflict to organizations and communities
- Explain how mediation programs can be developed and implemented to reduce economic and human costs and to help develop a culture of collaboration in organizations
- Identify a number of the individual, organizational, and societal challenges that mediation faces
- Understand the role of program evaluation in improving mediation processes and programs
- Identify some challenges facing the profession of mediation, and some proposed responses to these challenges

CHAPTER OUTLINE

Introduction 325
Measuring the Costs of Conflict 326
Types of Workplace: Competitive Versus Collaborative 328
What Is a Mediation Program? 330
Conflict Management Systems 336
Community Mediation Programs in Canada 338
Evaluation of Processes, Programs, and Systems 342
Challenges and Risks of Mediation 344
The Profession of Mediation 350
Summary 358

Sometimes the right response to evil is an appeal to powerful and effective social organization—an appeal to civilization itself.

P.J. O'Rourke

Introduction

In our competitive society, we are inclined to use an adversarial approach to disputes and conflicts. Most of our heroes are fighters, not peacemakers. In this chapter, we will examine the consequences of this for our organizations, our institutions, and our communities. These consequences include the high cost of unresolved conflict, both the direct, tangible costs and the intangible ones that usually go unaccounted for.

One of this chapter's principal topics is how organizations and communities develop mediation programs and conflict management systems, and how these programs contribute to the development of a culture of collaboration. We consider the factors that are critical in designing an organizational mediation program, and the need for evaluation of program outcomes to ensure the program meets its objectives for the organization or community.

Using mediation in any context involves challenges and risks, as well as potential criticisms. By identifying these challenges and risks, we can develop ways to respond to them. In the process, we can try to ensure that mediation is used in a way that is both beneficial and just for all.

Measuring the Costs of Conflict

What are the costs of conflict in organizations and communities? How can we identify and measure these costs, both the tangible (that is, direct and measurable) ones, and the intangible ones?

There are many direct, measurable costs of unresolved workplace conflict. They include the following:

- legal and other costs of pursuing or responding to grievances, harassment claims, and other employee disputes, including dismissal disputes;
- salary and benefit costs paid on behalf of an employee who, owing to conflict, is on paid leave;
- recruiting, orientation, and training costs that the organization incurs in paying for employees who are brought in to replace other employees who, owing to unresolved conflict, are either on leave or have been transferred;
- compensation paid to settle harassment and other conflict claims of aggrieved employees; and
- termination and severance pay paid to an employee who has been terminated owing to a workplace conflict.

As this list suggests, the direct costs of conflict to an organization are significant. Justice Canada (2010, p. 15) has reported that the cost to an organization of replacing an employee who has left the organization owing to conflict is 150 percent of the ex-employee's total compensation because of lost productivity and various additional expenses, including recruiting fees, orientation and retraining costs, and interviewing time.

What about the indirect or intangible costs of conflict in an organization—the costs that don't figure into the financial accounting? To understand these costs, we need to revisit some conflict theory covered in earlier chapters. As discussed in Chapter 4, conflict elicits the *fear response*, also known as the acute stress response. Even if parties do not actually experience fear in response to conflict, their physiological reaction will involve stress. The stress of unresolved conflict can produce the following effects for an organization and its members (Tangri, 2003; Rouble, 2014):

- mental health problems, including stress, frustration, anxiety, and depression;
- diminished morale and motivation;
- reduced productivity;
- poor or damaged working relationships;
- absenteeism;
- disability claims;
- presenteeism (in other words, when employees are physically present at the workplace but, due to a medical or emotional problem, are distracted to the point of reduced productivity) (see Goetzel et al., 2004, as well as Aronsson, Gustaffson, and Dallner, 2000); and
- loss of productive work time, because managers and employees have to discuss and deal with conflict.

Conflict Culture

An organization's conflict culture is a key factor in determining how negatively conflict will affect that organization. According to Gelfand, Leslie, Keller, and de Dreu (2012), there are three types of organizational conflict culture:

1. avoidant,
2. dominating, and
3. collaborative.

Avoidant

Organizations with an *avoidant conflict culture* assume that conflict is dangerous and ought to be suppressed in the interests of organizational harmony. In this kind of organization, agreeableness and passivity are the norms for conflict management (Gelfand, Leslie, & Keller, 2008), and individuals typically respond to conflict by "accommodating or acquiescing to the point of view of others, changing the subject, and smoothing over or otherwise evading open discussion of the issue" (Gelfand et al., 2012, p. 1133).

Dominating

In an organization with a *dominating conflict culture*, managers and employees tend to actively confront conflicts and disagreements in a win–lose way. The assumption here is that "individuals have the agency to openly deal with conflict and that disagreeable or competitive behaviors are appropriate and normative" (Gelfand et al., 2012, p. 1133). In this kind of organization, handling conflict typically involves "direct confrontations and heated arguments in which individuals are reluctant to give in, yelling and shouting matches, or threats and warnings" (Gelfand et al., 2012, p. 1133).

Collaborative

Finally, organizations with collaborative conflict cultures tend to address conflict through cooperative, active discussion (Gelfand, Leslie, & Keller, 2008). Here, as with dominating conflict culture, there is an assumption that individuals have the agency to deal with conflict. The difference is that, with a collaborative conflict culture, individuals are expected to resolve conflict with cooperative behaviour and openness. In this kind of organization, handling conflict typically involves "active listening to the opinions of all parties involved, mediation of different perspectives, open and honest discussion of the conflict, and demonstrations of mutual respect" (Gelfand et al., 2012, p. 1133).

Types of Workplace: Competitive Versus Collaborative

Traditional Competitive Organizations

Most North American organizations tend to follow the traditional 20th-century model of competitiveness. Employees compete for recognition and material rewards—promotions, higher remuneration, and career advancement. The competitive organization has mechanisms for evaluating the performance of all employees and for recognizing and rewarding its star performers. The conflict culture of such an organization could be either avoidant or dominating, but it is probably not collaborative.

Members of a traditionally competitive organization will have a reactive approach to conflict rather than a proactive plan for addressing it constructively. The organization will simply deal with conflicts as they arise, and in doing so will rely on traditional, formal processes for resolving disputes—grievance or complaint policies, such as a harassment in the workplace policy, or external litigation processes. It will not have developed a program of collaborative resolution processes for its workforce. Figure 11.1 illustrates the effects that increasing levels of conflict have on workplace productivity in a traditional workplace.

Conflict tends to be suppressed in a reactive workplace. Such suppression induces high levels of conformity and group-think, and it dampens individual initiative. When conflict levels are low in this kind of workplace, productivity is lower than it could be. When conflicts reach a point where they can no longer be avoided or suppressed and are confronted, productivity in a reactive workplace may actually increase marginally. As conflicts increase further, however, they are handled in an adversarial, competitive way, and this results in diminished productivity.

Modern Collaborative Organizations

The reactive organization has a long history. However, as we advance into the "knowledge age" of the 21st century, people are increasingly aware of the need for a

Figure 11.1 Effects of Conflict in a Traditional Workplace

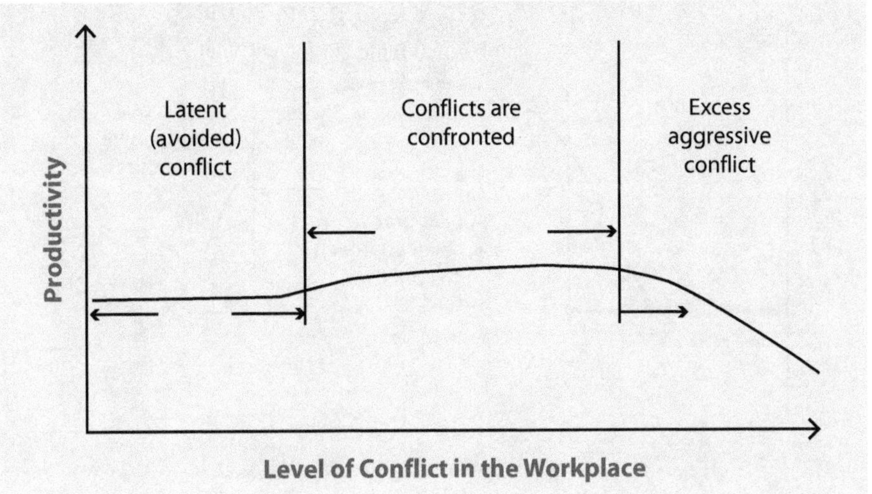

more collaborative model for organizations. Certain features define a collaborative organization, as writers in the area have noted (Logan & Stokes, 2004; Rosen, 2007; Rosen, 2009). Viewed in comparison with a reactive organization, a collaborative organization will

- be governed in a more democratic, egalitarian, and decentralized way;
- strive to develop a culture of collaboration, with higher levels of mutual trust and respect for all employees;
- encourage and value the ideas, knowledge, and contributions of all employees; and
- provide tools, skills, and processes for proactive conflict resolution.

In the collaborative workplace, people are encouraged to express their individual ideas and opinions. The organization provides its employees with the means of handling all types of conflicts proactively and collaboratively. When conflicts are confronted (that is, *expressed*, not *suppressed*) and handled collaboratively, productivity in that organization tends to be much higher. Many of the negative effects of workplace conflict listed above (low morale, high stress, psychological illness and disability, absenteeism, presenteeism) are reduced.

Figure 11.2 illustrates what happens in an organization that deals with conflict proactively, has developed a program of collaborative resolution processes for its workforce, and has taken steps to become a collaborative organization.

Instituting a workplace mediation program is among the initiatives that can help to develop a more collaborative organization.

Figure 11.2 Effects of Conflict in a Collaborative Workplace

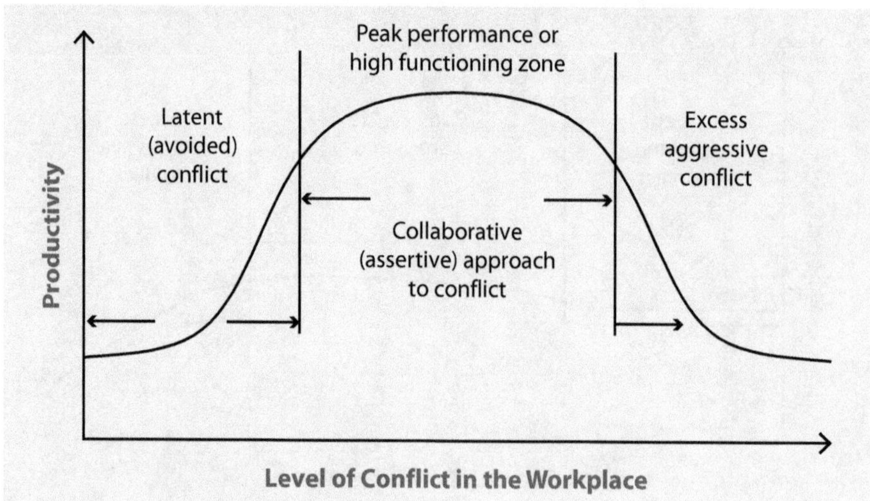

What Is a Mediation Program?

A mediation program is a system of resources, personnel (both operational and administrative), procedures, and practices for providing mediation services to people within a school, institution, or other organization, or within a community. These people will be clients of that program and will use it on an ongoing basis. Typically, an organizational mediation program will have some form of ongoing administration, perhaps with a full-time manager or administrator.

Mediation programs can be found in private sector companies, government departments or agencies, non-profit corporations, NGOs, elementary and secondary schools, colleges, and universities. These programs provide mediation services to a defined population within their organization. For example, a school-based mediation program (usually a "peer mediation" approach) will provide mediation services to students for student-to-student conflicts. Workplace mediation programs provide mediation services to employees for workplace conflicts between employees, including grievance or harassment disputes; however, typically they do not handle conflicts or disputes between employees and outside parties such as customers, suppliers, or family members. The mediation of the conflict between Danny and Teresa, in the Workplace Change scenario presented in Chapter 8 (see Box 8.1), would come from a workplace mediation program of this kind.

Mediation programs in organizations come in different forms and sizes, but they generally involve the following elements:

- a centralized manager or administrator,
- a roster of qualified mediators,

- a process for intake and convening,
- mechanisms for educating the population about the program and its services,
- procedures and guidelines for mediation processes provided to program clients, and
- mechanisms for evaluation and ongoing development of the mediation services provided by the program.

Those responsible for administering the mediation program need to be clear about the program's larger goals and objectives, which will transcend the local function of settling disputes among the target population it serves. For instance, many programs state that resolving underlying conflict will not only prevent or limit future conflicts but will improve working relations, morale, and productivity. Some mediation programs set goals that strive for transformation; their goal is to enable disputing parties to learn new and better ways to handle conflicts with others not only in the organization but also in their homes and communities. School-based mediation programs commonly aspire to help students learn collaborative life skills that will enable them to deal constructively with conflict today and in the future.

A mediation program within an organization, by helping the organization's members use mediation and develop their own collaborative skills, will promote a culture of collaboration and help reduce the direct and indirect costs of conflict.

Developing an Organizational Mediation Program

To show how mediation programs are developed, we present a hypothetical student-run mediation program (Student Mediation Services or SMS) that is being established by the students' council at Carleton University (CUSA) in Ottawa.

To ensure that the new program would have broad-based support within the student population, CUSA would form a program-planning group to design the main features of this new mediation program. The planning group would have a cross-section of participants from the student and university community and would include an outside consultant with organizational mediation and program development experience.

The planning group would undertake a number of activities to develop the design for its organizational mediation program. These activities would follow a process that is used in many types of organizations, including campus communities (Warters, 2000, p. 43). The process involves the following steps:

- conducting an organizational conflict-needs assessment;
- determining the initial scope and focus of the program, including what types of conflict cases will be handled;
- developing a statement of purpose;

- determining staff needs and responsibilities;
- establishing a program budget;
- deciding who the program mediators will be, how they will be selected or recruited, and what training they will require;
- developing various operational procedures and guidelines;
- developing a plan for educating the target population about the program and its services; and
- designing mechanisms for evaluation and ongoing development of the program.

Determining the Needs and the Scope of the Program

Designers of a new mediation program must first assess the conflict needs of its target population. A needs analysis will help determine, among other things, the most common types of conflicts the program will need to address. In the case of Carleton's SMS program, the needs analysis might reveal that a great many students have experienced conflict with roommates, either in residence or in off-campus housing. These conflicts have mainly been disagreements about kitchen cleaning and other housework, and disputes over payment of rent and utilities. The needs analysis might show that these conflicts among roommates have been serious enough to impair some students' ability to concentrate fully on their academic work, jeopardizing their grades, and that a smaller number of students have been so unsettled by these conflicts that they have dropped out of university altogether.

Another area where students have had conflict, according to the needs analysis, is in their work on group assignments. These conflicts interfered with their academic work and threatened their academic success.

SMS program planners would come to recognize that by providing volunteer mediation services, they could provide a valuable service to a large percentage of Carleton's student population. The program they would eventually establish would address a wide range of conflicts and disputes. These would include the following: roommate conflicts and conflicts arising from group assignments; disputes between students and instructors over classroom interactions; disputes between student tenants and their landlords; consumer disputes between students and local businesses (similar to the dispute described in the Car Repair Blues scenario from Box 1.1); and disputes involving accusations of bullying, harassment, and discrimination.

Recruiting, Selecting, and Training Mediators

Another task for the developers of mediation programs is to create a roster of mediators. The developers of Carleton's SMS program would create a roster of qualified student volunteer mediators whom the program administrator could call upon as needed. They would also create a roster of external, professional mediators who agree to provide their services pro bono in particularly challenging cases, and, when necessary, to coach or mentor the student mediators.

A workplace mediation program, such as the one at Danny and Teresa's Library (see Box 8.1, in Chapter 8), is likely to have a variety of mediator rosters, such as the following:

1. *Internal, volunteer mediators.* These would include volunteer employees of the organization who have been trained and otherwise qualified as mediators within the program.
2. *External, volunteer mediators.* This roster would include individuals within the surrounding community who have been trained and otherwise qualified as mediators within the program and who are willing to provide their services on a pro-bono, volunteer basis.
3. *External, professional, contract mediators.* This would be a roster of experienced mediation practitioners, often (but not necessarily) self-employed, who have met the requirements to be professional mediators within the program and who will provide their services on a fee-for-service, contract basis in complex cases.

How does a program coordinator or convenor decide which of these rosters to resort to? If the conflict is not serious, the individuals may be satisfied with an internal mediator. Or, to ensure privacy, they may prefer an external volunteer mediator. In conflict situations that could result in disciplinary action, reassignment, or termination, or that could have legal implications, the parties may need an external professional mediator who is retained by the organization on a fee-for-service basis.

Recruiting Volunteer Mediators

Criteria for selecting volunteer mediators vary from program to program. However, certain considerations are common to most programs. Most programs, such as our hypothetical SMS program at Carleton, recruit people from a variety of cultural backgrounds, ages, classes, and linguistic groups in order to ensure that the program reflects the diversity of the community it serves. They recruit individuals with prior community experience and a strong commitment to social justice. Generally, volunteer recruits have no formal academic requirements to meet; some of the best mediators are those with significant life experience and not a lot of formal education. People recruiting volunteer mediators also tend to look for the following: good interpersonal and communication skills; proven ability to work both independently and as part of a team; and availability and flexibility with respect to time. Mediation training and experience are looked for in a candidate but may not be required. The

Ontario Ministry of the Attorney General (2010) provides guidelines for selecting mediators, and their criteria are typical of those applied to volunteer mediators.

Training Volunteer Mediators

Most community mediation programs provide their own training for volunteer mediators. Minimum requirements range from 24 to 40 hours. This training covers the following:

- Conflict theory—an introduction to the nature of conflict, responses to conflict, conflict and emotion and how conflict affects communication;
- Communication process and skills—an overview of communication theory and an introduction to practical skills and techniques such as active listening, open-ended questioning, perspective-taking, and reframing; and
- Negotiation and mediation process and skills—theoretical foundations of negotiation and mediation, as well as the techniques needed to move parties from positional bargaining to interest-based communications and perspectives;

Volunteers are by no means fully trained after taking an introductory skills session. After basic training, they begin their apprenticeship in mediation and will likely conduct their first five or six mediations in co-mediation with a skilled and experienced volunteer. The more senior volunteer will help the novice by offering feedback and will report on his or her progress to the program coordinator.

Not all volunteers have an aptitude for mediating, and a significant proportion of the candidates considered will not be called upon for this work. Most community programs have a small (5–8 in number) core group of skilled mediators who provide most of the services to the community program and also mentor new volunteers. The latter may eventually join the core group. Good mediators are critically important to the community-based mediation program. They are the "face" of the program, and if they are not skilled, word will get out locally and the program will lose credibility in the community.

Some programs have implemented program evaluation frameworks, which include client assessments of mediators and the mediation process. These assessments provide ongoing feedback about volunteer performance and, in combination with the evaluations provided by other mediators (for example, by partners in co-mediation sessions), significantly contribute to developing new mediators' capacities and skills.

Mechanisms for Intake and Convening

It is essential for a mediation program to have guidelines and procedures for intake and convening. Most mediation referrals come in one of the following two ways:

1. A prospective client contacts the program directly.
2. A referral agent refers the conflict situation and/or one of the parties involved in it to the program.

As we explained in Chapter 6, the convenor in a mediation program is responsible for a number of tasks: determining whether the conflict situation meets the program criteria; helping the parties determine whether mediation is appropriate for them; and determining, with input from the parties, the logistics of the mediation process and what type of mediator the parties need. Effective convening is critical to the success of a mediation program.

After the program convenor or case manager has developed a good understanding of the conflict situation and the people involved, he or she will select a mediator or mediators with the appropriate skills and experience to conduct the session. Criteria in selecting mediators might include years of experience mediating; the complexity of the case; comfort and experience with high emotion; the parties' level of conflict; the cultural, religious, and/or linguistic background of the parties and/or the mediator; and the mediator's professional background (if the conflict requires substantive knowledge in a particular area).

Rarely do community programs allow the parties themselves to select mediators; the parties are neither likely to have much understanding of the skills and capacities required to mediate nor able to assess their own needs accurately within the process. Nonetheless, if the parties are unhappy with the convenor's selection, they may reject a mediator and request that the program find another before they consent to attend the process.

Educating the Target Population and Marketing the Program

Educating the target population about the services the program provides and marketing the program are two important aspects of every mediation program, as Warters (2000, p. 103) has noted.

A mediation program cannot confer its many benefits if people don't know about it. A program needs to educate the target population, through marketing, about its mediation services and about what types of cases are best suited to these services. In our hypothetical example, Carleton's SMS program would focus on making it known to the student population that certain types of cases—roommate conflicts, student academic group conflicts, tenant–tenant conflicts and landlord–tenant disputes—are well suited to the program's mediation services. A shrewd marketing effort will make it more likely that individuals involved in these kinds of conflicts will be referred to SMS or will contact the program directly.

Managers of mediation programs also need to educate organizational leaders about the qualitative goals of the mediation program—in particular, the goal of developing a culture of collaboration—and about the long-term benefits of achieving these goals. Showing the organization's executive members how its mediation program can contribute to transformation within the organization will ensure that the program gets the support and resources it needs to continue and expand.

Some organizations also provide conflict training to their target population and to their potential referral agents. In 1999, for example, when the newly formed Canada Customs and Revenue Agency instituted a mediation program and other collaborative conflict management methods, it provided its over 40,000 employees with training in interest-based negotiation and conflict resolution.

Referral Agents

In addition to educating and informing the target population, a mediation program needs to identify key referral agents and to develop "effective and consistent referral systems" (Warters, 2000, p. 114). The Carleton SMS program's referral agents might include faculty members, campus housing authorities, off-campus housing agencies, the campus safety service or university police, the student union, student associations, student counselling and health services, departmental chairs, and deans. For the workplace mediation of Danny and Teresa (see Box 8.1, in Chapter 8), possible referral agents could include departmental directors and managers, human resources staff, Employee Assistance Program personnel, union representatives, fellow workers, and others familiar with the situation. By educating potential referral agents on how mediation works and what it can achieve in certain types of cases, a mediation program will increase the likelihood that cases will be referred to it.

Interfacing with Other Programs and Systems

A mediation program will find itself having to interact with other systems within the organization, especially those concerned with dispute resolution, such as the organization's system of discipline. This interaction inevitably occurs when a conflict within the organization involves allegations of wrongdoing or misbehaviour. For example, consider the case of Melissa and Arnold from Chapter 4 (under the heading "Ignore"). To the extent that Arnold's conduct toward Melissa has been excessive, it may warrant some form of organizational discipline. At the same time, mediation may be used to good effect alongside such discipline.

Conflict Management Systems

All organizations have conflict management systems. While some are proactive and strategic, others are reactive and ad hoc, dealing with conflict situations only as they arise. An organization has an *integrated conflict management system* when it has a proactive and "systematic approach to preventing, managing and resolving conflict" within the organization (Society of Professionals in Dispute Resolution (SPIDR),

2001). It has been noted (Ford, 2003; Lynch, 2001; Lynch, 2003; SPIDR, 2001) that an integrated conflict management system or ICMS has the following features:

1. The organization has a centralized coordinating office that works to prevent, identify, and resolve all types of conflict problems and disputes at all levels and among all people within the organization.
2. The organization has multiple access points by which people within the organization may access the resources and processes of the conflict management system. People can "readily identify and access a knowledgeable person whom they trust for advice about the conflict management system" (SPIDR, 2001).
3. The organization has multiple options for resolving any conflict or dispute. These options will include both formal processes (for example, a grievance process or complaint investigation process) and informal ones (for example, negotiation and mediation). The organization will also have sufficient information and resources to help parties choose from among those options.
4. The leadership of the organization fosters a culture of collaboration—a culture that welcomes good-faith dissent and encourages resolution of all conflicts through direct negotiation (SPIDR, 2001). Lynch (2003, p. 104) refers to this as a "fostering and sustaining environment"—in other words, "social and cultural surroundings that empower, encourage and capacitate individuals and communities to … recognize, acknowledge, prevent, address, manage and resolve conflict in a productive, consistent and systematic manner."
5. The organization provides support and systemic access to various conflict resolution options, and it fosters, among all members of the organization, competence in dealing with conflict (SPIDR, 2001). Promoting competence involves providing education and training to all members of the organization.

From 1996 to 2003, there was much optimism that an organization could be transformed and become more collaborative and productive by designing and instituting an integrated conflict management system. In 2003, the Canadian federal government introduced the *Public Service Modernization Act*, one of whose goals was to "foster more collaborative labour-management relations to ensure a healthy and productive workplace" (Treasury Board, 2008). One of the statutory components of this Act was the *Public Service Labour Relations Act*, section 207 of which provides as follows:

> Subject to any policies established by the employer or any directives issued by it, every deputy head in the core public administration must, in consultation with bargaining agents representing employees in the portion of the core public administration for which he or she is deputy head, establish an

> informal conflict management system and inform the employees in that portion of its availability.

This provision required every department in the core public service to establish an informal conflict management system. It was an important step forward for the organizational culture of the government of Canada. Nonetheless, despite what the framers of this statute may have intended, the informal conflict management (ICM) systems introduced by some government departments did not always result in the *integrated* conflict management system we defined above—that is, a proactive and systematic approach to preventing, managing, and resolving conflict. Nor did these ICM systems always commit to or actively foster a culture of collaboration.

Lipsky and Avgar (2010) have identified significant resistance to organizational conflict management systems. This resistance comes both from those with a progressive view of conflict and from those with a traditional view. According to Lipsky and Avgar (2010, p. 11), the former, including unions, civil rights groups, and plaintiff's lawyers, view ICMS as an attempt by management to control the workplace and their employees without really responding to their interests. They view it as an approach instituted by management to appease—but also, ultimately, to control or even manipulate—the organization's employees. Those with a traditional view of conflict—managers and business leaders—believe that conflict management systems "help legitimize workplace conflict and inevitably lead to higher levels of employee participation in decision making than is desirable" (2010, p. 11). Corporate lawyers, too, according to Lipsky and Avgar (2010, p. 41), view ICM systems as undermining managerial authority. As long as the competitive, win–lose culture prevails, it seems that the transformative potential of the ICMS approach will be very limited.

Lipsky and Avgar conclude by saying (2010, p. 42) that designers of conflict management systems need to "move away from a 'one-size-fits-all' approach." The structures and cultures of organizations vary significantly, as do their objectives, so organizations have very different conflict management needs. Managers must design conflict management practices that suit the particular organization.

Community Mediation Programs in Canada

Aboriginal communities in Canada have a robust and lengthy tradition of taking disputes to tribal leaders, elders, and in some cases to the whole community for guidance in resolving conflicts. In mainstream Canada, however, as in most Western nations, the history of community-based dispute resolution is relatively short compared with non-Western nations. Nonetheless, community mediation emerged in this country well before mediation emerged in most other sectors—for example, family, commercial, civil, public policy, and institutional dispute resolution. Only the labour sector, where mediation and conciliation have been used to resolve disputes since the 1920s, has a comparable history. The labour relations field has produced a professional cadre of mediators who, in some cases, have lent their skills to community mediation. On the other hand, other mediators from this sector have taken up more lucrative opportunities in commercial and civil mediation once these latter areas developed.

Mediation and Justice in the Community

Community Justice Initiatives of Kitchener, Ontario claims to be the oldest community mediation service in Canada. Established in 1978, it was set up by Mennonite and Quaker communities. Today's programs reflect the distinct philosophical underpinnings provided by these peace-loving faith communities.

Early programming in community mediation was driven by disillusionment with the criminal justice system. This system, as discussed in Chapter 10, views crime as a deviance to be controlled and punished, sees victims as irrelevant to justice, and applies retributive measures to change behaviour. Various church and community groups, believing that an alternative was needed, sought to address criminal matters in communities actually affected by the crime. Early mediation proponents viewed crime in a new light—that is, as a social problem, and they believed that criminals needed not merely to be punished but to be transformed.

Communities were the foundation for this change—the notion that people who commit crimes should be accountable to their communities and to their individual victims. Where the formal justice system was faceless and anonymous, community processes would be personal, for criminals and victims alike. Community members, for their part, needed to be responsible for problems within their communities; they needed to be empowered to transform social inequities causing or contributing to crime; and they needed to develop empathy for criminals. The processes used in mediation programs were developed with these community-based considerations in mind.

Mediation programs in restorative justice promoted dialogue among the various parties touched by a crime—those who committed it, those who directly suffered its effects, and those living in the community where it occurred. These programs aimed to help people recently released from prison reintegrate into the community. They sought reconciliation between victims and perpetrators, and they sought to heal and repair the harm done to the community by the crime. Community mediation developed as a moral, and not a legal, movement within neighbourhoods. Programs soon expanded to deal with a range of issues in the community, including disputes between neighbours over property and noise, intergenerational and spousal conflict (excepting divorce and separation), tenancy issues, small claims disputes, petty criminal acts, and some public policy conflicts.

In Canada, community-based mediation thus developed as a communitarian and transformative project. Community mediation in the United States was strongly influenced by the civil rights movements. Mediation was viewed as an alternative to a justice system that had proved inaccessible and discriminatory for poor people and for racial and ethnic minorities. Church and community groups in the US developed community-based mediation programs, as they did in Canada. However, the majority of American community mediation schemes were primarily aimed at improving access and justice for the poor and marginalized. The American project had some influence over Canadian community mediation, most notably in its expansion of services, but the access-to-justice goals of American programs were not prominent in the Canadian context.

Canadian community-based programs have maintained their emphasis on having the community take responsibility for social conflict. This orientation is based on their belief that addressing conflict through restorative and healing processes and empowering community members to handle their own conflicts offer far more than does the traditional justice system. Community mediation has remained a social endeavour and a distinct alternative to the formal justice system. Because it was an expression of dissatisfaction with the state system of justice, community-based mediation has seen limited engagement by the state.

Funding Community Programs

In the 1990s, there were more than 100 community programs in Canada. Today, fewer than 30—possibly fewer than 20—of these programs remain. Our number is based on estimates from informed individuals in the field. The uncertainty about the number is owing to the fact that community-based mediation has never been nationally or provincially regulated in Canada and little data has been collected concerning it. When it existed, the Conflict Resolution Network of Canada included approximately 70 percent of community-based mediation programs as members. Today, Peacemakers Trust, a more recent network, lists 14 programs based on self reporting, and this number probably represents only about 50 percent or so of the real total. (For a current listing of programs, see the Peacemakers Trust website in the list of websites at the end of this chapter.)

The declining number of community-based mediation programs in Canada is owing to the lack of funding for these programs. From the mid-1980s to the late 1990s, charitable and community foundations, bar associations, municipalities, provinces, and the federal government's National Crime Prevention fund helped maintain them. In the early years of the 21st century, government funds shifted to support other forms of alternative dispute resolution, particularly court-referred or court-annexed ones, such as family mediation, civil litigation mediation, and ADR for commercial disputes. Spending constraints on the government were one factor in the withdrawal of state funds. Another factor, most likely, was some community mediation programs' stubborn insistence on independence from the state, a stance that was in line with their alternative philosophy.

Programs associated with the courts have continued to receive funding from the government. The restorative justice programs that focus on post-charge, pre-sentencing mediation and alternative measures for youth and Aboriginal peoples have developed closer ties to the police, the prosecutors, and the government officials responsible for ADR programming. Doing so has enabled these programs to maintain their existence. They rely on the police and prosecutors for referrals and on the government officials for funding. Some programs are associated with small claims courts, which refer certain cases to mediation. Other programs, if properly accredited, take on family law cases. All community mediation programs are creatively responding to their need for regular and consistent funding.

Sectors of Community-Based Mediation

Community-based mediation continues to serve a range of people and a variety of conflicts in communities. New sectors benefiting from mediation now include inheritance, health care, workplace, and elder care. Most community programs also take on small claims and small business disputes. Part of the funding in these new conflict areas comes from fees for service, particularly in the small claims, business, and workplace sectors. Public demand has produced a new service area called *conflict coaching*. Conflict coaches advise individuals on how to resolve their own conflicts. The operating expenses of mediation programs are also covered by training fees. Some of the websites listed at the end of this chapter reveal the extent to which fees in these new service areas provide necessary funds for certain mediation programs.

Most programs have a small paid staff to coordinate programs, including a coordinator (or director) and a head trainer. Typical operating budgets are between $40,000 and $65,000 CAD. Volunteer assistance is crucial to the survival of these programs. They are often run by a volunteer management board composed of community leaders and representatives, service providers within the community, and representatives from agencies that refer cases to the program—police, small businesses in the community, and health centres. Volunteers typically reflect the diversity—with respect to ethnicity, language, gender, age, class, and profession—of the community served by the program, and they come from these communities. This serves the ideal of community empowerment and responsibility that is a philosophical basis of mediation.

Mediation Programs in Schools

A number of schools in Canada and the United States have adopted peer mediation and restorative justice programs as a way to respond proactively to many forms of student misconduct, including bullying, violence, and vandalism (Nanavati, Powidajko, & Stalla, 2007; Reimer, 2011; Lewis, 2009; McCullough, 2007; Shafer & Mirsky, 2011). These programs are used in addition to or instead of traditional methods of punitive discipline. The goal of this approach is to empower all members of the school community—students, teachers, administrators, and parents—to take responsibility for creating a safer, more respectful school.

There are a number of different mediation and restorative processes that can be used in a school context. These include classroom circles, peer mediation, and multi-party restorative conferences (Nanavati et al., 2007, p. 24; Reimer, 2011, p. 7). Certain provinces have begun to adopt these processes. In Ontario, individual schools and even some school boards have introduced restorative practice programs. In Nova Scotia, this has been a province-wide collaborative initiative of the provincial government, the school boards, and the schools and communities (Llewellyn, 2009; Shafer & Mirsky, 2011). Much of the restorative practice training in Nova Scotia schools has been done by the International Institute for Restorative Practices Canada (IIRP Canada), which is based in Port Hope, Ontario. IIRP Canada is an organization that has developed and provided training for restorative practice programs in schools in Ontario, Nova Scotia, and other parts of Canada.

There is a growing body of evidence showing that restorative practice programs in schools, when properly funded and supported, can help make schools and communities safe, respectful, and inclusive. (Nanavati et al., 2007; McCullough, 2007; Lewis, 2009; Reimer, 2011; Shafer & Mirsky, 2011)

Evaluation of Processes, Programs, and Systems

While scholarship is moving us closer to understanding what we do when we mediate and why we do it, there are still relatively few studies that examine the extent to which mediation processes are effective at achieving their stated goals. Most of the research that has taken place has focused on client satisfaction in the context of court-mandated or institutional programs; see, for example, Macfarlane (1995) and Bingham and Pitts (2002.) Since these programs were established to respond to delays in the justice or regulatory system, researchers are most interested in whether clients receive timely service, how that affects the dispute, the effects of the process on their satisfaction levels, and the outcomes.

Evaluating mediation is made more difficult because most mediators believe that the qualitative difference between mediation and more formal dispute resolution mechanisms lies in the *process* and not, necessarily, the *outcomes*. Capturing and measuring philosophical differences is not an easy task—it is much simpler to compare outcomes than to compare processes. A further problem arises when contrasting formal court proceedings with the process of mediation, since measuring process benefits is a more subtle undertaking—often it is like comparing apples and oranges. These evaluations, which rely on client self-disclosure and self-assessment, are nonetheless useful in understanding client reactions to mediated processes.

Not all mediation programs, and certainly not all mediators, have the same objectives. Community mediation programs seek to transform social relations in their neighbourhoods, whereas commercial mediators are often more interested in ensuring that their clients arrive at settlements that they can live with. For mediators and mediation programs that have still other goals—moral growth, transformation through insights, or empowering those on the margins—it is important that they and others who wish to develop similar programs evaluate what they are achieving. We also need to learn more about the expectations of the parties themselves. Are parties able to achieve their objectives through mediated processes? Do their objectives change as they work through the process? Are they empowered and transformed? Data derived from qualitative research—and the documentation of different modes of mediation—is critical to the continued improvement of the field. We already know from one study (Welsh, 2001) that one of the key principles of mediation—namely, self-determination—can no longer be taken for granted, and that it needs to be protected if mediation is to continue to be qualitatively different from the dispute resolution process found in the courts.

A closely related issue is how the public, government, institutional, and corporate consumers of mediation services view the goals and objectives of mediation and mediation programs. A challenge in recent years, particularly for the non-profit, community-based mediation sector, has been the relatively low public and government support for such programs. This support is unlikely to increase without readily demonstrable economic and social benefits; program-outcome data is becoming more and more essential. In Canada, government funding is often required to establish and sustain these programs, to achieve the long-term "macro" or social benefits they can produce. To the extent that such mediation programs can be shown to produce long-term social and economic benefits, the weight of public opinion and political support will decide whether, and to what extent, they deserve short-term funding. Let's look at what an outcome evaluation of a mediation program would need to include.

Conducting an Outcome Evaluation

Outcome evaluation focuses on whether and to what extent the specific, tangible goals and objectives established for the program have been achieved. Such an evaluation focuses on the outcomes of the program and the program's ability to document them, with particular attention to the following goals:

1. to document *what happened* (rather than *how it happened*) in terms of utility or frequency; and
2. to document *what changed* as a result of the program.

Program outcome evaluations generally ask questions about the program's activity level with respect to mediating cases and training mediators. For example, how many mediators were trained? How many cases went to mediation? How many cases were resolved in mediation? Outcome evaluations also focus on showing what changes occurred, which is measured through pre-test and post-test designs. In other words volunteer mediators are tested before they have undertaken any training (pre-test) and then they are given the same test once their training is completed. This is a way of tracking their advances or changes in knowledge and attitude. This type of evaluation design could also be used to test transformation among clients, but it is less commonly used for that. The types of outcomes being evaluated generally include the following:

- skills and abilities learned;
- behaviours and attitudes changed;
- the extent to which the program was used; and
- the economic, relational, or infrastructure resources that were created as a result of the program.

The evaluation of a program may address tangible goals, such as participant satisfaction, cost-effectiveness, case management, and resolution time frames. It may also address intangible goals, such as the empowerment and transformation of the parties involved, the positive changes to their morale or psychological well-being, or the cultural change within an organization. Community mediation programs that rely on volunteers to act as mediators frequently look at whether volunteers have been transformed by their involvement in the mediation program.

Challenges and Risks of Mediation

To fully appreciate how mediation is used in organizations, institutions, and other contexts, we need to consider its challenges and risks, as well as the criticisms sometimes levelled at it. Recognizing the risks will help us to avoid them, and addressing the criticisms will help us to respond to and overcome them.

The risks and challenges of mediation exist at three levels:

1. individual cases (the micro level);
2. organizations, institutions, or communities (the systemic level); and
3. the whole society (the macro level).

Individual Risks

There are a number of reasons why there may be a risk of injustice to one or more of the parties in a given mediation, including the following:

- power imbalances,
- lack of procedural safeguards,
- cultural or other bias, and
- possible infringement of a party's legal rights.

Power Imbalances

In most if not all mediations, there is some power imbalance between the parties. Mediators need to be able to recognize and address the various power differentials, which may involve personal power, positional power, or social and economic power. In some relationships, such as those between spouses or between parents and children, there may be long-standing patterns of power-based interaction that the mediator will need to uncover.

In Chapter 6, we discussed convening as the process for determining whether mediation is appropriate for a given case. We discussed a number of situations where mediation may not be appropriate—for example, where one party has been subjected to violence, abuse, or intimidation by the other party; where one party is vulnerable to the other's manipulation, deceit, or harm; or where one party lacks mental or emotional capacity. In such cases, where one party has an unfair advantage over the other, the use of mediation may involve the risk of an unjust outcome. Even with good convening, there is a risk that cases that should be screened out will slip through. The mediator therefore needs to be vigilant throughout the mediation process to ensure that one party does not take unfair advantage of the other, either intentionally or unintentionally. Ensuring that the less powerful party's voice is heard and understood is an important role of the mediator. That said, he or she needs to be careful not to overcompensate or to address the needs of one party at the expense of the other. By ensuring that all voices are heard, all parties are understood, and that the interests and needs of all parties are revealed, the mediator contributes to a process that is mutually beneficial and just for all.

If at any time the mediator suspects that an unfair advantage may be developing, he or she should take steps to stop it—by, for example, meeting privately with one or both parties or even by terminating the mediation.

Lack of Procedural Safeguards

Courts and tribunals have established procedures to ensure due process and procedural justice. The rules of evidence ensure that only reliable types of information may be considered as evidence and that this information is presented in ways that are fair and consistent for all parties. The fact that legal hearings usually occur in a public forum—in "open court"—further ensures a process that is fair, accountable and just for all.

Mediation, by comparison, has no required standards or procedural safeguards, only voluntary ones that professional member associations set. Because mediation is a private, confidential process, it will only be the parties and those who accompany them who are aware of what a mediator does in the mediation process. Mediators are not openly accountable in the way that adjudicators are in the public court process. Therefore, mediation programs need to have ways to evaluate mediators and mediation processes. Many of the risks and challenges of mediation are resolved through sound mediation practices, along with checks and balances to ensure that these practices are being followed.

Cultural or Other Bias

Every mediator and every mediation process has some cultural bias; it is inevitable. As LeBaron and Zumeta (2003, p. 464) observe, "Since naming disputes is a cultural act, deciding how to frame and respond to them is also completely bound up with culture." Any form of bias, whether it is the mediator's own bias or an element that arises in the mediation process, may cause injustice, and mediators must be vigilant in this regard.

According to the 2011 Canadian census (Statistics Canada, 2011), 20.6 percent of the Canadian population is foreign-born. The proportion of foreign-born Canadians is expected to grow significantly in years to come. With this prospect, mediation practitioners need to work to achieve *cultural competence* in their practices (Barsky, Este, & Collins, 1996; LeBaron, 2003; Sue, Arrendondo, & McDavis, 1992). Possessing such competence involves the following:

- Learning to recognize possible cultural problems or sources of cultural bias (assumptions, values, world views) in mediation, especially the mediator's own expectations of others' behaviour and the meaning he or she attributes to that behaviour. (In other words, the mediator must have *self-awareness*).
- Being open and nonjudgmental in actively striving to understand the world views of clients from different cultural backgrounds. (In other words, the mediator must have *an open attitude*).
- Employing culturally relevant and sensitive skills and interventions with people from different cultural backgrounds. (In other words, the mediator must have *cultural skills*).

To be culturally competent mediators, we need to be aware of the cultural biases that will be inherent in our practice of mediation, and we must take steps to address them and adjust our approach accordingly.

Our cultural assumptions affect us reflexively and easily escape our awareness. For example, consider your responses to the following questions:

- *How are conflicts defined?* Consider a fistfight between two neighbouring children. Is it a problem of social relations or a problem involving the violation of rights (for example, an assault)? In Canada, individual legal rights are increasingly given priority over communal relations. Therefore, one child's family, especially if the child has been hurt, is quite likely to call the police and have the other child charged with assault.

- *What approaches should be used to resolve conflicts?* We have already discussed traditional methods for resolving community conflict. In many cultures, respected community leaders make decisions on behalf of the community. In a multicultural society, these methods coexist with more formalized third-party dispute resolution. In the case of the children's fistfight, which method or methods might be employed by the families to resolve the conflict?
- *Who do you consider to be directly involved in the conflict?* Is the conflict limited to the two children or does it also involve the families and perhaps other neighbours? The principle enshrined in the African proverb—"It takes a village to raise a child"—is practised in many countries. In these societies, if there were a fistfight between children, extended family and other community members might be found discussing the problem together. Who do *you* think should be present for such a discussion?
- *What are public versus private topics?* In any society, certain topics are considered too shameful to discuss in front of others. Many societies, for example, include rape or sexual assault in this category. Some societies are comfortable with queries about such matters as salaries, ages, or family status. Other societies are not. Some might consider it inappropriate to discuss children's aggressive behaviour in public? What is your view?
- *Which communication patterns and other interactions are common to the group?* In Chapter 5 (under the heading "Understanding Communication"), we discussed high- and low-context communication patterns, as well as the notions of assertiveness and directness. If one of the families talks about the children's behaviour by telling a story or parable to illustrate the problem of aggression, would you listen with interest or would you become impatient or, perhaps, consider that the storyteller was being evasive?

This list touches on key cultural differences in the way conflict is identified, discussed, and resolved. The questions should stimulate you to consider your own preferences and assumptions regarding these variable cultural values. Keep in mind that these values can change and evolve as people move in and out of their original cultural frameworks and are exposed to others. Still, our original values inevitably shape how we make sense of the world around us, organize our relationships, understand authority and rules, and deal with problems. We are often not conscious of our values concerning conflict until we are confronted by opposing ones.

Possible Infringement of a Party's Legal Rights

In many contexts, especially court-connected mediation, mediation is conducted within a legal framework in which parties' rights and obligations are articulated and understood. In Chapter 7 (under the heading "The Role of Lawyers in Mediation"), we discussed the role of lawyers and other advisers in helping to ensure that parties in mediation know their rights and make fully informed decisions. However, in cases where parties do not have legal advice, they need to know that the mediator cannot be their legal adviser.

A mediator may provide basic legal information. For example, in mediating the divorce dispute between Paul and Jo-Anne (see Exercise 1, at the end of Chapter 3), the mediator may inform the parties about the basic provisions of the *Family Law Act* and about the *Federal Child Support Guidelines*. However, it is not appropriate or ethical for the mediator to provide legal advice to either party. And, unless she is an evaluative mediator, the mediator will not express an opinion about the possible or likely legal outcome of the dispute.

Family Mediation Canada's (FMC) Members Code of Professional Conduct sets out the following responsibilities for mediators:

- To help the participants reach an informed and voluntary agreement that meets both their mutual needs, interests, and concerns, and those of other persons affected by the dispute (Article 3.3).
- To promote "the participants' awareness of the interests of others affected by the dispute and by the proposed agreement and to assist the participants to consider the separate and individual needs of such other persons" (Article 3.4).
- To help parties reflect upon and consider "how their proposed arrangements realistically meet the needs and best interests of other affected persons, especially vulnerable persons" (Article 8.2).
- To ensure that the participants "reach agreement freely, voluntarily, without undue influence, and on the basis of informed consent" (Article 9.1).
- To ensure procedural fairness—to ensure, in other words, "that each participant has an opportunity to speak and to be heard in mediation, and to articulate his or her own needs, interests and concerns" (Article 9.2).
- To ensure that each party "has had an opportunity to understand the implications and ramifications of available options and, if a party needs either additional information or assistance in order for the negotiations to proceed in a fair and orderly manner ... to refer the individual to appropriate resources" (Article 9.5).

Article 9, section 6 of the FMC Members Code of Professional Conduct sums up the mediator's responsibilities with respect to agreements that do not accord with legal guidelines or community expectations, but do reflect the parties' sense of fairness and their cultural values:

> It is a fundamental principle of mediation that competent and informed participants can reach an agreement which may not correspond to legal guidelines contained in the relevant statutes or case law or that does not correspond with

general community expectations and standards. The mediator, however, has a duty to assist the participants to assess the feasibility and practicality of any proposed agreement in both the long and short term, in accordance with the participant's own subjective criteria of fairness, taking cultural differences into account.

Organizational Risks

As we discussed in Chapter 6 (under the heading "Task 5: Determining Suitability for Mediation"), using mediation for certain types of disputes, such as workplace harassment or discrimination, may suppress wrongdoing and privatize injustice without resolving it. Because mediation is a private, non-public process, some allege that it does not always hold wrongdoers publicly accountable for the harm they have done.

Discrimination or active wrongdoing may be systemic within an organization, pervading its culture and structure. Regarding such cases, critics charge that mediation, though it may provide an individual complainant with some form of redress, is unlikely to change the deeper organizational defects that gave rise to the complaint. They say that mediation in such a context, by resolving the dispute privately and thereby removing the stimulus for reform, will effectively perpetuate or preserve the unjust status quo

Societal Risks

Many of the critiques of mediation concern its influence at the macro or societal level. Some of the early critiques came from those who were altogether opposed to mediation, asserting that it exerts covert state control (Abel, 1982) and that alternative dispute resolution has transformed disputes over facts and legal rights into conflicts over feelings and relationships (Merry, 1990; Nader, 1988; Harrington, 1985). According to these critics, certain features of mediation—its private nature, its lack of procedural rules, and the fact that most mediators come from the most privileged classes—result in mediated agreements that uphold the status quo of unequal social relations. Over two decades ago, Scimecca (1991) asserted that ADR, as a movement, had lost sight of its original purpose—to provide social justice, particularly to the poor.

Another criticism is that the transformative goal of mediation is mistaken. Retributive justice advocates, in particular, claim that restorative approaches are soft on crime and undermine the goals of the criminal justice system—deterrence, peace and order, and social security. In effect, they believe that the transformative promise of restorative justice is a false one. Retributive justice advocates point to cases where criminals have got off with a "slap on the wrist," only to offend again. And, in some cases, they are right; that has happened and will happen again. But it does not have to be that way. Restorative processes need not be soft or lenient on offenders. In fact, as we saw in Chapter 10 (see the case studies in that chapter), restorative processes have been successfully applied both before and after an offender has been held fully accountable by the standards of the retributive criminal justice system.

As mediation processes continue to be applied in new arenas of conflict, the question of how and to what extent these processes serve justice will always be raised. This is particularly true in societies that have just emerged from conflict and are trying to come to terms with past injustice and oppression. Martha Minow, in *Between Vengeance and Forgiveness* (1998), eloquently articulates the tension between restorative, reparative, and retributive practices of justice in her overview of how societies attempt to heal after large-scale atrocities and tragedies, such as those that occurred in Rwanda and the former Yugoslavia. Reviewing the various options—trials, truth and reconciliation commissions, and reparations—she concludes by encouraging us not to be silent about these issues.

Increasingly, healing processes that attempt to balance justice imperatives are being used for issues that warrant them, such as environmental mediation. However, these methods are not without critics, for many of the same reasons discussed previously, including the fear that entitlements, rights, and even social progress may be traded off.

Notwithstanding these important concerns, there is reason for optimism. Many of those who manage programs in mediation are believers in its ideals and transformative potential. Perhaps they have received training from outside institutions that promote relationship-enhancing mediation, or they might have been private practice mediators who have been convinced to join an institution in the hopes of shaping its programs in a meaningful way. Even if the leaders of institutions adopt mediation for the sole purpose of lowering costs, good consequences can result. Parties are able to preserve or enhance relationships through this process and, in most models of mediation, they do gain insight into themselves and into the parties with whom they are in conflict.

The Profession of Mediation

In this section, we consider how people wishing to be mediators enter the field and obtain training as mediators. We also discuss how mediation, as a profession, responds to the challenges and risks we have identified above.

Education and Training

Mediation practitioners have no single set of legal or national educational requirements. Training programs vary greatly, and, unlike other professions, mediators have no governing body mandated to establish and enforce minimum training qualifications. To complicate things, there is no proof of a correlation between education or training and successful mediation.

The standards that inform educational requirements for mediators exist only as recommended guidelines, which are non-enforceable. For the most part, professional mediation organizations set these guidelines, and these differ depending on the context in which mediation is being used. The discussion that follows is based on the standards set by three bodies (see Appendix C):

- Family Mediation Canada,
- the Association for Conflict Resolution, and
- ADR Institute of Canada.

Looking at the standards set by these three organizations, we see more common goals—confidentiality, impartiality, informed consent, and self-determination—than divergent ones.

Mediators seeking to enter the field should ask themselves the following questions:

- Why do I want to be a mediator?
- What education, training, and experience do I already have that will lend itself to this type of work?
- What types of conflicts am I interested in mediating—family, workplace, commercial, community, environmental, public policy?

With some sense of what they want in these regards, mediators will be better able to determine the educational or training resources that best suit their needs. Most people who currently work in private practice as full-time mediators in Canada have a professional degree in areas such as law, social work, business, education, or management to support their more specialized training in mediation.

What Specialized Training Do Mediators Need?

Mediators need to acquire theoretical knowledge as well as the skills and techniques required to intervene in a wide array of conflict situations and with diverse groups of people. They also need to develop a personal style that is rooted in their world views and cultural orientations. What's more, we concur with Lang and Taylor (2000) in affirming that mediators need to be aware of their core philosophy of human interaction to sustain them through the difficulties they will inevitably face.

The beliefs, knowledge, and skills required to be a successful mediator are developed through studies, coached practice, and ongoing interaction with others. It is a lifelong learning process of questioning, experimenting, discovering, and refining. As with any profession, some learning will be acquired through practical, on-the-job experience; other learning comes from books, lectures, group discussions, peer review, and other classroom or workshop activities.

Regardless of where mediators take their training, courses of study should cover three broad areas:

1. the process skills for analyzing, approaching, and resolving disputes;
2. the social and conflict theories embedded in these processes; and
3. the tools for becoming a reflective practitioner.

Typically, introductory mediation training programs cover basic conflict resolution, negotiation and mediation theory, communication skills, collaborative conflict resolution strategies, and principles of reflective practice. In addition to training in the science of mediation, mediators should also develop non-traditional skills. Introductory mediation rarely addresses this area, although advanced training courses are increasingly recognizing the importance of intuitive, somatic, and experiential knowledge. Training modules that address these topics can usually be found in courses that address emotional intelligence, creativity, and intuitive development. Mediators will be guaranteed to find at least a handful of workshops in this area if they attend a mediation conference. "Using Metaphors in Mediation," "Martial Arts and Mediation—The Yin and the Yang," and "Tapping into Your Creativity in Mediation" are just a few titles of workshops that have been offered at mediation conferences.

As a minimum requirement, many institutionalized professional programs suggest 40 hours of training—after training in such disciplines as law, social work, education, or business management. Given the requirements of other recognized professions, the 40-hour (or 5-day) training standard seems far from sufficient to realize the larger social and more holistic visions of mediation. Consider, for example, how much training someone who is learning to play a sport or a musical instrument typically receives. In Canada, a youngster who aspires to play hockey at a high or even a professional level will participate in literally thousands of hours of training and coaching sessions over a period of 10 or 15 years. To reach their full potential, mediators should consider basic or introductory training as only the beginning of their journey to becoming competent practitioners.

University and College Programs

In the early days of mediation training, most training programs were offered in the private sector by professional trainers. There were relatively few university or college programs that were dedicated to the study of conflict or that specialized in mediation or other conflict resolution skills and practices. Over the past decade, the fields of conflict resolution and peace studies have become institutionalized; they are recognized academic subjects within universities and colleges. Interestingly, there are more graduate-level programs than undergraduate ones. This is probably because individuals coming into the field tend to be mid- to upper-career professionals who are looking for a new career path, making plans for what they will do after they retire from their current positions, or who have been assigned responsibilities that involve conflict resolution work. Many already have undergraduate degrees, have taken professional development courses, and now want to support their skills-based training in conflict resolution with a theoretical foundation.

For the most part, these programs specialize in particular areas. For example, the master's program at the University of Victoria focuses on public policy dispute resolution, while the one at Royal Roads is directed toward peace and security. The master's program at Saint Paul's University in Ottawa focuses on international, ethnocultural, and religious conflicts. The joint Master of Arts in Peace and Conflict Studies offered by the Conflict Resolution Studies Program at the University of Winnipeg, in cooperation with the Arthur V. Mauro Centre for Peace and Justice at St. Paul's College at the University of Manitoba, educates students in the analysis of social conflicts. This program covers, among other topics, the structural roots of social divisions and inequalities, as well as strategies for transforming conflict and promoting social justice. Most law schools offer courses and opportunities to specialize in ADR. The University of British Columbia's Law School, for example, offers dispute resolution as a specialty. The University of Ottawa Law School has been a pioneer in introducing mediation and ADR to all of its first-year law school students.

At the undergraduate level, two of the more established programs are at Menno Simons University in Winnipeg and Conrad Grebel University College in Waterloo, Ontario. Although there are few degree programs, most if not all universities offer conflict resolution and mediation courses in a range of disciplines, including sociology, psychology, political science, international relations, law, and social work. Individuals can often enroll as special students, if they are not interested in embarking on a full program.

Some Canadian universities offer certificate and diploma programs rather than full degree programs. For example, Carleton University in Ottawa offers an academic, for-credit, diploma program at the graduate level. Various universities, including Queen's, Dalhousie, Toronto, York, Mount St. Vincent, McMaster, Prince Edward Island, and Sherbrooke, offer non-credit certificate programs through their continuing education departments. College programs include those offered through the Justice Institute of British Columbia, Laurentian University, Mount Royal, and Humber College. Certificate and diploma programs require students to take multiple courses and, in some cases, to participate in a practicum or pass a skills assessment to graduate.

To find out more about university-based programs, explore some of the websites listed at the end of this chapter.

Professional Development Programs

Until recently, professional development courses provided most of the formal training in mediation. Many courses span 40 hours and primarily focus on the acquisition of skills. As mediation practice has increased, private sector courses—offered by for-profit or non-profit charitable organizations—have begun to flourish. Increasing numbers of students want some form of certification in a designated area, even though certification of this kind only means that the student has completed a particular program of study in a particular organization. Some of these courses or programs provide some form of skills- and knowledge-based evaluation; others only provide certificates of attendance, without any assessment component. Individuals can find out about training courses in their area by consulting the home pages of Family Mediation Canada and the ADR Institute of Canada. The websites for these and other organizations are listed at the end of this chapter.

In-House Training Programs and Other Short Courses

Organizations wanting to build a culture that includes collaborative problem solving are beginning to offer their staff short courses in conflict resolution and mediation. These courses are useful in educating staff members about conflict resolution and how to access in-house mediation services and other resources for dealing with conflicts. They are also designed to provide employees with the management tools to deal with conflict when it first surfaces. These types of courses are generally not designed to train people to mediate.

Half- or full-day courses are often offered at professional conferences. Focused on specialized topics or issues, these workshops are led by individuals who practise in the field.

Mentoring Programs

Learning happens through experience; training alone is rarely sufficient. Students preparing to go into practice on their own still need—and want—some mentoring and developmental assistance after their training program is concluded. Our experience with community-based mediation programs that use volunteers bears this out. The number of volunteer applicants far exceeds the positions available.

As with other social and mental health professions, would-be mediators commonly search for mentoring and co-mediation opportunities to develop their skills. Unfortunately, mentoring is largely a hit-and-miss opportunity in Canada, because there are few mediators who offer this service, with few guidelines for mentoring if they do. Students can find the lack of mentoring opportunities frustrating and confusing. The reality is that it takes time to mentor properly and, because few practitioners mediate full time, the opportunities are limited. One approach is to find parties who want mediation and then call on an experienced practitioner to mentor and coach or, better still, to work as a co-mediator, with debriefing and feedback after the mediation. In this situation, any fees for the mediation would go to the mentor as payment for his or her time. In this way, the new mediator will take responsibility for getting the business, and gain experience and some one-on-one training in a real situation, while the mentor earns some income—a win–win arrangement.

New mediators often ask if they can observe a mediation. The answer is usually "no." In many cases, parties do not like to be observed in this way, and having observers may detract from the process. Instead, we sometimes offer to co-mediate with inexperienced mediators, as a way of giving them needed experience. Needless to say, we ensure that the person is capable of participating as a co-mediator. Once new mediators find someone they would like to learn from, they should create a mentoring plan, which should include learning goals and objectives, proposed roles and responsibilities, expectations, time frames, and fees. People should not expect experienced mediators to mentor for free.

Given the scarcity of established mediators willing to mentor someone new, and given a market that values reputation and experience, new mediators have few opportunities to get themselves experienced enough for practice. This problem will not solve itself. The field needs to find ways to address ongoing learning for would-be practitioners.

The Regulation of Mediation

Mediation practice contains a complex set of interrelated and sometimes contradictory goals. On the one hand, it has the potential to generate inexpensive, efficient, and speedy settlements. Additionally, it offers a forum where individuals have more opportunity to tell their stories, and more creative space to invent solutions (LeBaron, 1994). Those mediation advocates who call for regulation seek the legitimacy and recognition accorded to other professionals, fearing that if practitioners do not set their own standards, less informed bureaucrats and policy makers will try to do it for them. Those on the other side of the debate fear that inappropriate barriers for entry to the field will be created and broad dissemination of peace-making skills hampered. Picard (1994, p. 155) believes that "the fear of creating a monopoly lies at the heart of the credentials debate." She speculates that only mediators who deal with legal, corporate, public policy, and international disputes will become legitimized through certification, while those who work in community-based and volunteer programs will be marginalized. In turn, non-adversarial dispute settlement options will become available only to the elite and wealthy—the very situation that mediation originally set out to change. While the debate goes on, the reality is that professional organizations and government departments have gone ahead and set standards of practice. Although, for the most part, they are advisory, not mandatory, they do set the bar for what practicing professional mediators need to know and do.

Some researchers (Kolb, 1994; Moore, 2003) have examined the areas of education, training, skills, and experience to consider what may contribute to mediator competency. Others (for example, Honeyman, 1990) have gone further, by proposing minimum standards for developing a "professional" status for the field of mediation. Even current job postings for mediators have established minimum criteria for applicants. Yet, there is no consensus on which minimum standards are advisable or achievable (Picard, 1994; Waldman, 1996).

Even when there is agreement on the idea of minimum standards, considerable debate continues about the criteria that should be used in setting them. Given the variety of mediation models, there is no agreement in the field on generic standards of practice, let alone the qualifications that mediators need in order to meet these standards. Since what constitutes success in mediation is contested, how can we possibly set generic standards for achieving diverse goals and objectives?

Moreover, depending upon whether regulation is input- or output-oriented, the criteria would be quite distinct (Reeve, 1998). Output regulation would rest on quality standards for services, such as client satisfaction with the process and outcomes, and satisfaction with the mediator's comportment. Input regulation would refer to the qualifications required for a mediator to gain certification. Inputs would need to include certain levels of education, experience, training, and skills. Much of the current discussion about regulation concerns both input and output elements.

Standards of Mediation

In the future, regulation, if deemed necessary, could take two forms:

- standards could be set by the government, or
- the practice of mediation could become self-regulating, similar to the medical and legal professions.

Given the diversity of the field, no single area of practice is likely to be able to set standards for all mediation applications, since standards will vary depending on the context in which mediation is practised. A mediator for a divorcing couple who want to sort out custody arrangements will need competencies that are quite distinct from a mediator who is facilitating a healing circle within an Aboriginal community or one who is mediating a construction dispute.

To some extent, consumers do help to maintain quality control in the field, because ineffective mediators are unlikely to receive work, especially when clients are paying for the service. Reputations are important, and good mediators are recommended by former clients, mediation service coordinators, and other mediators. In fact, new mediators often have a tough time breaking into the field—they do not possess the experience needed to develop a reputation. That said, it is risky to rely only on word of mouth and a record of success when you are choosing a mediator, given the subjective nature of success in the differing contexts of the field.

Government licensing raises several problems. There is little agreement or knowledge about what qualifications produce effective mediators. In light of this, standards that are determined from one perspective could eliminate competent mediators from practising. Given the evolving nature of mediation, setting standards today could inadvertently "freeze" dynamic practice and eliminate innovation in the field. The new areas of practice and types of mediation that we have seen emerge over the past decade or so might not have been developed if rigid practice standards had been in place. Finally, there is a concern that, as a result of licensing, one particular group could dominate the field.

Whether provincial governments in Canada will ever legislate requirements for general mediator licensing or certification, or whether they should, remains an open question. In the United States, some states "license" mediators, while others "register" or "certify" them through institutionalized certification programs. In Canada, the marketplace is establishing such standards—and no doubt will continue to do so in the future.

The professional group that seems best placed to dominate the field is lawyers. The recent institutionalization of mediation within the legal field has produced a specialized field of ADR lawyering. Law schools now have significant mediation programs. Picard and Saunders (2002, p. 235) state that "the danger ahead for the regulation of mediation is not only that these groups will occupy and colonize the practice (or at least its profitable sectors), but also that they will do the same on the regulatory front." This would be a great loss to the transformative or communitarian goals of mediation, which have not been found in court-mandated or tribunal types of mediation. Court-mandated mediation is also one of the few areas where the process is mandatory, making the consumer a captive client. These clients are developing knowledge and experience of only one form of mediation practice. Picard and Saunders see that future standards of mediation are being set by legal and state professionals to the detriment of practitioners whose practices have broader social goals.

A number of mediation organizations have established mediation standards of practice and codes of conduct, including the following that are found in Appendix C:

- Family Mediation Canada,
- Association for Conflict Resolution, and
- ADR Institute of Canada.

Mediator Certification and Ethics

Although there is no centralized governing body for mediators, some universities, training institutes, mediation organizations, and mediation programs certify mediators. People who are certified usually have basic levels of mediator aptitude and competence, an understanding of a body of principles and ethical guidelines, and a commitment to a code of conduct.

Certification standards define requirements for training, experience, education, skills, and abilities to meet a minimum level of competence. They provide consumers with some level of assurance that these requirements have been met.

Certification Standards in Canada

The acceptance and institutionalization of mediation have expanded rapidly over the past few years, with a proliferation of court-connected, government, and community mediation programs. Most of these programs have certification requirements based on certain minimum qualification standards—for training, experience, and subject matter and process knowledge. For example, mediators with the Canadian Human Rights Commission are required to have, in addition to mediation training and experience, some level of knowledge and experience with human rights issues and cases. You will find the requirements and procedures for the certification processes of the following organizations on their websites listed at the end of this chapter:

- Family Mediation Canada,
- Association for Conflict Resolution, and
- ADR Institute of Canada.

Even if a mediator's practice area does not require certification, we advocate following standards that have been set by the mediation profession through various organizations, including Family Mediation Canada, the Association for Conflict Resolution, and ADR Canada, to name a few. These member associations reflect the collective knowledge, expertise, and efforts of many individuals and groups working in the field of mediation. Following these standards demonstrates a desire to be accountable and to hold a high level of practice.

Summary

In this chapter, we have expanded our discussion of mediation practices, considering the design and evaluation of structured mediation programs and conflict management systems in both public and private sector organizations and in communities. In organizations, the introduction of integrated conflict management systems is an important element in fostering a culture of collaboration, and it can help these organizations become more "conflict competent."

Within such conflict management systems, mediation programs often exist alongside other more formal approaches, such as formal disciplinary hearings or grievance processes. Referral agents within the organization play an important role in determining which kinds of disputes are suitable for mediation and which require more formal dispute resolution or investigative processes. Consequently, it is important for referral agents and other members of the organization or target community to be well informed about the advantages of mediation and the nature of the mediation process. Without effective marketing of the program and support from referral agents and other key personnel in the organization, the full potential of these mediation programs may not be realized.

We have also examined some of the challenges and risks facing mediation practitioners, and the forms of training available for would-be mediators. While early forms of mediation training were largely provided either by private sector trainers or by organizations seeking to train a cadre of volunteer mediators, over the past decade the field of conflict resolution and peace studies has become more entrenched in university and college institutions, with courses and programs at both the undergraduate and graduate levels. Despite this institutional acceptance of the profession of mediation, many people entering the profession continue to find it difficult to obtain mentoring opportunities with established mediators, or to obtain the practical experience in mediation or co-mediation they need to develop a professional reputation as a mediator. As a profession, mediation still lacks a centralized, official organization that establishes standards of competency, ethics, and professional training for mediators in all fields of mediation practice. Nor is there consensus among all mediation practitioners about the need for such standards, given the diversity of mediation practice styles and of mediation goals.

With no single authoritative standard, professional organizations such as Family Mediation Canada, the Association for Conflict Resolution, and the Canadian Bar Association have developed different standards of professional practice for specialized areas of mediation. We expect an ongoing conversation among mediators and mediation organizations about the need for standards of professional mediation practice, and we expect this conversation to be productive.

We hope that the knowledge you have gained from this book will enable you to respond more effectively to whatever conflict challenges you may encounter in the future, whether as a party, as a mediator, or as some other kind of conflict practitioner.

DISCUSSION QUESTIONS AND EXERCISES

1. Why should the leaders of any organization want to have a mediation program for all people within the organization? Why do all organizations with a population of 100 or more people not have mediation programs?
2. Why is it so important for a mediation program to have effective evaluation processes? What will this achieve for the mediation program and the organization or community it serves?
3. Think of a conflict that may require the services of a mediator.
   a. What questions would you ask of a mediator to ensure that he or she had the qualifications to intervene in this particular dispute?
   b. Do you think you would be able to determine who is or is not a good mediator for this conflict, based on your questions?
   c. If yes, explain why, and if not, why not?
4. You are starting a community-based mediation program.
   a. How might program evaluation help you in starting or maintaining your new program?
   b. What kinds of evidence would be most persuasive to potential funders of a mediation program in your community?
5. You are the manager of a mediation program in your organization.
   a. What are your primary responsibilities and challenges?

   b. What are some of the things you need to do to ensure that mediation is used in a way that is beneficial and just for all of the people in your organization?
6. A couple has been referred to you for mediation.* They are originally from another country and have asked to include their extended families in the mediation. At the mediation, the woman's family is highly participatory; they respond to the questions you are posing rather than allowing her to speak on her own behalf. As you watch the woman, you have the sense that she is uncomfortable with the direction that the mediation is taking—namely, trying to convince her not to leave her marriage. At the same time, she is appearing to agree with her family. The husband's family is more passive, leaving him to do the talking. When you discussed the prospect of the families attending the mediation, you didn't think that this would happen. Now you are concerned about the course the mediation is taking and the possible impact that it is having on the woman.
   a. What do you think is going on?
   b. How do you interpret this behaviour through your own values?
   c. What can you do? What do you think you should do?
   d. What lessons can you take away from this for the future?
7. You are providing training in effective communication in conflict situations to a small community in another country. Three older men from the training have come to see you about resolving a conflict in their community. They begin the discussion by asking you about your family and community. After an hour and a half, you have learned more about their families and some detail about the community, but you still don't know what the conflict is about. You only have another half hour before you resume the training workshop. You would like to learn more about the conflict, but you do not know how to get there.
   a. What do you think is going on?
   b. How do you interpret this behaviour according to your own values?
   c. What can you do? What do you think you should do?
   d. What are the lessons here for the future?

FURTHER READING

Costantino, C., & Merchant, C. (1996). *Designing conflict management systems: A guide to creating productive and healthy organizations*. San Francisco: Jossey-Bass.

Katsh, E., & Rifkin, J. (2001). *Online dispute resolution: Resolving conflicts in cyberspace*. San Francisco: Jossey-Bass.

Lang, M., & Taylor, A. (2000). *The making of a mediator*. San Francisco: Jossey-Bass.

LeBaron, M. (2003). *Bridging cultural conflicts: A new approach for a changing world*. San Francisco: Jossey-Bass.

* Thanks to Laura Cohen, who created this scenario for a training exercise with the Ontario Association of Family Mediators.

Noble, C. (2011). *Conflict management coaching: The Cinergy™ model*. Toronto: Cinergy Coaching.

Noble, C., Dizgun, L., & Emond, P. (1998). *Mediation advocacy: Effective client representation in mediation proceedings*. Toronto: Emond Montgomery.

Sue, D.W., Arrendondo, P., & McDavis, R.J. (1992). Multicultural counseling competencies and standards: A call to the profession. *Journal of Multicultural Counseling and Development, 70*, 66-48.

Websites

Information Resources

ADR Institute of Canada, Inc.—Professional Designations: http://www.adrcanada.ca/resources/designation.cfm

Campus Conflict Resolution Resources: http://www.campus-adr.org

Family Mediation Canada (FMC)—Practice and Certification Standards: http://fmc.ca/sites/default/files/sites/all/themes/fmc/images-user/CertificationStandards.pdf

Mediation Services—A Community Resource for Conflict Resolution (Winnipeg): http://www.mediationserviceswpg.ca

National Defence and the Canadian Armed Forces Conflict Resolution Program—Alternative Dispute Resolution: http://www.forces.gc.ca/en/caf-community-dispute-resolution-centres/index.page

Online Mediators.com—Global Online Mediation Services: http://www.onlinemediators.com

Peacemakers Trust: http://www.peacemakers.ca
Peacemakers Trust is a Canadian charitable organization for research and education on conflict resolution and peace-building. It features an internationally acclaimed bibliography of research materials on conflict resolution and peacebuilding.

St. Stephen's Community House—Conflict Resolution & Training: http://www.sschto.ca/conflict-resolution

Treasury Board of Canada Secretariat: http://www.tbs-sct.gc.ca/hrh/psmalmfp-eng.asp
This site provides an overview of the *Public Service Modernization Act* and its function.

UN Department of Political Affairs—Mediation Support: https://www.un.org/wcm/content/site/undpa/mediation support

Professional Associations

ADR Institute of Canada, Inc.: http://www.adrcanada.ca

apeacemaker.net: http://www.apeacemaker.net

Association for Conflict Resolution: http://www.acresolution.org

Association of Family and Conciliation Courts (AFCC): http://www.afccnet.org

Elder Mediation International Network: http://www.eldermediation.ca
The Elder Mediation Code of Professional Conduct may be obtained on the Family Mediation Canada website at http://www.fmc.ca/sites/default/files/sites/all/themes/fmc/images-user/Code%20of%20Professional%20Conduct%20-%20Feb%202014.pdf.

Family Mediation Canada: http://www.fmc.ca

Justice Institute of British Columbia: http://www.jibc.ca

Mediation Services—A Community Resource for Conflict Resolution (Winnipeg): http://www.mediationserviceswpg.ca

National Association for Community Mediation: http://www.nafcm.org

Restorative Justice Online—Mediation Information and Resource Centre: http://www.restorativejustice.org/webtour/alphalisting/mediate

Saskatoon Community Mediation Services: http://mediate.sasktelwebsite.net

St. Stephen's Community House: http://www.ststephenshouse.com/crs.shtml

Victim Offender Mediation Association: http://www.voma.org

Educational Programs in Mediation

Carleton University, Department of Law and Legal Studies—Graduate Diploma in Conflict Resolution: http://www.carleton.ca/law/conflict

Justice Institute of BC—Centre for Conflict Resolution: http://www.jibc.ca/programs-courses/schools-departments/school-community-social-justice/centre-conflict-resolution

Royal Roads University—Master of Arts in Conflict Analysis and Management: http://www.royalroads.ca/prospective-students/master-arts-conflict-analysis-and-management

University of Victoria Institute for Dispute Resolution: http://dispute.resolution.uvic.ca

University of Victoria, School of Public Administration—MA in Dispute Resolution: http://www.uvic.ca/hsd/publicadmin/graduate/future-students/grad-programs/dispute-resolution/index.php

University of Waterloo, Peace and Conflict Studies—Conrad Grebel Peace and Conflict Studies: http://uwaterloo.ca/peace-conflict-studies

York University Certificate in Dispute Resolution: http://dce.yorku.ca/dispute-resolution/dr

REFERENCES

Abel, R.L. (Ed.). (1982). *The politics of informal justice* (Vol. 1, pp. 267–320). New York: Academic Press.

Aronsson, G., Gustafsson, K., & Dallner, M. (2000). Sick but yet at work: An empirical study of sickness presenteeism. *Journal of Epidemiology & Community Health, 54*, 502–509.

Barsky, A., Este, D., & Collins, D. (1996). Cultural competence in family mediation. *Mediation Quarterly, 13*(3), 167–178.

Bingham, L.B., & Pitts, D.W. (2002). Highlights of mediation at work: Studies of the national REDRESS evaluation project. *Negotiation Journal, 18*, 135–146.

Ford, J. (2003, March). Organizational conflict management—What's a system? Mediate .com. http://www.mediate.com//articles/ford9.cfm.

Gelfand, M.J., Leslie, L.M., & Keller, K. (2008). On the etiology of organizational conflict cultures. *Research in Organizational Behavior, 28*, 137–166.

Gelfand, M.J., Leslie, L.M., Keller, K., & de Dreu, C. (2012) Conflict cultures in organizations: How leaders shape conflict cultures and their organizational-level consequences. *Journal of Applied Psychology, 97*(6), 1131–1147.

Goetzel, R., Long, S., Ozminkowski, R., Hawkins, K., Wang, S., & Lynch, W. (2004). Health, absence, disability, and presenteeism cost estimates of certain physical and mental health conditions affecting US employers. *Journal of Occupational and Environmental Medicine, 46*(4), 398–412.

Harrington, C. (1985). *Shadow justice: The ideology and institutionalization of alternatives to court.* Westport, CT: Greenwood Press.

Honeyman, C. (1990). On evaluating mediators. *Negotiation Journal, 6*, 23–36.

Justice Canada. (2010). *Informal conflict management system evaluation—final report.* http://www.justice.gc.ca/eng/rp-pr/cp-pm/eval/rep-rap/11/icms-sgice/index.html.

Kolb, D.M. (1994). *When talk works: Profiles of mediators.* San Francisco: Jossey-Bass.

Lang, M., & Taylor, A. (2000). *The making of a mediator.* San Francisco: Jossey-Bass.

LeBaron, D.M. (1994). The quest for qualifications: A quick trip without a good map. In C. Morris & A. Pirie (Eds.), *Qualifications for dispute resolution: Perspectives on the debate* (pp. 109–129). Victoria, BC: University of Victoria Institute for Dispute Resolution.

LeBaron, M., (2003). *Bridging cultural conflicts: A new approach for a changing world.* San Francisco: Jossey-Bass.

LeBaron, M., & Zumeta, Z. (2003) Windows on diversity: Lawyers, culture, and mediation practice. *Conflict Resolution Quarterly, 20*(4), 463–472.

Lewis, S. (2009). Improving school climate: Findings from schools implementing restorative practices. International Institute for Restorative Practices (IIRP) Graduate School. http://www.iirp.edu/pdf/IIRP-Improving-School-Climate.pdf.

Lipsky, D. & Avgar, A. (2010). The conflict over conflict management. [Electronic version]. *Dispute Resolution Journal, 65*(2-3), 38–43. http://digitalcommons.ilr.cornell.edu/articles/775/.

Llewellyn, J. (2009). Restorative collaboration: The Nova Scotia restorative justice program. Paper presented at the 12th world conference of the International Institute for Restorative Practices. http://www.iirp.edu/article_detail.php?article_id=NjI5.

Logan, R. & Stokes, L. (2004). *Collaborate to compete: Driving profitability in the knowledge economy*. Toronto: Wiley & Sons.

Lynch, J. (2001). Beyond ADR: A systems approach to conflict management. *Negotiation Journal, 17*(3), 207-216.

Lynch, J. (2003). Integrated conflict management programs emerge as an organization development strategy. *Alternatives to the High Cost of Litigation*, 21(5), 99–113.

Macfarlane, J. (1995). *Court-based mediation of civil cases: An evaluation of the Ontario Court (General Division) ADR centre*. Toronto: Ministry of the Attorney General.

McCullough, M. (2007). Restoring justice for safer schools. *Professionally Speaking: The magazine of the Ontario College of Teachers*. http://professionallyspeaking.oct.ca/december_2007/justice.asp.

Merry, S.E. (1990). The discourses of mediation and the power of naming. *Yale Journal of Law and the Humanities, 2*(1), 1–36.

Minow, M. (1998). *Between vengeance and forgiveness: Facing history after genocide and mass violence*. Boston: Beacon Press.

Moore, C.W. (2003). *The mediation process: Practical strategies for resolving conflict* (3rd ed.). San Francisco: Jossey-Bass.

Nader, L. (1988). The ADR explosion—The implications of rhetoric in legal reform. *Windsor Yearbook of Access to Justice*, 8, 269–290.

Nanavati, M., Powidajko, J., & Stalla, C. (2007). Using restorative practices in school: Creating a caring community. http://www.hpedsb.on.ca/ec/services/eds/documents/RestorativePracticesinSchoolArticle.pdf.

Newfoundland & Labrador Public Service Commission. (2013). The cost of conflict. http://www.psc.gov.nl.ca/psc/rwp/costofconflict.html.

Ontario Ministry of the Attorney General. (2010). Local mediation committee guidelines for selecting mediators—Ontario Mandatory Mediation Program. Toronto: Queen's Printer. http://www.attorneygeneral.jus.gov.on.ca/english/courts/manmed/guidelines.asp.

Picard, C.A. (1994). The emergence of mediation as a profession. In C. Morris & A. Pirie (Eds.), *Qualifications for dispute resolution* (pp. 141–164). Victoria, BC: University of Victoria Institute for Dispute Resolution.

Picard, C.A., & Saunders, R.P. (2002). The regulation of mediation. In M. MacNeil, N. Sargent, & P. Swan (Eds.), *Law, regulation and governance* (pp. 223–238). Toronto: Oxford University Press.

Public Service Labour Relations Act. SC 2003, c. 22, s. 2.

Public Service Modernization Act, SC 2003, c. 22.

Reeve, C. (1998). The quandary of setting standards for mediators: Where are we headed? *Queen's Law Journal, 23*, 441–474.

Reimer, K. (2011, March 11). An exploration of the implementation of restorative justice in an Ontario public school. *Canadian Journal of Educational Administration and Policy, 119*, 1–42. http://www.umanitoba.ca/publications/cjeap/pdf_files/reimer.pdf.

Rosen, E. (2007).*The culture of collaboration: Maximizing time, talent and tools to create value in the global economy*. San Francisco: Red Ape Publishing.

Rosen, E. (2009). *The bounty effect: Seven steps to the culture of collaboration*. San Francisco: Red Ape Publishing.

Rouble, G. (2014, April 2). Is there a measurable cost to workplace conflict? *Leading Indicator: Compelling Insights to Organizational Health, Alignment and Performance*. http://www.leadingindicator.ca/article/456221/is-there-a-measurable-cost-to-workplace-conflict.

Scimecca, J.A. (1991). Conflict resolution and a critique of alternative dispute resolution. In H. Pepinsky & R. Quinney (Eds.), *Criminology as peacemaking* (pp. 263–279). Indianapolis, IN: Indiana University Press.

Shafer, M., & Mirsky, L. (2011, April 1). The restorative approach in Nova Scotia: A partnership of government, communities and schools. International Institute for Restorative Practices (IIRP). http://www.iirp.edu/article_detail.php?article_id=Njg5.

Society of Professionals in Dispute Resolution (SPIDR). (2001). Guidelines for design of integrated conflict management systems within organizations—Executive summary. Mediate.com. http://www.mediate.com/articles/spidrtrack1.cfm.

Statistics Canada. (2011). Immigration and ethnocultural diversity in Canada. Analytical document: 99-010-X. http://www12.statcan.gc.ca/nhs-enm/2011/as-sa/99-010-x/99-010-x2011001-eng.cfm.

Sue, D.W., Arrendondo, P., & McDavis, R.J. (1992). Multicultural counseling competencies and standards: A call to the profession. *Journal of Multicultural Counseling and Development, 70*, 66-48.

Tangri, Ravi, (2003). *Stress Costs—Stress-Cures*. Victoria, BC: Trafford Publishing.

Treasury Board of Canada Secretariat. (2008). Public Service Modernization Act. http://www.tbs-sct.gc.ca/hrh/psmalmfp-eng.asp.

Waldman, E. (1996). The challenge of certification: How to ensure mediator competence while preserving diversity. *University of San Francisco Law Review, 30*, 723–756.

Warters, William. (2000). *Mediation in the campus community: Designing and managing effective programs*. San Francisco: Jossey-Bass, 2000.

Welsh, N. (2001). The thinning vision of self-determination in court-connected mediation: The inevitable price of institutionalization? *Harvard Negotiation Law Review, 6*, 1–96.

APPENDIX A

Agreement to Mediate

We, Chris Somerville, Dale Rochon (the parties), and Peter Bishop (the mediator) agree to proceed with a mediation of the dispute relating to the repair work done by Chris on the automobile owned by Dale, on the following terms:

1. The mediation will take place at Carleton University, Room D490, Loeb Building, on Wednesday, October 15, 2014 between 10:00 a.m. and 1:00 p.m. or, if required, such later time as all participants may agree to.
2. As an impartial facilitator, I will help you communicate about and negotiate the issues between you for the purpose of reaching a final agreement that will settle those issues. As your mediator, I will not make any judgment or decision about the issues in dispute and will not give or offer any legal advice.
3. We, Chris and Dale, understand and agree that mediation is a completely voluntary process; that we are going ahead with this mediation because we have freely chosen to do so; and that either one of us may choose to limit or terminate this mediation at any time, for any reason. If either of us wishes to terminate the mediation before it is concluded, we will notify you the mediator and, in private, discuss with you our reasons for wanting to end the mediation.
4. During the mediation, we will in good faith discuss the issues between us and will pursue the resolution process actively. Subject to any limits or conditions communicated to all participants at the commencement of the mediation, each of us has full authority and capability to determine and settle all issues in the mediation.
5. Subject to any agreement we may reach relating to specific information or matters to be communicated to others, all oral and written communications in this mediation process will be confidential. In particular, subject to paragraph 6 below, we understand and agree that the mediator will not communicate or report anything about the mediation or its outcome to anyone except that which is expressly agreed by all parties.

6. At the conclusion of the mediation, the mediator will report to ☐ the court, ☐ the sponsoring organization, or ☐ no one that the mediation has been completed and that either (1) the dispute has been fully settled and the matter is now closed or (2) the dispute has not been settled.
7. Except for any legally binding agreement resulting from the mediation, all oral and written communications in this mediation process shall be "without prejudice" and, as such, in any subsequent legal or administrative proceeding:
   a. Statements made and information provided in the mediation session or in pre-mediation exchanges, and which are not otherwise producible, are not required to be disclosed and are not admissible into evidence.
   b. The mediator may not give evidence, or be summoned or called to give evidence, or be required to produce any notes or records relating to the mediation.
8. The parties agree that the mediator's fee in accordance with the attached fee schedule will be shared equally between them and that they will pay their one-half share of this fee at the end of the mediation. [Remove this section if not required]

Dated: October 15, 2014

P. Bishop

PETER BISHOP

C. Somerville

CHRIS SOMERVILLE

Dale Rochon

DALE ROCHON

APPENDIX B

Memorandum of Understanding (MOU)

Having successfully concluded a mediation of the issues between them, Chris Somerville and Dale Rochon agree as follows:

1. Dale will pay Chris $800.00 in four (4) monthly instalments of $200.00 each starting today, October 15, 2014, and ending January 15, 2015, in full satisfaction of Invoice No. 5400819. This amount represents the actual costs of all parts replaced and one half of the labour costs previously billed.
2. Chris will return Dale's automobile (2007 Ford Focus) to her upon receipt of the first instalment cheque. Chris confirms that the car is in good running order and that there is a 30-day warranty on all parts and repair work as described in the original invoice.
3. To encourage further patronage and show appreciation, Chris will give Dale a 25 percent discount (to a maximum of $150.00) on her next automobile service invoice at Chris's shop.
4. Dale recognizes that Chris is a conscientious mechanic and when the opportunity arises, she will readily recommend Chris and his automobile service centre to others.
5. Both parties acknowledge and agree that
   a. they fully understand the terms of this MOU,
   b. all terms are reasonable, and
   c. they sign this MOU freely and without duress.

Dated: October 15, 2014

Dale Rochon — C. Somerville

DALE ROCHON — CHRIS SOMERVILLE

APPENDIX C

Standards of Practice

1. Family Mediation Canada Guidelines for FMC Family Mediators

Family Mediation Canada is an interdisciplinary association of lawyers, social workers, human services, and health care professionals, working together to create a better way to provide cooperative conflict resolution relating in a range of family issues. FMC's practice guidelines and certification process was approved in 1996. Detailed information on these standards, steps in the certification process, and an application form are available on its website (http://www.fmc.ca).

Family mediators generally deal with conflicts about pre-nuptial issues, the re-organization of the family after separation and divorce, the particulars of future parenting plans for children (including custody, access, and guardianship issues), financial support, property matters connected to separation or divorce, child protection matters, family business matters, and disputes within intact families about issues involving the division of responsibility for the care of elderly parents, parental conflict with or about children, family finances, estate matters, adoption, and educational matters. A family mediator is defined as an impartial third party who possesses expertise in non-adversarial conflict and dispute resolution processes and techniques. This professional assists in the management, control, and resolution of interpersonal conflicts. The following information (reprinted by permission) is from FMC's standards of practice guide, available online at http://fmc.ca/sites/default/files/sites/all/themes/fmc/images-user/CertificationStandards.pdf.

> Family mediators shall work with the participants to establish and maintain a mediation process that will:
>
> 1. Be client centered;
> 2. Facilitate the participants' involvement in the mediation while taking into consideration their respective:
>   a) Abilities to negotiate … ;
>   b) Abilities to make decisions in accordance with their own individual interests … ;

c) Power to influence family decision-making;
d) Psychological, emotional and economic states;
e) Access to and understanding of relevant information; and
f) Access to appropriate support services such as independent legal advice.

3. Ensure that the participants have adequate time to fully discuss, consider and resolve their disputes and conflicts;
4. [Ensure that families with histories of abuse or unmanageable power imbalances are assessed for appropriateness of mediation and are referred to other services if necessary];
5. Ensure that culturally appropriate forms of dispute resolution are included;
6. Ensure that the interests of all persons in the dispute or conflict are considered;
7. Ensure confidentiality of the process is discussed and maintained except when:
   a) the mediator suspects that a child is in need of protection; ...
   c) the mediator determines that there is a need to inform a potential victim and the police about an imminent danger;
   d) there is a mutual agreement that the information may be released, as in an open mediation;
   e) the mediator must breach confidentiality in order to comply with a duty to disclose the whereabouts of a child in cases of abduction;

   ...
8. Use language that is meaningful and appropriate to the participants;
9. Be fair to all participants;
10. Ensure that the special interests of children are recognized and considered by parents when they are making decisions about their children;
11. Assist participants to resolve family problems in a way that respects each family's interests, values, and rights to self-determination, while also respecting the interests and rights of others who may be affected;
12. Be sensitive to the participants' cultural perceptions, needs and understandings of fairness; ...
16. Ensure that agreements reached in mediation reflect the range of options considered acceptable in law and if the participants wish to enter an agreement falling outside that acceptable in law, strongly encourage the participants to obtain independent legal advice and reflect for a period of time before concluding any agreement; and
17. Attempt to ensure that no one suffers physical or emotional abuse as a result of participating in mediation.

2. Association for Conflict Resolution (ACR) Model Standards of Conflict for Mediators

ACR is a professional organization dedicated to enhancing the practice and public understanding of conflict resolution. Its mission is to promote peaceful effective conflict resolution. ACR represents and serves a diverse national and international audience that includes more than 7,000 mediators, arbitrators, facilitators, educators, and others involved in the field of conflict resolution and collaborative decision making. It hosts an annual conference, publishes a newsletter, and has chapter organizations and sector groups of special areas of interest. The following standards were adopted in 2005.*

Preamble

Mediation is used to resolve a broad range of conflicts within a variety of settings. These Standards are designed to serve as fundamental ethical guidelines for persons mediating in all practice contexts. They serve three primary goals: to guide the conduct of mediators; to inform the mediating parties; and to promote public confidence in mediation as a process for resolving disputes.

Mediation is a process in which an impartial third party facilitates communication and negotiation and promotes voluntary decision making by the parties to the dispute.

Mediation serves various purposes, including providing the opportunity for parties to define and clarify issues, understand different perspectives, identify interests, explore and assess possible solutions, and reach mutually satisfactory agreements, when desired.

Note on Construction

These Standards are to be read and construed in their entirety. There is no priority significance attached to the sequence in which the Standards appear.

The use of the term "shall" in a Standard indicates that the mediator must follow the practice described. The use of the term "should" indicates that the practice described in the standard is highly desirable, but not required, and is to be departed from only for very strong reasons and requires careful use of judgment and discretion.

The use of the term "mediator" is understood to be inclusive so that it applies to co-mediator models.

* This material is the result of a collaborative effort between the Association for Conflict Resolution (ACR), the Section of Dispute Resolution of the American Bar Association (ABA), and the American Arbitration Association (AAA). The Model Standards were originally drafted and adopted in 1994 by the ABA Section of Dispute Resolution, the AAA, and the Society of Professionals in Dispute Resolution (or SPIDR, which merged with two other organizations in 2001 to form ACR). Reproduced with permission from the Association for Conflict Resolution (ACR). www.ACRnet.org.

These Standards do not include specific temporal parameters when referencing a mediation, and therefore, do not define the exact beginning or ending of a mediation.

Various aspects of a mediation, including some matters covered by these Standards, may also be affected by applicable law, court rules, regulations, other applicable professional rules, mediation rules to which the parties have agreed and other agreements of the parties. These sources may create conflicts with, and may take precedence over, these Standards. However, a mediator should make every effort to comply with the spirit and intent of these Standards in resolving such conflicts. This effort should include honoring all remaining Standards not in conflict with these other sources.

These Standards, unless and until adopted by a court or other regulatory authority do not have the force of law. Nonetheless, the fact that these Standards have been adopted by the respective sponsoring entities, should alert mediators to the fact that the Standards might be viewed as establishing a standard of care for mediators.

STANDARD I. SELF-DETERMINATION

A. A mediator shall conduct a mediation based on the principle of party self-determination. Self-determination is the act of coming to a voluntary, uncoerced decision in which each party makes free and informed choices as to process and outcome. Parties may exercise self-determination at any stage of a mediation, including mediator selection, process design, participation in or withdrawal from the process, and outcomes.

1. Although party self-determination for process design is a fundamental principle of mediation practice, a mediator may need to balance such party self-determination with a mediator's duty to conduct a quality process in accordance with these Standards.
2. A mediator cannot personally ensure that each party has made free and informed choices to reach particular decisions, but, where appropriate, a mediator should make the parties aware of the importance of consulting other professionals to help them make informed choices.

B. A mediator shall not undermine party self-determination by any party for reasons such as higher settlement rates, egos, increased fees, or outside pressures from court personnel, program administrators, provider organizations, the media or others.

STANDARD II. IMPARTIALITY

A. A mediator shall decline a mediation if the mediator cannot conduct it in an impartial manner. Impartiality means freedom from favoritism, bias or prejudice.

B. A mediator shall conduct a mediation in an impartial manner and avoid conduct that gives the appearance of partiality.

1. A mediator should not act with partiality or prejudice based on any participant's personal characteristics, background, values and beliefs, or performance at a mediation, or any other reason.
2. A mediator should neither give nor accept a gift, favor, loan or other item of value that raises a question as to the mediator's actual or perceived impartiality.
3. A mediator may accept or give *de minimis* gifts or incidental items or services that are provided to facilitate a mediation or respect cultural norms so long as such practices do not raise questions as to a mediator's actual or perceived impartiality.

C. If at any time a mediator is unable to conduct a mediation in an impartial manner, the mediator shall withdraw.

STANDARD III. CONFLICTS OF INTEREST

A. A mediator shall avoid a conflict of interest or the appearance of a conflict of interest during and after a mediation. A conflict of interest can arise from involvement by a mediator with the subject matter of the dispute or from any relationship between a mediator and any mediation participant, whether past or present, personal or professional, that reasonably raises a question of a mediator's impartiality.

B. A mediator shall make a reasonable inquiry to determine whether there are any facts that a reasonable individual would consider likely to create a potential or actual conflict of interest for a mediator. A mediator's actions necessary to accomplish a reasonable inquiry into potential conflicts of interest may vary based on practice context.

C. A mediator shall disclose, as soon as practicable, all actual and potential conflicts of interest that are reasonably known to the mediator and could reasonably be seen as raising a question about the mediator's impartiality. After disclosure, if all parties agree, the mediator may proceed with the mediation.

D. If a mediator learns any fact after accepting a mediation that raises a question with respect to that mediator's service creating a potential or actual conflict of interest, the mediator shall disclose it as quickly as practicable. After disclosure, if all parties agree, the mediator may proceed with the mediation.

E. If a mediator's conflict of interest might reasonably be viewed as undermining the integrity of the mediation, a mediator shall withdraw from or decline to proceed with the mediation regardless of the expressed desire or agreement of the parties to the contrary.

F. Subsequent to a mediation, a mediator shall not establish another relationship with any of the participants in any matter that would raise questions about the integrity of the mediation. When a mediator develops personal or professional relationships with parties, other individuals or organizations following a mediation in which they were involved, the mediator should consider factors such as time elapsed following the mediation, the nature of the relationships established, and services offered when determining whether the relationships might create a perceived or actual conflict of interest.

STANDARD IV. COMPETENCE

A. A mediator shall mediate only when the mediator has the necessary competence to satisfy the reasonable expectations of the parties.

1. Any person may be selected as a mediator, provided that the parties are satisfied with the mediator's competence and qualifications. Training, experience in mediation, skills, cultural understandings and other qualities are often necessary for mediator competence. A person who offers to serve as a mediator creates the expectation that the person is competent to mediate effectively.
2. A mediator should attend educational programs and related activities to maintain and enhance the mediator's knowledge and skills related to mediation.
3. A mediator should have available for the parties' information relevant to the mediator's training, education, experience and approach to conducting a mediation.

B. If a mediator, during the course of a mediation determines that the mediator cannot conduct the mediation competently, the mediator shall discuss that determination with the parties as soon as is practicable and take appropriate steps to address the situation, including, but not limited to, withdrawing or requesting appropriate assistance.

C. If a mediator's ability to conduct a mediation is impaired by drugs, alcohol, medication or otherwise, the mediator shall not conduct the mediation.

STANDARD V. CONFIDENTIALITY

A. A mediator shall maintain the confidentiality of all information obtained by the mediator in mediation, unless otherwise agreed to by the parties or required by applicable law.

1. If the parties to a mediation agree that the mediator may disclose information obtained during the mediation, the mediator may do so.
2. A mediator should not communicate to any non-participant information about how the parties acted in the mediation. A mediator may report, if required, whether parties appeared at a scheduled mediation and whether or not the parties reached a resolution.

3. If a mediator participates in teaching, research or evaluation of mediation, the mediator should protect the anonymity of the parties and abide by their reasonable expectations regarding confidentiality.

B. A mediator who meets with any persons in private session during a mediation shall not convey directly or indirectly to any other person, any information that was obtained during that private session without the consent of the disclosing person.

C. A mediator shall promote understanding among the parties of the extent to which the parties will maintain confidentiality of information they obtain in a mediation.

D. Depending on the circumstance of a mediation, the parties may have varying expectations regarding confidentiality that a mediator should address. The parties may make their own rules with respect to confidentiality, or the accepted practice of an individual mediator or institution may dictate a particular set of expectations.

STANDARD VI. QUALITY OF THE PROCESS

A. A mediator shall conduct a mediation in accordance with these Standards and in a manner that promotes diligence, timeliness, safety, presence of the appropriate participants, party participation, procedural fairness, party competency and mutual respect among all participants.

1. A mediator should agree to mediate only when the mediator is prepared to commit the attention essential to an effective mediation.
2. A mediator should only accept cases when the mediator can satisfy the reasonable expectation of the parties concerning the timing of a mediation.
3. The presence or absence of persons at a mediation depends on the agreement of the parties and the mediator. The parties and mediator may agree that others may be excluded from particular sessions or from all sessions.
4. A mediator should promote honesty and candor between and among all participants, and a mediator shall not knowingly misrepresent any material fact or circumstance in the course of a mediation.
5. The role of a mediator differs substantially from other professional roles. Mixing the role of a mediator and the role of another profession is problematic and thus, a mediator should distinguish between the roles. A mediator may provide information that the mediator is qualified by training or experience to provide, only if the mediator can do so consistent with these Standards.
6. A mediator shall not conduct a dispute resolution procedure other than mediation but label it mediation in an effort to gain the

protection of rules, statutes, or other governing authorities pertaining to mediation.

7. A mediator may recommend, when appropriate, that parties consider resolving their dispute through arbitration, counseling, neutral evaluation or other processes.
8. A mediator shall not undertake an additional dispute resolution role in the same matter without the consent of the parties. Before providing such service, a mediator shall inform the parties of the implications of the change in process and obtain their consent to the change. A mediator who undertakes such role assumes different duties and responsibilities that may be governed by other standards.
9. If a mediation is being used to further criminal conduct, a mediator should take appropriate steps including, if necessary, postponing, withdrawing from or terminating the mediation.
10. If a party appears to have difficulty comprehending the process, issues, or settlement options, or difficulty participating in a mediation, the mediator should explore the circumstances and potential accommodations, modifications or adjustments that would make possible the party's capacity to comprehend, participate and exercise self-determination.

B. If a mediator is made aware of domestic abuse or violence among the parties, the mediator shall take appropriate steps including, if necessary, postponing, withdrawing from or terminating the mediation.

C. If a mediator believes that participant conduct, including that of the mediator, jeopardizes conducting a mediation consistent with these Standards, a mediator shall take appropriate steps including, if necessary, postponing, withdrawing from or terminating the mediation.

STANDARD VII. ADVERTISING AND SOLICITATION

A. A mediator shall be truthful and not misleading when advertising, soliciting or otherwise communicating the mediator's qualifications, experience, services and fees.

1. A mediator should not include any promises as to outcome in communications, including business cards, stationery, or computer-based communications.
2. A mediator should only claim to meet the mediator qualifications of a governmental entity or private organization if that entity or organization has a recognized procedure for qualifying mediators and it grants such status to the mediator.

B. A mediator shall not solicit in a manner that gives an appearance of partiality for or against a party or otherwise undermines the integrity of the process.

C. A mediator shall not communicate to others, in promotional materials or through other forms of communication, the names of persons served without their permission.

STANDARD VIII. FEES AND OTHER CHARGES

A. A mediator shall provide each party or each party's representative true and complete information about mediation fees, expenses and any other actual or potential charges that may be incurred in connection with a mediation.

1. If a mediator charges fees, the mediator should develop them in light of all relevant factors, including the type and complexity of the matter, the qualifications of the mediator, the time required and the rates customary for such mediation services.
2. A mediator's fee arrangement should be in writing unless the parties request otherwise.

B. A mediator shall not charge fees in a manner that impairs a mediator's impartiality.

1. A mediator should not enter into a fee agreement which is contingent upon the result of the mediation or amount of the settlement.
2. While a mediator may accept unequal fee payments from the parties, a mediator should not use fee arrangements that adversely impact the mediator's ability to conduct a mediation in an impartial manner.

STANDARD IX. ADVANCEMENT OF MEDIATION PRACTICE

A. A mediator should act in a manner that advances the practice of mediation. A mediator promotes this Standard by engaging in some or all of the following:

1. Fostering diversity within the field of mediation.
2. Striving to make mediation accessible to those who elect to use it, including providing services at a reduced rate or on a pro bono basis as appropriate.
3. Participating in research when given the opportunity, including obtaining participant feedback when appropriate.
4. Participating in outreach and education efforts to assist the public in developing an improved understanding of, and appreciation for, mediation.
5. Assisting newer mediators through training, mentoring and networking.

B. A mediator should demonstrate respect for differing points of view within the field, seek to learn from other mediators and work together with other mediators to improve the profession and better serve people in conflict.

3. ACR Standards of Practice for Family Mediators

The following standards are available in their entirety online at http://www.acrnet.org (go to "About ACR," then "ACR Standards of Practice and Ethical Principles," then "Model Standards of Practice for Family and Divorce Mediation").

The Standards incorporate much of the best of the previous standards, and update them to include topics such as domestic violence and child abuse. In addition, the Standards address the issue of the best interests of the children and how mediation can help parents to address them in divorce.

The Symposium, which developed the Standards, included representatives from Academy of Family Mediators (AFM), Association of Family Courts and Community Professionals (AFCC), American Bar Association (ABA) Family Section, and other national, state and regional organizations. The Standards represent a consensus of the best suggestions made over a period of two years in which the Symposium met to develop them.

The Standards had previously been adopted by the ABA Family Section and by AFCC, as well as several state mediation organizations. The adoption of these standards by ACR rounds out the trio of major national organizations whose members are family and divorce mediators.

The General Standards

STANDARD I: A family mediator shall recognize that mediation is based on the principle of self-determination by the participants.

STANDARD II: A family mediator shall be qualified by education and training to undertake the mediation.

STANDARD III: A family mediator shall facilitate the participants' understanding of what mediation is and assess their capacity to mediate before the participants reach an agreement to mediate.

STANDARD IV: A family mediator shall conduct the mediation process in an impartial manner. A family mediator shall disclose all actual and potential grounds of bias and conflicts of interest reasonably known to the mediator. The participants shall be free to retain the mediator by an informed, written waiver of the conflict of interest. However, if a bias or conflict of interest clearly impairs a mediator's impartiality, the mediator shall withdraw regardless of the express agreement of the participants.

STANDARD V: A family mediator shall fully disclose and explain the basis of any compensation, fees and charges to the participants.

STANDARD VI: A family mediator shall structure the mediation process so that the participants make decisions based on sufficient information and knowledge.

STANDARD VII: A family mediator shall maintain the confidentiality of all information acquired in the mediation process, unless the mediator is permitted or required to reveal the information by law or agreement of the participants.

STANDARD VIII: A family mediator shall assist participants in determining how to promote the best interests of children.

STANDARD IX: A family mediator shall recognize a family situation involving child abuse or neglect and take appropriate steps to shape the mediation process accordingly.

STANDARD X: A family mediator shall recognize a family situation involving domestic abuse and take appropriate steps to shape the mediation process accordingly.

STANDARD XI: A family mediator shall suspend or terminate the mediation process when the mediator reasonably believes that a participant is unable to effectively participate or for other compelling reason.

STANDARD XII: A family mediator shall be truthful in the advertisement and solicitation for mediation.

STANDARD XIII: A family mediator shall acquire and maintain professional competence in mediation.

4. ACR Criteria for Training Programs Approved by the ACR Family Section

The ACR Family Section has also approved the following standards for mediation training programs. These standards state that participants should be able to demonstrate the following knowledge and skills:

1. Ability to explain what mediation is (within the dispute resolution context) and what a mediator does;
2. Awareness of theories and current research and literature underlying conflict and its resolution, and their application to family mediation;
3. Ability to contract for mediation services;
4. Ability to screen for appropriateness of mediation, including knowledge and ability to screen for domestic violence and an awareness of appropriate responses when domestic violence or its potential has been identified;
5. Ability to assist the parties in surfacing and framing the topics to be discussed in mediation;
6. * Awareness of the consequences of separation/divorce for adults and children;

7. * Ability to work with the substantive information encountered in separation/divorce mediation;
8. Ability to build a working relationship and a constructive process with the parties;
9. Ability to facilitate communication between the parties by using specific skills (e.g., active listening, reframing);
10. * Ability to facilitate problem solving between the parties, especially in the areas of divorce including, but not limited to, parenting, support, division of assets/liabilities, insurance, tax filing, etc.;
11. Knowledge of conflict management skills;
12. Understanding concepts of mediator influence and neutrality;
13. Knowledge of standards of practice and how ethical issues are resolved;
14. Ability to recognize when the assistance of other professionals might be helpful to the mediation process and to facilitate this discussion with the parties; and
15. Awareness of what additional knowledge/skills/experience/supervision may be necessary for the successful practice of mediation and how to get it.

* *For 30-hour Family Mediation Programs, substitute appropriate content area(s).*

5. ADR Institute of Canada: Code of Conduct for Mediators (2011)

The following code of conduct is available online at http://www.adrcanada.ca/resources/documents/CodeOfConduct2012August30.pdf.

> This Code of Conduct for Mediators (the "Code") applies in its entirety to every Mediator who is a member of the ADR Institute of Canada, Inc. (the "Institute") or any of its Regional Affiliates, or who accepts from the Institute an appointment as Mediator. While Mediators come from varied professional backgrounds and disciplines, every Mediator must adhere to the Code as a minimum. Being appointed as a Mediator confers no permanent rights on the individual, but is a conditional privilege that may be revoked for breaches of the Code … .
>
> **1. Code's Objectives**
>
> 1.1 The Code's main objectives are:
>
> (a) to provide guiding principles for the conduct of Mediators;
>
> (b) to promote confidence in Mediation as a process for resolving disputes; and
>
> (c) to provide protection for members of the public who use Mediators who are members of the Institute.

2. Definitions

2.1 In the Code:

(a) "Mediation" means the use of an impartial third party to assist the parties to resolve a dispute, but does not include an arbitration; and

(b) "Mediator" means an impartial person who is a member of the Institute or accepts from the Institute an appointment as Mediator and who is engaged to assist the parties to resolve a dispute, but does not include an arbitrator unless the arbitrator is acting as a Mediator by consent of the parties.

(c) "Regional Affiliate" means a regionally based alternative dispute resolution ("ADR") organization designated by the Institute to provide ADR services in a specific region as requested by the Institute.

3. Principle of Self-Determination

3.1 It is the right of parties to a Mediation to make their own voluntary and non-coerced decisions regarding the possible resolution of any issue in dispute. Every Mediator shall respect and encourage this fundamental principle of Mediation.

3.2 The Mediator shall provide the parties at or before the first Mediation session with information about the Mediator's role in the Mediation. The Mediator shall discuss the fact that authority for decision-making rests with the parties, not the Mediator.

3.3 The Mediator shall not provide legal or professional advice to the parties. The Mediator may express views or opinions on the matters at issue, and may identify evaluative approaches, and where the Mediator does so it shall not be construed as either advocacy on behalf of a party or as legal or professional advice to a party.

3.4 The Mediator shall, where appropriate, advise unrepresented parties to obtain independent legal advice. The Mediator shall also, where appropriate, advise parties of the need to consult with other professionals to help parties make informed decisions.

4. Independence and Impartiality

4.1 Unless otherwise agreed by the parties after full disclosure, a Mediator shall not act as an advocate for any party to the Mediation and shall be and shall remain at all times during the Mediation:

(a) wholly independent; and

(b) wholly impartial; and

(c) free of any personal interest or other conflict of interest in respect of the Mediation.

5. Potential Disqualification

5.1 Before accepting an appointment as Mediator and at all times after accepting such an appointment, a Mediator shall disclose in writing any circumstance that could potentially give rise to a reasonable apprehension of a lack of independence or impartiality in the Mediation of a dispute.

5.2 Any Mediator who makes a disclosure of any circumstance under section 5.1 shall continue to serve as Mediator if all parties to the dispute waive, in writing, the right to object to any reasonable apprehension of a lack of independence or impartiality or conflict of interest that arises as a consequence of that disclosure.

6. Confidentiality

6.1 The Mediator shall inform the parties and any experts, advisors, and any other persons who accompany a party to a Mediation session of the confidential nature of Mediation.

6.2 The Mediator, the parties, their experts and advisors, and any other persons who accompany a party to a Mediation session shall keep confidential and shall not disclose to any non-party all information, documents, and communications that are created, disclosed, received, or made available in connection with the Mediation except:

(a) with the parties' written consent;

(b) when ordered to do so by a court or otherwise required to do so by law;

(c) when the information/documentation discloses an actual or potential threat to human life;

(d) in respect of any report or summary that is required to be prepared by the Mediator;

(e) where the data about the Mediation is for research and education purposes, and where the parties and the dispute are not, nor may reasonably be anticipated to be, identified by such disclosure; or

(f) where the information is, or the documents are, otherwise available to the public.

6.3 If the Mediator holds private sessions (including breakout meetings and caucuses) with one or more parties, he or she shall discuss the nature of such sessions with all parties before commencing such sessions. In particular, the Mediator shall inform the parties of any limits to confidentiality that may apply to information disclosed during private sessions.

6.4 The Mediator shall maintain confidentiality in the storage and disposal of Mediation notes, records, files, information, documents and communications.

7. Quality of the Process

7.1 The Mediator shall make reasonable efforts before Mediation is initiated or at the start of the Mediation to ensure that the parties understand the Mediation process.

7.2 The Mediator shall conduct Mediations in a manner that permits the parties to participate effectively in the Mediation and that encourages respect among the parties.

7.3 The Mediator shall acquire and maintain professional skills and abilities required to uphold the quality of the Mediation process.

7.4 The Mediator shall act professionally at all times, and the Mediator shall not engage in behaviour that will bring the Mediator or the Institute into disrepute.

7.5 A Mediator who considers that a Mediation in which he or she is involved may raise ethical concerns (including, without limitation, the furtherance of a crime or a deliberate deception) may take appropriate action, which may include adjourning or terminating the process.

8. Advertising

8.1 In advertising or offering services to clients or potential clients, the Mediator shall:

(a) refrain from guaranteeing settlement or promising specific results; and

(b) provide accurate information about his or her education, background, mediation training and experience, in any oral or written representation or biographical or promotional material.

9. Fees

9.1 The Mediator shall give the parties as soon as practicable after his or her appointment a written statement of a fee structure, likely expenses, and any payment retainer requirements.

9.2 The Mediator's fees shall not be based on the outcome of Mediation, or on whether there was a settlement, or (if there was a settlement) on the terms of settlement.

9.3 The Mediator may charge a cancellation or a late/delay fee within the Mediator's discretion, provided the Mediator advises the parties in advance of this practice and the amount of the fee.

10. Agreement to Mediate

10.1 The Mediator and the parties shall prepare and execute a mediation agreement setting out:

(a) the terms and conditions under which the parties are engaging the Mediator;

(b) if the National Mediation Rules of the Institute apply to the Mediation, any of the Rules that the parties agree shall not apply to the Mediation; and

(c) any additional rules that the parties agree shall apply to the Mediation.

11. Termination or Suspension of Mediation

11.1 The Mediator may suspend or terminate the Mediation if requested, in writing, by one or more of the parties.

11.2 The Mediator may suspend or terminate the Mediation with a written declaration by the Mediator that further efforts at mediation would not be useful at this time.

12. Other Conduct Obligations

12.1 Nothing in the Code replaces or supersedes any other ethical standard or code that may govern the Mediator. Where there are multiple such standards or codes, the Mediator shall be bound by the stricter or strictest of them.

Index

accommodation, 103
active listening, *see* reflective listening
ADR Institute of Canada, 255, 351, 357–358, 382–386
adjudication
  as a rights-based dispute resolution process, 38–39
  compared to arbitration and mediation, 80
adversarial dialogue, transformation, 207
adversarial system, 14
agreed outcomes, 66–67
agreement, *see also* final negotiations; settlement
  completion, 275–276
  legal effect of, 276–279
Agreement to Mediate, 182, 185, 202, 367
alternate story, 76, 77, 243
alternative dispute resolution (ADR), 78–79, 316, 349, 357
anchoring assumptions, 261, 283
appeal to authority, 100–102
appearance, 134
arbitration, 22, 24, 34, 35, 39–40
Arbitration Act, 1991, 40
Aristotle, 94
assertive communication, 148
assertiveness, 99
assisted negotiation, 41
Association for Conflict Resolution, 351, 358, 373–382
assuming ownership, 269
assumptions, identification of, 46, 108, 200, 208, 211–212, 231, 234, 347
  see also anchoring assumptions; limiting assumptions
attribution errors, 260–261
authoritative command
  majority vote, 36–37
  power-based method, 35–36
  problems, 37
authoritative mediator, 70
Avgar, A., 338
avoidance, 99, 103, 104
avoidant conflict culture, 327
awareness, 15, 117, 208, 231–234, 264
Axelrod Robert, 261

Band-Aid solution, 226
bargaining power, 33, 66, 293
BATNAs, 52, 173, 256–257, 271, 273
Benjamin, R., 11, 16, 230
best alternatives to negotiated agreements, *see* BATNAs
bigger picture, 234
Bingham, L.B., 342
bluffing, 49, 103
Bodtker, A.M., 234
body language, 134
bottom-lining, 103
Boulding, K.E., 94
Boulle, L., 279
brainstorming, 47, 243, 265–266
Braithwaite, J., 299–301
breaks, 273
Brett, J., 33, 100, 101
Burton, John, 98
Bush, Robert Baruch, 4–5, 71, 76, 86, 234, 303, 309

Cadman, Dona, 311
Cadman, Jesse, 310
Canadian Bar Association, 359
Carnevale, P., 42
caucusing
  co-mediation and, 181–182
  defined, 215
  dialogue preparation and, 204
  guidelines, 216–217
  reasons to caucus, 215–216, 259
Center for Restorative Justice and Peacemaking, 309

Chan, Cheryl, 310
CHEAP BFVs, 229–230
Child and Family Services Act, 315
Christie, N., 83
chronemics, 134
Church Council on Justice and Corrections, 299
circle of conflict, 192
claiming tactics, 49, 103
Cloke, K., 143
co-mediation
  advantages of, 180–181
  effectiveness, 180
  process of, 181–182
Cobb, S., 243
Code of Conduct for Mediators, 255
cognitive dimensions of conflict
  conflict cycle, and, 111–112
  learning process, and, 112–113
  narrative composition, 108–109
  schemas, 109–111, 128
  self-fulfilling prophecy, 111–112
  social nature of cognition, 109
cognitive misers, 109
cognitive schemas, 109–111, 128
cold contacts, 168
collaboration
  conflict behaviour, and, 103
  factors influencing, 198–200
  factors limiting
    anchoring assumptions, 261
    attribution errors, 260–261
    judgmental overconfidence, 262
    loss aversion, 262
    partisan perceptions, 259
    reactive devaluation, 262
    tunnel vision, 259–260
    zero-sum thinking, 260
  mediator's role in, 200–201
  workplace type, 328–330
collaborative conflict culture, 328
collaborative organization, 328–330
Common Ground, 240
common interests, 51, 67
communication
  aggressive versus assertive, 148
  attack–defend pattern, 131
  blockers, 131–132
    assumptions, limiting, 133–134
    conflict emotions, and, 134
    giving advice, 132–133
    judging, 132
    minimizing, 133
  conflict resolution, role in, 125
  creative communicator, 239–248
  cultural roots of, 127–128
  "Feelings" conversation, 129
  high-context, 127–128
  human interaction, and, 128–131
  "Identity" conversation, 129
  low-context, 127
  mediator skills
    connecting skills, 146–148
    non-blaming skills, 148–149
    non-defensive skills, 148, 149–151
    productive questioning skills, 143–146
    reflective listening, 137–143
  metaphor, use of, 239–242
  miscommunication, reasons for, 130–131
  non-verbal communication
    cues, 127, 130
    inclusions, 134–136
  opening message, 129
  stories, use of, 108–109
  "What happened?" conversation, 129
communication bridge, 14
community-based conflict resolution programs, 338
community-based mediation programs, 4, 156, 165, 167–168, 298, 338–342
Community Justice Initiative, 297–298, 310, 339
competition, 103
competitive organization, 328, 329
compromise, 103
conciliation, 22, 40–41
confidentiality
  caucusing, and, 216
  closing the mediation, and, 280
  convening and, 179
  core element, mediation, 65
  interview stage and, 170
  professional standards, mediators, 351
conflict, *see also* conflict behaviour
  17th-century philosophers and, 94
  behaviour of people during, *see* conflict behaviour
  categorization by type, 102–104
  choices, and, 104–108
  classical philosophers, and, 94
  constructs
    conflict is dynamic and emergent, 96–97

conflict is relational, 95–96
conflicts are value-based, 97–98
costs, measurement of, 326–328
culture of in organizations, 327–328
definitions of, 21, 93–95
getting to the heart of, 8, 227, 229–230
key element of, 119
latent differentiated from manifest, 94–95
parties to, 26
responses to
appeal to authority, 100–102
choice of, 27, 98–99
cognitive dimensions of, 108–113
dysfunctional, 104
emotions and, 113–117
fear response, 117–120
fight, 99–100
functional, 104
ignore, 99
negotiate, 102
withdraw, 99
sources of
data conflicts, 190
interest conflicts, 191
mediator strategies, and, 191–194
relationship conflicts, 191
structural conflicts, 191
value conflicts, 190
conflict behaviour, *see also* conflict
cognitive dimensions of
conflict cycle, 111–112
insight and learning, 112–113
mental programming, 109–111
social nature, 109
defined, 93
emotions, and
functions of, 114–115
influence on, 113–114
negotiation, and, 115–117
fear response, and
fight-or-flight physiology, 117–118
mediation, effect on, 118–120
types of
accommodating, 103
avoiding, 103
collaborating, 103–104
competing, 103
compromising, 103
conflict coaching, 341
conflict competence, 20, 21
conflict culture
avoidant, 327
collaborative, 328
dominating, 327
conflict cycle, 111–112
conflict emotions, 134
conflict management systems, 336–338
conflict narratives, 22, 108, 205–207
Conflict Resolution Network of Canada, 340
conflict story, 108–109
connected intelligence, 15, 16
connecting skills
bridging, 146–147
discrepancy confronting, 147–148
immediacy, 147
consensual dispute resolution process, 24
consensus, 64–65
consideration, 265
content intervention, 70
content level, 112
context level, 112
continuum of mediation goals, 71
convening, *see also* mediators
convenor
as mediator, 155, 157, 180
choice of, 156–158
distinct from mediator, 156
decision making and planning, 178
defined, 22–23, 155
first contact, 166–169
framework, 165–178
homework, 176, 183, 307
individual interviews and assessment
comfortable climate, importance of, 170
conflict, exploration of, 171
mediation suitability, determination of, 175–177
party coaching and motivation, 173–174
party education about mediation, 172–173
mediator, selection of, 156, 178–182
modified process, 156
phases of, 158–159
pre-mediation meeting
Agreement to Mediate form, 182, 185, 202, 367
communication during, 184
homework, 183
information collection, 184–185
mediation scheduling, 185
reporting requirements, 183

convening, pre-mediation meeting (cont.)
questions that arise, 160–161
reasons for
informed choice of parties, 163
mediation suitability, determination of, 163
preparation of parties, 163–164
reflection of parties, 162–163
trust building, 162
situational variations
community-based mediation, 156, 165
court-connected mediation, 164
international disputes, 165
multi-party disputes, 164
restorative justice programs, 165
workplace mediation, 165
skills required, 179–180
conversations, categories of, 129–131
cooling-off period, 176
cooperative behaviour
origins, 194
theory of, 195–197
cooperativeness, 99
Cormier, Robert, 296
Cornelius, H., 132
corrective justice, 290–291
Cory, Peter, 314
Coser, L., 94
costs of conflict
direct costs, 326
indirect costs, 326–327
court-connected mediation, 55–57, 64, 157, 164, 357
Covey, S.R., 131
creativity, 83–84
Crum, Thomas, 63
cultivating dialogue, 7, 190, 197–200
cultural bias, 346–347
cultural competence, 346
culture and negotiation, 127–128

Dahrendorf, Ralf, 94
Damasio, Antonio, 98, 113
data conflicts, 190
de Dreu, C., 327
deadlines, 273–274
Deas, Supriya, 311
decision-making authority, 23, 32, 66–67, 255–257
deep culture, 97
Deutsch, Morton, 95, 196, 288, 292–293
dialogue cultivation
communication and collaboration, facilitating, 200
party collaboration, assessment of, 198–200
party education, 198
process, establishment and management, 197–198
differences, types of, 268
discrepancies, 234, 236
dispute, 24
dispute resolution processes
categories, 24
interest-based methods
distinguishing feature, 40–41
key presumption, 41
mediation
benefits of, 82–87
core elements, 64–67
defined, 52, 63–64
forms of practice, 68–78
hybrid methods, 54–57
mediator's role, 53
modern mediation movement, 53, 63–64
neutrality of mediator, 67–68
reasons to choose, 78–81
success, defined, 81–82
negotiation
essential elements, 42
types of, 43–52
power-based methods
authoritative command, 35–37
majority vote, 36–37
unilateral action, 34–35
power/right/interests, relationship of, 32–33
rights-based methods
adjudication, 38–39
arbitration, 39–40
dispute resolution spectrum, 33–35
distressed system, 33
distributive justice
concerns of, 292
power imbalances, and, 293
principles of
equality principle, 292–293
equity principle, 293
need principle, 293
dominating conflict culture, 327
dynamic and emergent conflict, 96

education, 86
Einstein, Albert, 1, 13
Elmira case, 297–298, 339

emotion
awareness of, 130
functions of, 114–115
minimization, 113
negotiation, and, 115–117
neuroscience, and, 113–114
owning, 184
reflecting, 139–140
emotional communication, 134
emotional intelligence, 15, 200
empowerment, 75
equality principle, 292–293
equity principle, 293
evaluation of mediation programs
difficulty, 342
outcomes, 343–344
evaluative approach to mediation, 71–75
expand the pie, 258
externalizing the conversation, 243–244

face saving, 79
facilitative approach to mediation, 71–75
fairness, 197, 292–295
fairness standards, 271–272
Faire, S., 132
family group conferencing, 315–316
Family Mediation Canada, 156, 348, 351, 357, 358, 359, 371–372
fear response
fight-or-flight, physiology of, 117–118, 326–327
mediation, and, 118–120
"Feelings" conversation, 129
fight, as a response to conflict, 99–100
fight-or-flight response, 117–118, 326–327
final negotiations
breaks, usefulness of, 273
deadlines, 273–274
human dimension, and, 274
incremental convergence, 274
leap-to-agreement approach, 274
objective criteria, application of, 271–272
one-text procedure, 272
procedural methods to reach agreement, 274
reality check, 272–273
reflection on progress, 273
settlement range procedure, 271
Fisher, R., 42–44, 46, 52, 103, 104, 148, 150, 173, 239–240, 243, 258, 271–272, 276
Fiske, S.T., 109
flexibility, 82–83
flexible dispute resolution process, 40
flip chart, use of, 266–267
Folger, Joseph, 4, 71, 76, 86, 126, 234, 309
Ford, Henry, 189
framing the problem, 19, 227–228
see also reframing the problem, 213–214, 234, 238
Fuller, Lon, 53

gacaca courts, 299–300, 317
Gelfand, M.J., 327
genuine listening, 137
Ghandi, Mahatma, 93
Gladue, R v, 314
Goldbach, T., 314
Goldberg, S., 33, 100, 101
Goleman, Daniel, 15, 114
Gordon, Thomas, 129, 137
Gulliver, P., 127

Hall, E.T., 127
hard bargaining, 103, 148
Harvard Program on Negotiation, 48
Heen, S., 128
high-context communication, 127
Himes, J., 94
Hobbes, Thomas, 94
Hocker, J., 94, 239
Hofstede, G., 127
holistic approach to mediation, 10–15
homework, 176, 183, 307
Howse, R., 300
humanistic mediation, 309–311
hybrid methods of mediation, 54–57
hypothesizing, 231–232

"I" messages, 149
Iacobucci, Frank, 314
"Identity" conversation, 129
ignorance as a response to conflict, 99
impartiality, 65–66
implementing decisions, 281–283
in-house mediation training programs, 354
"in principle" statements, 267
incremental convergence, 274
independent mediator, 69–70
Indian Residential Schools Adjudication Secretariat, 318
individual risks, 347–349
informal conflict management system, 338

informality, 82–83
insider-partial, 66
insight, 86, 234
Institute for Multitrack Diplomacy, 240
Institute for the Study of Conflict Transformation, 4
integrated conflict management system, 336–337
integrative paradigm, 24
interdependence, 102, 195
interest-based dispute resolution processes
  development of, 33
  differentiated from rights-based, 40
  distinguishing feature, 40–41
  key presumption, 41
  underlying arguments, 41
interest conflicts, 191
interest dominant system, 33
international conflict, 157, 165, 167, 246, 263
International Institute for Restorative Practices Canada, 342
intervention, 214–215
intuitive-imaginative intelligence, 15, 16
issue, 24

James, William, 109
Jameson, J.K., 234
Johnson, M., 130, 239
joint action, 42
joint problem statement, 265
Jones, T.S., 126
judgmental overconfidence, 262
justice
  aspects of
    justice as fairness, 292–295
    justice as punishment, 289–390
    justice as reconciliation, 296
    justice as restitution, 290–291
  mediation, applied to, 339–340
  restorative versus retributive justice, 296–297
justice gap, 288
justice perspective, 22, 25

Kahneman, D., 262
Keller, K., 327
Kelly, K.J., 279
Kerry, John, 157
key interests, 46–47
Kilmann, R.K., 102
kinesics, 134
King, Martin Luther King, Jr., 287
Kolb, Deborah, 70
Kressel, Kenneth, 70
Kruk, E., 54
Kydd, J., 247

Labour Relations Act, 39
Lakoff, G., 130, 239
Lang, M., 18, 19, 247, 351
latent conflict, 94–95
lawyers, 73, 82–84, 164, 167, 173, 184, 217–220, 275–276, 278, 280, 299, 338, 347, 357
lawyer's dilemma, 220
Lax, D., 48–49, 50, 103, 220, 268
leap-to-agreement approach, 274
LeBaron, M., 15–16, 230, 239, 241, 242, 247, 346
Lederach, J.P., 66, 240, 243
LeDoux, J., 113
legal rights infringement, 347–348
Leslie, L.M., 327
limiting assumptions, 133–134
linking and de-linking, 234–235
Lipsky, D., 338
listening
  as a communication skill, 126, 131
  as a two-way process, 130
  difficulty of, 131
  for discrepancies, 234, 236
  reflective, *see* reflective listening
Llewellyn, J.J., 300
Locke, John, 94
logic of mediation, 225–228
loss aversion, 259, 262
low-context communication, 127
lower costs, 85

Macfarlane, J., 342
Mack, R.M., 194
Maggiolo, W., 17
majority vote, 36–37
management decision, 36
manifest conflict, 94–95
Marx, Karl, 94
Maslow, A., 97–98
material issue, 25
Mayer, B., 5
mediation, *see also* mediator
  advisers to parties, role of, 217–220
  applications of, 2–4
  approaches to, 4–5, 70–71

dualism and, 70–71
evaluative, 71–73
facilitative, 71–75
insight, 77–78
narrative, 76–77
transformative, 75–76
art of, 9–16, 231–232
assisted negotiation as, 52–53
benefits of
creativity, 83–84
education, 86
flexibility, 82–83
informality, 82
insight, 86
lower costs, 85
openness, 83–84
challenges and risks, 344–350
closing, 279
co-mediation
advantages of, 180–181
effectiveness, 180
process of, 181–182
continuum of goals, 71
convening, *see* convening
core elements
confidentiality, 65
consensus, 64–65
decision-making power, 66–67
impartiality, 65–66
court-connected mediation, 55–57, 157, 164, 357
definitions of, 63–64
differentiated from other forms of dispute resolution, 53–54
evaluation of
difficulty, 342
outcomes, 343–344
forms of practice, 68–70
goals of, 5–6, 71
holistic approach to, 10–15
humanistic, 309–311
hybrid methods, 54–57
limitations, 86–87
online dispute resolution, 4
profession of
certification and ethics, 357–358
education and training, 350–355
regulation, 355–356
standards of, 356–357
reasons to choose, 78–81
regulation of, 355–356
restorative justice approach to, *see* restorative justice
risks associated with
individual risks, 344–349
organizational risks, 349
societal risks, 349–350
scheduling, 185
stories, *see* stories
successful, defined, 81–82
suitability determination, 163, 175
victim-offender, 78, 167, 287–288, 303–309
mediation-arbitration, 54–55
mediation program
defined, 25, 53, 330
development of
intake and convening mechanisms, 334–335
marketing program, 335–336
mediators, recruitment, 332–333
mediators, training, 334
needs and scope, determination, 332
other programs, interfacing with, 336
referral agents, identification, 336
target population, education of, 335–336
elements of, 330–331
mediator, *see also* convening; mediation
advanced practitioner, 19
agreement
completion, 275–276
legal effect of, 276–279
tactics used to reach, 270–275
types of, 270
artistry, development of, 231–232
attributes, 17–18
authoritative mediator, 70
beginning mediation, 201–205
caucusing, *see* caucusing
CHEAP BFV questions, 229–230
closing mediation, 279–280
collaboration, 258–263
communication, and
connecting skills, 146–148
creativity, 239–248
management of, 126
non-blaming skills, 148–149
non-defensive responses, 148, 149–151
productive questioning, 143–146
reflective listening, 137–143
competence, development of, 19–20
connecting through ritual, 246

mediator (cont.)
convenor as mediator, 155, 157, 180
cultural competence, and, 346
differentiated from judge, 67
doing the unexpected, 246–247
ethics, 357–358
expansion of party awareness, 232–239, 258
externalizing the conversation, 243–244
framing the problem, 227–228
humanistic mediation, and, 309
in-house mediation training programs, 354
independent mediator, 69–70
insights, eliciting, 234–235
intelligence, types needed, 15–16
liability, 278–279
linking and de-linking strategies, 235, 237
listening for discrepancies, 234–235, 236
measures of success, 82
mediator as neutral, 67–68
mentoring programs, 354–355
metaphor, use of, 239–242
mind, heart, body, and spirit, use of, 247
peer mediator, 53, 179, 330
process framework
cultivating dialogue, 7, 189
getting to heart of conflict, 8, 189, 229–230
logic of, 225–228
options, generation of, 254–263
post-mediation, 8, 189, 280–283
pre-mediation, 7, 159, 182–185, 189
process completion, 8, 270–280
reaching decisions, 8, 189, 270–280
stages, 6–7
professional associations, 362
professional development
dynamic four-stage model, 248
professional training, and 354–355
questions, types asked, 244–245
reflective practice, importance of, 18–19
resolution phase strategies, 263–269
assuming ownership of idea, 269
brainstorming, 265–266
flip chart/whiteboard, use of, 266–267
future, focus on, 267
"in principle," idea consideration, 267
joint problem statements, 265
non-participating parties, involvement of, 263–265
party role reversal, 268
"some people" comparison, 269
trading on party differences, 268
"what if?" requests, 269
"what would it take?" request, 267
ritual, establishing connections and, 246
selection of, 178–182
self-determination, principle of, 255
skills development, 17–20
social network mediator, 68–70
specialized training requirements, 351–352
stories, use of, 242–243
strategies to move parties forward, 238
strategies used to transform negative influences
acknowledgment of feelings, 209
affirmation of parties' efforts, 209
conflict sources, effect on, 191–194
consequences, exploration of, 211
creative intervention, use of, 214–215
education of parties, 208–209
expression of feelings, invitation, 210–211
naming conflict perceptions, 211–212
normalization, parties' assumptions, 209–210
reframing, use of, 213–214
response, invitation for, 212
suggestions, requests for, 210
techniques, 72–75
training facilities
in-house training programs, 354
mentoring programs, 354–355
professional development programs, 353–354
university and college programs, 352–353
types of
authoritative mediator, 70
independent mediator, 69–70
social network mediator, 68–69
visualization, use of, 245
ways of knowing, 15–16
Melchin, K.R., 86, 112, 234
memorandum of understanding, 275, 276, 369
Menin, B., 264
Menkin, Betty, 305
mentoring programs, 354–355
Merry, S.E., 70
metaphor, 239–242
mind, heart, body, and spirit, 247
Minow, Martha, 350
misunderstanding, 130
Mnookin, R., 220, 268

Monk, Gerald, 234, 244, 245, 246
Moore, Christopher, 65, 68, 185, 190–192, 258, 265, 271, 274
Moses, R v., 314
multi-party mediation, 164, 185
Myers, Elaine, 305

naming process, 211–212
narrative approach to mediation
  defined, 76
  externalizing conversation, 243–244
  goals, 76
  phases, 77
  questions, types asked, 244–245
  stories, use of, 108–109, 242–243
National Crime Prevention, 340
need principle, 293
negotiation
  as a response to conflict, 42, 102
  best alternative to a negotiated agreement (BATNA), 52, 173, 256–257, 271, 273
  defined, 42
  emotions and, 115–117
  essential elements, 42
  Negotiator's Dilemma, 48–52, 195, 220
  positional negotiation, 43
  principled negotiation, 43–48
  types of, 43–48
Negotiator's Dilemma
  BATNA, 52
  claiming tactics, 49, 220
  trust creation, 195
  value creation, 49–52
neuroscience, 113–114
neutral evaluation, 54, 257
neutrality, 67–68
Nichols, M., 130, 137
non-blaming statements, 148–149
non-defensive responses, 148–151
non-verbal cues, 130
non-verbal expression, 134–136

objective criteria, 271
one-text procedure, 272
online dispute resolution (ODR), 4
Ontario Association for Family Mediation, 156, 316
Ontario Child Protection Mediation Roster, 316
Ontario's mandatory mediation program, 56
openness, 83–84
organizational risks, 349
organizations
  collaborative, 328–330
  competitive, 328–329
  conflict culture, types of, 327–328
  costs of conflict, 326–327
  mediation programs, and
    defined, 25, 53, 330
    development of, 330–336
    elements of, 330–331
O'Rourke, P.J., 325
outsider-partial, 66

paralanguage, 134
paraphrasing, 138
partisan perceptions, 259
party
  advisers, participation in mediation, 217–220
  collaborating knowledge, assessment, 198
  conflicting perspectives, 200–201
  defined, 26
  differences, types of, 268
  education, 198, 208–209
  non-participating, involvement, 263–265
  preparation by convener, 163–164
  with disability, 176
Patton, B., 128
Pauchay, Christopher, 314
Peacemakers Trust, 340
Peachey, D., 290
Peppet, S., 220, 268
personal filters, 130
Picard, Cheryl, 5, 53, 72, 86, 112, 137, 234, 355, 357
Pitts, D.W., 342
Plato, 94
positional negotiation, 43
positional paradigm, 24
positions, 46
post-mediation
  co-mediations and, 280
  decisions, implementation of
    informal conflicts, 282–283
    with constituencies, 283
    with formal proceedings, 281–282
    without formal proceedings, 282
  monitoring of agreement, 280
  reports, 280–281

power-based response to conflict
  authoritative command, 35–36
    majority vote, 36–37
    problems, 37
  unilateral action, 34–35
power imbalances, 176, 345
pre-mediation phase
  Agreement to Mediate form, 182
  communication during, 184
  homework, 183
  importance, humanistic mediation, 309
  information collection, 184–185
  mediation scheduling, 185
  reporting requirements, 183
  variations in, 159
presenting problem, 95
Price, Marty, 305
principled negotiation
  collaboration as, 104
  defined, 43
  interests, focus on, 46
  objective criteria, use of, 47–48
  options, generation of, 46–47
  separation, people from problem, 45
problem-solving model, 71
procedural safeguards, 345
profession of mediation
  education and training
    in-house training, 354
    mentoring programs, 354–355
    professional development, 353–354
    required specialized training, 350–352
    university and college programs, 352–353, 362
  mediator certification and ethics, 357–358
  professional standards, 356–357
  regulation of, 355–356
professional associations, 362
professional development programs, 353–354
proxemics, 134
Pruitt, D., 42, 70
Public Conversation Project, 240
Public Service Labour Relations Act, 337
Public Service Modernization Act, 3, 337
punishment, 289–290

questions posed by mediator
  broadening, 144–145, 229
  CHEAP BFV, 229–230
  closed, 143
  deepening, 144–145, 229
  open-ended, 143
  types used by narrative mediators, 143–146

reactive devaluation, 262
reality check, 272–273
recognition, 75–76
reconciliation, 299
referral agents, 336
reflect on progress, 273
reflection, 231–232
reflective listening
  attending, 137
  identifying emotion, 139
  paraphrasing, 138
  steps involved, 137
  tips for, 140
  tools
    confusion clarification, 141
    effort validation, 142
    encourage conversation, 140
    facts restatement, 141
    feelings, reflection of, 141
    major ideas, summarization, 142
reflective practice, 18–19
reframing the problem, 213–214, 234, 238
  see also framing the problem
regulation of mediation, 355–356
relational conflict, 95–96
relationship conflicts, 191
reporting requirements, 183
resolution, 27
resolution phase strategies
  non-participating parties, involvement, 263–265
  option-generating methods
    assuming ownership, 269
    brainstorming, 265–266
    flip chart/whiteboard, use of, 266–267
    future, focus on, 267
    "in principle" statements, 267
    joint problem statement, 265
    role reversal, 268
    "some people" suggestions, 269
    trading on differences, 268
    "what if?" questions, 269
    "what would it take?" questions, 267
resolution wheel, 33, 35
response, 231–232
response to conflict, 27

responsive intentionality, 260
restitution agreements, 311–312
restorative circles, 312–313
restorative justice
  approach to offender accountability, 300–302
  convening and, 165
  defined, 25
  family group conferencing, 315–316
  in Canada, 297–298
  other mediation processes and, 302–303
  principles, 296
  programs, 297–298
  regular justice system, compared with, 298–301
  restorative circles, 312–313
  sentencing circles, 313–315
  shaming, use of, 300–302
  transitional justice processes, 316
  versus retributive justice, 296–297
  victim–offender mediation and, 303–312
retributive justice
  aspect of, 290–291
  defined, 25
  restorative justice, compared with, 296–297, 301
Retzinger, S., 129
right relations, 311
rights-based response to conflict
  adjudication, 38–39
  arbitration, 39–40
  decision-making authority and, 32
  development of, 32
  methods, common features of, 38
Riskin, L., 71–72
risks of mediation
  individual, 344–349
  organizational, 349
  societal, 349–350
ritual, 246
Rogers, Kenny, 31
role reversal, 268
rule of law, 32

safety valve, 204
Satir, V., 170
Saunders, R.P., 5, 357
scheduling mediation, 185
Scheff, T., 129
Schelling, T.C., 196
school mediation programs, 341–342
Schuller, Robert H., 155
Serrell, Peter, 305
Schwerin, E.W., 71
scientific method
  new, 10
  old and new compared, 12
  traditional, 9
Scimecca, J.A., 349
Sebenius, J.K., 48–49, 50, 103, 220, 268
self-determination principle, 26
self-fulfilling prophecy, 111
sentencing circles, 313–315
settlement, 27
  see also agreement; final negotiations; resolution
settlement range, 271
shaming, 300–302
Shapiro, Dan, 318
Shon, D.A., 18–19
shuttle mediation, 175
Silbey, S., 70
silence, power of, 310
Simmel, Georg, 94
Snyder, R.C., 194
social network mediator, 68–69
societal risks, 349–350
socioeconomic mediation, 70
soft bargaining, 148
somatic intelligence, 15, 16
"some people," 269
split the difference, 103
stakeholder, 26
standards of practice, 356–357, 371–386
Stein, Janice Gross, 110
Stone, D., 128
stories
  conflict behaviour, and, 108–109
  use in mediation, 242–243
  used to define "justice," 288–289
    corrective justice story, 290–291
    distributive justice story, 292–295
    restorative justice story, 296–302
    retributive justice story, 289–290, 301
structural conflicts, 191
Stuart, Barry, 314
Student Mediation Services, 331–332, 335–336
subjective experience, 14
substantive issue, 25

talking back, 176
Tannen, D., 24

task-oriented mediation, 70
Taylor, A., 18, 19, 109, 247, 351
third-party dispute resolution process, 24
Thomas, K.W., 102
tit for tat, 108, 261
transformative approach to mediation, 70–71, 75
transitional justice processes, 316–318
Trudeau, Pierre, 25
trust building, 162, 195
Truth and Reconciliation Commission (Canada), 318
Truth and Reconciliation Commission (South Africa), 317
truths, identification of, 129
Tulumello, A., 220, 268
tunnel vision, 259–260
Tversky, A., 262
Twain, Mark, 253

Umbreit, M., 170, 309
underlying problem, 95
unexpected, use of the, 246–247
unilateral action, 34–35
unique account questions, 244
unique circulation questions, 245
unique outcome questions, 244
unique possibility questions, 245
unique redescription questions, 245
university mediation programs, 352–353
Ury, W., 33, 42–44, 46, 52, 100, 101, 103, 104, 148, 150, 173, 243, 258, 271, 272, 276

value, creation of, 49–52
value-based conflict, 97–98
value-claiming process, 49
value conflicts, 190
value-negating process, 52
vested-interest mediator, 70
victim impact statement, 290
victim–offender mediation, 78, 167, 287–288, 303–309
visualization, 245
volunteer mediators
  recruitment, 333
  training, 334

Warters, W., 335
Wehr, P., 66
"What Happened?" conversation, 129
"what if?", 269
"what would it take?", 267
Wheatley, M.J., 10, 225
whiteboard, use of, 266–267
Wilmot, W., 94, 239
Winslade, John, 234, 244, 245, 246
withdrawal as a response to conflict, 99
without prejudice, 204
workplace mediation, 165
workplace
  collaborative, 328–330
  competitive, 328–329
Worth, Dave, 297

Yantzi, Mark, 297
"you" messages, 148–149

Zehr, H., 299–300
zero-sum outcome, 52
zero-sum thinking, 260
Zumeta, Z., 346